Grand-Guignolesque

Exeter Performance Studies

Series Editors:
Helen Brooks, Reader in Theatre and Cultural History, University of Kent
Jane Milling, Professor in Drama at the University of Exeter
Steve Nicholson, Emeritus Professor, University of Sheffield
Duška Radosavljević, Reader in Contemporary Theatre and Performance,
Royal Central School of Speech and Drama, University of London

Exeter Performance Studies explores performance in relation to historical
context. The series is a home for a wide variety of work engaging with
processes of making and doing, as well as materiality, policy and cultural
practice. It publishes the best new scholarship, presenting established authors
alongside pioneering work from new scholars, including titles which
provide access to previously unavailable material and engage in processes
of decolonisation and methodological innovation.

Selected previous titles:

Grand-Guignolesque

Classic and Contemporary
Horror Theatre

Richard J. Hand

and

Michael Wilson

UNIVERSITY
of
EXETER
PRESS

First published in 2022 by
University of Exeter Press
Reed Hall, Streatham Drive
Exeter EX4 4QR
UK

www.exeterpress.co.uk

Exeter Performance Studies

British Library Cataloguing in Publication Data
A catalogue record for this book is available
from the British Library.

https://doi.org/10.47788/EQDI2918

ISBN 978-1-80413-015-5 Hardback
ISBN 978-1-80413-080-3 Paperback
ISBN 978-1-80413-016-2 ePub
ISBN 978-1-80413-017-9 PDF

Cover image: adapted from Licence to Thrill's poster for
'Tis the Season 2016 © Les Williams

Typeset in Chennai, India by S4Carlisle Publishing Services

To the Grand-Guignoleurs of the world,
past, present and future...

Contents

Illustrations

Acknowledgements

We would like to express our heartfelt thanks to the numerous writers, directors, producers, actors and other aficionados of the Grand-Guignol who have made this volume possible. The number of people who have helped us through interviews, informal conversations, letters and email correspondence, as well as by giving us access to archival materials and inviting us to performances, are far too numerous to mention individually, but you know who you are, and we are immensely grateful for your enthusiastic support and enormous generosity.

We would also like to thank our colleagues and students at the University of East Anglia and Loughborough University and, as always, our erstwhile collaborators in the Grand-Guignol Laboratory we established at our former institution where this long journey began: the University of South Wales (formerly the University of Glamorgan).

Preface

It is now more than twenty years since we first started to research the Théâtre du Grand-Guignol*—that most intimate of theatres, half-hidden at the end of a dark alleyway in the red-light district of Pigalle in Montmartre, Paris—and the particular blend of horror, comedy and eroticism for which it became famous during its sixty-five-year life from 1897 to 1962. Since then, we have written three books (this being the fourth) and several articles, translated and adapted numerous plays from the French, run workshops, given talks, had long discussions (often involving beer and occasionally *tartare de boeuf*, that most Grand-Guignolesque of dishes), staged performances, spilled (fake) blood, and directed, performed and watched many plays with several generations of students.

In the introduction to our first book (*Grand-Guignol: The French Theatre of Horror*, 2002) we claimed that the Théâtre du Grand-Guignol was one of the world's great forgotten theatres. We don't think that was any exaggeration. At the time there was Mel Gordon's survey book *The Grand Guignol: Theatre of Fear and Terror*, which had recently gone out of print (now republished in a revised edition), and a handful of short articles in academic journals, but that was the limit of the literature in English on the subject. Agnès Pierron's large collection of scripts had also been recently published in French but was not widely known in the UK.

Despite its subsequent neglect, the Grand-Guignol had an international reputation during its lifetime, frequented and loved by the Montmartrean underclass, as much as the crowned heads and leading diplomats of Europe. It was a favourite with the occupying German forces during the Second World War and then equally so with the liberating Allies in 1944. It was on the 'must-do' list, along with the Eiffel Tower and the Louvre, of every self-respecting tourist to Paris in the first half of the twentieth century.

This volume presents another way of assessing the importance of the Grand-Guignol by looking at its contemporaneous imitators and the long shadow of its influence. What we have tried to do is to assess the influence of the Grand-Guignol and the state of play of current horror performance, focusing principally upon experiments and enterprises in the UK and the USA. While the original Théâtre du Grand-Guignol has long since closed its doors and the actors who trod the boards in the rue Chaptal have all but made their exit, attempts at reviving the form have come and gone with varying degrees of success.

---

* As with our previous books, we have adopted the convention of using the hyphenated Grand-Guignol when referring to the specific theatre in the rue Chaptal and as the default spelling when referring to the genre more generally. We have used the non-hyphenated Grand Guignol when either a citation demands it, or when referring specifically to the London Grand Guignol or other manifestations where the hyphen has not been used in official publicity.

Part One

An Overview of Classic and Contemporary Horror Theatre

1

Establishing the Grand-Guignolesque

Despite the demise of the Grand-Guignol, the cultural form of horror has never gone away. Across all art forms and media, horror has been a major genre for the remainder of the twentieth century and into the twenty first. An interesting case in point is Hammer Films, a doyen of British cinema that enjoyed international success with its distinctive brand of 'Hammer Horror'. Although it had existed as a film company since the 1930s, it was with films such as *The Quatermass Experiment* (1955), *The Curse of Frankenstein* (1957) and *Dracula* (1958) that Hammer found popular and commercial success with the formula of horror. This 'discovery' of horror is reminiscent of the Grand-Guignol's own revelation in its earliest days that it was the more horrific spectacles that commanded an audience, a phenomenon capitalized on by the entrepreneurial genius of Max Maurey who would brand the venue as the 'Theatre of Horror'. It is also worth noting that Hammer Films and its prolific production of melodramatic horror films played no small part in centring popular horror performance on the cinema screen rather than the stage.

After Hammer Films's heyday came to an end in the 1970s, it ventured into television with the anthology series *Hammer House of Horror* (1980) and did not return to the cinema until well into the twenty-first century. Starting with *Let Me In* (2010), a remake of the Swedish vampire film *Let the Right One In* (2008), the revamped and rebranded Hammer Studios had returned. Hammer's film version of *The Woman in Black* (2012) enjoyed enormous success. The film capitalized on two factors: it was an inspired star vehicle for Daniel Radcliffe; and the film adapted the Susan Hill novel (1983) and its arguably more famous stage version by Stephen Mallatratt (1987) which had been a West End and touring stalwart since the late 1980s. Despite Hammer's successful return to the cinema screen, it is interesting to note that when the company relaunched in 2008, its first output was a free-to-access vampire drama series titled *Beyond the Rave*, which was released in twenty four-minute episodes on the largest social media platform at the time, Myspace. This represented a transmedia approach to horror culture that was reflected further when Hammer ventured into the world of horror theatre with productions of *The Turn of the Screw* (2013) and *The Haunting of Hill House* (2015) at the Liverpool Playhouse. In 2017, Hammer produced a work of immersive theatre in

London with a vampire play, *The Soulless Ones*, at the restored Victorian music hall, Hoxton Hall. In the same year, Hammer announced a deal with the messaging platform Skype to produce a series of iconic Hammer Horror emoticons and stickers. As we can see, the brand that is Hammer has remained in the cinema while embracing other examples of horror culture, from social media and the digital to 'traditional' and immersive theatre. In this regard, Hammer stands as a paradigm of contemporary horror culture where the form can be found across the fullest range of media. In our own time, horror is a major genre across literature, cinema, television, audio drama, gaming (digital, board and role playing), fashion and beyond. A significant manifestation of horror culture continues to be found in theatre.

Horror in theatre is no longer confined to an intimate Grand-Guignolesque stage but is a genre that runs the full gamut of performance. We have already mentioned the phenomenal success of *The Woman in Black* in the West End, where audiences have also patronized the neo-Gothic world of Andrew Lloyd Webber's musical adaptation of (occasional Grand-Guignol playwright) Gaston Leroux's *The Phantom of the Opera* since 1986. Richard O'Brien's *The Rocky Horror Show* (1973), an alternative musical, which opened at the Royal Court Theatre, has toured internationally ever since, while the cult following that surrounds the film adaptation, *The Rocky Horror Picture Show* (1975), and its elaborate practices of audience participation signals a narrowing of the boundary between cinema and theatre. A repertory theatre such as the Liverpool Playhouse produced Andy Nyman and Jeremy Dyson's *Ghost Stories* (2010) before it enjoyed great success in London and on tour and in subsequent revivals, as well as a 2017 film adaptation. *Ghost Stories*' journey from stage to screen happened in reverse in the case of John Pielmeier's stage adaptation of the 1973 horror film *The Exorcist* (2012), which has enjoyed numerous international productions. Aside from mainstream theatre, horror has flourished in 'fringe' contexts. The Edinburgh Fringe and other festivals will typically have some horror offerings, ranging from intense experiences to comic parodies.

Horror has been presented in experimental performance work from the Netherlands, including Jakop Ahlbom Company's physical theatre mime show *Horror* (2015) and Dries Verhoeven's ghost train installation *Phobiarama* (2017), both of which enjoyed international acclaim on extensive tours. Verhoeven's appropriation of an authentic carnival ghost train for an arresting work of modern, politicized horror reflects the carnivalesque traditions of popular horror that playfully challenge rational behaviour and bourgeois morality. The mainly American tradition of Halloween culture in the form of haunted attractions has become internationalized with similar walkthroughs and site-specific events growing in popularity from theme parks to community productions. Similarly, we might consider ghost walks, zombie runs or the 'edutainments' of The London Dungeon and its wider franchise. Even immersive theatre companies such as Punchdrunk and its many imitators can be seen as drawing on traditions of haunted attractions in pushing the potential of spatial and temporal experience in live performance to the limit.

In recent years, we have also seen a rise in nostalgia for the interwar period of the 1920s and 1930s, a golden age for the Grand-Guignol, but also a period when the thriller and the crime story dominated page, stage and screen. This is evident not only in the number of films that have been released in the past few years that are set in this period, but also ventures such as the British Library's Crime Classics series and Collins's revival of the Crime Club imprint, both of which are reissuing large numbers of long out-of-print 'Golden Age' detective novels and thrillers, which had for a long time been deemed rather quaint and highly unfashionable (not to say politically dubious) and have now found a whole new readership. The wider resurgence of interest in all things noir also manifests in the success, in the UK in particular, of crime fiction and crime television drama that has come out of the Scandinavian countries, so-called Nordic or Scandi Noir. A similar appetite can be detected in the 'true crime' genre in the world of podcasting; the extraordinarily successful *Serial* (2014 onwards) is just one example in a growing and extensively downloaded form. These examples of the crime genre may not seem to be horror per se, but when we look at them as we would the Grand-Guignol, we see the affinity: a world of real or possible horrors. Moreover, what is significant is the hybridization of horror. If we consider screen media, quality television programmes such as *True Detective* (2014–19) or *Gangs of London* (2020 onwards) can seem to stray across the boundaries of the crime genre into horror as deftly as *Them* (2021) or *Lovecraft Country* (2020) are simultaneously horror narratives set in historical contexts as well as critiques of racial injustice in contemporary America.

Whether mainstream or cult, horror seems to be ubiquitous. Arguably, we can detect the Gothic in this, a continuum that has always flourished at times of social crisis. We would like to argue that the Gothic and neo-Gothic pleasures of horror have a special place in live performance, where we might coin it the Grand-Guignolesque. At times of global uncertainty, be that environmental, economic, political or pandemic-related, when face-to-face and real-time interactions were increasingly replaced by on-line or technologically enabled relationships, the prospect of the thrills, emotional rollercoasters and frissons of live horror theatre provided an irresistible prospect. In this book, we collate some recent examples of Grand-Guignolesque theatre, but will begin by returning to the original Grand-Guignol and its rivals.

2
The Grand-Guignol's Contemporary Imitators and Competitors

It is said that imitation is the sincerest form of flattery, and it is a mark of its success that the Théâtre du Grand-Guignol always had its imitators, even from its early days. Established in 1897 by Oscar Méténier, a writer of gritty naturalist dramas, who had worked for André Antoine at the radical Théâtre Libre until its closure in 1896, and who by day worked as a secretary to the Police Commissioner of Tour Saint-Jacques in the 4th arrondisement, the Théâtre du Grand-Guignol began life as a venue for radical Zola-esque naturalist theatre, but was soon transformed into a full-blown theatre of horror under his successor, Max Maurey. It was under Maurey's direction that the Grand-Guignol developed its signature programme of short plays that alternated horror plays and comedies (usually sex farces), with each horror play becoming increasingly terrifying as the evening progressed, which became known as *la douche écossaise* or the 'hot and cold shower'. The formula proved such a popular and commercial success that a number of imitators emerged, most importantly the Théâtre du Grand-Guignol's greatest rival, the Théâtre des Deux Masques.

Le Théâtre des Deux Masques: Rivalry in Montmartre

By the turn of the century, Montmartre had long since supplanted the Left Bank as the artistic and intellectual heart of Paris and 'had developed into a veritable entertainment industry, boasting over forty venues comprised of cabarets, café-concerts, dance halls, music halls, theaters, and circuses' (Myers 2007). At the same time, what had begun as a home for subversive and anti-bourgeois experimentation, had begun to enter the commercial mainstream, following the 1900 World Fair. By the 1920s and *les années folles*, the entertainments on offer in Montmartre were as likely to be enjoyed by the social elite as the Montmartrean working class, and such was the case in the theatres, including the Grand-Guignol. As Myers says, 'What had begun as a critique of decadent society had become a symbol of decadence itself' (Myers 2007).

Consequently, the Montmartrean theatre owners, in constant competition with each other for audiences, would always be looking to imitate the success of their competitors. The most successful of these was arguably

Figure 1. Pierre Palau and Jean Velu's *Une Main dans l'ombre* (*A Hand in the Shadows*), a horror play about revenge, Le Théâtre des Deux Masques, May 1923, *Le Théâtre et Comoedia Illustré* No. 19, July 1923 (out of copyright)

Le Théâtre des Deux Masques (popularly known as the Deux Masques), which opened in July 1905, and was located literally just around the corner in the rue Fontaine in a theatre that had been established seven years earlier as Le Nouveau Tremplin. Rue Fontaine (and its neighbourhood of Saint-Georges) was a district long associated with Bohemian artists: Toulouse-Lautrec, Edgar Dégas and Camille Pissarro all either lived or had studios here. The Deux Masques (representing not comedy and tragedy per se, but fear and laughter) was promoted specifically as a rival to the Grand-Guignol, under the direction of Paul Garbagni, who came from the highly respectable Théâtre Odéon. While the Deux Masques enjoyed some success, it was dogged by instability and uncertainty, moving venues and changing names several times. Garbagini's tenure lasted until 1908. In 1921, under Marcel Nancey, the Deux Masques once again enjoyed a period of success, as is evident in reviews that describe the theatre as the 'competitor of the Grand Guignol as a chamber of horrors' (*Variety* 30 June 1921). However, it is interesting to note that among the showcase of largely new plays in the Deux Masques' May/June show, the *Variety* reviewer deems the most successful play to be René Berton's *Tics* (1908), a comedy that had premiered at the Grand-Guignol a significant number of years before. Later in 1921, another review assesses the Deux Masques: 'This house is running as a sort of opposition to the Grand-Guignol and giving a similar program with equal success' (*Variety* 25 November 1921). However, if this review is anything to go by, the purpose of the Deux Masques caused some bemusement even if the audience was suitably pleased. Certainly, the comedies presented are judged as 'not as humorous as intended' (*Variety* 25 November 1921). The horror plays of the evening comprised an adaptation by Robert Numes of W.W. Jacobs's 'The Monkey's Paw' (*La Main de Singe*); and E.M. Laumann and Paul Carrière's *Le Diagnostic*, about a bacteriologist who convinces his wife's lover that he is afflicted with an incurable disease causing him to take his own life. These works could easily be imagined on the little stage in rue Chaptal, but for the reviewer this begs the question of the Deux Masques' originality and purpose: 'There is nothing particularly novel about the new program' of this theatrical rival (*Variety* 25 November 1921).

Even if the Deux Masques could not pretend that its style and format were entirely original, it nevertheless produced work of comparable quality, often imitating the production techniques of its neighbour and commissioning plays from writers who had made their names at the rue Chaptal. Henri Bauche, André Mycho, Charles Hellem and Pol d'Estoc, for example, all had works performed at the Deux Masques. Jean Aragny, who went on to co-write the highly successful *The Kiss of Blood* (*Le Baiser de sang*, 1929) with Francis Neilson for the Grand-Guignol and, according to Pierron, was thought of as the successor to André de Lorde as horror theatre's principal writer (1995: 1,113), had previously written *Eyes*

of the Phantom (*Les Yeux du spectre*) for the Deux Masques in 1924.[1]
Furthermore, *Les Détraquées* (*The Unhinged*) in 1921, arguably the
Deux Masques' most successful piece, which relied upon an up-to-date
psychological understanding of sexually deviant behaviours, followed the
Grand-Guignol's tried and tested process of pairing an established playwright (in this case Pierre Palau, who would become a successful actor
from the 1930s until his death in 1966) with Joseph Babinski, the emi-
nent psychologist, concealing his identity behind the pseudonym 'Olaf'.
It is a testament to the success with which the Deux Masques managed
to replicate the offering of the Grand-Guignol that Pierron includes *Les
Détraquées* in her substantial collection of Grand-Guignol scripts (1995),
and the play was revived by the modern Parisian Grand-Guignol company
acte6 as part of its programme in 2012.

An American correspondent reviewing *Les Détraquées* for *Variety*
seemed to find the play by this 'sort of rival to the Grand Guignol' somewhat disagreeable, saying that the subject matter deals with a 'pathological
problem which might have been left to the medical profession' (*Variety*
25 March 1921) rather than given a spotlight on the stage. Nevertheless,
the same reviewer enjoys other elements of the *douche écossaise*, namely
the satirical *La Petit Maud* (*Little Maud*) by Guy de Teramond in which a
bankrupt lady becomes the live-in cook for her former, now *nouveau riche*,
servant; and P. Despras and Willemetz's *Le Dindon de la Farce* (*The Butt
of the Joke*), in which an insanely jealous husband groundlessly accuses
his wife and best friend of having an affair only to be filled with guilt and
remorse (only for an affair to actually begin). The other horror play in the
showcase with *Les Détraquées* was Jean Sartène's *La Griffe* (*The Grip*) in
which a paralysed peasant, once renowned for his powerful hands, sees his
daughter-in-law abuse and finally murder his son: the shock of the crime
is enough to reawaken the old man's strength and he exacts his revenge
on the guilty woman. *La Griffe* is evidently a melodrama with echoes of
Émile Zola's *Thérèse Raquin* (novel 1868; play 1873), and it is interesting
that the *Variety* review found this and the comedies 'Far more entertaining' (*Variety* 25 March 1921) than the contemporary psychological horror
of *Les Détraquées*. We can see a *douche écossaise* of a satirical comedy
of manners, a melodramatic horror play, a sex farce and a psychological
horror drama that would have been just as comfortable on the boards of
the Grand-Guignol.

Other nights at the Deux Masques presented similar hot and cold 'pack-
ages'. In July 1923, the Deux Masques presented a double-bill of *Adultère*

---

[1] According to Pierron, 'Les Yeux du spectre' premiered in November 1923 at
the Deux Masques (1995: 1,426). However, the script, published by Librairie
Théâtrale in 1926 gives the premiere as taking place the following year, on
3 November 1924.

Figure 2. Yoris d'Hansewick's *Pâques juives* (*Jewish Easter*), a horror play about antisemitic brutality and revenge, Le Théâtre des Deux Masques, July 1923, *Le Théâtre et Comoedia Illustré* No. 26, September 1923 (out of copyright)

(*Adultery*), a sex farce by Léo Marchès and Clément Vautel, and the iron-ically titled *Pâques juives* (*Jewish Easter*) by Yoris d'Hansewick, a drama about antisemitic persecution in a pre-revolutionary Russian ghetto. In *Pâques juives*, the body of a young Russian man is discovered and the Jewish community is accused of sacrificing him in a ritual. The town governor torments a Jewish family by force-feeding them pork and raping a woman in front of her husband. A drunken Cossack officer gouges out the eyes of the patriarch of the family. Twenty years later—in the (contemporary) tumult of the Russian Revolution's aftermath—a fleeing colonel seeks asylum in the same family's house. The Jewish family recognize the officer as the sadistic Cossack who tormented them many years before. They exact revenge on him, ultimately gouging out his eyes. The reviewer in *Le Théâtre et Comoedia Illustré* likened the play to the Grand-Guignol's *Le Baiser dans la Nuit* (*The Final Kiss*, 1912) by Maurice Level, observing that it 'executed the same kind of torture' (July 1923). Level's classic play is, of course, a crime of passion, whereas *Pâques juives* presents a more socially critical play about antisemitism and political upheavals (both historical and contemporary) in which the perpetrators of a sadistic regime get their comeuppance. In this regard, *Pâques juives* is more reminiscent of André de Lorde and Pierre Chaine's *Au Rat mort, cabinet 6* (1908), which enjoyed success at London's Grand Guignol as *Private Room Number 6* (1920). In this play, another Czarist officer is paid back for former atrocities.

In fact, in March 1923, the Grand-Guignol had presented an even more similar play. *Les Crucifiés* (*The Crucified*), by A-P. Antoine and Charles Poidlouë, is a play set in Ireland during the Great Famine. There is a desper-ate rebellion—*Le Théâtre et Comoedia Illustré* could not help but notice the parallels with the contemporary Civil War in Ireland—that is ruthlessly crushed by British troops, who go as far as to crucify one young rebel. In reprisal, the rebels capture an isolated soldier (played by Georges Paulais) and crucify him on the front door to their house. *Le Théâtre et Comoedia Illustré* is impressed that after the intense violence of the first act, which offered the novelty of Paulais being tortured as opposed to torturing, the second is more psychological in its terror. Years later the rebels are haunted by their crime and denounce each other, convinced that the spec-tre of their victim is rising from the dead just outside the fateful door. *Le Théâtre et Comoedia Illustré* comments that the effect on the audience—who apparently leaped out of their seats—was so powerful because they did *not* see a ghost, just the meticulously calibrated performances of the Grand-Guignol ensemble.

In addition, the Deux Masques itself had already exploited a similar narrative formula earlier in the summer with Pierre Palau and Jean Velu's *Une Main dans l'ombre* (*A Hand in the Shadows*) in May 1923, in which a French victim of wartime torture disguises himself as a Dutch journalist to infiltrate the home of a retired German general. When finally alone the

'Dutchman' reveals his true identity and exacts revenge on the general's crimes of rape and murder by strangling him to death. Unmistakably similar to the forthcoming *Pâques juives* and *Private Room Number 6*, the image we reproduce from the production, with the long rope and avenger gaining leverage with his foot upon the table, gives a sense of the physical intensity of the performance. While the Deux Masques sought to imitate the Grand-Guignol repertoire, it evidently could match it in the intensity of its performances.

If we return to *Pâques juives*, although the reviewer in *Le Théâtre et Comoedia Illustré* may detect a degree of Grand-Guignol influence, he praises the play for two distinctive elements: the strong performance from an old widow—including roars of sheer terror—when she sees the Cossacks enter their home; and the trajectory of the colonel's monologue in the denouement, interspersed with responses of complete and ominous silence, as it gradually dawns on him that this was the location of one of his many crimes. Undoubtedly, the risqué romps in *Adultère* offered a counterbalancing light relief to the horrors of *Pâques juives*. Although only two plays, the evening afforded the 'hot and cold' of a Grand-Guignol *douche écossaise* or, more aptly, the two masks of the Deux Masques. Other evenings at the Deux Masques were more of a Grand-Guignol feast of plenty. In February 1922, the Deux Masques offered its audience no fewer than five shows, including four comedies of different styles and a major drama: *L'Ile du Docteur Moreau*, Laumann and Henri Bauche's two-act adaptation of H.G. Wells's 1896 novel. *Le Théâtre et Comoedia Illustré* found the drama of Moreau's atrocious experiments and his '*animal-homme*' to be very ably done.

Despite its successes, the Deux Masques struggled to find a permanent venue and, in this respect, did not have the glorious advantage of the Grand-Guignol's extraordinarily evocative deconsecrated chapel. After relocating from Le Nouveau Tremplin to the Théâtre Fontaine in 1924, the Deux Masques closed the following year, re-emerging briefly in 1930 and between 1935 and 1938. While the Deux Masques struggled to find itself a permanent home, the Grand-Guignol continued to enjoy its reputation as the *original* theatre of horror, and had established itself as a seemingly enduring feature of the Parisian theatrical landscape.

The continuing success of the Grand-Guignol itself and the intermittent but nonetheless significant rivalry of the Deux Masques as a Grand-Guignol imitator impacted elsewhere in Paris in the early 1920s. In February 1921, Irénée Mauget (who was the director of the open-air Théâtre Pre-Catelan at the Bois de Boulogne) opened the Théâtre Nouveau, which was literally inside the celebrated Paris wax museum Musée Grevin. Transforming the museum's auditorium into a public theatre, the atmospheric venue was evidently suitable for Grand-Guignolesque performance. A press review makes it clear that Mauget has 'adopted the policy of the Grand Guignol and Deux Masques' (*Variety* 4 November 1921) with its evenings of *douche écossaise*. As an example, in October 1921 the Théâtre Nouveau presented four plays, including two comedies: Johannes Gravier's *A bas des auteurs!* (*Down with Authors!*), a satire about theatre directors; and Paul Giafferi's *Trois Types* (*Three Chaps*), about a group of wartime civil servants and the contrast between their austere working relationship and their genuine friendship after hours. These plays were complemented by two horror plays: *Dans la Jungle* is E.M. Laumann's adaptation of Rudyard Kipling's 'The Return of Imray' (1891), an eerie short story about the mysterious disappearance of a successful man and the eventual, gruesome discovery of his corpse within his home; and Isabelle Fusier's *L'Execution*, which is based on the satirical writings of Henri Monnier, in which a crowd surrounds a guillotine and a street urchin (played by Fusier herself) scales a lamppost and describes the decapitation of four condemned men in lurid detail. The producer Irénée Mauget was to be found presenting the Grand-Guignolesque elsewhere in Paris: in 1923, he staged the full-length play *L'Ombre des Lauriers* (*The Shadow of the Laurels*) at the Théâtre Albert. One theatre reviewer was less than impressed: 'The plot unfolds the story of a wife's repugnance at resuming marital relations with her husband, who returns horribly wounded from the war. It is a distressing subject, poorly handled' (*Variety* 24 May 1923). The theme of this play is reminiscent of H.F. Maltby's *The Person Unknown* (1921), a play written for the London Grand Guignol about a brutally disfigured veteran of the First World War who returns to receive the 'kiss' promised to him by the female singer during a military recruitment drive.

The Grand-Guignol Abroad

While the most significant attempt to establish a permanent Grand-Guignol theatre across the Channel in Britain was the collaboration between José Levy and the Thorndike-Cassons at The Little Theatre between 1920 and 1922, this experiment was itself built upon a visit to London by the Parisian Grand-Guignol Company in 1908. Max Maurey brought the Grand-Guignol ensemble to London to perform a programme of plays in French, presumably also as a way of promoting the theatre to the middle- and upper-class English tourists who would visit Paris as the nearest and most easily reached foreign destination. Levy subsequently staged English versions of two Grand-Guignol adaptations—*Seven Blind Men* (*L'Atelier d'Aveugles*) by Lucien Descaves and *The Medium* (*L'Angoisse*) by Mme de Vylars and Pierre Mille—at the Palladium in 1912. In the same year, examples of the Grand-Guignol repertoire appeared elsewhere in Britain, as in the actor-manager Arthur Bourchier's *Striking Home* in Glasgow—an adaptation of Charles Hellem, W. Valcros and Pol d'Estoc's *Sabotage* (1910)—in which a strike leader's daughter needs an emergency operation, only for the striking workers to switch off the city's power supply, which kills the patient.

In June and July 1915, around a dozen plays formed part of the repertoire during the French Grand-Guignol's residency at the Coronet Theatre
in Notting Hill (Hand and Wilson 2007: 12–15). The plays were, of course,
in French, yet still had to be subjected to the scrutiny of the Lord Chamberlain's Office in order to secure a licence. The dislike for the form that
came to blight José Levy's enterprise in the early 1920s is clearly foreshad-
owed in the handling of the famous company on tour. For example, when
Maurice Level and Étienne Ray's script for *Sous La Lumière Rouge* (*In the
Dark Room*, 1911) was submitted, it was only with 'extreme reluctance'
that the inspector G.S. Street approved the play:

> [This is a] horrible play, and it is almost incredible that in such dread-
> ful times as these there can be any demand for artificial horrors. I do
> not think a license [*sic*] would be given to the play if it were English;
> however, since we have the Grand Guignol here I suppose a certain
> latitude must be given it and I hesitate to recommend rejection.
> (https://www.greatwartheatre.org.uk/db/script/501/)

The season at the Coronet may have been for just a few weeks, but the
Grand-Guignol appeared elsewhere in London soon afterwards. In August
1915, the Garrick Theatre presented a performance of Grand-Guignol
plays including André de Lorde's *La Dernière torture* (*The Ultimate
Torture*, 1904), which the inspector Ernest A. Bendall—seemingly less sen-
sitive than his colleague G.S. Street—approved for licence with this verdict:
'Necessarily painful; but with no offence either of taste or discretion in its
tragic thrills' (https://www.greatwartheatre.org.uk/db/script/606/).

The Garrick's Grand-Guignol season ended the same month that it
began, with *Variety* concluding that 'It has been an artistic success and a
financial failure' (*Variety* 20 August 1915).

Despite these examples, it was not until the interwar period, under the
direction of Camille Choisy, however, that the Théâtre du Grand-Guignol
reached the height of its fame, in the atmosphere of decadence and excess
that prevailed in Jazz Age Paris, and various attempts were made to establish Grand-Guignol theatres in other major cities. The most famous (and
successful) of these was undoubtedly London's Grand Guignol, which presented eight seasons of plays at the Little Theatre in John Adam Street, off
the Strand, between 1920 and 1922, followed by a short provincial tour.
Managed by José Levy and headed by the leading couple of the English
theatrical world at the time, Sybil Thorndike and Lewis Casson, the venture was no little success until it exhausted the patience of the Lord Chamberlain's Office, the official theatre censor. Further seasons were staged
in London in 1928 at the private Arts Theatre Club and in 1945 at the
Granville Theatre, when the censor had become a little more relaxed about
such things, but nothing was able to sustain itself in the way that Levy's

experiment had done. The Little Theatre continued to have some significance in other examples of horror, being the venue that staged the highly
successful run of John Balderston's dramatization of *Dracula* in 1927,
which was the template used by Universal Pictures in their landmark film
version in 1931 starring Bela Lugosi.

Other attempts to establish permanent Grand-Guignol theatres, or at
least regular programmes of horror theatre, were made in Rome and New
York. Interestingly, although the New York venture in 1923 ultimately
failed, as late as 1934 the writer F. Scott Fitzgerald felt that the reason
for this was an insistence on a programme of pure horror plays, rather
than an adoption of the *douche écossaise* model of alternating horror
and comedy, and that there was still potential for establishing a successful
Grand-Guignol model in New York City. Writing to his friend, the author
and critic Gilbert Seldes, Fitzgerald says:

> it seems to me an evening of five nonsense plays would be monoto-
> nous no matter how funny they were, but just suppose taking over the
> technique of the Grand Guignol, two of those plays were alternated
> with something macabre. When the Grand Guignol failed in N.Y.
> it seems to me that I remember that all the plays were plays of hor-
> ror and the minute the novelty wore off it closed up shop. Mightn't
> some enterprising producer be interested in a thoroughly balanced
> program if we could get the material together? I don't know whether
> there are any good horror one-acters in America but we might pick
> up a couple of the Grand Guignol hits very cheaply or get somebody
> to dredge something out of Edgar Allen [*sic*] Poe. What do you think
> of this idea? (31 May 1934)

It is unclear what Seldes's response to Fitzgerald was, but it appears that
the proposition went no further.

Of course, one of the key challenges for producers wishing to establish
Grand-Guignol theatres at the time in England and the USA, in particular,
were the different cultural approaches and levels of tolerance afforded to
matters of displays of violence and eroticism, especially when represented
on the stage. In London, for example, the Lord Chamberlain kept a watchful gaze and paternalistic guardianship over what was being presented on
the nation's stages in order to protect the institution of the theatre as much
as public sensibilities. Certainly, if it was ever felt that the Lord Chamberlain had failed in his duty to police an enterprise as inherently morally
dubious as the theatre, there was no shortage of religious and moral insti-
tutions on hand to remind him of his obligations.

Even after the curtain finally fell on the Little Theatre seasons in June
1922, and the completion of a provincial tour in the summer of that same
year (Hand and Wilson 2007: 76–77), there were sporadic attempts to

re-establish a Grand-Guignol in London and individual Grand-Guignol plays continued to be staged within more general programmes, taking advantage of the appetite for thrills and chills among British theatre audiences. After staging an experimental season at the private Arts Theatre Club in November 1927, Levy himself attempted a revival at the Little Theatre in 1928, reassembling a company of many of the veterans of 1920–22, although, crucially, neither Sybil Thorndike nor Lewis Casson, who had both moved on to other projects by that time (Hand and Wilson 2007: 78–79). In spite of the involvement of the 73-year-old Arthur Wing Pinero, the success of six years earlier was not repeated and the season closed down after three weeks. Levy made no further attempts, dying in 1936, aged 52.

Of particular interest, however, are the seasons staged at the Granville Theatre in Fulham between May and November 1945, as the Second World War finally drew to a close. These were primarily vehicles for the playwright Frederick Witney who was instrumental in persuading A.A. Shenburn, the manager at the Granville, otherwise principally a venue for Variety, to take a gamble with a programme of Grand-Guignol plays with a distinctly British flavour. Of all the plays performed at the Granville that year, nine were by Witney himself, eight of them premieres. Witney's enthusiasm for Grand-Guignol can be traced back to the early 1920s, when he submitted two plays to Levy for consideration for inclusion in the Little Theatre seasons. The two plays, *The Anniversary* (1947: 45–58) and *Coals of Fire* (1947: 61–73) were both banned outright by the censor, although *Coals of Fire* was included in Levy's programme at the Arts Theatre Club in November 1927, but not in the Little Theatre revival the following year. The experience undoubtedly hit Witney hard, and while he enjoyed a modicum of success throughout the 1930s as a writer of comedies, his notes to his collection of Grand-Guignol plays published by Constable in 1947, in the aftermath of the Granville seasons, betray a thinly disguised, lingering bitterness towards the official censor.

In addition to *Coals of Fire*, which played in both the first and third seasons at the Granville, Witney's other contributions to the 1945 seasons were *Nuit de Noces* (1947: 127–36), which premiered on 2 May with Ellen Pollock and Hugh Miller taking the leading roles and co-directing; *The Bitter End*, which also premiered in the same first season; *Coral Strand* (1947: 95–110), which premiered on 28 June under the direction of John Hanau; *Rococo* (1947: 3–21), which opened on 2 August; and *The Celibate* (1947: 77–92), *Weekend Cottage* (139–54), *The Last Kiss* (113–23) and *Say It With Flowers* (1947: 189–203), all of which premiered on 26 October. Of this last group of plays, the first three featured the renowned Shakespearean actress Jean Forbes-Robertson in key roles, and the last two were adaptations from Maurice Level. It is significant that this 1940s British revival of Grand-Guignol incorporates brand new works but also showcases works by Level, one of the giants of Grand-Guignol playwriting during the original theatre's golden age.

Another key member of the Granville company was the melodramatic actor of stage and screen Tod Slaughter, who played (among other parts) the role of La Borgnesse in a revival of André de Lorde's *The Old Women* in the third programme in August. This was the play that had become infamous during Levy's 1920–22 seasons, where it was credited to an unknown writer called Christopher Holland, almost certainly a pseudonym of Lewis Casson, who had translated de Lorde's as yet unperformed play as part of an elaborate ruse to secure a licence from the Lord Chamberlain.[2] It was widely acknowledged as being the most daring of all the Grand-Guignol plays staged at the Little Theatre, and was remembered as much for the harrowing publicity posters produced by Aubrey Hammond that were banned from the London Underground as for Russell Thorndike's gripping performance in the same role as Slaughter took nearly a quarter of a century later.

The inclusion of *The Old Women* is also indicative of how Witney's plays were interleaved with other Grand-Guignol classics, including Eliot Crawshay-Williams's *E. & O. E,*[3] and St John Ervine's *Progress* in the first season,[4] and *Private Room Number 6,*[5] by André de Lorde, and Pierre Chaine and C. de Vylars's *The Kill* in the second season. In addition, *Something More Important* by H.F. Maltby, which had contributed to the programme at the Little Theatre in 1928, was included in the third programme at the Granville, with Slaughter in the lead role. Maltby had written four plays for the 1920–22 seasons, one of which (*I Want to Go Home*) was refused a licence, and he was a prolific writer for both stage and screen, most notably for Tod Slaughter's series of film melodramas.[6]

Reviews for the Granville seasons were broadly positive, if not overly enthusiastic, and the fact that Shenburn ran four seasons of Grand-Guignol plays over a six-month period suggests that the experiment was moderately successful, while not successful enough to ensure a continuation into

---

[2] For the full story see Hand and Wilson (2007: 63–66).

[3] First performed in Levy's fifth series at the Little Theatre in October 1921 and arguably the playwright's most popular and commercially successful play.

[4] First performed in Levy's seventh series in April 1922. Its staging, as an anti-war play that depicts the murder of a scientist who has developed a 'weapon of mass destruction' on 2 May 1945, a mere six days before VE Day and three months before the dropping of the atom bomb on Hiroshima, must have been poignant, if not controversial.

[5] First performed in Levy's second series and credited solely to de Lorde.

[6] *The Crimes of Stephen Hawke* (1936); *Sweeney Todd, The Demon Barber of Fleet Street* (1936); *It's Never Too Late to Mend* (1937); *The Ticket-of-Leave Man* (1937); *Crimes at the Dark House* (1939).

the following year.[7] Again Witney's resentment shows itself in his notes to *Rococo*, probably the least successful of all of the plays, where he bemoans the use of a stock company to perform the seasons, which can lead to poor casting decisions, since 'stock companies (are) death to plays, whatever they may be for actors' (1947: 1). This seems to be a particularly unfair criticism given that the Grand-Guignol in Paris and Levy's earlier experiment had both operated successfully with stock companies and also taking account of the high quality of actors that Shenburn had recruited. By this time, although the horror genre continued to develop in cinematic and literary forms, there was only one further serious attempt to restage Grand-Guignol plays in London during the rest of the twentieth century, when Kenneth Tynan staged a programme of five plays at The Irving Theatre in November 1951 (Hand and Wilson 2007: 80), which included a revival of Witney's *Coals of Fire*.

The Grand-Guignol in England: Writers

The Grand-Guignol always attracted its specialist writers who became famous within the genre. André de Lorde or Charles Méré, for example, are just two among many who forged their careers at the rue Chaptal. Across the Channel in London, H.F. Maltby, who had a successful screenwriting career in the 1930s, not least adapting Tod Slaughter's barnstorming melodrama performances for the screen, and the former MP Eliot Crawshay-Williams were prolific contributors to London's Grand Guignol. At the same time the genre also attracted more widely renowned playwrights. At the rue Chaptal one thinks of Gaston Leroux, Octave Mirbeau and Maurice Renard, while Levy secured contributions from Noël Coward, albeit a young and impecunious writer at the time, and A.W. Pinero. There were, however, a number of other writers who had greater reputations for their prose fiction but who were influenced by the Grand-Guignol. Among them were writers who were better known in their time than now, such as F. Tennyson Jesse, the criminologist and detective novelist, who co-wrote a number of plays with her husband H.M. Harwood, including *The Mask* (1912), which, as well as having been adapted by John Raphaël for presentation at the rue Chaptal in March 1916 under the title *Le Masque*, appeared on the third programme at the Granville in 1945, as well as in Tynan's revival six years later.[8] Two better-known novelists, however, stand

---

[7] In our earlier volume on *London's Grand Guignol* (2007) we stated that the Granville Theatre hosted two seasons in 1945. Further research has since revealed that, in fact, there were four seasons of Grand-Guignol plays, launched respectively in May, June, August and September of that year.

[8] It is interesting that another crime writer from the Golden Age, John Dickson Carr, while never writing for the Grand Guignol, named an early novella after

out for their having tried their hand at the Grand-Guignolesque: Joseph Conrad and Agatha Christie.

Well into his sixties when London's Grand Guignol opened in 1920, Joseph Conrad was regarded as a major living English literary figure with a highly regarded canon of novels to his name. Conrad was primarily seen as a writer of prose fiction who made occasional forays into essay writing, but two successful adaptations of his work in 1919 encouraged him to become a scriptwriter in earnest.[9] In 1919, he dramatized *The Secret Agent* (1907), which received a high-profile but short-lived run in the West End in 1922, and in 1920 he was commissioned by Hollywood to adapt the short story 'Gaspar Ruiz' (1906) into the unproduced screenplay *Gaspar the Strong Man*.

On Thursday 2 December 1920, Conrad attended the Grand Guignol at the Little Theatre and was inspired enough to complete his experiment in horror theatre: the two-act play *Laughing Anne*, an adaptation of his short story 'Because of the Dollars' (1915). The play presents the decent, if not heroic, Captain Davidson and his old friend the prostitute 'Laughing' Anne in their confrontation with a trio of gangsters, led by the diabolical 'Man Without Hands', who seek to rob Davidson of his cargo of currency. The play builds up an atmosphere of intimidation and danger to the climax in which Davidson takes on the mob in a gunfight and prevails, although Anne is bludgeoned to death by the maimed ringleader who has iron weights strapped to his stumps. Conrad submitted the play to the Little Theatre only for it to be rejected by Levy. In assessing the play for its publication after Conrad's death, John Galsworthy was highly critical of the work, saying that the play reveals Conrad's naivete about what was possible or acceptable on stage. Galsworthy gives a specific example:

> Conrad probably never realised that a 'man without hands' would be an almost unbearable spectacle; that what you can write about freely cannot always be endured by the living eye. (Galsworthy 1924: 7)

---

the theatre. 'Grand Guignol' first appeared in *The Haverfordian* in 1929 and was an early outing for his series detective Henri Bencolin, prefect of the Paris Police. Dickson Carr, an American by birth and an Anglophile by nature, spent some time in Paris as a young man in the mid-1920s, and this gruesome locked room mystery is a homage to one of his favourite Parisian haunts. He later expanded the story into his first novel, *It Walks by Night*, first published in 1930 and recently republished in the British Library Crime Classics series.

[9] In 1919, Basil Macdonald Hastings's stage dramatization of Conrad's novel *Victory* (1915) enjoyed a large-scale and successful run at the Globe Theatre in the West End produced by, and starring, the actor-manager Marie Löhr. In the same year, an entirely unrelated film version of *Victory* was produced in Hollywood featuring Lon Chaney. This major release was directed by Maurice Tourneur, who was a well-established French theatre director who had worked at the Grand-Guignol in Paris before moving into motion pictures and emigrating to the USA in 1914.

However, in his own account of the play's rejection, Conrad gives a rather different reason:

> Mr Levy did not see his way to produce it—at which I was not surprised—the second Act being very difficult to stage with convincing effect. Too much darkness; too much shooting. (Partington 2000: 179–80)

It seems evident that Levy rejected the play on the grounds of its technical demands and not because of Galsworthy's 'unbearable spectacle'. In fact, *Laughing Anne* makes perfect sense once assessed through a genre-specific lens. As a whole, *Laughing Anne* presents conflict and cruelty with bloodshed, including the unexpected and brutal demise of the eponymous character. It is unmistakably a Grand-Guignol play that seeks to find a frisson of thrills within the 'shuddering' of shock. If anything, Levy's alleged criticism of the play for containing 'too much shooting' perhaps reveals that Levy desired more suitably imaginative modes of murder for London's Grand Guignol. Despite being in print with performing rights available for decades, *Laughing Anne*—in all likelihood served no favours by Galsworthy's disparaging preface—did not grace the stage until it was premiered in 2000 (Knowles and Moore 2001: 225) as part of the Grand-Guignol Laboratory established by the authors at the University of Glamorgan.

Agatha Christie first established her reputation with *The Mysterious Affair at Styles* (1920), which was followed at the rate of approximately one novel per year during the 1920s, increasing to two or three per year during the 1930s. It was during this period that the detective novel, framed largely as a kind of protracted crossword puzzle during which readers were invited to play detective and pit their wits against the writer and the fictional detective, reached significant heights of popularity. It was also the age of the stage thriller in Britain, which began in earnest with Sir Gerald du Maurier's portrayal of Bulldog Drummond for the first time in 1921. As James Harding says, this captured the spirit of the age with its 'crude thrills, spectacular villainy, titillating horror and sadism unashamed' (Harding 1989: 112), and John Stokes argues that this new fascination with stage violence was an inevitable response to the traumatic legacy of the war (Stokes 2000: 47–48). Of course, both the stage thriller and the detective novel have much in common, not least their subject matter, but it is this coming together of the fashions for both thrills and game-playing that also heralded the Golden Age of the Grand-Guignol in Paris and the establishment of London's Grand Guignol by José Levy.

Christie was also a keen and avid theatregoer from an early age (Green 2018: 33) and 'was passionate about the theatre' (5) and 'the collaborative nature of the process, enabling her as it did to exchange ideas with others in a way that her largely solitary work as a novelist did not' (4). Christie was living in London during the 1920–22 seasons at the Little Theatre and, as a dedicated theatregoer and Francophile, it seems highly likely she would have attended. Further circumstantial evidence that Christie attended Levy's London seasons in the early 1920s comes in the form of a letter that she sent to her mother from Melbourne on 9 May 1922 in which she wrote: 'I've been rather idle—but have written a Grand Guignol sketch and a short story' (Agatha Christie Archive and quoted in Green 2018: 48).

In January 1922, Christie had accompanied her husband, Archie Christie, on a ten-month tour of South Africa, Australia, New Zealand and Canada to promote the British Empire Exhibition that was planned for 1924,[10] and she clearly had horror on her mind. While in South Africa she wrote a short story entitled 'The Wife of the Kenite' (Medawar 2018: 313–22). Set on the South African veldt, it is a revenge tale that ends with the gruesome image of a nail being hammered into a victim's skull. This was the story that Christie was referring to in her letter to her mother, and it was an idea she later reworked for the radio play *Butter in a Lordly Dish* (1948).[11] The 'sketch' that is being referred to is *The Last Séance*, an unpublished and unperformed playscript that was eventually turned into a short story and published in the UK in the collection *The Hound of Death* in 1933.

The Last Séance is (perhaps significantly) set in Paris; it concerns a spiritual medium who is being exploited by her fiancé and is persuaded to perform a private sitting for a bereaved mother who wishes to make contact with her deceased daughter. The medium has sat for the woman before and on each occasion the apparition of the daughter has been increasingly realistic, but the séance has left the medium progressively exhausted and frail. This will be the last sitting, but the medium is frightened that a terrible fate waits her. As the séance unfolds, the daughter's spirit materializes and, reunited with each other, the mother and daughter flee. As the curtain behind which the medium is sitting is drawn back, she is collapsed on the floor, dead and 'literally "awash with blood"' (Green 2018: 558).

Julius Green suggests that Christie did very little with the playscript to adapt it into short story form. 'The dialogue', he complains, 'which simply appears to have had speech marks put around it, works well when spoken, but not when read, and the highly theatrical denouement, when briefly described on the page, goes for nothing' (Green 2018: 50). Green's observation is a fair one and it makes for a curious read as a short story, only making sense if the reader imagines the scenes playing out on the stage. The story's origins as a stage play are evident.

---

[10] For further information see Christie (2013).
[11] The play was the first in a series of six radio plays broadcast as *Mystery Playhouse Presents The Detection Club*, each written by a different member of The Detection Club to raise money for the society's coffers.

One can only guess why the play never saw the light of day, but it seems quite probable that Christie wrote the play with London's Grand Guignol in mind. It is not clear whether Christie had any correspondence with either José Levy or Lewis Casson, but when she left London it was a highly successful venture and there was no sign that it would come to an end six months later. It seems likely that Christie's intention was to submit the play to Levy upon her return to England at the end of the year, only to find that when she returned, London's Grand Guignol had already closed down in June. Undoubtedly, without the London Grand Guignol there would have been very limited, if any, opportunity to stage a one-act horror play of this kind, and the script appears to have been filed away until it was brought back into service as a short story four years later.[12]

As we can see, the Théâtre du Grand-Guignol was an inspiration for imitators who created rival theatres in Paris and homage-venues in London, but most important and influential was the *idea* of the theatre and its trademark formula. The *concept* of this genre of theatre captured the imagination of writers as diverse as Joseph Conrad, F. Scott Fitzgerald, Agatha Christie and John Dickson Carr. The cultural importation of the structural and narrative concepts underpinning this very French form of theatre was exciting to many in the Anglophone theatre from producers to actors and writers. Moreover, it is this idea, this concept of horror theatre, that has continued to cast a shadow over theatre into the twenty-first century.

---

[12] The Grand-Guignol continued to play an influence on Christie. *The Rule of Three* (1962), a set of three one-act plays, very clearly adopts a typical *douche écossaise* structure. The opening play, *The Rats*, described by C.D. Heriot, the Reader from the Lord Chamberlain's Office in his report as 'quite a good Guignol' (quoted in Green 2018, 503), is a story about a pair of lovers who become trapped in a room with a trunk that contains the body of the woman's husband. Julius Green (502) suggests that this is drawing from Maurice Level's *Le Crime*, which opened at the rue Chaptal in March 1918 and was featured in Levy's fifth season at the Little Theatre in October 1921 as *Crime*, an adaptation by Lewis Casson.

3

The New Wave

The Théâtre du Grand-Guignol may have closed its doors at the end of 1962, but the genre, as opposed to the building, has never really gone away. We have seen there have been sporadic experiments in horror theatre, and one can explore the thin boundaries between thrillers, crimes and whodunits and the horror genre. Even the great totemic play of mainstream, West End theatre, Agatha Christie's *The Mousetrap* (1952), the world's longest running play, presents a play of claustrophobic realism with murder, humour and intensely disturbing psychology that would not have been out of place in rue Chaptal. We saw in Chapter 1 that horror as a genre frequently treads the boards. Mainstream producers have doubtless been encouraged by the success of *The Woman in Black*, *The Exorcist* and *Ghost Stories* to invest in a horror play. Venues such as the Noël Coward Theatre in the West End returned to activity after the COVID-19 pandemic—an era that spelled near disaster for live performance—with Danny Robins's *2:22* (2021), a haunted house drama, clearly hoping that it would have enough appeal to bring back its audiences. As well as having box office appeal, developments in theatre technology have facilitated the realization of horror and the uncanny: these plays and others frequently hybridize classic stage trickery (Pepper's Ghost and trapdoors to 'Kensington gore' stage blood effects) with ingenious advances in audiovisual digital technology.

A particularly interesting example in contemporary mainstream theatre is Peter James. A prolific and popular novelist, James has co-created a number of stage adaptations of his crime fiction with the playwright Shaun McKenna. As Robins did with *2:22*, James strove to break the stalemate of cultural lockdown with a national tour of *Looking Good Dead* (2021), a play about bankruptcy, blackmail and livestreaming 'snuff' porn. This, like several of James's plays, brings the intrepid yet troubled detective Roy Grace from the page to the stage. If we consider a play such as *Dead Simple* (2015), this may be a tale of crime and detection with Grace on the case, but it explores very dark territory indeed: at its heart is a stag night prank gone wrong with a groom-to-be buried alive in a coffin (presented in the original production with inventive scenography), as well as disturbing scenes of torture and violent murder. It is an excellent example in the rich tradition of the crime thriller, but in its disturbing scenario, characters and gore can be easily interpreted through a Grand-Guignolesque lens. James's/McKenna's plays have also strayed into stage horror of a different kind with *The House on Cold Hill* (2019), a haunted house story: this presents a classic neo-Gothic narrative of a family moving into a very old house but, like the aforementioned *2:22*, updates some of these conventions with possessed Alexa devices as well as traditional haunted mirrors and other tropes of the uncanny.

As a final example of horror in contemporary theatre, Carl Grose's *Grand Guignol* (2009) is a fascinating and playful homage to the history and practices of the Parisian horror theatre that premiered at The Drum at the Theatre Royal Plymouth in 2009 and was later successfully revived in 2014, playing again at Plymouth, before moving for a run at the Southwark Playhouse in London. Carl Grose is an actor, writer and director, as well as (until 2021) Co-Artistic Director of Kneehigh Theatre, with whom he has worked extensively for many years. Drawing heavily on the first book in this series (Hand and Wilson 2002), Grose created not an authentic Grand-Guignol horror drama as such, but a horror comedy that is set at the theatre in the rue Chaptal and draws heavily upon its history, albeit creatively rather than accurately. André de Lorde, Max Maurey, Paul Ratineau and Alfred Binet, as well as the actors Maxa and Paulais all make appearances, as a story based around de Lorde's nightmares and his relationship with Binet plays out against a backdrop of scenes from the classic repertoire of the Grand-Guignol.

While using the Grand-Guignol, its history and its key personalities as his raw material, Grose's homage to, and affection for, the Grand-Guignol is more evident in the playfulness that ran throughout the production. With its mix of melodrama, naturalism and farce, the production employed a series of well-executed technical tricks of which Ratineau himself would have been proud, as it 'plays neatly on the difference between fakery and reality' (Lyn Gardner, *The Guardian* 2 November 2014). Its playfulness echoed that which was evident at the rue Chaptal (see Hand and Wilson 2002: 69–72) and caused Howard Loxton, reviewing for the *British Theatre Guide*, to remark on how Grose made 'the audience feel part of some elaborate game'.[13] In its mixture of drama, comedy and extracts, Grose's *Grand Guignol* offered its own *douche écossaise* within a single, scripted play. Being staged in the intimate auditoria at The Drum and Southwark Playhouse worked well for this play of horror and hilarity. Grose, a significant figure in contemporary British theatre, has continued with his interest in horror, as both theatrical form and device. This is evident in his *The Grinning Man* (2016), a playfully grotesque neo-Gothic musical based on Victor Hugo's *The Man Who Laughs* (1869) and his adaptation of John Willard's comedy horror *The Cat and the Canary* (1922), which toured

---

[13] https://www.britishtheatreguide.info/reviews/grand-guignol-southwark-playh-10851, accessed 17.11.20.

the UK in early 2020, prior to the national closure of theatre owing to the COVID-19 pandemic, in a production with Britt Ekland and directed by Roy Marsden.

All these examples demonstrate that horror theatre is never far from the stage as a viable option in contemporary theatre. Some companies, however, have dared to go beyond the odd foray into horror. Since the 1990s, a succession of self-proclaimed horror theatre companies have emerged in what might be thought of as a vibrant revival or continuation of the tradition of the Grand-Guignol theatre. Many of these attempts have, like José Levy's time-limited enterprise at the Little Theatre in London in the early 1920s, been short-lived, two- to three-year experiments that have come and gone, but no less important for all that. The most successful of these companies have thrived over many years. They have predominated in the USA, UK and Ireland, but can also be found in the non-anglophone world, and in this chapter we include examples from Brazil, Italy and France. The companies mentioned in this chapter are not meant to comprise an exhaustive list—far from it—but are simply a representative snapshot of professional, semi-professional and amateur groups that have sought to continue the Grand-Guignol tradition since the 1990s. Like all tradition bearers, they have produced work that both conforms to and challenges the established orthodoxies of the genre.

It is worth noting at this point that the Grand-Guignol was always a rewarding form for female artists: this is evident in the celebration of Paula Maxa and Sybil Thorndike as what we would call 'scream queens' in Paris and London respectively, Eva Berkson as the artistic director of the Théâtre du Grand-Guignol in the 1940s, and countless rich roles for women in the French and English repertoire, from victims to villains to victors. In discussing contemporary horror film, Samantha Holland argues that although horror is sometimes dismissed as being 'about a blonde girl trying to escape capture and torture' (Holland 2019: 2) it is much more than that: 'horror is always based on contemporary anxieties and so will always find new ways to tell those stories and new styles to do so' (Holland 2019: 1). The Grand-Guignol is an example of how this is emphatically the case in theatre too: the original Grand-Guignol tapped into the anxieties of its time and some of its plays can be adversely judged now for their redundant stereotypes regarding race, mental illness, sexuality and other themes. Nevertheless, the original theatre's concerns about personal security, medicine and science continue to chime. The contemporary Grand-Guignolesque has, by default, updated itself and treats the representation of many subjects with more sophistication and nuance than the original repertoire. At the same time, fear remains at the core of the genre: we witness in the Grand-Guignolesque the age-old tradition of telling tales of terror to tap into our personal or collective anxieties, albeit in new and evolving styles.

Grand-Guignolesque USA

In this section, we will address the (re)discovery of the Grand-Guignol form in the USA. There are two key companies in this story: one on the West Coast (Thrillpeddlers) and another on the East (Molotov Theatre Group). These two companies have produced Grand-Guignol, and Grand-Guignolesque, work with energy and ambition and have secured audiences—and awards—in the process. After telling the stories of these distinct companies, we will give further examples of how the Grand-Guignol has manifested across a wide range of American theatre.

Thrillpeddlers

Thrillpeddlers, based in San Francisco, was arguably the foremost Grand-Guignol company in recent times. Formed in 1996 by Russell Blackwood and Daniel Zilber, it became a feature on the San Francisco alternative theatre scene, running the annual Halloween Shocktoberfest from 1999 until its demise in 2017, following the loss of the lease on the Hypnodrome, which had been its home since 2004.

Blackwood and Zilber had been childhood friends in Kansas City, producing homegrown theatre and horror movies, sometimes under the name Belle Nouveau Productions. Zilber's father had spent his childhood until his early teenage years in Paris before moving to the USA, and it was from him that the two young horror fans learned about the Théâtre du Grand-Guignol. By 1991 Blackwood had moved to San Francisco, where he was working full time for the San Francisco Shakespeare Festival and establishing a name for himself as a theatre director. That year, under the Belle Nouveau banner, Blackwood staged a version of de Lorde's *Laboratory of Hallucinations*, audaciously adapting the script that had been recently published in Mel Gordon's book on the Grand-Guignol, while forgetting to credit Gordon, who had himself recently moved to take up a chair at the University of California Berkeley. In what turned out to be a serendipitous occasion, Gordon turned up to see the show and challenged Blackwood. Blackwood tells of how Gordon generously forgave the transgression, saying 'It's just the kind of thing I would have done when I was young' (interview, 31 August 2017).

Belle Nouveau Productions evolved into Thrillpeddlers in 1996, when Blackwood left his role at the Shakespeare Festival after five years, and he spent the next three years staging occasional Grand-Guignol and other plays, including a residency in South Africa in 1999, where he directed a free adaptation of de Lorde's *A Crime in the Madhouse*, which had become available in English through the revised edition of Gordon's book in 1998. It was when he returned in 1999, however, that Thrillpeddlers really began to find its own unique identity, after Zilber joined him in San Francisco and they staged the first Shocktoberfest.

Figure 3. Thrillpeddlers, poster for *Shocktoberfest 13:*
The Bride of Death (image credit: Flynn DeMarco)

The 1999 Shocktoberfest programme consisted of four plays: de Lorde's *A Crime in the Madhouse* and *Dr Tarr and Professor Feather*, Frederick Witney's *The Celibate*, which had been first staged in October 1945 at the Granville, after having previously banned by the Lord Chamberlain for Levy's 1920–22 seasons, and a Victorian fetish play called *A Visit to Mrs Birch and the Young Ladies of the Academy*. This blend of reworked and adapted classic Grand-Guignol scripts mixed with high camp erotica and fetishism became part of the Thrillpeddlers trademark style that built them a substantial and loyal following over the next sixteen years of Shocktoberfests, as well as attracting both new and established performers, such as Jill Tracy (who became their leading performer after first appearing in Charles Méré's 1928 play *The Beast* (*L'homme nu*) in 2004).

The secret of this success—in addition to the consistent high quality of the productions—can be attributed to two things. First, Blackwood and Zilber

Figure 4. Thrillpeddlers, production still, *The Orgy in the Lighthouse*, 2000
(photo credit: David Allen)

did not try to recreate the Parisian Grand-Guignol in twenty-first-century San Francisco, but instead created a version of the Grand-Guignol that was unapologetically San Franciscan. As Blackwood says, 'Halloween in the Castro was always a major, major thing', but the arts community hadn't really started catering for it (interview, 31 August 2017). What Thrillpeddlers were able to do was to fill that particular gap, and Shocktoberfest became a celebration of San Francisco as a city of tolerance that embraced alternative cultures and as a community emerging from the trauma of AIDS, which had particularly affected San Francisco and the gay community living in the Castro. According to Blackwood, 'from the get-go Daniel and I felt like this could only be happening here and that we only wanted to try and make a go of it here' (interview, 31 August 2017). In the same way that the Parisian Théâtre du Grand-Guignol necessarily emerged in fin-de-siècle Montmartre, Thrillpeddlers were equally successful because of their ties to time and place, becoming '*what* it did because it emerged *when* it did and *where* it did' (Hand and Wilson 2002: x).

The second factor in their success was the acquisition of their own venue, the Hypnodrome, an empty former antiques warehouse, in time for the 2004 season, which was titled as *Welcome to the Hypnodrome*. Up until that point the cost of renting theatre space to perform had meant that every season existed on a financial knife edge. Thrillpeddlers were given a

free lease on the warehouse for an initial period of two years, which became thirteen years, before the building was sold and, in an echo of what
happened at the rue Chaptal in early 1962, the company disbanded and
disposed of its props and other assets in February 2017. However, for thirteen years the Hypnodrome enabled Thrillpeddlers to maintain a constant
physical and visible presence in the city and develop an auditorium that
was particularly suited to their particular style of Grand-Guignol. While
the new seating capacity was much smaller than they had had at other
theatres, only forty-five in total, the lack of rent meant they could extend
runs and maximize audiences by keeping ticket prices low and still avoid
losing money. Blackwood's stage designer father was recruited to design
the new auditorium, constructed largely out of repurposed materials, including Thrillpeddlers' unique version of the rue Chaptal's *loges grillées*.
These were the 'shock-boxes', semi-private theatre boxes at the back of
the auditorium (as at the rue Chaptal), which were designed in a way that
allowed actors to creep up behind them and poke sticks or squirt water,
for example, through strategically placed holes in a reimagining of the
Grand-Guignol's playfulness, San Francisco style. Like the introduction of
the *médecin de service* (house doctor) at the Théâtre du Grand-Guignol,
this additional gimmick helped build the Thrillpeddlers' identity and reputation, as well as a uniquely playful audience experience.

Between 1996 and 2017, the Thrillpeddlers combination of 'authentic
Grand Guignol horror plays, outrageous Theatre of the Ridiculous musicals, and spine-tingling lights-out spook shows' (www.thrillpeddlers.com)
won the company both critical acclaim and awards, including the Best of
San Francisco Award in 2015 for *Creepshow Camp*. It also provided the
foundation for collaborations, both locally (such as creating musicals with
The Cockettes, the (in)famous 1970s drag troupe) and internationally. For
example, they collaborated with Brazilian Grand-Guignol company Vigor
Mortis, resulting in a tour to Rio de Janeiro in 2013, and also with various
Grand-Guignol practitioners in the UK. They performed the American pre-
miere of Noël Coward's *The Better Half* in March 2011, directed by Eddie
Muller, 'the czar of noir', who had previously provided translations of French
scripts for the company. For Shocktoberfest in 2013 Carl Grose contributed
an adaptation of André de Lorde and Pierre Chaine's 1934 play *Jack the
Ripper* (*Jack L'Éventreur*) to 'an evening of Horror, Madness, Spanking and
Song commemorating the 125th anniversary of the Jack the Ripper Mur-
ders in London' (https://www.brownpapertickets.com/event/445136) that
also featured a new play, *The Wrong Ripper*, by Rob Keefe and a revival
of *A Visit to Mrs Birch*. All of this provided Thrillpeddlers with an international visibility and reputation, enhanced by their own websites (www.
thrillpeddlers.com and www.grandguignol.com), which not only promoted
their own work, but also acted as an important online introduction and
resource for those interested in the genre. Over a period exceeding twenty

years, Thrillpeddlers are the only company to have successfully established a viable Grand-Guignol theatre outside Paris, achieved through a combination of learning from the tradition, while simultaneously innovating and adapting it for its own modern and San Franciscan audiences.

Molotov Theatre Group

Probably the most established horror theatre company in the USA, second to Thrillpeddlers, is Molotov Theatre Group. Indeed, the two companies have collaborated in exchanges, with Molotov mounting a production of *Mondo Andronicus*, Thrillpeddlers' adaptation of Shakespeare's *Titus Andronicus*. Molotov was founded in Washington DC in 2006 with a conscious interest in horror performance. This specialism had already begun before the company developed, as Alex Zavistovich (co-founder and artistic director of Molotov) puts it, 'a deep understanding, of Grand-Guignol' (interview, 24 April 2015). This is revealing: contemporary theatre companies are frequently attracted to the *idea* of the Grand-Guignol before they have a detailed knowledge of the genre itself. Part of the pleasure in exploring a company such as Molotov is detecting their process of 'research and development' as they have immersed themselves in the genre and subsequently pushed it forward into a twenty-first-century iteration of horror theatre, one that has roots in the traditional Grand-Guignol but is also an achievement all of its own.

Interestingly, Zavistovich admits that their detailed research into Grand-Guignol began after they had become successful as 'the horror theatre' on the DC theatre scene. Molotov had capitalized on their reputation with gimmicks such as 'Blood-Proof Ponchos' and 'Splash Zone' seating. This incarnation of theatre as 'thrill-ride' was indubitably popular, but these were stunts that Molotov began to shift away from. Their scholarly and practical research revealed that there was more to Grand-Guignol than stage blood and they began to develop a more sophisticated (re)construction of the genre.

Following Molotov's research work, Zavistovich began to see something of a sea change when it came to audience and reception. A novelty factor remained for regular theatregoers who might be used to live performance but not when it is presenting horror. As Zavistovich assesses:

> (The typical theatre audience) would rather spend money to see another revival of a musical or either a relationship comedy or a comedy of manners or something that they feel challenges them intellectually and doesn't ask them for much of a visceral reaction other than a feeling of 'isn't this pretty'. But we didn't want that kind of theatre right from the very beginnings. Molotov began also because at the time we started every theatre mission statement had some version

of 'to explore the human experience' to the point where it became a joke to us. Seriously, how much exploration of the human experience can you have in ninety minutes, with or without an intermission? (Interview, 24 April 2015)

Looked at like this, Molotov may seem to be the *enfant terrible* in the Washington DC theatre scene, but it has had success in drawing an audience. It has won multiple awards, not least with the 2013 revival of William Mastrosimone's *Extremities* (1982), a violent and morally complex drama about rape and revenge, which enjoyed phenomenal success at the DC Metro Theater Arts Best of 2013 awards, winning across the categories of Best Play, Best Director and Best Actor and Actress (both lead and supporting).

If Molotov's output continues to challenge and surprise regular theatre-goers, they have made considerable efforts to broaden out the demographic of their audience, such as their production of Jennifer Haley's *Neighborhood 3: Requisition of Doom* in 2015, a horror play about digital gaming, which drew in a swath of audience more experienced in videogames than theatre. With this and other productions wherein Molotov attempts to capture a spectator more used to a cornucopia of screen horror, the distinctiveness and specificity of Molotov's brand of stage horror came to the fore. To this end, the company created 'The Molotov Manifesto' (see Chapter 4), which stands as an enlightening and tangible expression of twenty-first-century horror theatre and the Grand-Guignolesque.

Molotov has produced numerous Grand-Guignol seasons, featuring productions of classic Grand-Guignol plays as well as modern horror plays written by a wide range of contemporary playwrights. These plays have strayed into areas the traditional Grand-Guignol would have avoided, such as adaptations of H.P. Lovecraft or plays about psychic investigation, but the performance practice of Molotov has always adhered to its carefully realized post-Grand-Guignol aesthetic in terms of effect and the dramatic structure of live horror performance. An extremely important part of this is the pre-show and framing of a Molotov show. The company has produced many of its shows in the studio theatre within the DC Arts Center in the Adams Morgan district of Washington, which is accessed through the Center's art gallery. This itself creates an interesting journey into the performance space that has frequently been consolidated with Zavistovich acting as host at the beginning of the show, ratcheting up the suspense and humour to the event with suitable warnings, macabre jokes and other gimmicks (including merchandise). Zavistovich signals the importance of this 'packaging': 'Early on, we decided to capitalise on the shock factor and we would give people vomit bags, barf bags, which were just paper bags with the Molotov logo printed on them. We put out a press release about this to exploit the "camp" factor' (interview, 24 April 2015).

In using a host to frame the shows, Molotov is not alone. Indeed, it is notable how frequently contemporary horror companies use a framing host or master of ceremonies to engage the audience but also to 'explain' the Grand-Guignol and its formula. It can add a successful sense of cabaret, breaking down the barrier between the audience and the ensemble, traversing the fourth wall to ensure that the spectators are co-creators in the live horror experience. The function of a host when used at a Molotov night is centrally to emphasize the purpose of the *douche écossaise* and the essential interpolation of horror with comedy. As Zavistovich explains:

> When I give a curtain speech, I have to give people permission to laugh. They think they're there for completely different reasons. They can often resist the temptation to laugh even when the comedy is written large in the script. When you give them permission to laugh, not only do they get more involved in the show, the scares are so much bigger because their guard is down. (Interview, 24 April 2015)

When time has not permitted a host speech, the atmosphere is apparently much more 'leaden', with the actors having a lot less to play off. On such occasions, Zavistovich feels that the audience leaves the theatre saying 'Well, that was weird, why was all that comedy in the show? (interview, 24 April 2015).

We can see that an acute interest in audience reaction and engagement is of paramount importance in the intimate performances of Molotov. Zavistovich discusses the potency of live theatre when he gives advice to actors regarding the targeting of audiences:

> Break that fourth wall, find the person in the audience who's having the hardest time with it and focus on them. Prolong the agony, distort the time. Don't break eye contact with that person. If you can touch them, even better. We've had fights, wherein trying to scramble to escape, we've had an actor put his hand on someone's knee. They hate it. They hate it and they love it in that most delicious way. Then it palpably ramps things up, because the rest of the audience thinks 'I could be next!' And they sit on the edge of their seats, wondering what the interaction is going to be. In breaking down that imperious fourth wall, that is where the magic actually happens in that voyeuristic connection. (Interview, 24 April 2015)

Like many modern theatre companies, Molotov cannot survive on its intimate nights of Grand-Guignolesque horror alone. Consequently, Molotov has offered specialist acting training and educational work, including 'Shakespeare Flesh and Blood' high school workshops (exploring *Hamlet* via Grand-Guignol techniques). In 2014, Molotov's production of Eric Coble's *Nightfall with Edgar Allan Poe* enjoyed particular critical and popular success. This eventually led to Alex Zavistovich heading up a major initiative in the nearby city of Baltimore (which has strong Poe associations) at the National Edgar Allan Poe Theatre, 'a theatre production and entertainment organization focused on presenting the works of Edgar Allan Poe for the stage, for broadcast, and for education' (https://www.poetheatre.org/our-shows). The initiative has extrapolated the counter-cultural foundations of Molotov, audaciously performing excess, gore and horror in the nation's capital city, into a project affiliated with urban regeneration, heritage industry and education. The National Edgar Allan Poe Theatre might seem far from the notorious horrors of Molotov at its goriest, but we should remember that Poe was a key influence on the original Grand-Guignol, even being described as the theatre's 'patron saint'.

Grand-Guignolesque USA: Other Examples

The USA has seen other attempts to explore the Grand-Guignol. Notable examples include Nosedive Productions in New York City, which was established in the early 2000s.[14] Other examples have included Pandemic Collective in Denver, Colorado, which, its 'Mission Statement' explains, is 'dedicated to infecting the masses through horror theatre' (http://www.pandemiccollective.org/mission-statement.html). Since the 2010s, Pandemic Collective has delivered frequent seasons of horror theatre, spanning productions of *The Woman in Black* to recurrent *Nights of Grand Guignol*, which present modern horror plays in homage to the Grand-Guignol tradition.

On the West Coast, performer-producer Debbie McMahon established the Grand Guignolers in Los Angeles, which presented horror theatre in a dynamic hybridization of popular performance traditions. Their first show was *An Evening of Grand Guignol* (2007) at the celebrated Moth arts venue in Hollywood, which featured the classic Grand-Guignol plays *The Final Kiss* and *A Crime in the Madhouse* with an all-new play *The Kiss of Death*. Other successful seasons followed soon afterwards, including *A Very Grand Guignol Christmas* (2007), which similarly mixed classic plays with all-new works, and *A Grand Guignol Children's Show* (*NOT For Children)* (2008), which effectively 'Grand-Guignolized' fairy tales and folk tales.

Arguably, the Grand Guignolers' most successful show was *Absinthe, Opium and Magic: 1920s Shanghai* (2009). The production had a three-month sell out run at the ArtWorks venue, which it converted into a journey

---

[14] For an account of this company's successful history as a horror theatre, please see the preface to *A Room With No View* by James Comtois in the Plays section of this volume.

by ship to decadent Shanghai, echoing the original Grand-Guignol's fascination with setting plays in the 'Exotic East', permitting rich opportunities for
design and no small measure of 'Orientalism' (Hand and Wilson 2002: 199).
The *Los Angeles Times* was very impressed by the production, praising its immersivity, recommending that audience get in the spirit by dressing in 1920s
cocktail attire and summing it up as 'all in all, the most fun you're likely to
have at a decapitation' (19 December 2009). The review goes on to say:

> Exploring the less wholesome appetites of the psyche has always been
> near and dear to the hearts of these macabre purveyors of horror and
> humor. But in four inventively interlocking segments showcasing her
> unique stylistic fusion of Grand Guignol with commedia dell'arte,
> puppetry, music and dance, McMahon and her hard-working ensem-
> ble also offer some (literally) sharp-edged social commentary.

The beautifully designed production captured the decadent allure of the
1920s with humour, song and an intoxicating 'exoticism'. It is interesting that the reviewer signals the 'social commentary' of the plays. Grand-
Guignol is so often thought of for the shock factor and titillation of its
horror and hilarity, but often could make a political point. In *Absinthe,
Opium and Magic*, this included the play *The Cabinet of Hands* by Chris
Bell, in which an entitled Western tourist receives a gruesome comeuppance
when patronizing a 'quaint' opium den. This drama is in the tradition of an
original Grand-Guignol play such as Pierre Chaine and André de Lorde's
adaptation of Octave Mirbeau's *Torture Garden* in 1922: both plays can
be regarded as brutal satires of Western colonial attitudes.

A key ingredient in the Grand Guignolers' repertoire is Les Petits
Guignolers, an ensemble of finger puppets who are charged with presenting their own vignette or full play within the overall *douche écossaise*. The
name 'Grand-Guignol', of course, references the traditional Lyonnais 'guignol' puppet show, which draws upon the commedia dell'arte and is similar to the English Punch and Judy show. Accordingly, one translation of
'Grand-Guignol' might be 'puppet show for adults'. The Grand Guignolers
have taken this literally with their Les Petits Guignolers company within
the ensemble, taking over proceedings with their bawdy and/or gruesome entertainments. Les Petits Guignolers are not the only examples of
Grand-Guignol puppetry in the USA. Every autumn since 2005, the Center
for Puppetry Arts in Atlanta, Georgia, has staged an annual Halloween
celebration, *The Ghastly Dreadfuls*. The show takes the form of a variety
or vaudeville programme, presenting a series of short ten-minute stories
and songs, or turns, performed by multi-skilled puppeteers and musicians,
employing a range of puppetry forms (shadow puppets, marionettes, etc.).
The puppeteers themselves adopt camp horror personas and often perform
alongside, and interacting with, the puppets themselves. Their repertoire

draws widely on a range of Halloween-appropriate material, relying heavily upon the supernatural and the Gothic, but in 2016 included in the programme was an adaptation of André de Lorde and Alfred Binet's *The Horrific Experiment*, using the adaptation included in our earlier volume (2016). The programme also included adaptations of Oscar Wilde's 'The Canterville Ghost', Patricia McKissack's children's story 'The 11:59', 'The Ghost on the Trapeze' (an original story by the company), along with a rendition of 'Riders in the Sky' and a 'traditional calypso' entitled 'Zombie Jamboree'. The incorporation of Grand-Guignol horror drama into the programme was well received by its audience and resulted in a revival of the piece in the following year's show. Les Petits Guignolers and *The Ghastly Dreadfuls* prove that the Grand-Guignol can be popular and effective when presented in puppet form—as well as a rather satisfying journey back to the etymological roots of the term.

Grand-Guignolesque UK

There have been many theatre ensembles in the UK that have specialized as horror theatre companies. Significant companies such as Theatre of the Damned from London; Dreamcatcher Horror Theatre from Devon; Tin Shed Theatre Company from Newport, Wales; and License to Thrill, Liverpool, are all represented in the Plays section of this volume, and we direct you to look at the Prefaces of their plays for overviews of their respective achievements. Among other companies, we might consider Le Nouveau Guignol, which was the first professional company to emerge directly from our work with the Grand-Guignol Laboratory at the University of Glamorgan (now the University of South Wales). Graham Townsend, a former Glamorgan student, established the company in London in 2010 and enjoyed a degree of success for the two years they ran. In that time, they produced a number of thematically organised shows (such as *Ladies Night: Femmes Fatales and Wayward Women* and *Strange Love: Romance . . . The Guignol Way*), generally following the *douche écossaise* formula of alternating horror and comedies, and created programmes of rarely performed plays from the repertoires of both the rue Chaptal and Levy's Little Theatre. These included Reginald Berkeley's *Eight o' Clock* (2010) and H.F. Maltby's *I Want To Go Home* (2011), both from Levy's London seasons, and Level's *The Final Kiss* (2011), Eugène Héros and Léon Abric's *Chop-Chop* (2011) and Alfred Machard's *Orgy in the Lighthouse* (2011), the latter two as part of the programme they presented at the London Horror Festival in 2011 at the Courtyard Theatre in Hoxton, a major festival we will be looking at in due course. Unfortunately, this was to be their last production, as the key players moved on to other projects.

Another company that regularly served up productions of Grand-Guignol plays between 2010 and 2015 was Exeter Alternative Theatre, based in the south-west of England, and led by its producer and creative director Louis Ravensfield. Making their debut in 2010 at the Barnfield Theatre in Exeter with a programme of four plays (Eliot Crawshay-Williams's *The Nutcracker Suite*; André de Lorde's and Eugène Morel's Boxer Rebellion play *The Ultimate Torture*; René Berton's sex comedy *Tics*; and *Voluptuous Atrocity*, a new translation of *L'Atroce Volupté* by Georges Neveux and Max Maurey), they followed up in 2011 with a show consisting of André de Lorde and Pierre Chaine's adaptation of Octave Mirbeau's *The Torture Garden*, Frederick Witney's *Weekend Cottage* and a new play, *An Eye for an Eye*, by Rosie and Midge Mullin. This formula, consisting of a blend of original French and British Grand-Guignol plays, and a newly commissioned piece, served them well over five years.

By 2013 their reputation as a Grand-Guignol company had grown to the extent that they were able to stage a mini-tour of Devon in June of that year (Barbican, Plymouth; Phoenix, Exeter; Little Theatre, Torquay; as well as their 'home' at the Barnfield), as well as accept an invitation to appear at the London Horror Festival with a programme consisting of Level's *The Last Kiss*, Witney's *Coals of Fire* and *The Death of Love*, a new play written by Ravensfield. Their fifth and final Grand-Guignol show took place in May 2014 with a four play programme of Gaston Leroux's *The Man Who Saw The Devil*; an adaptation of W.W. Jacobs's well-known short story of the supernatural 'The Monkey's Paw'; Witney's *Nuit de Noces*; and *A Dangerous Love*, a new play by Malcolme Littler.

Nine Knocks Theatre, established in 2020 by Loughborough University graduates George Cooper and Ellie Hardwick, is a new addition to the Grand-Guignol fold and, like Le Nouveau Guignol, has emerged from our own practice-based research with our students into the Grand-Guignol. Cooper had become interested in Grand-Guignol while an undergraduate, performing as Henri in Robert Scheffer and Georges Lignereux's *The Little House at Auteuil*, which played at Loughborough as part of the 'Thirty Minute Theatre' programme, before participating in a Halloween Double Bill in Norwich with community and student performers from the University of East Anglia in October 2017. He followed this by staging a *douche écossaise* of Grand-Guignol translations, including Paul Atelier and Paul Cloquemin's *The Lighthouse Keepers*, Benjamin Rabier and Eugène Joullot's *Short-Circuit* and *The Eyes of the Phantom* by Jean Aragny at Loughborough University the following year.

Nine Knocks have veered from the traditional Grand-Guignol formula in that they have fully embraced the supernatural within their work. Their first venture, originally intended for the Edinburgh Fringe Festival in 2020, became part of Online@TheSpaceUK, after the cancellation of the festival owing to COVID-19. What had originally been proposed as a stage adaptation of Henry James's classic ghost novella *The Turn of the Screw*, *After the Turn: The Mystery of Bly Manor* was presented as an online series of linked monologues in the form of a documentary interviews and 'found footage' in the style of *The Blair Witch Project* (1999). The play was nominated for an OnComm Award in 2020. Still operating under COVID-19 restrictions, the company followed up this success with another online show, *The Unfinished Tales*, a series of six separate ghost stories, delivered as monologues on the company's YouTube channel and released at fortnightly intervals between March and June 2021.

Perhaps most interesting in the UK context of the Grand-Guignolesque is the place of the festival. Many of the horror theatre companies we have already mentioned have thrived in the rich British traditions of fringe festivals and pub theatre. The attempt to create a permanent horror theatre like the original Grand-Guignol in Paris or the Hypnodrome in San Francisco is a delightful prospect but hard to make practical or feasible for various reasons, including economic.[15] Therefore, the attempt to pool efforts and talent into festivals of horror theatre that could command a captive audience of fans and the curious could be a viable solution.

The London Terror Seasons

The London Terror Seasons were an attempt to establish an annual horror theatre festival in London and ran at the Union Theatre, Southwark, between 2004 and 2008, before moving to the Southwark Playhouse for the 2009 and 2010 seasons, and then finally finding a home at the Soho Theatre Downstairs for its final two seasons. The last season took place in 2012. During its nine years it gradually grew its reputation and audience, as reflected in its move to increasingly large and established venues, its nomination for a Peter Brook Empty Space Award and its commissioning of new work from several well-known dramatists. During its nine years, it clearly both created and met a growing demand for live horror performance with great success.

The London Terror Season was the brainchild of Adam Meggido, an actor and director who has since made a name for himself as co-director and co-creator of the long-running *Showstopper! The Improvised Musical* (2008 onwards). In 2004 Meggido was running The Sticking Place, a London-based theatre company dedicated to new writing and improvised performance, and the first Terror Season presented what they called

---

[15] Perhaps the nearest to it in London are the resident tourist attractions The London Dungeon (1974 onwards) and The London Bridge Experience (2008 onwards), which feature a very large ensemble of actors in their exploration of the more gruesome history of the capital city: straying into the territory of scare attractions, these examples of ostensible 'edutainment' are immersively theatrical more than theatre, per se.

'a varied programme of one-act plays including original adaptations of cult and classic horror and new writing in a modern "Grand Guignol" idiom'.[16] On the programme of seven plays was a mixture of new writing, an adaptation from H.P. Lovecraft, a version of Charles Dickens's *The Signalman* and Maurice Level's *Le Baiser dans la nuit*, in a new translation by Tristan Langlois, titled *Goodnight Kiss*.

The season ran from 19 October until 12 November, over the Halloween period at the Union Theatre, Southwark, an intimate, if basic, theatre space built beneath a railway arch. In many ways it was a perfect theatre for Grand-Guignol—on the less fashionable south side of the river, and with the faint but noticeable rumblings of the trains overhead merely adding to the uncanny atmosphere. The season was a great success with its audience and the company revelled in the mixed critical reviews it received, which gave it a somewhat transgressional character.

The formula was repeated in 2005, with a changing nightly programme from a repertoire of short plays, which included adaptations of H.G. Wells's *The Red Room* and Edgar Allan Poe's *The Premature Burial*. By 2006, a year in which the season celebrated the seventieth anniversary of the death of M.R. James, the run was extended to a whole month, running from 24 October until 25 November and was advertising itself as 'Britain's only annual horror theatre festival'. The programme that year also included a revival of Anthony Neilson's 1991 play, *Normal*, which dealt with the case of Peter Kurten, the so-called Vampire of Düsseldorf, and was turned into a film in 2009.

The Terror Seasons have now established a growing audience, as well as a faithful crowd of its own 'guignoleurs', and its reputation was further cemented in 2007, when it staged the first production of Noël Coward's *The Better Half*, since its production at the Little Theatre, as part of Levy's London Grand Guignol seasons, in 1922, as well as *Le Baiser de sang* (translated as *Kiss of Death* by Tristan Langlois), by Jean Aragny and Francis Neilson, a classic of the French repertoire. In addition, they were able to boast the inclusion of a new play, *Ripper*, by Mark Ravenhill, and Lucy Kirkwood's *Guns or Butter*. By this time, the shows occasionally included improvised performances by School of the Night, an informal improvisation company set up by Meggido and the great theatre maverick Ken Campbell. Interestingly, Ken Campbell visited the Grand-Guignol on a trip to Paris in 1962 to catch a performance there before it closed down. On the programme he saw was the adapted stage version of Georges Franju's film *Les Yeux sans Visage* (*Eyes Without a Face*, 1960).

When Meggido moved the Terror Season to the larger Southwark Playhouse in 2009, the year following Campbell's death, it focused entirely on

---

[16] http://www.extemporetheatre.com/past-productions/the-terror-seasons/terror-2004/ (accessed 26.04.21).

new writing with further plays from Ravenhill (*The Experiment*), Kirkwood (*Psychogeography*) and Neilson (*Twisted*), along with *Some White Chick* by Neil LaBute, all well-established and successful playwrights. Ravenhill and LaBute contributed further plays the following year. By its final year, the company had become much more comfortable in its own success and less edgy and risk-taking in its programming. That place had by now been taken over by the London Horror Festival, which once again offered a space for new, more experimental, more transgressional work to take place. In its early days at the Union Theatre they had enjoyed the controversy, but in 2012 when Sarah-Louise Young, an actor with the company was interviewed by the BBC, she explained that a play about a real murder in Ukraine that used 'internet footage of people reacting to the video of a killing' was pulled from the programme at a late stage. She said it was 'a line that we couldn't cross . . . people would have probably walked out'.[17] The Terror Season did not return in 2013 as Meggido had moved on to other things in improvised theatre, especially, and as a director. He had also effectively handed over the mantle of London Terror Seasons to the London Horror Festival, an even more ambitious and long-running cultural event.

The London Horror Festival

The London Horror Festival began as an initiative by Theatre of the Damned's co-founders Stewart Pringle and Tom Richards to provide a regular platform for new horror theatre in London, following the company's early success at the Etcetera Theatre in Camden (see preface to *The Ghost-hunter* for a discussion of the work of Theatre of the Damned). Pringle and Richards had always entertained the dream of establishing a long-term horror theatre presence in London, but were equally aware that in order to do so would require a more stable platform for supporting that ambition and a venue that could hold larger audiences in order to generate more significant revenues. With this in mind, they established the London Horror Festival in 2011 at the Courtyard Theatre in Hoxton, a five-week programme during October and November of that year (to include Halloween) and featuring the participation of ten companies. The programme included Theatre of the Damned's *Revenge of the Grand-Guignol*, and Le Nouveau Guignol, with a programme that included *Orgy in the Lighthouse.*

In spite of this early success at the Courtyard, Pringle felt that the move to a larger venue had not served their performances well. Although the Courtyard itself only has a capacity of 150—still classifying as a small venue—it lacked the intimacy of the Etcetera auditorium, where there was

---

[17] https://www.bbc.co.uk/news/entertainment-arts-20095581 (accessed 26.04.21).

always a risk of the audience getting splattered with stage blood, and the specially designed special effects, into which the company had made a significant investment, lost much of their immediacy. For example, they had a particularly gruesome set piece that involved a victim's head and a lathe, but the effect became somewhat lost in the larger auditorium of the Courtyard. As Pringle explains:

> Our huge brutal lathe ending [. . .] Our first year's show ended with a woman being dismembered in a packing crate and blood spurting out the side and severed arms being pulled out. It's a very simple, junky sort of effect, but it blew people's minds at the Etcetera because it was inches away. This lathe which cost £400, and which was a nice bit of engineering, didn't look like anything much when you're sitting at the back row of a 180-seat raked auditorium, and so that was a question for me of what the limits of upscaling Grand Guignol are.
> (Interview, 31 August 2016)

At the same time, Pringle acknowledges that their interest in horror led them to focusing their efforts on the horror plays and the climactic special effects. This led to an overuse of blood and horror and a neglect of the importance of comedy in the Grand-Guignol mix. As Pringle says, 'We were relentlessly brutal in a slightly nihilistic way', and even before the inaugural festival had completed its run, they were already planning for the following year when 'we were going to see if we could have the most blood ever on stage'. The experience of that first season, however, and taking on board the reviews and audience feedback, they realized that they had pushed things as far as they could, and to be continually ratcheting up the horror would have exhausted both their audiences and themselves.

Instead they began to be more experimental and bolder about reimagining what a successful and sustainable Grand-Guignol theatre might be like for the twenty-first century. For a start that meant a return to the smaller, more intimate venue, and the following year the Etcetera Theatre was brought back into commission as a festival venue. Nevertheless, in 2012, for their own contribution to the London Horror Festival, Theatre of the Damned tried something much more ambitious. *The Horror, The Horror* was not a piece of Grand-Guignol, as such, but a piece of Grand-Guignolesque that used the form of a programme of music hall turns for a series of horror and ghost stories that unfolded during a promenade performance in the ramshackle, labyrinthine and mid-renovation Wilton's Music Hall in Whitechapel.

Pringle handed over the running of the Festival in 2014, yet it has continued as a celebration of horror performance and remained loyal to its roots of attracting young and experimental performers and audiences to small venues, running a new writing competition alongside its programme.

In 2016 it transferred to the Old Red Lion Theatre in Islington, where it remained until 2019 when it spread to The Pleasance Theatre, Islington, to become a two-venue festival. While Pringle moved on to other things with his dramaturgical work, at first at the Bush, and then at the National Theatre, the Grand-Guignol remains an influence and even maintains a ghostly presence in his work. The original dream of a permanent, full-time Grand-Guignol theatre in London may have foundered on the rocks of economic necessity, but Pringle now sees the Grand-Guignolesque mix of horror, dark comedy and the weird as having an important place in a wider horror cultural landscape that has established itself in the 2010s and beyond. Furthermore, the London Horror Festival remains part of the Theatre of the Damned's legacy and continues as an important and enduring experimental platform for new and horror writing and performance. The event has since spawned a sister in the London Lovecraft Festival (2018 onwards), a similar conglomeration of Lovecraft-inspired theatre, installations and other events that typically occurs in the early part of the calendar year, ensuring fans of horror-based live performance can feast on horrors at other times than the long Halloween season.

Global Grand-Guignolesque

There is not scope in this present volume to explore the significance of the Grand-Guignolesque beyond the Anglophonic nations. However, we would like to signal a couple of very important companies. Vigor Mortis is a long-established and prolific horror company, spanning both theatre and film, based in Curitiba, Brazil (the country's eighth-largest city). After completing his master's dissertation on the Théâtre du Grand-Guignol at Royal Holloway, University of London, in 1993, the company's founder and artistic director, Paulo Biscaia Filho, returned to Brazil, recruited an ensemble of actors to his vision for a contemporary Grand-Guignol company and established Vigor Mortis in 1997. Their breakthrough came in 2004 with the show *Morgue Story*, which toured nationally. They also established a close working relationship with Thrillpeddlers, with both companies touring to each other's home cities and sharing their developing artistic practice. Vigor Mortis have similarly had a productive relationship with Molotov Theatre Group, which premiered an English-language version of *Morgue Story* in Washington DC in 2011.

Vigor Mortis styles itself as an unapologetically Grand-Guignol theatre company, although its work is distinctly contemporary, drawing upon modern horror tropes and elements of the supernatural, macabre and fantasy literature (for example, *Lobos Nas Paredes/Wolves in the Walls* was based upon the work of Neil Gaiman). They have also produced work more directly in homage to the Parisian Grand-Guignol, such as *Duplo Homicídio Na Chaptal 20/Double Homicide in Chaptal 20*, but—unlike

Thrillpeddlers—have not generally sought to retranslate and revive plays from the classic Grand-Guignol repertoire. Instead, what distinguishes Vigor Mortis from other Grand-Guignol companies is that they are also filmmakers. Their cinematic work includes the reworking of their theatre shows for film, as well as purely cinematic projects, but increasingly they have incorporated the use of film into their theatrical productions, more readily embracing the performative possibilities afforded by multimedia technology for horror performance. During the grim period of the global theatre lockdown caused by COVID-19, Vigor Mortis gave some relief to fans of horror performance with their short film experiment #*vigor-mortischallenge* (May 2020): this breath-taking montage brought together horror performers from around the world in presenting a continuous, gruesome relay of Grand-Guignolesque attacks and effects, partly horrifying, frequently hilarious and entirely compelling (vimeo.com/420009526).

In Italy, the Grand Guignol de Milan was formed in 2014 by the actor-director Gianfilippo Maria Falsina and the Convivio d'Arte Company in Milan. This was the most significant attempt to revive horror theatre in Italy since the original venue that imitated the Parisian theatre, Alfredo Saintini's Le Compagnia del Grand-Guignol established in Rome in 1908, closed down in 1946. The company's signature style of creating a horror variety show, combining monologues, live music, pantomime and burlesque was developed for their first show, *Grand Guignol de Milan: Le Cabaret des Vampires*. In the tradition of the *douche écossaise*, the company relishes breaking the fourth wall and switching from comedy to drama and from prose to popular music. The shows can be as shocking as any horror theatre can be, but interpolates the pantomimic, taking inspiration from commedia dell'arte *lazzi* as well as cinematic effects such as slow motion.

Typically, the performances of the Grand Guignol de Milan feature four short plays or vignettes inspired by true crime stories in a technique reminiscent of the original Grand-Guignol's use of *faits divers*. The plays—which can range in duration from fifteen to forty-five minutes—are self-contained but are linked by an overarching character-host, 'Asmodeus, The Prince of Darkness' (played by Falsina himself) who effectively mixes storytelling with stand-up comedy as he leads the audience into a cathartic journey into the evils of humankind. The Grand Guignol de Milan repertoire features a growing number of plays, exploring subjects such as homicidal doctors in *Angels of Death* or murderous churchmen in *Bloody Cassocks*. Plays such as *The Bloody Benders* presented the family of serial killers in 1870s Kansas; and *Holmes Horror Hotel* presented the astonishing story of Henry Howard Holmes, who constructed a hotel with multiple lethal devices to slaughter his guests in 1890s Chicago. The plays also explore the factual basis behind legends and folklore, as in *A History of Vampires: The Facts behind the Myth* and *Italian Horror Stories: The Italian Origins of Gothic Horror*. The latter play was a successful touring show that played the San Diego Fringe Festival in July 2018 and the London Horror Festival at the Old Red Lion Theatre in October of the same year. The show returned to the subsequent London Horror Festival in November 2019, where it played at the Pleasance Theatre Main House.

It is only appropriate to conclude by noting that the Grand-Guignol has recurred where it all began: in France. The theatre company acte6 has been one of several occasionally performing revivals of plays from the Grand-Guignol canon. Formed in 1999, they have performed throughout France and Switzerland, but also regularly at Théâtre 13, a small (280 seats in eight rows, giving an intimacy not unlike that at the rue Chaptal), modern theatre on a housing estate in the thirteenth arrondissement. Under the direction of co-founder Frédéric Jessua, the company began its experiments with the Grand-Guignol in 2008 with productions of Gaston Leroux's *L'homme qui a vu le diable* (*The Man Who Met The Devil*) and René Berton's *Tics*. In 2012, the company toured Switzerland with a programme of Maurice Level and Etienne Rey's *Sous la lumière rouge* (*In the Darkroom*), *Sabotage* by Charles Hellem, William Valcros and Pol d'Estoc and André de Lorde and Alfred Binet's classic *Un Crime dans une maison de fous* (*A Crime in the Madhouse*).

This was followed by another programme of three plays in April 2013, which completed a run of thirty-six shows at the Théâtre 13. The plays—Maurice Renard's *L'Amant de la morte* (*The Lover of Death*), Olaf and Palau's *Les Détraquées* (*The Unhinged*) and Jean Aragny and Francis Neilson's *Le Baiser de sang* (*The Kiss of Blood*)—were performed with comic interludes, featuring the character of Paula Maxa introducing each play, thus maintaining a sense of the *douche écossaise*, even though the programme contained no comedies as such. Jessua also incorporated moments within the plays that were performed with comic effect, undisguised playfulness and unconcealed eroticism. Jessua continues to stage Grand-Guignol plays, and in 2021 was scheduled to direct a programme consisting of Georges Neveux's *L'Atroce volupté* and de Lorde's *Le Laboratoire des Hallucinations* at the Festival du Nouveau Théâtre Populaire in Fontaine-Guérin.

Afterword

It was a sad day in 1962 when the Théâtre du Grand-Guignol closed down. As the interior of the venue was stripped and gutted like many a hapless victim in its repertoire, it was clearly the end of an epoch. The glory days of the Grand-Guignol must have seemed eons away and the theatre seemed no longer relevant: the days when the Deux Masques and other rivals desperately sought to imitate the Grand-Guignol were long gone. The Grand-Guignol was perhaps a venue and a genre that belonged to a bygone era: blighted by the Second World War's horrors (and in spite of the fact that the theatre remained open and earned an income during the Occupation), the Grand-Guignol seemed old fashioned and was losing its audience who could feast on thrills, horrors and laughter at the cinema or simply stay at home and watch television. However, as a *concept* the Grand-Guignol refused to die. The term has never left the languages of French or English but, just as importantly, the extraordinary notion of a permanent venue specializing in horror theatre has fascinated many people with a penchant for horror culture and live performance. It was a concept so irresistible that a significant number of creatives across the world have attempted to make a resurrection of the form a reality.

This book has offered a mere snapshot of a prolific and ever-evolving form that we have labelled the Grand-Guignolesque. Horror theatre companies have risen, buoyed by obsession and passion, only to fall owing to the challenges of gaining an audience, critical approbation or, most typically, economic viability. On this latter point, it remains difficult to make a commercial success from a permanent, or regular, specialist horror theatre company. All of the contemporary companies we have cited run to a large degree on goodwill and commitment. Some groups work on profit-share as graduate companies, where making a living is less important than making the work. Others are diverse in their programming and horror theatre is only one part of what they do.

There is, nevertheless, a significant degree of kudos in working with some of the more established horror companies, which have attracted performers not by the promise of a large income (there will not be) but the opportunity to work with well-known horror companies and the chance to experiment with things on stage that they are generally unlikely to experience in the mainstream. In this respect, it is also important to celebrate the remarkable stories of success: companies such as Thrillpeddlers, Molotov Theatre Group and Vigor Mortis—as well as Festivals in London—have proved that horror theatre can be viable, award-winning and influential. Some examples of horror theatre have thrived in cities such as San Francisco; Washington DC; New York City; Los Angeles; Denver, Colorado; Curitiba, Brazil; Milan, Italy; Liverpool and London, establishing stages in the less salubrious and more arty parts of town reminiscent of the mood and spirit of Pigalle. At the same time, it is interesting how some horror theatre companies have thrived in more surprising places such as Newport, Wales; and Devon in the UK. With all these theatres, they have, to varying degrees, recreated or paid homage to the original Grand-Guignol, but many have forged their own path in a way that would have been alien to the original theatre—such as exploring the supernatural or hybridizing multiple practices of popular performance and physical theatre.

Like the best kind of monsters in horror culture, the Grand-Guignol refuses to die. It returns from the grave when one least expects it, like a cultural jump scare. The theatre might have seemed a potentially moribund form in the early 1960s, when television was coming of age and cinema was pushing boundaries in an irreversible way. For fans of horror, however, the concept of live horror theatre is as irresistible as it is exciting. We live in an age where the screen is hegemonic and horror fans have a wealth of options from films to television shows to digital games. But the prospect of seeing horror on stage, the ultimate three-dimensional entertainment, in a collective experience of unified time and space that cannot be paused or switched off remains a delectable concept. In addition, even non-horror devotees have continued to enjoy the novelty of live horror in its visceral exploitation of the dynamics of the stage and the frisson the genre can create at a night in the theatre. The Grand-Guignol may be dead, but the Grand-Guignolesque is coming soon to a theatre near you.

4
'The Molotov Manifesto'

Molotov Theatre Group enjoyed success as a contemporary horror theatre company before they had an in-depth knowledge of the Grand-Guignol as a specific form. Consequently, the company embarked on an extensive research process to understand the complexities of the Grand-Guignol form across writing and design and, above all, effects and acting. This work culminated in the creation of 'The Molotov Manifesto', an essential credo for experienced Molotov performers and an important primer for actors new to the company. We include the Manifesto in full as it gives a valuable insight into contemporary horror performance practice from the perspective of a successful company. Written with humour and colour, it gives us a privileged view of what happens 'behind the scenes', revealing that although horror theatre can sometimes appear unruly, unpredictable and spontaneous, it is actually disciplined, calculated and emphatically *safe*.

THE MOLOTOV MANIFESTO, OR ACTING GRAND GUIGNOL, MOLOTOV STYLE
Molotov Theatre—Art Imitates Death

We're often asked about the "style" of acting in Grand Guignol theatre. Most trained actors come to us with preconceived notions of "stripping away," which means they're taking a wrong turn right out of the gate. We strip away the stripping away.

The Molotov Grand Guignol style is stylized. As with the style of the original Theatre du Grand Guignol, it has a foot in both naturalism and melodrama. The Molotov Grand Guignol style is surreal in the purest sense of the word: a layer of something on top of reality, like the morning dew glistening on a cow pie (ah, poetry).

The most important things to keep in mind with the Molotov Grand Guignol style are to stay open-minded, and to put logic behind you. When it comes to acting this brand of theatre, it's not how it feels onstage; it's how it looks—and how it makes the audience feel. (Remember that phrase; it comes up a lot.)

The Molotov Grand Guignol style is divided into three aspects, each distinct but inter-related. We refer to these aspects as "Acting the Effect," "Gore" and "Brawling." (For a slack bunch, we've actually given this stuff a fair amount of thought. That's why we're great.)

Before we go into any more detail on these aspects, it's important to keep in mind that actors in the Molotov Grand Guignol style are responsible for more than just delivering their lines. They must be able to handle the artistic demands of Acting the Effect and the technical demands of Gore and Brawling at the same time—otherwise the overall effect is diminished.

For that reason, the Molotov Theatre Group puts great value in developing an ensemble of players who, through their common understanding of these aspects of style, can become comfortable enough with one another to take more risks and go to more disturbing places in their performances.

With that as background, let's look at the principal aspects of the Molotov Grand Guignol style:

Acting the Effect: The most brainy and least physical of the three aspects, "Acting the Effect" itself has three components: "The Moment of Horror," "Fourth Wall Ambiguity," and "Distortion of Time." The director and the actors may not agree on The Moment of Horror at the outset. The strongest voice wins, and after that it's a matter of tying it to the other components. Even if the director does not agree with The Moment of Horror, he or she usually is best at tying it all together. Why? Because it's not how it feels onstage; it's how it looks—and how it makes the audience feel (sound familiar?).

The Moment of Horror—As the saying goes, the difference between comedy and tragedy is tragedy happens to you. Whether it's comedy or tragedy, there is ALWAYS a Moment of Horror. A businessman who spills coffee down the front of his pants right before an important presentation has just experienced The Moment of Horror, even though it's comedy to everyone else. The Molotov Grand Guignol style identifies The Moment of Horror for each character, and puts a picture frame around it with techniques such as Fourth Wall Ambiguity and Distortion of Time.

Fourth Wall Ambiguity—This is not simply direct address to the audience. Fourth Wall Ambiguity means actually breaking down the illusion of a separate on-stage reality. An actor may even step out of character to take a line directly to an audience member (preferably one who is already affected by what's happening on-stage). This can be used to foreshadow The Moment of Horror to come, or to underscore The Moment of Horror as it is happening. In creating that ambiguity, the separation between the audience and the actors dissolves. The audience is pulled into the action, creating a voyeuristic connection that heightens the effect.

Distortion of Time—Have you ever been in an accident and experienced "time standing still?" That's the key to Distortion of Time. In the

Molotov Grand Guignol style, time may slow down or speed up around The Moment of Horror. This is not just a matter of action and pacing, but even line delivery. The original Grand Guignol actors noted that at times they delivered their lines with difficulty, as if the act of speaking was itself physically demanding. Together with distortion in physical action, Distortion of Time heightens the tension around The Moment of Horror. No matter how slowly things are moving, there is still nothing you can do to stop it. That's crucial. Remember: It's not how it feels onstage; it's how it looks—and how it makes the audience feel.

Gore: To say that the Molotov Grand Guignol style is dripping with gore is a gross understatement. Blood flows by the quart, liquid latex is involved in practically everything, and clean-up is definitely NOT a breeze. Excess is indulged, indulgence is excessive, and messiness is expected. Actors and make-up (or effects) people typically are involved together in refining the Gore effect—usually because the effect has never been done before on the stage with its limited resources (as compared to films).

As with "Acting the Effect," "Gore" also has multiple components, which in Molotov Grand Guignol style are called "The Gimmick" and "The Reveal." These components are important to understand, because ideally, Gore must be perceived to be happening in plain view of the audience. Gore also is integrated with the last element of Molotov Grand Guignol style, namely "Brawling" (more on that later).

The Gimmick—Taken from the vocabulary of street magicians, The Gimmick is the device or means by which Gore happens. (Gore in the Molotov Grand Guignol style means more than just blood. Any bodily fluid or semi-fluid is fair game.). Often The Gimmick is retrieved in nearly plain view of the audience, with misdirection drawing the audience's attention long enough to set the effect.

Because some Gore effects require The Gimmick to be attached to the actor's body before the show begins, the actor and the effects person often collaborate on placement of The Gimmick, its triggering, and comfortable wearing. Molotov has found that actors may have the best ideas on how to make The Gimmick the most comfortable to wear.

The Reveal—None of us really knows what it feels like to have acid thrown in his face, or his hand sliced open with a razor, or a toenail ripped out with pliers. We do know, however, that it is instinctive to protect the injured part of the anatomy, to draw yourself inward, to prevent further injury.

That's pointless in the theatre of horror. What good does it do to conceal the effect? It's like a joke with no punch line, or kissing your sister.

The Reveal happens when The Gimmick has been deployed and the actor is Acting the Effect—that is, using The Moment of Horror, Fourth Wall Ambiguity, and Distortion of Time to heighten the dramatic (or comedic) effect. This can be one of the most difficult things for an actor to remember, because it is a total departure from natural instinct. The actor has to find a way to revel in The Reveal, to put the violence on display, and not to prevent further injury. This is counter-intuitive but essential. Remember: It's not how it feels onstage; it's how it looks—and how it makes the audience feel.

Brawling: Maybe it's gallows humor or whistling in the graveyard, but Molotov's unofficial motto has evolved into "Safety Is Right Up There." That's why the Molotov Grand Guignol style refers to stage combat as "Brawling," not "fight choreography." There's something a bit more real to the fight work of the Molotov Grand Guignol style. If it's not real-looking, it's stylized for deliberate effect.

Certainly, punches are pulled and "naps" are sounded in Brawling. Training in stage combat by accredited instructors of the Society of American Fight Directors is both desirable and encouraged. As an ideal, though, the Molotov Grand Guignol style would be more like professional wrestling than traditional stage combat. The director's wet dream would be having trained actor/combatants willing to play rough, and to throw themselves into the action with a bit more abandon than your typical thespian. As long as all parties realize that they may occasionally get their bells rung, everyone should be OK with ramping up the intensity, right? Having said that, it's worth repeating that Safety Is Right Up There—definitely in the top five things we consider important.

The aspects of Brawling in the Molotov Grand Guignol style are "Contact" and "Integrating 'The Gimmick.'"

Contact: The victim is in control, but that doesn't mean the victimizer uses no measured force. The victim establishes control in rehearsal, by dictating the amount of force he or she is willing to take—defining limits, which ideally are close enough to the real thing to make reactions as genuine as possible.

- Pushing down is better than guiding down.
- A solid slap to the face is better than a nap to the face.
- A real punch is better than a fake punch.
- We NEVER really punch the face. Ever.
- Real spit is better than fake spit.
- Real spit to the face is awesome.

Integrating 'The Gimmick': Because The Gimmick in Gore often is worn by the actor from the very opening of the show, Integrating 'The

Gimmick' in Brawling is essential as early as possible in working the Brawling, to limit the possibility of accidentally triggering The Gimmick. There is some conceptual overlap in Integrating 'The Gimmick' in Brawling and The Reveal in Gore, because some moves that may not actually be truly "fight-worthy" must be done to prevent The Gimmick from being accidentally triggered by Contact while Brawling.

As with The Reveal in Gore, it is the actor's responsibility to sell every Brawling move to the audience, and not to question the logic of the move, because every move happens for a reason. Remember: It's not how it feels onstage; it's how it looks—and how it makes the audience feel.

Part Two

Thirteen Plays of Grand-Guignol and the Grand-Guignolesque

In this section, we present thirteen plays of the Grand-Guignolesque. We have deliberately included both old and new plays: first translations of plays from the original Grand-Guignol; plays from the Deux Masques; and representative examples from the contemporary Grand-Guignolesque, generously provided by contemporary playwrights of horror theatre in the USA and the UK.

The plays are divided into three sections and presented chronologically within each section. We begin with translations of plays that were originally performed at the Théâtre du Grand-Guignol or the Deux Masques but have enjoyed a revival in recent years. The inclusion of Alfred Machard's *Orgy in the Lighthouse* in Eddie Muller's translation for Thrillpeddlers, provides us with the link to the next section, which is a sample of modern Grand-Guignolesque plays that have emerged from the work of American companies in the first decade of the twenty-first century. The final section comprises of plays that have been written for, or devised by, UK practitioners and theatre companies in the past ten years, The final play in this selection is the most recent, but draws upon the history of the Théâtre du Grand-Guignol during the early twentieth century, so bringing the Grand-Guignolesque neatly back to its Parisian origins.

The collection should be regarded as offering plenty of options for a *douche écossaise*, with the first two plays being classic comedies from the original Grand-Guignol repertoire, followed by eleven horrors of varying gruesomeness. Many of the plays are uncompromising, some of the plays are humorous, a few of the plays are satirical; some even manage to blend all of these qualities. Hopefully, it will become evident how the Grand-Guignolesque can be adrenaline-fuelled, escapist entertainment but can also take an audience into a very dark psychological space with a cathartic purpose.

Professor Verdier's Operations

(Les Opérations du Professeur Verdier, 1907)

by

Élie de Bassan

Preface

Élie de Bassan was a banker who became a playwright and wrote a number of one-act comedies for the Grand-Guignol including *Un frère* (1901), *Une Présentation* (1908) and *Les Mines de Ganeffontein* (1911). De Bassan also wrote a few horror plays including *La Terreur du Sébasto* (1905), a horror play set during the Crimean War in the 1850s, and *Pour la République* (1903), which was revived on French radio in 1936. This radio production was part of a trend in radio drama in which some of the older Grand-Guignol repertoire was broadcast live. For example, the aforementioned comedy *Les Mines de Ganeffontein* was performed by the veteran stage and screen actor Madeleine Guitty as part of an evening of 'Humorous Sketches' on French radio in April 1935, along with a number of other works including André de Lorde's *L'Attaque nocturne* (1920). De Lorde's play is an interesting example of a comedy written by the 'Prince of Terror', albeit suitably dark in theme. In this play, a woman in a panic enters a police station late at night and informs a police officer that her lover has died during a rendezvous at her house and her husband is returning home. The officer is charmed by the woman and offers to help her dispose of the body.

De Bassan's *Professor Verdier's Operations* is a similarly dark comedy, set in a surgeon's practice. The rich and successful surgeon Verdier has lost his prized pair of golden tweezers and is convinced he may have sewn them up when completing one of his many operations. The play is a farce, and we watch Verdier conduct various consultations while preoccupied over the recovery of his beloved instrument. It is a work with great potential for comic characterization in the parade of diverse patients and the eccentric Verdier. Contemporary medical practice provided a rich context for the Grand-Guignol, frequently in horror plays that presented horrifying 'true stories' of medical accidents, anomalies or malpractice. But as *Professor Verdier's Operations* demonstrates, medicine is ripe with comic potential. To some extent, all members of an audience can relate to the world of the doctor's surgery. It is a place where we can be (literally) exposed or need to 'confess' our most personal secrets and anxieties. It is a realm we trust is confidential and professional. In de Bassan's play, Verdier exploits the trust of his patients and his personal status in his desperate search for his lost treasure. From charlatans peddling fake cure-alls in commedia dell'arte, the mischievous concocting of elixirs in Ben Jonson's *The Alchemist* (1610) or the self-diagnosing protagonist in Molière's *Le malade imaginaire* (*The Hypochondriac*, 1673), medical comedy has a long tradition. In more recent times, medicine has been at the heart of screen comedy such as the British *Doctor* . . . films (1954–70), based on Richard Gordon's comic fiction, or darker examples of Channel 4 comedy such as Chris Morris's GP sketches in *Jam* (2000) or the sitcom *Green Wing* (2004–07).

PROFESSOR VERDIER'S OPERATIONS

(*Les Opérations du Professeur Verdier*, 1907)

by

ÉLIE DE BASSAN

Translated by Richard J. Hand and Michael Wilson
Premiered at the Grand-Guignol on 16 May 1907

Cast
Professor Verdier, 45
Count de Vieubois, 50
John, 30
A Patient, 40
Virginia, 35
Alice, 20
Blanche Verdier, 30
Rose, 18

SCENE ONE

The richly furnished study of a successful surgeon. A desk is centre stage; a chaise longue stage left; an armchair, chairs and a screen are stage right; a bookshelf and a telephone are on the wall behind the desk. Doors to the left and right.

Professor Verdier is sitting at his desk in consultation with a Patient.

PATIENT: Oh dear, doctor . . . At first I didn't think anything of it, but the swelling got bigger and bigger . . . And now, as you can see, it's very uncomfortable when I sit down . . .

VERDIER   (*very distracted*): Yes, quite bizarre . . .

PATIENT: Quite so! I'm in perfect health otherwise, and my family has three octogenarians and another who is a hundred years old!

VERDIER   (*reading his notebook*): It gets more and more mysterious . . .

PATIENT: There's been nothing like this in my family before.

VERDIER   (*still distracted*): Nothing . . . Nothing at all.

PATIENT   (*plaintively*): Please tell me doctor, why does this horrible abscess keep coming back? I mean I am—
           Verdier stands up quickly and turns his back on the Patient who stops talking

VERDIER: Please continue. It is most interesting.

PATIENT: The horrible thing always comes back in exactly the same place.
            Silence

VERDIER   (*heads over to the bookshelf*): And these headaches never go away?

PATIENT   (*puzzled*): Er . . . doctor, it's not my head—

VERDIER   (*quickly*): I know! I know! But it is very common for an abscess
            on the bottom to cause a headache.

PATIENT: I never knew that . . . Forgive me, doctor, I might be mistaken but
            you seem to be rather distracted . . .

VERDIER: I have lost one of my surgical instruments. One that I use all the
            time. A pair of golden tweezers.

PATIENT: That is a shame.
            Telephone rings. Verdier rushes over to it.

VERDIER: Please excuse me . . .! Hello . . .! Hello . . .! Saint Benoit Hospital
            . . .? Yes, yes, I'll wait . . . Is that you Dubois . . .? Oh, I'm fine
            thank you . . . Patient 120 is not doing too well . . .? Oh, never
            mind, just stuff him with morphine . . . My tweezers . . .? No, still
            nothing, I'm very sorry to say . . . Please continue searching, leave
            no stone unturned . . . Telephone me immediately if they turn up
            . . . Goodbye. (*Hangs up.*)

PATIENT: I hope you find them.

VERDIER: We've *got* to find them!

PATIENT: What should I do, doctor?

VERDIER   (*randomly*): Oh, confine yourself to bed and eat . . . spinach . . .
            only spinach, mind!

PATIENT: But . . . I can't stand spinach!

VERDIER: These are my strictest orders. And in four days' time, I will
            operate on you.

PATIENT   (*terrified*): Are you sure it's that serious . . .?

VERDIER: An operation is an operation . . . And you will need to move out
            of your apartment.

PATIENT   (*still frightened*): Move out of my apartment? For an abscess?
            Really?

VERDIER: As long as the risk of deadly infection does not frighten you, you
            can do what you like.

PATIENT: Very well, doctor, I understand! (*He stands up and we finally see
            the agony he is in as he hobbles to the door.*) Oooh! Aaah!

VERDIER: Oh, while I remember . . . Don't forget to pay the fee *before* the
            operation . . .

PATIENT: Yes, of course . . .

VERDIER: Good . . . If you pay before it saves us any trouble with your
            family when it comes to your will.

PATIENT   (*panicked*): My . . . will . . .?

VERDIER   (*shakes the Patient's hand*): Come on, old chap . . . Chin up . . .!
            And I'll see you on Wednesday . . .
            Patient exits.

VERDIER: What a bore!
            John enters

VERDIER: Anything?

JOHN: Nothing. Still nothing.

VERDIER: It is impossible!

JOHN: I know for a fact you had them last month.

VERDIER: Yes, I remember that only too well . . . But where have they gone!?

JOHN: Well, you have done an awful lot of operations lately.

VERDIER: Yes, and that makes it all the more difficult to locate them.

JOHN: Do you remember there was that incident when you left a sponge in the head of a patient after brain surgery? They found it during the post mortem. Maybe I'll go and check at the morgue.

John exits stage left. Blanche enters stage right.

BLANCHE: Well? Any sign of your tweezers?

VERDIER: No. I am lost for words.

BLANCHE: It's so annoying . . . They were worth a fortune!

VERDIER: Oh, it's not just the value.

BLANCHE: Don't upset yourself.

VERDIER: I have a strong personal attachment to them! They are like my lucky charm! Do you remember? I used them on my first millionaire . . . You never forget something like that.

BLANCHE: You have no memory of what you may have done with them?

VERDIER: I definitely used them at the hospital last month.

BLANCHE: You'd lose your head if it wasn't screwed on! Last week you lost the cigarette case I gave you for your birthday and now you can't find your golden tweezers!

VERDIER: There's no need to get personal about it! What we must do is work out where they have gone! I don't know—maybe I stitched them up into somebody's tummy!?

BLANCHE: You have no idea?

VERDIER: I've been so overworked lately. Sixty operations in a fortnight . . . That's nothing to be sniffed at.

BLANCHE: And you can't count on any of your patients to be honest enough to return them!

VERDIER: Dubois is on the case. I left the hospital this morning having done twelve operations in an hour. That's a record . . .! And you know what, they were all a great success . . . in the circumstances.

BLANCHE: Do you at least know the names of all the patients you operated on?

VERDIER: Pretty much.

Bell rings

VERDIER: A patient! Off you go. I can hardly think about consultations at the moment! Oh well . . . Come in!

John enters

JOHN: It's the Count du Vieubois to see you, sir.

VERDIER: Send him in.

John exits and the Count enters, a distinguished gentleman very smartly dressed.

COUNT: Good day, my dear doctor.

VERDIER: Good day, Count!

They shake hands

COUNT: You're well, I take it?

VERDIER: Oh, I could be better. I have been having terrible migraines.

COUNT: How unpleasant . . . Any nosebleeds?

VERDIER: Thankfully not.

COUNT: You need to take the pressure off your head a bit. If I were you, I'd soak my feet in a warm bath, have a strong black coffee and inhale an infusion of camphor.

VERDIER (*smiles*): Thank you . . . But what about you, my dear Count, what seems to be the problem? I assume you didn't take the trouble to come here just to give me a consultation on *my* woes!

COUNT (*sitting on the armchair*): You see, doctor . . . I feel rather peaky . . . And my legs feel rather—

VERDIER: Oh, that's nothing to worry about.

COUNT: And every night, I get a constant pain in my kidneys . . .

VERDIER: That's just the weather. It will pass.

COUNT: But what causes me the most discomfort is a persistent pain in my abdomen . . .

VERDIER (*suddenly, very interested*): In your tummy . . .? What kind of pain are you feeling . . .?

COUNT: I'd describe it as heavy waves of discomfort . . .

VERDIER: Really? Can you remind me when I operated on you?

COUNT: About a month ago, I think.

VERDIER: And these waves of discomfort . . . where exactly are they?

COUNT (*points at tummy*): It hurts mostly around here.

VERDIER (*quickly*): I can believe it! And would you describe the pain as being acute . . .?

COUNT: Sometimes, yes. It depends.

VERDIER: Do you get a particular sensation . . . (*Struggles for words.*) As if—just for argument's sake obviously!—as if there was some *sharp object* stuck in your abdomen . . .?

COUNT (*hesitates*): It's . . . possible . . . I suppose . . . Although—

VERDIER (*nervous*): I beg you, my dear Count, don't hold anything back from me. I am your doctor, you can trust me . . . And don't worry about your legs, that's nothing . . . So, let's carry on, when you suffer this intense pain, these waves of discomfort, perhaps a stabbing sensation in your tummy, the pain in your kidneys and legs is probably just a distant echo, that's all . . .

COUNT (*timidly*): Maybe I exaggerated that a bit . . .

VERDIER (*on his feet, aside*): My tweezers! I know where they are! (*Pacing, loudly.*) Worrying. Very worrying indeed.

COUNT (*unnerved*): Is it serious, doctor?

VERDIER: I hope not. I sincerely do. But it's clear that I will have to operate. It's not just necessary—it is *urgent*!

COUNT (*frightened*): What are you saying, doctor?

VERDIER: Hmm, I wonder . . . Maybe we should operate here, right now . . .

COUNT: That's impossible—I'm going on holiday!

VERDIER: Holiday!? In your condition!?

COUNT: But I'm packed and ready.

VERDIER: Don't even think about it. I'm sorry to say this but you might die.

COUNT   (*rises and heads over to the chaise longue*): Doctor, I assure you, I feel fine really . . .! It's nothing serious, I'm sure of it!

VERDIER: So if you are the medical expert why on earth did you come and see me?

COUNT: Oh dear, doctor, forgive me, I am just so upset . . .!

VERDIER: After the operation you will be able to do anything you want.

COUNT   (*stunned*): Good heavens . . .
         Telephone rings

VERDIER: Please excuse me . . . Hello? Saint Benoit Hospital . . . Very well . . . (*Silence.*) Dubois . . .? Well . . .? What . . .? Really. . . .!? It can't be possible . . .? Someone's found them . . .? A lady? She's spoken to the caretaker about it . . .? That is wonderful news! Send her over as soon as you can . . . That's fine, I'll be only too happy to wait . . . Thank you. Goodbye . . . (*Hangs up the telephone delightedly then is embarrassed when he remembers the Count, who sits in torment. Verdier scratches his head then ambles over to the Count.*) You've planned this holiday for a while, have you?

COUNT: Yes.

VERDIER: Let me check you over again. (*Swiftly puts his ear to the Count's chest.*) Pulse. Very strong. (*Grabs his wrist.*) Yes, excellent . . . Stick out your tongue . . . (*Count does so.*) Perfect . . . Well, everything looks in perfect order to me . . . You can go on your holiday now . . .

COUNT: But . . . the operation . . .

VERDIER   (*ushering the Count to the door*): It can wait until you come back . . .

COUNT   (*resisting*): But doctor, you told me that—

VERDIER: An operation is only necessary as a last resort . . .

COUNT: But, doctor, you absolutely insisted that—

VERDIER   (*jovially*): Oh, I may have overegged the pudding a bit! Nothing to worry about! Have a wonderful time . . .! Goodbye!
         Count exits. Verdier rings bell and John enters

VERDIER: My wife will be delighted, John!

JOHN: How come, sir?

VERDIER: The hospital called. You can tell her they have found what we have been looking for. She'll be so happy!

JOHN: Is it possible?
         Bell sounds

VERDIER: Send the next patient in immediately.
         John hurries out

VERDIER: Thank God! I was starting to get desperate. (*Door knocks. Cheerfully.*) Come in!
         Virginia enters. Standing at the door, she waves in a friendly way.

VIRGINIA: Hello, doctor . . . It's me . . . Virginia.

VERDIER   (*keenly*): Please come in, come in!

VIRGINIA: You're too kind. (*She enters the room.*) You remember me, don't you?

VERDIER: Your face is familiar but . . .

VIRGINIA: Oh, doctor! You're one of my best customers!

VERDIER: Um, I'm still trying to place you . . .

VIRGINIA: Virginia! I look after the public toilets next to the hospital.

VERDIER   (*takes her hand*): Delighted to see you! Please, do sit down! On the armchair, there!

VIRGINIA: I don't know if I dare!

VERDIER: All my patients are at home here, never forget that.

VIRGINIA: Oh, you're so kind, sir! I came here straightaway.

VERDIER: Delighted to hear it!

VIRGINIA   (*stands and wanders around*): The caretaker gave me your address. I'm sure he told you what I've brought with me.

VERDIER: Yes, yes, he has! Wonderful!

VIRGINIA: I'm an honest lady you see, doctor.

VERDIER: Who would have the audacity to doubt it?

VIRGINIA: You see, if I wasn't honest I couldn't have the job I've got.

VERDIER: Absolutely!

VIRGINIA   (*noticing a bottle of madeira on the side*): Is that medicine?

VERDIER: No, madeira. It's a kind of wine.

VIRGINIA: Is it any good?

VERDIER: Would you do me the honour of accepting a glass?

VIRGINIA: How could I say no, but just wet the bottom of the glass. (*Sits down again*)

VERDIER   (*handing her a full glass*): You are a fine and noble lady and I am honoured to drink to your health. (*They drink.*)

VIRGINIA   (*gulps it down in one and smacks her lips*): Delicious!

VERDIER: Another finger or two?

VIRGINIA   (*Holds out her glass*): How could I say no. (*It is refilled, and she drains it in one again.*) While I'm here, doctor, I haven't been feeling too well . . .

VERDIER: Really, madam? I'm sorry to hear that.

VIRGINIA: I'm in good health by and large, doctor, but I do have a little problem, if you know what I mean.

VERDIER: Of course! I'd be only too happy to examine you! As a token of my gratitude!

VIRGINIA   (*surprised*): Oh, thank you!

VERDIER: By the way, when did you find them?

VIRGINIA: Last week . . . Tuesday . . .

VERDIER: Interesting . . . (*Back to check-up.*) Hmm. You've probably been working too hard . . . However, you look well. (*Takes her wrist.*) Perfect. (*Listens to her chest*) Breathe in . . . Breathe out . . . (*Virginia gasps in and out very loudly. Verdier sits up.*) I'd appreciate it if you didn't breathe all over me. (*He listens again.*) What a chest! (*Squeezes her waist.*) How about when I touch you here?

VIRGINIA   (*giggles nervously*): Ooh . . . Ooh . . .

VERDIER: What is it?

VIRGINIA: It tickles, doctor!

VERDIER   (*aside*): I'm sure it does! (*Aloud.*) Why did you wait so long before coming to see me?

VIRGINIA: I didn't know what to do.

VERDIER: You should have handed them in to the hospital.

VIRGINIA: I preferred to see you here because I know you're more likely to be kind enough give me a little something.

VERDIER   (*feels in pocket*): Of course! A reward! Here you go, fifty francs.

VIRGINIA: You're too kind, doctor.

VERDIER   (*going to chaise longue*): There's no need to keep you any longer, but I would like to have my tweezers back now.

VIRGINIA: Your tweezers . . .? I think you have misunderstood me . . .

VERDIER: I beg your pardon?

VIRGINIA: What I found. (*Taps her tummy.*) It's your cigarette case.

VERDIER   (*leaping up*): What on earth are you talking about . . .!?

VIRGINIA   (*pulls the case from her dress*): Don't worry—here it is! Your cigarette case!

VERDIER   (*shocked*): Oh! Good grief! What is that doing there!?

VIRGINIA: You left it at my toilets . . .

VERDIER   (*furious*): You could have told me sooner!

VIRGINIA: Sorry, my dear doctor, I don't understand—

VERDIER: Don't you 'my dear doctor' me . . .! And what a nerve you have!

VIRGINIA: Me!?

VERDIER: You come here all mysterious, you drink my madeira, you extort money out of me—all for nothing!

VIRGINIA   (*annoyed*): I didn't ask you for anything!

VERDIER: And pretending that you needed a check-up—complete fantasy!

VIRGINIA   (*raising her voice*): How would you like it if you had a boil on your buttock! I'll show you it just to prove I am not a liar! (*Starts to pull up her skirt*)

VERDIER   (*stopping her*): Oh! Stop right there! Be off with you!

VIRGINIA   (*furious*): I'll go when I'm good and ready . . . When you come to my toilets I'm always very nice to you!

VERDIER: Your toilets . . .!? I'll never go there again!

VIRGINIA: I'll happily let you walk on by—I will never let you in my toilets again!

VERDIER   (*pushing her to the door*): Get the hell out of here!

VIRGINIA: You're nothing but a villain! Good for nothing! A thug! (*Exits in distress.*)

VERDIER   (*going to telephone in a rage*): Hello! Hello! Wake up will you! Give me 14847 . . . Saint Benoit Hospital . . . Get me Mr Dubois . . .! Dubois, is that you? No . . . That stupid woman who cleans the bogs next door . . .! Found my stupid cigarette case, that's all! Keep looking, Dubois . . .! Leave no stone unturned . . .! (*Slams the telephone down.*) It's appalling! My poor tweezers! I'm desperate! It's breaking my heart, it really is . . .! (*Looks at diary.*) Well, if I have to cut open sixty abdomens, so be it! (*Stands up.*) It's obviously some wretch of a patient at the hospital who's nicked them! And it's too much to expect a simple act of honesty from scoundrels like them! (*Bell rings.*) It is an absolute disgrace! (*Goes to door and shouts.*) John . . .! Bring in the next patient, they can wait for me here! (*Exits.*)

Enter John with Rose and Alice

JOHN: If you ladies would be so kind as to wait here I will call the doctor for you.

ALICE (*insulted*): Wait a minute . . .! We want to see some references first.

JOHN: Doctor Verdier is one of the greatest physicians in-

ALICE: I couldn't care less about that. What about his *character*?

JOHN: Charming. And he has a very good clientele.

ALICE: I see . . . I bet he's a rogue.

JOHN (*stunned*): I don't think I understand what-

ALICE: Come off it, you don't fool me. We have come to ask a favour of him.

JOHN: Oh, so it's not a consultation?

ALICE: No. My sister here was in the hospital where the doctor does his operations.

JOHN (*suddenly colloquial*): Oh . . . and you're here for cash are you . . .? Forget it, darling, you're wasting your time . . . He's a miserable, old skinflint . . .

ALICE: Do you think we're beggars?

ROSE (*shy and gentle*): I just want a certificate.

ALICE: Ever since the operation, she's been tired and now she's ill again.

JOHN: You're ill? What's wrong with you?

ALICE: It's her tummy. That's right, isn't it, Rose?

ROSE: Yes, yes, it's horrible.

JOHN (*subtly excited*): When did the doctor operate on you?

ROSE: Last month. I was in bed number 36.

JOHN: And you've got pain in the tummy . . .? Oh, the boss will be delighted to see you . . .! (*Exits very quickly.*)

ALICE: You heard what he said . . . The doctor will be happy . . . Maybe he's not such a bad fellow after all.

ROSE: I'm so stressed . . .

ALICE: What a child you are!

ROSE: You're not my mother and don't you forget it!

ALICE (*goes over to the desk and snoops around*): You have got to say that you are in constant pain . . . You're always tired . . . Otherwise, when he claps eyes on you he will know it's not true!

ROSE: I know!

ALICE: Lay it on thick!

ROSE: Easy for you to say!

ALICE: Tell me, yes or no, do you want some time off work?

ROSE: What a stupid question!

ALICE: Well, without a doctor's certificate, you have no chance.

ROSE: We'll do our best.

ALICE: Very well . . . I can hear him coming . . . (*Sits down quickly.*) Get ready and don't move . . .

The door opens and Verdier appears

VERDIER (*very friendly, to Rose*): Hello, my dear. . . . (*Takes her hand.*) Mademoiselle is with you?

ROSE: This is my sister. . . .

Alice curtsies.

VERDIER: *Enchanté*, mademoiselle . . .! Please, please, sit down . . .
Rose and Alice sit together on the chaise longue, Verdier sits on a chair.

VERDIER: How *are* you?

ROSE: Doctor . . .

ALICE: She's not at all well, doctor.

VERDIER *(to Rose)*: You certainly do look peaky.

ALICE: She's definitely out of sorts.

VERDIER: You clearly have a fever.

ROSE: I feel exhausted all the time.

VERDIER: Only to be expected. *(Hesitates.)* My . . . assistant told me that you have been having stabbing sensations in your tummy . . .

ROSE: Yes, doctor, I have.

VERDIER: And I, er, operated on you?

ROSE: Last month.

VERDIER: It was appendicitis, wasn't it?

ROSE: Yes, doctor.

VERDIER *(beaming)*: Hmm . . . Oh dear . . . Stick out your tongue . . .
(Rose sticks out her tongue, Alice does the same by reflex.)
Bad . . . Very bad . . . Thank God you came to see me . . .
Verdier goes over to his desk.

ALICE *(stands up)*: As you agree she's not well, doctor, we were wondering if you could do us an enormous favour and give us a certificate . . .

VERDIER: What for?

ALICE: For her boss. She won't give Rose sick leave without it.
She's a right cow!

ROSE: She is, you know.

VERDIER: Of course, only too happy to do it . . . *(Scribbles a note.)* But before you go, you must listen to what I have to tell you.

ROSE: Of course, doctor.

ALICE: We are most grateful, thank you doctor!
Rose and Alice stand to leave

VERDIER: Please . . . Wait a moment . . . *(Takes a jar of sweets.)* Here, have a sweet.

ALICE: We don't want to take up any more of your time, doctor.
(To Rose.) Come along . . . We need to be on our way . . .

VERDIER *(Stands and gives certificate to Alice)*: Here you go, my dear.

ROSE: Thank you very much, doctor.
Rose and Alice head to the door.

VERDIER: Just a moment. Tell me, my dear . . . How do you feel when you walk? Any discomfort at all?

ROSE *(nervous)*: I . . . I don't know.

ALICE: My sister is very shy, doctor.

VERDIER: Come on, you can tell me . . . Is there any discomfort when you walk?

ROSE: I get very tired when I walk a lot.

VERDIER *(delighted)*: Good! And when you sit down?

ROSE: I feel much better.
VERDIER: Hmm, that's not good!
            Rose and Alice make to leave again.
VERDIER: Did they give you anything when you left hospital?
ROSE: Nothing.
VERDIER: That must have been an oversight . . . (*Feels in his pocket.*)
            Here you go—twenty francs!
ROSE: For me?
ALICE: You're too kind, doctor!
VERDIER: Tell me . . . The pain in your abdomen . . . Where exactly does
            it hurt?
ROSE   (*nervous*): In the middle . . .
VERDIER   (*aside*): Better and better . . . (*Aloud.*) Not up by your heart then?
ROSE: No. Before I eat I get terrible cramp in my stomach.
ALICE: It's true, she does.
VERDIER: All the symptoms. And what about sleep?
ALICE: She's always writhing around in bed when she's asleep.
VERDIER: You poor thing . . .! Don't worry, we will sort everything out in
            no time. (*to Alice.*) May I have a word, mademoiselle?
            He leads Alice away from Rose.
VERDIER: Your sister desperately needs treatment.
ALICE   (*slightly mockingly*): You really think it's something serious?
VERDIER: Very serious.
ALICE   (*still disbelieving*): Well, what can it be?
VERDIER   (*embarrassed*): You wouldn't have heard of it . . .
            But she must come and see me.
ALICE: But we live miles away and we don't have much money.
VERDIER: Bring her in a taxi. . . . (*Goes to desk and takes money from a
            cashbox.*) Here, a hundred francs . . .
ALICE   (*waves the cash at Rose*): Oh doctor, that's too generous of you!
ROSE   (*hurries over*): We can't thank you enough!
VERDIER: No need to thank me . . . I am President of the Ancient Order of
            Surgeons of the Appendix and these are funds from the society.
ALICE   (*heading to door*): A million thanks!
VERDIER: Wait a moment . . . (*To Rose.*) Before you go, I must examine you.
            Rose and Alice stare at Verdier.
ALICE: She'll come back soon, I promise you, doctor, but at the moment
            we really must—
VERDIER: It'll only take five minutes. Your wellbeing is of the utmost
            importance to me. (*He rings the bell. John enters.*) Bring us some
            tea . . . Please, make yourself comfortable . . . Take off your clothes
            . . . I'll go and wash my hands . . . Back in a minute . . . (*Exits*)
ROSE: (*takes off her hat and dress*) We're done for now! He'll soon find
            out we've been lying!
ALICE: Calm down. When he touches you there, grimace and writhe . . .
            It's bound to work.
            Verdier returns.
VERDIER: Hello ladies, let's get on with it . . .!

Knock on door.

VERDIER: Come in! (*John enters with tray. He puts it on the desk and looks bemused when he sees Rose in her underwear.*) Thank you! Would you care for some tea?

John exits

ALICE: May I be mother? Rose. (*She goes to the tray.*)

VERDIER: Sit down, my dear.

ROSE: (*shy*) I daren't!

VERDIER: Oh, but I'm a doctor!

Rose sits on the chaise longue. Verdier sits on a chair in front of her. Alice pours tea.

ALICE (*bringing cup over*): Here you go, Rose, a lovely cup of tea will make you feel better.

VERDIER: How about some cake as well?

ROSE: I'm so nervous!

VERDIER: There's no need to be! My patients are my friends!

ALICE: Would you like any sugar, doctor?

VERDIER: Two lumps, please.

ALICE (*opening the sugar bowl, she takes the sugar tongs and looks puzzled*): How strange! I've never seen tongs like this. Very strange sugar tongs, doctor! They look more like tweezers . . .!

VERDIER (*slowly turns his gaze*): My . . . God . . .! It's them . . . It's my golden tweezers . . .! (*Pause. He looks from Rose to Alice to the tweezers.*) What on earth are you two doing here?

ALICE (*friendly*): Um . . . We've come to see you doctor, having a nice cup of tea.

VERDIER (*livid*): Tea!? TEA!? I'LL GIVE YOU TEA!! (*He goes over to Rose and Alice and grabs the cups out of their hands.*) What on earth have you been playing at!? Pretending to be ill!

ROSE: No, doctor, I promise you!

VERDIER: Making up all kinds of fictitious symptoms to get money out of me!

ALICE (*hurries over to Rose*): But doctor . . .!

VERDIER: Come on, give me my money back!

Enter Blanche.

BLANCHE: What on earth is going on!?

VERDIER (*pointing at the tweezers in the sugar bowl*): Look! There they are!

BLANCHE (*pointing at Rose*): Oh! It was her!?

VERDIER: No, they're in the sugar bowl. (*To Rose and Alice.*) Well, what are you looking at? Are you going to give me my money back!?

ALICE: Oh, I don't think so!

VERDIER (*furious*): Oh, it's like that, is it!? Very well—clear off then! Both of you! As quick as you can!

Verdier opens the door and gestures them out. Rose holds her clothes in her arms.

ROSE: I can't go out like this!

VERDIER: So you want to use my office like a dressing room!? Go on, get lost!

ALICE: Come on, Rose. You can change on the stairs . . . You can see what he's like . . . He's a lunatic . . .! We won't stay here another second! Good riddance!
Rose and Alice exit.

VERDIER: They got 120 francs out of me!

BLANCHE: You are so naïve! Well, all that matters now is that you've got the tweezers back. You said they're . . .?

VERDIER: In the sugar bowl . . . I mean, what a place to leave them! Is that an appropriate place to leave an extremely valuable surgical instrument!? Which idiot did that? (*Rings the bell.*)
John enters.

VERDIER: Did you leave my tweezers in the sugar bowl?

JOHN: Oh, how can you think such a thing, sir!?

VERDIER: It must have been that stupid chambermaid . . . (*The telephone rings.*) Answer that!
John goes to the telephone.

JOHN: Hello? Hello? Is that the hospital? Yes, Mr Dubois, I'm listening . . . Don't speak so fast . . . I'll repeat it to Professor Verdier . . . (*Very slowly.*) You have reopened the stomach of patient 43 . . . the thigh of 89 . . . the throat of 48.

VERDIER   (*calmly*): What did he say?

JOHN: The intestines of 132 and 77 and 83 and you haven't found anything at all . . .?

VERDIER   (*goes to the telephone*): Hello, Dubois . . . Thank you so much for all your efforts, but you'll be pleased to hear I have found my tweezers . . . They were in the sugar bowl! (*Roars with laughter.*) Hilarious, isn't it . . .? You can stitch everyone up now, my friend, stitch them up!
Puts down the receiver. Bell chimes.

VERDIER: What a farce!

BLANCHE: Hurry up . . . We need to go soon.

VERDIER: Don't worry . . . I'll get rid of them as soon as I can.
The door opens and the Count enters.

VERDIER   (*surprised*): Ah, my dear Count!

COUNT: Doctor, I was thinking about what you said, and I've decided to postpone my holiday.

VERDIER: But . . .

COUNT: I will go on holiday after the operation.

VERDIER: But I told you there was no need to do that!

COUNT: I thank you for your tact, doctor. It is hard to imagine a more honourable gentleman!

VERDIER   (*resisting*): Quite seriously, there is no—

COUNT: I absolutely insist that we get the operation done as soon as possible.

VERDIER   (*resigned*): Very well, if you insist . . . This time tomorrow?

COUNT   (*shakes Verdier's hand*): Excellent! This time tomorrow!

CURTAIN

Short Circuit

(*Le Court-Circuit*, 1916)

by

BENJAMIN RABIER AND EUGÈNE JOULLOT

Preface

Dedicated in part to Camille Choisy, *Le Court-Circuit* premiered at the Théâtre du Grand-Guignol on 15 February 1916 and was later revived in March 1918 and August 1923. Neither of its authors wrote prolifically for the Grand-Guignol: this was Rabier's only piece of work for the rue Chaptal and Joullot produced one further piece, *Le Tendon d'Achille* (*The Achilles Tendon*), a 'vaudeville' play that he co-authored with his son Edmond Joullot and which was staged at the Grand-Guignol in July 1938. Benjamin Rabier wrote mainly vaudeville, burlesque comedies and comic fantasies for the theatre, but is best known as the illustrator and creator of Le Canard Gédéon (Gédéon the Duck), a series of comic books that appeared from 1923 until Rabier's death in 1939, and was later made into an animated TV series in 1976. Eugène Joullot was a writer of vaudevilles, revues and plays, as well as a lyricist and *chansonnier* in his own right.

On one level *Short Circuit* is a tightly written sex farce: Mina, an actress of limited ability, seeks to progress her career through a series of affairs with important and influential men, and the action of the play revolves around her dismissing her current lover (Robert) in order to effect a rendezvous with a new admirer (a minor foreign royal), while Robert, suspicious of Mina, seeks to spy on her (by adopting a disguise with truly awful incompetence) and so thwart her plans. For an audience at the Grand-Guignol, located as it was in the heart of the red-light district of Pigalle, the link between the theatre and illicit sex (be that the bars and brothels that lined the streets of Pigalle, or the *loges grillées*, the private boxes at the back of the theatre auditorium, where lovers would meet free from prying eyes), would have been an irony that was not lost on them.

At its core, however, this is not a play about sex, but about class, and particularly about the relationship between Robert and the working-class electrician, Anatole Loupy, whom he persuades to adopt the role of the mysterious Prince of Inertia. While none of the characters emerge from the play unscathed (with the exception perhaps of Félicie, the well-educated and insightful maid), particular disdain is reserved for bourgeois and aristocratic manners and those who aspire to a higher social status. Robert's desire to appear more sophisticated than he is and Mina's pretensions of refined conversation are mercilessly ridiculed. Through their affairs they are both seeking to gain social advantage—for Mina this is largely financial; for Robert it is the status that goes with having an actress as a mistress—but they are in fact both exposed as being duplicitous, foolish, self-obsessed, profligate, self-serving and incapable of making any sort of useful contribution to society.

By contrast Anatole, like Félicie the maid, is portrayed as being capable, pragmatic, adaptable, unpretentious and honest, while also knowing how and when to take advantage of any opportunity that comes his way. There is both ridicule and admiration for someone who is able to recite verbatim their socialist principles, while happily abandoning them if there are a few francs to made, especially at the expense of those with more money than sense, of whose buffoonish behaviour Robert and Félicie are remarkably tolerant.

In addition to moments of physical comedy typical of the farce tradition (based on fast-paced action, quick entrances and exits and near-misses), much of the comedy in *Short Circuit* is actually verbal in nature. There is no shortage of puns and word play. For example, Anatole's surname, Loupy, references both 'loup' (wolf), suggesting a certain proletarian lack of refinement, and also 'loupé' (failure) or 'louper' (to mess up or do a botch job), implying that, although he appears to be a competent and trained electrician, his name suggests otherwise. It is, however, the distinctions in the manner of speaking between the different social classes that provides the richest material for verbal comedy. What the play exposes in this manner is the whole set of social behaviours and codes, from ways of speaking to ways of dressing, and the rules of etiquette that determine which class each person belongs to. The fact that the behaviours and codes of one social class are largely incomprehensible to a member of a different social class means that Robert, Anatole and Mina each find themselves in a social situation they are completely incapable of navigating, and the comedy derives from their painful attempts to do so.

While this is, therefore, primarily a comedy about class, it is also worth remembering that in the play each of the characters is given to playing a role. Anatole plays the Prince of Inertia; Robert plays an electrician; Mina plays a sophisticated, cultured and refined actress. And they all play the roles very badly. So, in line with the Grand-Guignol's ability to reference and make fun of its own enterprise, it is also a play about (bad) acting.

SHORT CIRCUIT

(*Le Court-Circuit*, 1916)

by

BENJAMIN RABIER AND EUGÈNE JOULLOT

First performed at the Théâtre du Grand-Guignol on 15 February 1916
Translated by Richard J. Hand and Michael Wilson
To Monsieur Choisy and Monsieur Sevos

Cast
Anatole Loupy, working-class electrician
Robert, a pleasure seeker
Mina de Coursac, an actress
Félicie, her maid

---

*The drawing room of Mina de Coursac. Downstage left is the door
to the bathroom. Upstage left the door to the bedroom. Downstage
right a fireplace with a mirror over it. On each side of the mirror
is an electric light. Upstage right is a window that opens with two
curtains. At the back is a door that leads out to the vestibule.*

*Between the two doors on the left a dressing table with various
toiletries and make-up. On the left an armchair. On the right a
small pedestal table with a telephone and an encyclopedia. There
is a chair on each side of the table. Other chairs and small items of
furniture. Next to the fireplace is an electrical fuse-box. An electric
bell is on the right of the doorway.*

FÉLICIE   (*entering from the back*): The post and newspapers for Madame.
           (*She throws it all down onto the table and then goes to listen
           at the bedroom door.*) Midday! She's still fast asleep. It's only
           loose women who sleep so soundly. (*Going back to the table and
           examining an envelope.*) It's from that tenor, the little blond one
           that costs Madam so much. (*Examining a second letter.*) I don't
           know this handwriting . . . Someone on his last legs no doubt.

MINA   (*entering from the bedroom in an elegant dressing gown*): Ah,
           there you are, Félicie. (*Taken by surprise* Félicie *quickly puts
           down the letter.*) Why haven't you brought me the post?

FÉLICIE: I didn't want to wake you, Madame . . . the day after an opening
           night, I thought Madame would be very tired.

MINA: It's true. I was such a success last night . . . (*She sits down at the dressing table and opens the letters that* Félicie *has given her.*) What do the newspapers says about me? Read them to me, Félicie.

FÉLICIE: If Madame wishes . . .

MINA: You know how to read, I suppose.

FÉLICIE: Madame won't forget that I have my higher diploma.

MINA: Ah yes, you've already told me that. It's strange that with this thingumajig, you don't have more ambition. You could be in the music hall and have friends. You're no worse than anyone else. Perhaps you lack a little in style . . .

FÉLICIE: Madame is very kind, but I don't really have the figure for debauchery. I don't think I'm really cut out for it.

MINA: I think perhaps you're wrong . . . Anyway, I'm listening, Félicie.

FÉLICIE   (*reading*): 'The delicious Mina de Coursac, in the role of Watercress, showed us nature at its most fertile. With vegetation such as this, one could never regret spending time in the countryside.'

MINA: It's witty, but it's nothing to write home about. Which newspaper?

FÉLICIE: *Le Figaro*.

MINA: Let's have a look at *Le Matin*.

FÉLICIE   (*reading*): 'The delicious Mina de Coursac, in the role of Watercress, showed us nature at its most fertile. With vegetation such as this, one could never regret spending time in the countryside.'

MINA: It's exactly the same.

FÉLICIE: Probably all the critics are of the same opinion as regards Madame's talents.

MINA   (*sniffing the air*): Can you smell something, Félicie?

FÉLICIE   (*playing along*): Yes, a vague smell of burning onions. (*Picks up another newspaper.*) Ah, here's a review that's not the same as the others. 'Mademoiselle Mina de Coursac cuts a gracious figure, whose intelligence reminds us of the holy geese who saved the Capitole all those years ago.'

MINA: Ah, that's very kind. Which newspaper?

FÉLICIE: *The Theatre Echo*.

MINA: I shall send them a thank-you card.

FÉLICIE: I think it might be better if you didn't.

MINA: You think I might give the impression that I hadn't understood the review?

FÉLICIE: Perhaps Madame does not know the Capitole being referred to?

MINA: I can certainly tell you that. Why, I performed a revue there last year. It's the biggest music hall in Toulouse.

FÉLICIE: But no, Madame, this is the Capitoline Hill in Rome . . . the geese . . .

MINA: Ah, yes, the geese, everyone knows that that refers to people with academic qualifications. My dear, Félicie, you don't have to try and show off to me, just because you've got your higher diploma.

FÉLICIE: Oh, not at all, Madame.

MINA   (*sniffing the air, again, she gets up and goes towards the table*): It's strange how this smell persists.

FÉLICIE: It must be coming from the kitchen downstairs. (*The bell rings.*)

MINA: See who that is.

FÉLICIE   (*in no particular hurry*): And is Madame receiving guests?

MINA: I don't know. Go and see who it is first . . . but hurry up . . .
           go on, run!

FÉLICIE   (*going slowly to the door*): I'm not an athlete, you know, Madame.
           *Mina continues to open the letters. Robert enters, places his cane
           and hat on a chair, then approaches Mina from behind and kisses
           her on the back of the neck.*

ROBERT: Hello, old thing!

MINA: Robert! What are you doing here?

ROBERT: What sort of question is that?

MINA: Did you not get my message?

ROBERT: No, I had breakfast at the club this morning.

MINA: That explains it.

ROBERT: And what did you want to tell me in this message?

MINA: That I couldn't see you today.

ROBERT: Charming! And here was I ready to devote my whole afternoon
           to you.

MINA: Ah, my darling, I'm even more disappointed than you are, but I've
           had such rotten luck.

ROBERT: They've cut your parts in the revue?

MINA: No, my Uncle the Bishop is arriving today.

ROBERT: Again?! That's the third time this month. It seems to me that your
           Uncle the Bishop spends rather a lot of time in Paris.

MINA: He has some business to sort out with the Archbishop . . .
           you know, darling, it would never do if he found you here. If he
           ever suspected me of having a lover or working in the theatre . . .
           there'd be a right palaver!

ROBERT   (*who also momentarily sniffs the air*): Can you smell something
           burning?

MINA: That's what I just said to Félicie.

ROBERT   (*approaching the fuse box*): By Jove! There's a short circuit.
           You must ring an electrician immediately.

MINA: Really?! Oh no, I can't be left without lights with my Uncle the
           Bishop. (*Picking up the telephone from the pedestal table, whilst
           still sitting.*) Hello! Hello! 8-4-0-6-5. (*Shouting.*) 6-5. I believe I
           am speaking French . . . Hello! Is that the Ampère House? Would
           you please send an electrician straight away to the house of
           Mademoiselle Mina de Coursac, the famous Parisian artiste—I don't
           think there's more than one of us. (*To Robert.*) These electricians
           know nothing. (*Into the telephone.*) A short circuit . . . it's urgent.
           (*Replacing the receiver.*) They're sending somebody round.

ROBERT: Mina?

MINA: Yes, my darling?

ROBERT: Is your Uncle the Bishop staying long in Paris?

MINA: At least twenty-four hours.

ROBERT   (*pacing in front of her*): It's just that I was thinking . . . you won't
           be going to the theatre then tonight?

MINA: Of course not. I'll telephone the director to tell him that I have a migraine. He'll pass it on to my understudy.

ROBERT: Mina, I don't like this at all. At the very moment when you're on the verge of a breakthrough, when all the press are unanimously writing about your success. (*Aside.*) After I paid for the press notices. (*Aloud.*) At the very moment, I tell you, when your artistic career is opening up before you, the road strewn with bouquets of flowers and wreaths of laurels, you sacrifice your future because of some mundane family obligation.

MINA: What do you expect me to do? My Uncle the Bishop is always riding his moral high horse.

ROBERT: What a terrible way for a bishop to go riding. But since I haven't been able to convince you in the name of art, we'll both have to sacrifice ourselves.

MINA: What do you mean, 'both'?

ROBERT: Art and Yours Truly!

MINA: Oh, you're so stupid! (*Pause.*) At least you still want me, darling?

ROBERT: No . . . this evening I will go and cheer your understudy.

MINA: I forbid it . . . besides you'll only be disappointed. She's a bit of an old wreck . . . by the way, you know that the author has promised me a very important part in his next revue.

ROBERT: No!

MINA: A scene written especially for me . . . there's a train full of passengers and me . . . I watch them go past . . . whilst singing a couplet of course! What do you think of that?

ROBERT: I think you're made for the role.

MINA: Aren't I? (*With pride.*) I am the child of my art!

ROBERT: I hope your mother didn't have to suffer much.

MINA: Don't joke about such serious things . . . tell me, darling, do you forgive me for not letting you stay? (*She leads him to the door at the back, handing him his hat and his cane, as if in a hurry to see him leave. He exits.*) There we are! My Uncle the Bishop—it works every time. (*To* Félicie *who enters.*) Why didn't you show the gentleman out?

FÉLICIE: I was going to, Madame, but the gentleman told me that he was big enough to find his own way out, so I didn't insist.
The sound of a door slamming violently.

MINA: There he goes! (*She goes to sit down next to the dressing table.*)

FÉLICIE: The gentleman didn't look very happy!

MINA: The poor darling. However, I couldn't tell him that I was expecting a visit from the Prince of Inertia at four o' clock.

FÉLICIE: The Prince of Inertia?

MINA: Exactly. Yesterday during the second interval, the prince's private secretary came to my dressing room and said to me, word for word, 'Mademoiselle! His Majesty would like to make your acquaintance. Just name a time.' And I replied, 'Tomorrow at four o' clock at my place, 545, avenue de Villiers.' I don't know if the prince is young or old, but he's a real prince. As his secretary said, 'You only have to look him up in the phone book.'

FÉLICIE (*correcting her*): You mean the *Who's Who.*

MINA: Yes, *Who's Who,* the telephone directory, whatever . . . really Félicie, you hardly need your higher diploma to move in these circles.

FÉLICIE (*resigned*): As Madame wishes . . . in any case it's a good contact for Madame. Madame is going places.

MINA: I'm counting on it. Fortune favours the brave . . . whoever it might be. Whilst I'm waiting for His Majesty, I am going to soak myself in a scented bath. (*She goes into the bathroom.*)

FÉLICIE (*following her out*): I shall run your bath, Madame.
Robert *enters at the back, being careful to make sure that he is alone.*

ROBERT: I'm not falling for this thing with the bishop. I slammed the door, but only pretended to leave. (*The sound of running water. He goes to listen at the bathroom door.*) Mina is going to take a bath. That confirms my decisions . . . these hydrotherapeutic preparations hardly seem compatible with a visit from her Uncle the Bishop. (*The telephone rings. He quickly lifts the receiver.*) Hello! Hello! Mademoiselle Mina de Coursac? Perfectly, everything is fine . . . what did you say? The Prince of Inertia wants to know if Mademoiselle Mina will be free at four o'clock, as agreed? (*Aside.*) That explains everything. (*Into the telephone.*) Hello! Hello! Am I Mademoiselle Mina's butler? I don't have that honour! Hello! Who am I? Her Uncle the Bishop! Hello! You're the Prince's secretary! Now, listen to what I'm going to say. If the Prince makes the mistake of coming round to Mademoiselle Mina's place, I will knock him down the stairs with a boot up his backside. (*Replacing the receiver.*) There! That's better! A bishop who kicks a prince up the arse! It's perhaps a little risky, but that will teach the Prince to intrude on my territory. (*The doorbell rings.*) Oh! For God's sake! (*He hides behind the curtains. Félicie comes out of the bathroom to answer the door.*)

FÉLICIE: Right then, who's this coming to disturb us now? (*Félicie shows in Loupy, an electrician, his bag slung over his shoulder.*)

FÉLICIE: The short circuit's over here.

LOUPY (*entering and throwing his hat on the chair to the left of the table*): Don't you worry about it, love, I'll have it fixed in a jiffy.
Félicie exits. Loupy puts his bag down by the window, takes out various tools and, as he stands up, finds himself face to face with Robert, who has come out from behind the curtain.

LOUPY: Where on earth did you come from?

ROBERT: Ah! Are you the electrician?

LOUPY: Anatole Loupy, at your service! Is it possible to speak to the lady of the house?

ROBERT: You'll have to wait. She's currently abluting.

LOUPY: Abluting? Now, if you've quite finished speaking in riddles.

ROBERT: That's not my intention . . . she's having a bath, if you prefer.

LOUPY   (*giving him a poke*): Ah . . . a joker!

ROBERT   (*mopping his brow with his handkerchief*): There's no point in disturbing her anyway. The fuse box is over here. Get on with your work. (*Loupy examines the fuse box and begins to explain to Robert.*)

LOUPY: The fuse has blown. If the current has no resistance, that can cause havoc, so we have to insulate the wires because the rubber has burned through, and when the rubber has burned through . . . game over!

ROBERT   (*watching him attentively*): Now there's an idea! (*Going over to the electrician.*) Monsieur Loupy.

LOUPY: Yes, boss?

ROBERT: Would you like to earn 100 francs?

LOUPY   (*stepping back and falling into the chair on the right of the table*): A hundred nicker! What do I have to do?

ROBERT: Pull yourself together . . . You can't be well-off, I suppose?

LOUPY: You can say that again . . . what with all the business with the strike and unemployment, I've become a vegetarian.

ROBERT: A vegetarian?

LOUPY: Well, I'm just vegetating at least.

ROBERT   (*holding out a banknote*): I see we understand each other.

LOUPY   (*taking the money*): It's not a dud is it?

ROBERT: No, it's quite genuine.

LOUPY: What do you want me to do for this? Something illegal?

ROBERT: Something very simple! Take your clothes off!

LOUPY: What?!

ROBERT: Yes, give me your work shirt and overalls.

LOUPY: Very well. (*Aside.*) A hundred nicker! (*He takes off his overalls and his shirt, underneath which he is wearing vest and trousers.*) Well, you seem to have some peculiar ideas.

ROBERT: Now, Loupy, you are going to be a prince.

LOUPY: A prince? Is that all?

ROBERT: Don't you want to be a prince?

LOUPY: It's not something I aspire to. You see I'm a socialist. I'm for the people, the people work and work means freedom . . . the day when there are no more big investors who sit around doing sod all.

ROBERT   (*giving him another 100 francs*): Here's something to ease your socialist conscience.

LOUPY   (*pocketing the money*): You're a man of the people, you are! What do I have to do for two hundred nicker?

ROBERT: First of all, change your clothes. Yours are of a cut that leaves a little to be desired.

LOUPY: Well not everyone can afford to go to the top fashion houses!

ROBERT: Listen, on the corner of the street, there's a secondhand clothes shop that hires out costumes.

LOUPY: Old Abraham, yes, I know him. I repaired a leak for him less than a week ago.

ROBERT: Well, then. Go and see Old Abraham and choose yourself a suit with a frock coat, complete with gloves and top hat . . .

LOUPY: Are you absolutely sure about the top hat?

ROBERT: And add a row of medals to the frock coat . . . that'll be a nice touch. And once you are transformed, come straight back here and when the maid introduces you, all you have to say is, 'I am the Prince of Inertia.'

LOUPY   (*repeating with emphasis and making grand gestures*): I am the Prince of Inertia.

ROBERT: There's no need to overdo it. Put yourself inside the skin of your character . . . a little more of the Inertia.

LOUPY   (*repeating, simply this time*): I am the Prince of Inertia . . .

ROBERT: You've got it.

LOUPY: And then?

ROBERT: Then? Well, you reply as best you can to any questions you are asked. I'll be here to help you out. The Prince is supposed to be here at four o' clock. What time do you make it?

LOUPY: What time? Hang on, I'll find out. (*He goes to the telephone.*) 'Hello! . . . Hello! . . . Temple 609.

ROBERT   (*sitting down without noticing the hat that Loupy put on the chair when he came in*): Who are you calling?

LOUPY: The pawnbroker to ask him what time my watch says. I put it in hock three months ago.

ROBERT: What an idiot! Just hang up and get yourself off to Old Abraham's. Mina will be getting out of the bath any minute.

LOUPY: I'll be off then . . . and you know, you're a decent bloke, you are! (*Goes to leave, then goes towards Robert, as if he's looking for something.*) Excuse me, but what would you call a man who sits on your hat?

ROBERT: I'd call him an idiot!

LOUPY: Thank you! Would you give me back my titfer? You're sitting on it.

ROBERT   (*getting up*): Oh, I'm sorry.

LOUPY   (*taking his hat*): See you soon, Boss. (*He exits.*)

ROBERT   (*alone, putting on the shirt and overalls*): If, after this, Mina has not had enough of princes . . . But if I'm going to enjoy my revenge, I'll need to be able to remain here completely unrecognized. (*Sitting down at Mina's dressing table.*) A little make-up. (*He applies rouge to his face.*) A false moustache will complete the transformation. Here we go, I'll just borrow Mina's crimping tongs. (*He crimps the false moustache, then takes an old cap from Loupy's bag and puts it on his head, and a scarf that he ties round his neck, so achieving a half-decent disguise.*)

MINA   (*enters wearing an elegant negligee and notices Robert*): What are you doing here?

ROBERT   (*by the fuse box, imitating Loupy's voice and mannerisms*): I've come for the short circuit.

MINA: Well, hurry up, then, you're not planning to take all night, I hope.

ROBERT   (*aside*): More or less.

MINA: What did you say?

ROBERT: Nothing . . . I'm just looking . . . where exactly is your short circuit?

MINA: How should I know? Isn't that your job to find out?

ROBERT: I see what the problem is. The fuses have blown. (*Getting muddled up with his explanation.*) If the current no longer has any resistance . . . it will mess up the rubber insulation on the wires . . . and then . . . game over!

MINA: Well, do whatever you have to do . . . how long will it take to repair?

ROBERT: Some time this afternoon . . . it depends on how quickly I get on with it.

MINA   (*ringing the bell*): Well, get on with it quickly then . . . I'm expecting a visitor. (*Giving him a coin.*) Here's your tip.

ROBERT: Forty sous! (*Putting it in his pocket.*) That's the first time I've been given money by a woman.

FÉLICIE   (*entering*): Madame rang?

MINA: When the prince arrives, will you show him in?

FÉLICIE: Very good, Madame.

MINA: Tell me Félicie, since you're so clever, where exactly is Inertia?

FÉLICIE: It's a little bit everywhere . . . but to be more precise, we can look it up in the encyclopedia. (*She picks up the encyclopedia from the table and reads.*) Inertia. Small North American principality, situated between 26 and 45 degrees longitude and 38 and 50 degrees latitude. The royal family comprises of several family trees of which the current prince is the last branch.

MINA: The last branch . . . (*The bell rings.*) That's him! Quickly, Félicie, go and let him in. (*She takes a final look at herself in the mirror, whilst Robert carefully watches for the prince entering.*)

FÉLICIE   (*opening the door at the back and announcing*): His Highness! *She stays at the back. Loupy enters, dressed grotesquely in a badly fitting frock coat, his chest resplendent with medals. Félicie and Mina curtsy respectfully to him. Robert is doubled up with laughter.*

LOUPY: I am the Prince of . . . Prince of . . . (*Aside.*) Oh God, I can't remember where I'm the Prince of . . . (*Aloud.*) So here I am, it's me, the Prince!

MINA: I've been expecting you, your Highness.

LOUPY: Well, if you've been expecting me, you won't need to be told where I'm the Prince of.

MINA: You are welcome, your Highness.

ROBERT   (*aside*): What a hussy!

LOUPY   (*noticing one of his tools on the floor by Robert*): What's this tool doing over here?

MINA: That's the electrician who's repairing the short circuit. Félicie, offer his Highness the armchair.

LOUPY   (*aside*): They're going to offer my Highness the armchair. (*Félicie brings the chair forward.*)

MINA: Are you waiting for something, your Highness?

LOUPY: The armchair.

MINA: It's holding out its arms to you. (*Loupy tries to feel for the armchair for a moment, then finally sits down, rather baffled.*)

MINA: Now, my Prince, with your permission, let us have some tiffin.

LOUPY (*who doesn't understand*): Tiffin?

MINA: Don't you like tiffin?

LOUPY: On the contrary!

MINA: Félicie, His Highness would like tiffin. (*Before exiting, Félicie curtsies respectfully before Loupy, who gets up and politely bows.*) A Flower of the Harem, my Prince?

LOUPY: With pleasure.

MINA: I will go and get you one myself. (*She disappears for a moment into the bedroom.*)

LOUPY (*aside*): A Flower of the Harem! She's going to offer me a woman! (*Going towards Robert.*) Hey you, tell me, who is it you're working for?

ROBERT: I was going to ask you the same question!

LOUPY (*recognizing him*): It's the posh bloke from earlier . . . that's an amazing disguise.

MINA (*coming back in and presenting Loupy with a box of cigarettes*): Here are the Flowers of the Harem!

LOUPY (*disappointed, as if expecting something else*): Ah! They're just a brand of cigarette!

MINA (*holding out a match for him*): May I light your fire, your Highness?

LOUPY: By all means!

ROBERT (*aside*): You'll be lucky!

MINA: What are you still muttering about, electrician?

ROBERT: Me? Nothing! (*Looking into the fireplace.*) I'm looking for the mains cable.

LOUPY (*outraged at such incompetence*): He's bonkers, looking for the mains cable in the fireplace . . . you'll find it by the staircase.

MINA: You heard, by the staircase! Now, leave us alone, electrician. Go and finish your work on the landing. Well? What are you waiting for?

ROBERT: All right! All right! (*Aside.*) I'll leave, but I'll be keeping my eyes open. (*He exits at the back.*)

LOUPY: That bloke's a complete idiot!

MINA: These workers have no tact.

LOUPY: Let's not talk about that, my dear.

FÉLICIE (*bringing in a tray*): Tiffin for your Highness.

LOUPY (*sitting down on the left-hand side of the table*): Oh, is that what you meant?

MINA: A finger of port, your Highness?

LOUPY: Many fingers. (*Félicie pours. Mina takes a glass from the tray and passes it to Loupy.*)

MINA: Leave us, Félicie, I'll ring when I need you.

FÉLICIE: Very good, Madame. (*Curtseying to Loupy.*) Your Highness. (*Loupy gets up and politely bows, as before Félicie exits.*)

MINA: What do you think of the port, your Highness?

LOUPY: Excellent! (*Pulling a face.*) I'm getting a tincture of iodine.

MINA: Another cigarette?

LOUPY: Thank you, but they are a little mild. I prefer something with a bit of a kick. (*He takes out a rough tobacco pouch and starts to roll himself a cigarette.*)

MINA: You have such democratic ways!

LOUPY: Yes, I am for the people because the people work and work means freedom . . . the day when there are no more big investors who sit around doing sod all . . .

MINA   (*under his spell*): How beautifully you express yourself.

LOUPY   (*striking a match on his trousers*): Perhaps you'll now allow me to light your fire?

MINA   (*jumping onto his lap and taking a light*): Light my fire, your Highness! Light my fire! That's all I ask!

LOUPY: That's fine by me!

ROBERT   (*returning with a small stepladder*): Don't mind me!

MINA   (*sitting on Loupy's left knee and turning to Robert without getting up*): You again, electrician!

ROBERT: Do you want me to repair the short circuit or do you not want me to repair it?

MINA: Repair it but do hurry up! You can see perfectly well that we're busy.

ROBERT   (*climbing the ladder*): I can see! I can see! (*He disentangles—or rather tangles up—the wires.*)

MINA   (*getting up*): I beg your pardon, your Highness, this work is absolutely necessary. Without it we'll soon be without any light.

LOUPY   (*aside*): Does she really think he's going to manage that?

MINA: Your Highness, I am both happy and proud that you have deigned to even look at someone as modest as myself. May I speak frankly with you?

LOUPY   (*pointing out Robert's presence to her*): Perhaps you should wait until he has left?

MINA: The electrician? He's of no importance . . . Your Highness, I am deeply moved . . . just to think, a prince, a royal highness, paying me a visit . . . someone whose name is in the telephone directory.

LOUPY: Would you credit it?!

ROBERT   (*aside*): The silly goose!

MINA   (*pacing importantly in front of Loupy*): Oh, I'm familiar with your beautiful country . . . it's a country with lots of longitudes . . . and, where there are lots of longitudes, there's always plenty of latitude.

LOUPY: Evidently. (*Aside.*) She's a good talker.

MINA   (*aside*): I think he's impressed. (*Aloud, turning to Loupy.*) It's a beautiful country, very shady . . . with all those family trees of which you are the last branch.
           (*Robert, aside, doubled up over Mina's stupidity.*)

LOUPY   (*aside*): Why is she telling me all this?

MINA: Also, when your secretary explained to me your Highness's desires yesterday, I was quick to send away my boyfriend.

LOUPY: You have a boyfriend?

MINA:	Not that it matters. A Parisian lady cannot live alone—there are the dressmaker's and milliner's bills to pay . . .
ROBERT	(*aside, on the ladder*): What a cow!
MINA:	As for him, he's my last fling and you are my first true love.
ROBERT	(*aside*): Unbelievable!
MINA:	He is as stupid and disagreeable, as you are charming and distinguished.
LOUPY	(*aside*): She shouldn't say that in front of him.
MINA:	And on top of all that he is so gullible . . .
LOUPY:	You deceived him?
MINA:	And he fell for it . . . big time.
LOUPY:	That can't have been easy.
MINA:	Just imagine! So that I could see you today, I told him I was expecting a visit from my Uncle the Bishop.
LOUPY	(*doubled up*): The Bishop! Oh, that's a good one, all right!
ROBERT	(*aside, dropping his tool bag*): The old bag!
MINA:	Hey, electrician! Haven't you finished your work yet?
ROBERT:	Do you think it's easy trying to find a short circuit?
LOUPY:	Idiot! You just need to unscrew the ceramic cover.
MINA:	Just unscrew it, like the Prince says!
ROBERT:	I'm unscrewing!
LOUPY:	There, now check the connections. (*Robert follows Loupy's instructions. A huge spark flies and Robert is thrown onto the floor.*)
ROBERT:	Aaagh! I've been electrocuted! (*He starts to twitch as if he's doing some kind of dance.*)
LOUPY:	You prat! You haven't a clue. You made the connection before insulating the . . . You could have burned the bloody house down, you idiot!
MINA	(*to* Robert): Go away!
ROBERT:	I'd better just finish my work.
MINA:	Just clear off! I've had quite enough of you.
LOUPY:	Just make yourself scarce, before I make you scarce myself! (*He pushes Robert outside and closes the door behind him.*)
MINA:	That electrician is starting to get on my nerves.
LOUPY:	He doesn't know his job . . . You'll see, I'll have it sorted for you in a couple of ticks.
MINA:	Thank you, my Prince, but don't go to any trouble.
LOUPY	(*taking the ladder and replacing the fuses by the back door*): No problem, I know what I'm doing. That idiot would have messed up your wiring . . . You see, the fuses have blown. If the current has no resistance, that can cause havoc, so we have to insulate the wires because the rubber has burned through, and when the rubber has burned through . . . game over!
MINA	(*astounded, repeating mechanically*): Game over!
LOUPY:	There we go! It's all working now. You can put the lights on now without fear of causing havoc.
MINA	(*turning on the lights*): It's a good thing that you're so clever for a prince.
LOUPY:	In our line of work you have to know a whole heap of things.

MINA: But enough about short circuits . . . My Prince, let's talk about
            more pleasurable things.
LOUPY: I would wish for nothing else. (*Aside.*) I think I'm in here.
MINA: What do you think of me, your Highness?
LOUPY: What do I think of you? As far as good-looking girls go, you're a
            good-looking girl.
MINA: So, you like me, my Prince?
LOUPY: I think I like you very much. Your eye, your nose, your mouth,
            your ears . . . and then . . . and then everything else too.
MINA: Well then, your Highness, it's all yours!
LOUPY   (*incredulously*) Really?
MINA: Of course. (*She retreats to stage left, as if she's embarrassed by
            having perhaps said too much.*)
LOUPY: Perhaps there's a short circuit over here as well. (*Following Mina
            into the bedroom.*) Oh, my God!
ROBERT   (*coming in through the window*): When the door to the sitting
            room is locked, you just have to make use of the window.
            (*Advancing, his fists raised, as if he's going to break the door
            down.*) The scoundrels!
FÉLICIE   (*appearing at the door at the back with a letter in her hand*):
            Who are you looking for?
ROBERT: Nobody! I'm looking for the short circuit.
FÉLICIE: You're taking your time!
ROBERT   (*furiously*): I like taking my time.
FÉLICIE: Keep your voice down. There's a prince in the house.
ROBERT: I don't give a damn.
FÉLICIE: Well, that's not very nice!
ROBERT: All right! I'd better leave . . . otherwise I don't know what I might
            do. (*He exits furiously by the door at the back.*)
FÉLICIE: What a strange electrician!
MINA   (*in the doorway of the bedroom*): What's going on, Félicie?
FÉLICIE: It's the electrician, Madame.
MINA: What again?! Kick him out once and for all.
FÉLICIE: A letter for Madame.
MINA: Give it to me.
            *Félicie gives her the letter and exits. Mina looks for a letter opener
            on the table, whilst Loupy enters, dressed in Robert's pyjamas.*
LOUPY: She's quite a high-class hooker, what with all these perfumed
            sheets and what have you, smelling like a bouquet of flowers.
MINA   (*opening the letter*): Ah, I see you've risen, my Prince.
LOUPY: I was waiting for you, my Princess.
MINA: A letter with your Highness's coat of arms. It's from your private
            secretary. (*Reading.*) 'Madame, you are a silly little goose.'
            (*Speaking aloud.*) He's not very polite, your secretary. I think you
            should give him a lecture about it when you get back.
LOUPY: She must think I'm a professor.
MINA   (*reading*): 'You are a silly little goose and your Uncle the Bishop is
            ignorant and uncouth.' (*Speaking.*) My Uncle the Bishop? I don't
            have an Uncle the Bishop! How do you explain this, my Prince?

LOUPY   (*embarrassed*): You know, there are some things that are best left unexplained.

MINA   (*reading*): 'This man of the church said on the phone that he would knock his Highness down the stairs with a kick up the backside if he came to your house.' (*Speaking.*) The Bishop said that?

LOUPY: I can well believe it! (*Aside.*) There are going to be ructions!

MINA   (*continuing to read*): 'After such threats his Highness will never set foot in your house.' (*Speaking.*) You're not the Prince then?

LOUPY: Well, I would say that I both am and am not the Prince.

MINA   (*impatiently*): Well, explain yourself.

LOUPY: Well, it's like this. I was told that I had to be the Prince, but, you know, deep down, I'm not suited to it . . . I'm a socialist.

MINA: So, who are you?

LOUPY: An electrician.

MINA: Another electrician? And here I am . . .

LOUPY: Excuse me! I have asked for nothing that you didn't first offer me.

MINA: And to think I've been making love to this oaf.

LOUPY: Oaf! Just now you were calling me your sweet darling! How quickly women change their minds!

MINA: That's enough! Now make yourself scarce. My boyfriend may come back any minute and I have no desire to compromise myself any more.

LOUPY   (*gathering up his tools*): All right then, enough said!
         Robert enters at the back, having taken off the work-shirt and overalls.

MINA: Robert! There you are, and you didn't say a thing!

ROBERT: I didn't want to disturb you, Madame.

MINA: Not at all, my darling.

LOUPY   (*aside*): Her darling! She's got a nerve!

MINA: I was just here with the electrician who came to fix the short circuit.

ROBERT   (*looking at Loupy*): Wearing my pyjamas? Enough of this short circuit and enough of these lies! I know now what you really think of me. There is a saying, Madame, that one shouldn't try to ride two horses at the same time. You're nothing but a strumpet and I bid you farewell. (*He reaches the door at the back.*)

LOUPY: Well said!

ROBERT   (*to Loupy*): And as for you! You have gone beyond what we agreed. You're a complete swine! (*He exits.*)

LOUPY: Ah, I'm sorry, but there are plenty bigger swine than me!
         (*To Mina.*) Now then, about these two horses . . .

MINA: You! Beat it!

LOUPY: No hard feelings. (*At the door, turning around*) If ever you have another short circuit, remember me. (*He exits.*)

MINA   (*at the back door*): Bastards! Bastards!

CURTAIN

The Little House at Auteuil

(*La Petite Maison D'Auteuil*, 1917)

by

ROBERT SCHEFFER AND GEORGES LIGNEREUX

Preface

La Petite Maison D'Auteuil was premiered at the Théâtre du Grand-Guignol on 24 March 1907 and was produced again in July 1917, this time with Maxa in the role of Emma Fédon. Robert Scheffer was better known as a poet and a novelist than as a dramatist, and although his collaborator was much more a man of the theatre, Georges Lignereux was equally prolific as a librettist and translator of Greek folksongs.

Pierron describes the play as 'so violent that the publisher normally assigned to the Grand-Guignol did not dare publish it' (2011: 67). The publisher, Ondet, was not one to take such things lightly and was well known among writers for his liberal attitudes, acquiring the nickname of 'Ondet the benign'. And it certainly appears to be a graphic play, in terms not only of its violence, but also for its explicitness as regards the Baron's sexual proclivities.

The play is set in the fashionable, well-to-do Parisian suburb of Auteuil, one-time home of Victor Hugo and Molière, and birthplace of Marcel Proust in 1871, in the westernmost sixteenth arrondissement of the city. A young woman, Emma Fédon, returns home one evening in the company of the Baron, clearly a man of some wealth. It is not entirely clear whether or not Emma is a prostitute (although Pierron claims that in the 1917 production Camille Choisy dressed Maxa in a fashion that erased any ambiguity on that account), but when the Baron reveals his interest in sadomasochism, she is persuaded to accept money from him in return for allowing him to stab her in the arm with a needle and draw blood. When it transpires that Emma has been previously involved in a famous murder case, the Baron pays yet more money for them to re-enact the murder together for his sexual gratification. No sooner is the Baron bound to the chair by the laces of her corset, another of Emma's lovers, Henri, enters, reveals his own sadistic desires and proceeds to torture the Baron to death. The play ends with Emma being dragged off stage by the sexually aroused Henri.

It is an interesting play for a number of reasons. First, it is an extremely short play. Even for the Grand-Guignol, which specialized in the short-form drama, it is essentially a single scene play that unfolds in real time in a single location. Its running time is only about thirty minutes, yet it does not feel rushed and there is an extraordinary amount that happens in that time, both in terms of the exposition of the back-story and also in the playing out of violence. In fact, the brevity of the piece serves to intensify the violence, making it appear to be more horrific than it actually is. This use of brevity and economy of writing in order to intensify the emotional impact of the play is a key feature of Grand-Guignol drama and no more so than here.

Second, it is a fine example of the amoral (or at least morally ambiguous or complex) universe that the Grand-Guignol inhabits. On the surface one might describe the Baron as being the victim of the piece insofar as it is he who is tortured and murdered. At the same time, however, we are unlikely to harbour much sympathy for the arrogant and self-obsessed pleasure seeker. In fact, his treatment by Henri might be seen as just retribution for his own treatment of Emma (and presumably countless other women before her). It is rather Emma with whom our sympathies lie, as she is brutally exploited and abused by a continual stream of men. Arguably, the real horror is that which will happen off stage, perpetrated by Henri, after the curtain has fallen, rather than anything inflicted upon the Baron.

Third, the play is an excellent example of how the writers of the Grand-Guignol drew on real-life, sensationalized crime for their stories. In relation to the play, Pierron points out:

> The scenario is not without its parallels to the Bompard Affair, also called 'The Bloody Trunk', or 'Gouffé's Trunk'. In 1889 a woman of questionable virtue, Gabrielle Bompard, with her accomplice, a certain Eyraud, her lover at that time, had killed another of her lovers, Gouffé the bailiff. The body was carried in a trunk as far as the outskirts of Lyon in a mail coach, the driver of which was never found. The affair inflamed opinions and, bizarrely, the public sided with Gabrielle. (2001: 67)

Pierron further explains that after their arrest, having fled to America, the affair became a *cause célèbre* that captured the public imagination. Shortly afterwards a prostitute set up a service for clients whereby she constructed a replica of the room where the killing took place (just a few streets way from the actual murder scene) and offered to replay the events, with herself in the role of Gabrielle and the client as Gouffé, including the strangulation scene, in a moment of erotic asphyxiation. It seems she operated the service for a number of months before she was arrested, but such was its popularity that several other brothels took up the idea as well.

While the play was not performed at the rue Chaptal again after 1917, Pierron refers to a programme of plays performed in 1990 by Aboutface Theatre Company in New York, entitled *Return of the Grand-Guignol,* which comprised of adaptations of five classic Grand-Guignol plays (1995: LIII). Four of those were adaptations of de Lorde plays, including *La Dernière Torture* and *Au petit jour.* The fifth play was an adaptation of *La Petite Maison D'Auteuil,* entitled *House of the Rising Sin.* More recently students from Loughborough University in the UK staged a Grand-Guignol Laboratory production in October 2017, which played at both Loughborough University and at The Garage in Norwich.

THE LITTLE HOUSE AT AUTEUIL

(*La Petite Maison D'Auteuil*, 1917)

by

ROBERT SCHEFFER AND GEORGES LIGNEREUX

First performed at the Théâtre du Grand-Guignol on 24 March 1907
Translated by Richard J Hand and Michael Wilson

Cast
The Baron
Henri
Emma Fédon

A room, half-living room, half-boudoir, on Emma Fédon's ground floor. Upstage left a door leads out into the garden at the same level. Upstage right there is a window.

Stage left a curtain hangs over a doorway that leads to a bedroom. Upstage, against the wall, is a dressing table. On the table is a lamp, Chairs, armchairs, a pedestal table, etc.

As the curtain rises the stage is empty and dark. Through the half-open window, the greenery of the garden can be seen in the moonlight. Flashes of lightning. In the distance there are rumbles of thunder. Almost immediately there is the sound of a key turning in the lock. The door opens. Enter Emma.

EMMA: This way, my love. (*The Baron enters and misses his step.*) Look out, there's a step.
BARON: I've got it! Phew! We've got here just in time.
EMMA: You can say that again! A big drop of rain, the size of a five-franc piece, splashed on my hand as I opened the door. It's going to pour down.
BARON: So much the better! If the storm doesn't blow up, I'll be properly fed-up.
EMMA: Why? Do you like it when there's a storm?
BARON: It makes my day!
EMMA: How very strange!
BARON: What do you mean? I love the spectacle.
EMMA: Well, as far as I'm concerned, it puts me on edge, that's all there is to it.

BARON: Good grief! That's the same with me, but that's exactly why I like it!

EMMA: Possibly! Damn! There's lightning. (*She goes to the window and closes the curtains.*) There, that's better. That's nice and homely.

BARON   (*looking around*): A nice place we have here.

EMMA: At least I suppose it's better than being out on the street.

BARON: Even if it's a street in Auteuil, like the one we just left . . . silent, unnerving in its conspiratorial silence, impregnated with the nightly scents from the neighbouring gardens . . .

EMMA: Haven't you the gift of the gab!

BARON: Oh, don't flatter me!

EMMA: So, why is it that you always keep your hands in your pockets?

BARON   (*embarrassed*): Me? No reason . . . it disguises my nervousness.

EMMA: Tell me, am I making you nervous?

BARON: Eh? Well . . . perhaps . . .

EMMA: Well, that's the first time I've ever made anyone nervous.
        At that moment a long blow of a whistle can be heard in the distance.

BARON   (*shivering*): What was that?

EMMA   (*quite unconcerned*): That? It's the Circle Line train. It's only fifty metres from here, along the embankment.

BARON: What a fool I am! But you know, that whistle . . . in the night . . . I had no idea . . . Don't you get scared at all, here by yourself?

EMMA: Me? Why would I be scared?

BARON: Why indeed! It's terribly quiet round here . . . there are no other tenants in the building, we are set well back off the road. One night you could be murdered and you could cry out for all your worth, but nobody would hear you out on the street . . .

EMMA: You are funny, once you get started.

BARON: This could be a real House of Horrors.

EMMA: Well look, why don't we talk about something else?

BARON: Oh, I'm only saying it for your own benefit.

EMMA: Don't you worry about that . . . in any case, I have no money or jewellery. Why would anyone break into my place?

BARON: People don't always kill for money, you know.

EMMA: Yes, I know . . . They sometimes kill for revenge.

BARON: They also kill for *pleasure*! You should take care. There are some very strange people around. Do you ever really know who you're dealing with? Take me, for example, do you really know me? I could be a dangerous, raving maniac . . .

EMMA: You?

BARON: I love to see people suffering.

EMMA: You're certainly a man of passion.

BARON   (*slowly getting closer*): What if I were to hurt you? Very badly?

EMMA: Just try and you'll find out!

BARON: Ah! It would be stupid of me to stick a pin just here—I'd prick myself.

EMMA: It would serve you right!

BARON: Exactly. It would serve me right. But you're making fun of me. But what if I were to prick you with a pin as well, let's say, with my tie-pin?

EMMA: There you go again!

BARON: I think it would bring me some relief.

EMMA: Keep your hands off or else!

BARON: Oh, your pretty white arm! . . . Those pretty little veins that run beneath the skin. Look! (*He pricks her.*)

EMMA   (*crying out in pain and pulling away*): Ow! What kind of brute are you?! (*She immediately retreats behind the settee.*) Oh, you're going to pay for that!

BARON   (*pursuing her*): It's all the same to me! But let me see, let me see where I pricked you. (*He takes her by the wrist.*) Oh, what a beautiful red mark. Like a ruby. My beauty, it would be very nice of you, if you were to let me carry on.

EMMA: Ah! No! Never!

BARON: Don't refuse me when it gives me such pleasure . . . Look . . . Would you like twenty francs?

EMMA: Leave me alone!

BARON: I'll be very gentle. How about forty francs?

EMMA: Forty francs! All right but be careful. You won't hurt me too much? Promise me!

BARON: Not at all. Like this. You see, it's fine, there'll just be a little shiver.

EMMA: Ah! Bastard!

BARON: There. That wasn't so bad, and it was for twenty francs above the going rate. What's your name?

EMMA: Emma.

BARON   (*approaching the dressing table*): Well, Emma, you are a good girl. (*Noticing a photograph on the dressing table.*) Look! What's this then?

EMMA: It's a portrait.

BARON: I can see that. Of whom?

EMMA: What's that got to do with you?

BARON: One of your lovers?

EMMA: Leave it alone!

BARON: Your one and only true love perhaps?

EMMA   (*nervous*): Not at all! Put it back where it was!

BARON: Well then, who is it?

EMMA: It's Emile!

BARON: And who is Emile?

EMMA: My fiancé. There!

BARON: Gosh! You're engaged! For how long?

EMMA: Four years.

BARON: Why hasn't he married you?

EMMA: Because he's dead.

BARON: That's a good reason. (*Examining the portrait.*) Not bad . . . he has something of a shifty look about him, which is a shame . . . something dubious. Where the devil have I seen his face before?

You know, your fiancé really has a crazed look in his eye—quite
disturbing!

EMMA   (*almost violently snatching the photograph from him*): Right,
that's enough!

BARON   (*a little surprised*): Eh? Don't be like that! I'm only having a little
joke with you.

EMMA: Well, I don't find it at all funny!

BARON: Very well . . . very well! For goodness sake! I think you're
making something of a cult of his memory. (*He takes a few steps
forward and notices on the wall a framed collection of newspaper
cuttings.*) And this . . . what's this? (*He examines it more closely
and suddenly turns around, gripped by an intense unease and
scrutinizes, in turn,* Emma *and the newspaper cuttings.*)
No . . . but there's no mistake. It's . . . it's really you!

EMMA: What do you mean?

BARON: It's you . . . Emma Fédon!

EMMA: You must be joking!

BARON: Oh, don't deny it! This courtroom sketch leaves no shred of
doubt! You are Emma Fédon, the woman who was tried last year
for strangling some unfortunate well-to-do chap with the help of
your accomplice, your lover.

EMMA: Don't talk rubbish.

BARON: And that's why I also recognized him just now. And perhaps
this is the place . . . My God, yes, I remember now. 'The Crime
at Auteuil'! . . . The little house, set back at the bottom of a
garden . . . It was here! It was here that the poor chap was
ambushed and killed! Admit it!

EMMA: Very well! Yes, it was me! And so what? Does that story upset
you? There are plenty of others like it. Besides I hardly had
anything to with the whole business . . . Emile didn't tell me
anything beforehand. I know nothing . . . I'm innocent!

BARON: Innocent?

EMMA: Of course! And the proof is that I only got one year in prison.
As for Emile, he was put inside for life! Ah! He was lucky to get
away with only that!

BARON: Yes, yes, I know . . . you were in prison. From the very outset it
was a revelation to me that a sweet kid like you had . . . had been
capable of committing a crime . . . but now, I like you even more
for it . . . you interest me . . . will you tell me how it all happened?

EMMA: Never!

BARON: But you must . . . you must . . . I'll make it worth your while . . .
After all, the memory can't be that painful or you wouldn't have
put those cuttings up on the wall.

EMMA: Ah, well, that's another question. It's always flattering to have
your picture in the papers!

BARON: I'll tell you what, my dear, I have another idea. Would you like
to do me a favour? Well, instead of telling me how it happened,
show me, right here!

EMMA: What?

BARON: Reconstruct the scene for me . . . exactly as it happened.

EMMA: You're mad!

BARON: Perhaps! It's a little fantasy, I admit, but I'm not in the habit
        of being denied my little fantasies, and I always pay for them—
        I'm good for it. Come on then!

EMMA: No!

BARON: The last time you did it, it was for real—now you can do it just
        for fun!

EMMA: But why would you want me to?

BARON: To be afraid! Ah, I'm a complicated soul, I am. A little kiss on the
        lips—that leaves me cold! I need something else—a sense of fear
        that goes deep into the heart and under the skin, that makes you
        deliciously and horribly dizzy, and whose terrible stranglehold
        makes you moan out loud. Ah, I would risk everything just to
        experience the emotional intensity that fear brings. It won't
        surprise you that I spent nights walking along the embankments,
        mixing with the riff-raff, partying with the down-and-outs,
        I roamed the city walls . . . but I did more than this . . . me too,
        I almost killed someone.

EMMA: You?

BARON: Yes . . . a kid like you . . . but younger. As she was dying, as
        I strangled her, a marvellous feeling . . . but enough, I've told
        you too much . . . Besides, I didn't actually kill her . . .!

EMMA: You're frightening me . . .

BARON   (laughing nervously): Ah, yes, that's where I'd like to take you!
        But don't worry. People like me know their position and we never
        go as far as committing a crime. We stop at the very limit and
        content ourselves with the thrill of it, or it is our own blood that
        is spilled.

EMMA: Blood?

BARON: Look, just now, when I followed you down the empty street,
        I wallowed in the mystery of this sinister street, where the
        unexpected could suddenly appear, out of the blue, a crime! As
        I came in I had my hand in my pocket, holding my revolver . . .
        and suddenly I discovered that this was a place where blood was
        really spilled, that a pitiful ghost roams within these walls and
        by this tiny little hand a man met his death! Ah, I was frightened,
        terribly frightened. But for me that's not enough. You must give
        me the complete illusion of the drama. You must re-enact it for
        me . . . with me . . . and I will play the role of the victim! Did he
        cry out? I'll cry out! Did he put up a fight? I'll put up a fight! And
        . . . yes . . . perhaps we'll change the ending, my little murderess,
        so that you get something other than prison!

EMMA: No . . . I don't want to . . . I don't like thinking about it . . .

BARON   (who has opened his wallet): Look, here's two hundred francs!

EMMA   (dizzily): Two hundred francs!

BARON: Yes, two hundred francs. Here, take it.

EMMA: I'm so on edge . . . I have a headache . . . it must be the storm.

BARON: It's your choice.

EMMA (*giving in*): Everyone has to make a living.

BARON: Very well, let's begin . . .

EMMA: All right, so the day before his departure for Monte Carlo, the old man came around to my place for dinner.

BARON: Ah yes, I understand.

EMMA: Yes. Emile had given me a drug to put into his wine and had told me, 'Once he's fallen asleep, let me know.' After dinner he sat down in this armchair.

BARON: In this armchair?

EMMA: Yes.

BARON: Ah! (*He goes to sit down.*)

EMMA (*continuing*): And almost immediately he fell asleep, so I called Emile.

BARON (*impatient*): And then what? Get a move on! You're such a slowcoach!

EMMA: Well just to be sure I bound his hands and feet . . . I tied him to the chair.

BARON: Eh? You tied him up? Well then, you'll have to tie me up as well so that the excitement is magnified, the fear is more intense.

EMMA: What? You want me to tie you up?

BARON: Yes, yes . . . I've paid you . . . do as I ask . . .

EMMA: If that's what you want . . . It's neither here nor there to me . . . but what am I going to tie you up with?

BARON (*noticing the lace of a corset on the dressing table*): The lace of the corset.

EMMA: Good idea. The lace is flexible. That'll do the job.

BARON: And strong. Go on then, tie me up.

EMMA: There we are!

BARON: Don't be afraid, you can make it nice and tight. I want it so that when I hear you approaching, your hands ready to strangle me, I want it to be impossible for me to get away. That's it, now I'm well and truly trussed up . . . and now, carry on . . . what happened when the old man was tied up?

EMMA: To call Emile, I clapped my hands twice like this.

BARON: And then?

EMMA: I went and got the curtain tie.

BARON: Go and get it.

EMMA: And then I walked around the . . . oh . . . the floorboard just creaked . . .! The curtain is moving . . .! There's somebody behind it!

            Henri *enters from behind the curtain.*

EMMA (*to* Henri): It's you! Here!

HENRI: Well, yes, that's right, it's me.

BARON: Who is that? Emile!?

HENRI (*to the* Baron): No. Henri.

EMMA: You can see perfectly well that I'm not alone. How did you get in?

HENRI: I saw you in the distance with this gentleman. Only as it was raining I didn't feel like waiting outside in the street, so I came in through the kitchen window.

EMMA: What do you want?

HENRI: Some cash. I lost mine at the races. I came to ask you for some.

BARON: Emma, this is a good . . . a very good joke . . . you and your friend, you cooked up a nice little scheme. You gave me a fright and it was worth every penny . . . Now, untie me!

HENRI   (*walking around the Baron*): You! Don't interrupt our little heart-to-heart. I'll be talking to you soon enough.

EMMA: Henri! What are you going to do?

HENRI: None of your business.

EMMA: Tell me, I want to know.

HENRI: Ah, just leave me alone! Hop it! Get lost! I want to talk to the gentleman. (*He pushes her violently towards the door.*)

EMMA: Henri! Henri! You're not going to . . .

HENRI   (*pushing her out*): Go on, clear off! (*He closes the door and locks it.*) Now then, let's get all this sorted.

BARON: What do you want? Untie me!

HENRI: Oh, there's plenty of time for that. I've been waiting for quite a while, I have, in the next room, before I came in. Now it's your turn to wait. For the time being we're going to have a chat . . . yes, I was behind the door and I said to myself, 'My Emma, she's working like an angel, preparing a nice little job for me.'

BARON: You're not going to . . . murder me?

HENRI: As I said, we're just going to have a chat, as friends, yes, a friendly chat. How about that then? You see, it's just that you and I are very much alike . . . Like you, I enjoy the sensation of an orgasmic shudder running up and down my spine . . . it's quite a turn-on . . . For example, as I'm no millionaire, I can't do as you do, I can't afford the luxury of this game-playing. If I want to treat myself to that exquisite pleasure of fear you were just chattering about now, I have to put my neck on the line . . . but it's the danger that turns me on . . . Once, on a night very much like this one, I was walking around Neuilly, the breeze in my face, breathing in the sweet smell of the linden trees in the gardens of the big houses . . . Suddenly, thirty paces ahead of me, I noticed four old lags and I said to myself, if they see you, they'll do you in, for sure. Fortunately, it was a dark night . . . I pressed myself up into a corner . . . I flattened myself as much as I could, holding my breath . . . they went past and into the distance . . . I was fine! Ah, what a sigh of relief! But also what a fantastic feeling of fear. So you see, I'm right when I say I'm just like you . . . but that's not all . . . I not only like to feel frightened, but I also like to watch suffering and again to treat yourself to that you have to be rich . . . her? . . . No way will I damage her . . . she has to work . . . she's sacrosanct . . . but you . . .

BARON   (*his throat contracting with fear*): Me?

HENRI: A mug like you, that's totally different . . . and since I have you at my mercy, without your being able to defend yourself, well, we're going to have ourselves a bit of fun.

BARON: You're not going to . . . torture me!

HENRI: Have you ever imagined burning someone with a cigarette? That would be fun! Look! Like this! (*He stubs out his lit cigarette on the Baron's forehead.*)

BARON   (*crying out*): Aagghh!

HENRI: That's good isn't it? But that's nothing, nothing at all. I'm going to prepare something better . . . how about her curling tongs? I'll put them on the spirit stove and when they're red hot . . . (*As he is speaking, he lights the stove and places the curling tongs on it.*)

BARON: Help! Help!

HENRI: Oh you can shout all you like, no one will hear you.

BARON: Murder!

HENRI: And whilst I'm waiting, why don't I pull out some hairs from your beard, and some of your eyelashes? (*He carries out his threats.*)

BARON   (*crying out in pain*): Aagghh! Aagghh!

HENRI: What's that? That's a pretty song!

BARON: Bastard!

HENRI: What?

BARON: You monster! You maniac!

HENRI: What if I were to slash your face with my knife . . . oh yes, that would be fun! . . . A little gash here! A little gash there!

BARON   (*crying out*): Aagghh! Aagghh!

HENRI   (*gradually getting carried away in his sadistic madness*): Blood! Here's some blood! Oh the blood is so beautiful the way it runs down your cheeks like hot tears! It's intoxicating!

BARON: Help! Help! (*He struggles and tried to bite Henri.*)

HENRI: Ah! You filthy animal! You want to bite me! Wait a minute! I'm going to take out your teeth! (*He presses the blade of his knife into the Baron's gums.*)

BARON   (*moaning*): Aagghh! (*In the struggle he scratches Henri.*)

HENRI: So you're scratching me now? Give me your fingernails, so that I can pull them out.

BARON   (*cries out*): Aagghh!

HENRI: And the curling tongs! They must be hot by now!

BARON: Ah! No, no! Not that! For pity's sake! Mercy!

HENRI   (*approaching him with the red hot tongs*): What are you looking at me like that for? Your eyes . . . close them! They're scaring me! You won't do it? Very well, I'll close them for you! Like that! And that! (*He presses the tongs into the Baron's eyes.*)

BARON: (*final cry*): Aagghh!

          He passes out. During the last lines Emma can be heard crying out, 'Henri! Henri!' from behind the door, which she is trying to open. Henri goes to the door and opens it. Emma enters.

HENRI   (*triumphantly pointing at the Baron*): There! Look! (*Manic laugh.*) Ah, what a hideous fellow!

EMMA: Ah! That's horrible! You disgust me! You disgust me! (*She turns her back on the horrific scene.*)

HENRI: And now, come on my darling little Emma, my darling girl. (*He tries to lead her off into the bedroom.*)

EMMA: But him? . . . What about him?

HENRI: We'll chuck him in the river . . . the Seine's not far from here . . . but come on! I love you! I want you! I'll have you moaning with pleasure, just as I had him moaning in agony,

EMMA: Henri! You disgust me! You disgust me!
         She struggles, as he leads her off.

CURTAIN

The Unhinged

(*Les Détraquées*, 1921)

by

PALAU AND OLAF

Preface

Les Détraquées (*The Unhinged*) was *not* actually performed at the Théâtre du Grand-Guignol, but was a successful play premiered in February 1921 at the Théâtre des Deux Masques, the Grand-Guignol's most significant rival. *Les Détraquées* is nevertheless recognised as an important example of the Grand-Guignol genre and as such earns a place in Agnès Pierron's extensive collection of Grand-Guignol plays (1995). It was also performed in 2013 by contemporary professional French Grand-Guignol company acte6 at Théâtre 13/Jardin on the boulevard Auguste Blanqui in the thirteenth arrondissement (on the south side of the Seine), as part of a triple bill that also included Maurice Renard's 1925 drama *L'Amant de la Mort* (*The Lover of Death*) and Jean Aragny and Francis Neilson's 1929 classic *Le Baiser de Sang* (*The Kiss of Blood*), a translation of which appears in *Grand-Guignol: The French Theatre of Horror* (2002: 244–64).

The central link, however, between the play and the Théâtre du Grand-Guignol, beyond the play's obvious main thematic concerns, is that Pierre Palau, one of its authors, was a regular contributor to the seasons at the rue Chaptal as both an actor (he played the leading role in the 1907 premiere of *Les Opérations du Professeur Verdier* [*Professor Verdier's Operations*]), part of the same programme that premiered *La Petite Maison d'Auteuil* (*The Little House at* Auteuil), and a playwright known as much for his horrors as his comedies (Pierron 1995: 808). His co-author, the enigmatic Olaf, was the pseudonym of the renowned neurologist Joseph Babinski, who, like Alfred Binet, protected his identity and professional reputation by wearing a false beard to attend the performance of the play. His identity was first revealed in 1956 by André Breton in *Le Surréalisme, même*. As such, the play is a fine example of the *théâtre medical*, championed by de Lorde in his collaborations with Binet. Far from being a purely erotic play, the piece seeks to explore a specific mental and sexual (medical) disorder, based upon the latest scientific theories of the time.

Having said that, the play did cause shock and outrage when it was first performed, even in the notoriously liberal Montmartre. It was fiercely attacked by the critics, and were it not for the robust defence of the play launched by André Breton, the piece might have sunk ignominiously into obscurity. In their biography of Babinski, Jacques Phillippon and Jacques Poirier offer the following reasons on Breton's involvement:

> Fascinated by mental pathology and attracted by the intensity of attacks in the press against *Les détraquées*, André Breton went to see the play. He was captivated by the actress Blanche Derval, saying that he had been deeply moved and had had one of the greatest theatrical experiences of his life.[18] (2009: 44–45)

To put this into some perspective, however, one might consider that *Les Détraquées* was being performed on the Parisian stage at the same time that José Levy, the producer of the London Grand Guignol seasons, was having such tussles over censorship with the Lord Chamberlain's office, over such matters as a simple love-bite on an actor's neck (Hand and Wilson 2007: 58) and that Aubrey Hammond's posters were being banned from the London Underground for indecency and their harrowing nature.

As in many examples of the Grand-Guignol genre, *The Unhinged* offers excellent female roles. The two central roles of Madame de Challens and Mademoiselle Solange are clearly the most challenging for an actor—these are the roles that demand the carefully judged chronometric performance, the balanced and managed tension of the journey from naturalism to melodrama. Even the subsidiary role of Mademoiselle Claire has more depth than the rather two-dimensional characters of Police Superintendent Bernier and Doctor Levron, not to mention the working-class caricature Jean, the caretaker. Furthermore, the female characters are certainly not submissive or, indeed, domestically situated or restricted. They are articulate, professional and authoritative. Even the young and inexperienced Mademoiselle Claire is quite ready to assert her authority over Jean in the way she admonishes him for the use of slang.

Nevertheless, before getting carried away with its feminist credentials, this must also be balanced by the fact that the play can be read as continuing to pedal the stereotype of women as emotional, irrational and prone to hysteria, while men will remain logical and clear-headed. It is the very two-dimensional nature of Bernier and Levron that underpins the underlying assumption that it is men who are best suited to apply scientific rationalism to a situation and to solve and resolve the mystery. Yet one mustn't forget that the subject matter of the drama undoubtedly plays to male sado-masochistic lesbian fantasies, in spite of Pierron's slightly curious assertion that 'The Grand-Guignol is puritan. It hardly ever deals with

---

[18] Agnès Pierron also speculates as to whether Breton ever saw Maxa perform at the rue Chaptal, so much is his enthusiasm focused on Derval, who is associated solely with the Deux Masques (2011: 74).

homosexuals, transvestites, lesbians and seems closed to the trouble caused by sexual ambivalence' (2011: 271).

To merely understand the play as a piece about sex and sexuality (albeit from a detached psychoanalytical and psychosexual standpoint) is to ignore the importance of class. Stark contrasts are drawn between the sympathetically portrayed, salt-of-the-earth working-class honesty of Jean, the middle-class professionalism of the Superintendent and the Doctor and the aristocratic background of de Challens and Solange. There are numerous references to the purely aristocratic nature of the closed world of the boarding school and its role in nurturing the country's future nobility. And while the pupils are portrayed as innocent victims (as is consistent with the melodramatic code), they are as much victims of their rotten and depraved class, as they are of de Challens and Solange. Indeed, the behaviour of the two main protagonists is seen as being both depraved *and* aristocratic. Their debauchery is a direct result of their nobility and, as a result, they become not only unhinged from mental stability, but also from decent French, republican society. Their crimes are arguably both sexually abusive and anti-democratic—a double depravity.

In 1986 the play was adapted for film by Catherine Breillat, a writer and actress who had previously appeared as Mouchette in *Last Tango in Paris* (1972). Directed by Jacques Baratier, the film was released to mixed reviews under the title *L'Araignée de Satin* (*The Satin Spider*). Although some characters names were changed and some additional characters added, the basic premise of the plot remains, as do the names of the central protagonists. Ingrid Caven played the role of Madame de Challens with Catherine Jourdan as Solange. Colette Godard, writing in *Le Monde*, described the film as 'Gaston Leroux via Lewis Carroll, but even more deliciously perverse' (https://www.lemonde.fr/archives/article/1985/05/11/l-araignee-de-satin-filles-fleurs-pour-baratier_3047470_1819218.html).

THE UNHINGED

(*Les Détraquées*, 1921)

by

PALAU AND OLAF

First performed at the Théâtre des Deux Masques, Paris, February 1921
Translated by Richard J. Hand and Michael Wilson

Cast
Madame de Challens
Solange
Lucienne
Mademoiselle Claire
Madame Le Goff
Doctor
Police Superintendent
Jean, the caretaker

ACT ONE

The office of Mme de Challens, headmistress of 'Les Fauvettes' Boarding School at Versailles.

MLLE CLAIRE   (*on the telephone*): Hello? Yes . . . pardon? No, Madame isn't here. It's Mademoiselle Claire. Hello? Ah, it's you, Mademoiselle Edmée. What can I do for you? Yes . . . yes . . . yes. Indeed, it's terribly hot. Yes, I quite understand what you're saying. In principle, I don't think Madame would object. On the contrary. (*There is a knock at the door.*) Come in! (*The caretaker enters. Mademoiselle Claire indicates he should come in.*) Hallo? Mademoiselle Edmée, I hear what you're saying. Do whatever necessary to ensure that the children are not given homework for tomorrow. Yes, I'll check with Madame. What is it, Jean?
The caretaker (*handing her some letters*): It's the post, Miss.
MLLE CLAIRE: Is there anything for me?
CARETAKER: No, it's all for Madame and the pupils. (*Mademoiselle Claire starts to sort through the letters.*) There's one here that's scented! It's like a flower bed! Exactly the same! And look at this! There's one here with a wax seal with a napkin ring underneath it. Have a look!

MLLE CLAIRE: That's not a napkin ring. Look, Jean, it's a baronial crown.
CARETAKER: Ah, well, I wouldn't know that.
MLLE CLAIRE: It's for the Le Goff girl.
CARETAKER: Ah, yes, little Lucienne.
MLLE CLAIRE: She's a pretty one.
CARETAKER: All the young ladies here are pretty.
MLLE CLAIRE: Well, they're not exactly the children of paupers.
CARETAKER: That's for sure. They're more like spoiled brats, as the saying goes.
MLLE CLAIRE: Yes, as the saying goes. But I'd rather you didn't use such vulgar and coarse expressions. You know that Madame hates that kind of thing.
CARETAKER (*lowering his voice*): Is Madame here?
MLLE CLAIRE: No, she's gone out. To do the shopping.
CARETAKER: Well, that's odd.
MLLE CLAIRE: What?
CARETAKER: Eh?
MLLE CLAIRE: You just said, 'That's odd.' What's odd?
CARETAKER: Well, I never saw her go out and I haven't budged from my seat all day. (*Pause.*) It's so hot! In here it's just about bearable, but out there you could fry an egg. You don't mind if I sit down for five minutes to catch my breath?
MLLE CLAIRE: Five minutes and no longer. Madame won't be late coming back and you know that she doesn't like having men around where the girls are.
CARETAKER (*smiling*): Oh, at my age there's nothing to worry about. (*Pause.*) The boss isn't always that easy-going, is she?
MLLE CLAIRE: She's anxious.
CARETAKER: How long have you been here now?
MLLE CLAIRE: Well, let's see, I came shortly before Christmas, 15th December to be exact. Now it's the end of July.
CARETAKER: That's seven months then.
MLLE CLAIRE: Yes, seven months.
Pause.
CARETAKER: Do you like it?
MLLE CLAIRE: Of course. Why do you ask?
CARETAKER: No reason. Just idle chit-chat.
MLLE CLAIRE: Conversation. Just for conversation.
CARETAKER: What?
MLLE CLAIRE: One should say 'for conversation'. 'Chit-chat' is slang.
CARETAKER: Ah, I see!
MLLE CLAIRE: Oh, I'm not unhappy here. Of course, it's hard work and there's all the responsibility. And Madame doesn't always seem to give credit where it's due.
CARETAKER: That's bosses for you. They're all the same!
MLLE CLAIRE: In any case, I'm happy enough in spite of everything. That's not to say I'm not very much looking forward to the holidays.
CARETAKER: Normally we finish earlier. Why is the year so late?

MLLE CLAIRE:	It's because of the School Fair.
CARETAKER:	What fair?
MLLE CLAIRE:	Well, the one that Madame wants to organize. There'll be prize-giving too.
CARETAKER:	Again?
MLLE CLAIRE:	What do you mean 'again'? *The telephone rings.*
CARETAKER:	Well, you see, last year . . .
MLLE CLAIRE:	Hang on a second. Hello? Yes, it is. Ah, Madame de Chéroy, good morning, Madame. No, Madame. No, this isn't Madame de Challens. It's the school nurse. I'm afraid she's not here just at the moment. Oh, I'm sure she won't be long. I'm expecting her any minute. Would you like me to give her a message at all? The exact date of the prize-giving? I can't be precise, I'm afraid, Madame, but it will certainly be before the end of the month. Yes. Yes. Of course. Yes, I understand. It's a nuisance when you're trying to arrange the holidays. Very well, I will speak to Madame immediately for you. Yes, yes, Armelle is doing wonderfully. Ah, I see. Her work is going less well. Yes. Yes. Goodbye, Madame. (*She hangs up.*)
CARETAKER:	Let's hope that this year won't be like last year.
MLLE CLAIRE:	Last year? Why shouldn't it be like last year?
CARETAKER:	Ah, we don't want a repeat of that, you do know . . .
MLLE CLAIRE:	Not at all.
CARETAKER:	Don't you remember what happened?
MLLE CLAIRE:	You know full well that I wasn't here then.
CARETAKER:	Of course, I know that. But I thought you might have heard the gossip. The conversation, the gossip, whatever. It was certainly loud enough.
MLLE CLAIRE:	No, I was living out in the country.
CARETAKER:	Ah, in which case I'd better fill you in. You see, last year for prize-giving, Madame had the idea of throwing a fancy-dress ball. With a Louis XV theme. She arranged for a teacher of dance and deportment to come. She was called Mademoiselle Solange.
MLLE CLAIRE:	For what purpose?
CARETAKER:	To teach the boarders the dance steps and movements.
MLLE CLAIRE:	Of course . . .
CARETAKER:	Well, one of the pupils was a young girl . . . thirteen years old and pretty, very pretty. You might even say that she was beautiful. I can still see her standing there. Poor little mite.
MLLE CLAIRE:	Why 'poor little mite'?
CARETAKER:	She's dead!
MLLE CLAIRE:	Dead?
CARETAKER:	She killed herself!
MLLE CLAIRE:	Killed herself . . . at thirteen?!
CARETAKER:	Yes, out of despair.

MLLE CLAIRE:	Out of despair?
CARETAKER:	I'm afraid so.
MLLE CLAIRE:	That's impossible.
CARETAKER:	But it's true. It seems that on the very evening that she arrived, Mademoiselle Solange was very critical of her. Nobody knows why. The next day I found her body, covered in blood, at the bottom of the well near the allotment.
MLLE CLAIRE:	That's horrible!
CARETAKER:	You can say that again. If I were to live for a hundred years, I'd never forget the sight of it.
	A long pause. A clock chimes half past the hour.
MLLE CLAIRE	(*thoughtfully*): It's odd that this child died by her own hand.
CARETAKER:	Yes, but it happens. She was all alone. Her parents lived in Brazil. She never went out. Madame was her guardian. She was always sad, in a dream, anxious. (*Pause.*) It didn't surprise me.
MLLE CLAIRE	(*to herself*): I suppose it can happen. There are children who are melancholic, anxious, impulsive.
CARETAKER:	Yes, that's how it is. It's not that unusual. The press have loads of stories, as do the police, all well documented. And so the whole business was shelved, as they say.
MLLE CLAIRE:	And didn't this tragic accident cause a lot of trouble for the school?
CARETAKER:	You might think that Madame would have been worried about that. But at the end of the day, she wasn't to blame.
MLLE CLAIRE:	And what about this woman Solange?
CARETAKER:	She left again, shortly afterwards.
MLLE CLAIRE:	And she's never been seen again?
CARETAKER:	Never! (*Long pause.*) In any case, if Madame wants to hold a ball again this year, I'm happy with that. As long as that Solange woman isn't involved! Madame!
	Mme de Challens appears, her arms full of flowers. She is blonde and in her forties.
MME DE CHALLENS:	What is it?
CARETAKER:	It's . . . it's . . .
MLLE CLAIRE:	The post, Madame. Jean has just brought it across.
CARETAKER:	That's right, Madame.
MME DE CHALLENS:	Very good. Off you go then.
MLLE CLAIRE:	There's a telegram.
MME DE CHALLENS:	Ah. Jean, wait a moment. (*Excitedly she opens the telegram.*) Jean—the train that leaves Paris at twenty past three, what time does it get in?
CARETAKER:	Twenty past three . . . isn't that the one from Saint-Lazare?
MME DE CHALLENS:	Yes, from Saint-Lazare.
CARETAKER:	Well, with a change at Saint-Cloud, that would make it around four o'clock. Yes, it gets in at four.
MME DE CHALLENS:	Good. It's now half past three. You've got plenty of time. Go straight to the station and wait there for a lady. You can bring her luggage back as well.

CARETAKER: Very well, Madame. (*He goes to leave, then returns.*)
How will I know the lady that I'm supposed to . . .

MME DE CHALLENS: You've seen her before. You'll recognise her. And if you're worried that you won't, just ask for Mademoiselle Solange.
A reaction from Mademoiselle Claire and the caretaker.

CARETAKER: Mademoiselle . . . Solange? The lady who was here last year?

MME DE CHALLENS: That's right. Off you go then and don't be late.

CARETAKER: Of course . . . yes . . . no . . . yes . . . Madame.
He leaves in a state of deep confusion.

MME DE CHALLENS   (*recovering her sense of urgency*): Mademoiselle Claire, has the bedroom next to mine been made ready?

MLLE CLAIRE: Yes, Madame. That's to say it's prepared for a guest. Everything is ready.

MME DE CHALLENS: Put some flowers in there. Lots of flowers. Immediately.

MLLE CLAIRE: I'll do it now.

MME DE CHALLENS: And take the pupils' mail with you. You can hand it out at playtime.

MLLE CLAIRE: Very good, Madame. Ah, Mademoiselle Esmée asked for permission not to give homework to the girls tomorrow, so that they're not overworked in this temperature. I thought it was right to let them off this once.

MME DE CHALLENS: You should have spoken to me first. I wouldn't have been against it, but you should have checked.

MLLE CLAIRE: I'm sorry.
A pause.

MLLE CLAIRE: Mme de Chéroy telephoned to enquire about the date of the prize-giving.

MME DE CHALLENS: And what did you tell her?

MLLE CLAIRE: That I wasn't that well informed.
She leaves. Mme de Challens re-reads the telegrams, stares into space, puts down the flowers she has been carrying and picks up the telephone.

MME DE CHALLENS: Hello? Four-zero, please. Forty—two times twenty. Yes, here in Versailles, of course. Hello? Hello? Monsieur Gautret? It's Madame de Challens, Monsieur Gautret, I'd like to see you about the decorations for the ball. Yes, it's urgent. When could you call by? As soon as possible. Yes. Tomorrow morning around ten o'clock. Without fail. I'll be expecting you. Goodbye, Monsieur Gautret. (*A knock on the door.*) Come in!
Enter Mademoiselle Claire.

MLLE CLAIRE: Madame it's little Christine in Mademoiselle Esmée's class. She's had a major nosebleed. Would you like me to give her some ether?

MME DE CHALLENS: Don't even consider it! Ether for a nosebleed! (*She goes to the cupboard and takes out a small bottle.*) Take this and get her to inhale it. Where is she now?

MLLE CLAIRE: In the bathroom.

MME DE CHALLENS: Take the child down to the sick bay.

MLLE CLAIRE:	She's also complaining of a headache.
MME DE CHALLENS:	Very well. If it's no better in an hour, send for Doctor Bernier. Open the shutters please. It's stifling in here. (*A bell rings.*) A visitor! Go and see who it is. *Mlle Claire leaves, then reappears.*
MLLE CLAIRE:	Madame Le Goff would like to speak with you.
MME DE CHALLENS:	Madame Le Goff?
MLLE CLAIRE:	Yes, little Lucienne's grandmother.
MME DE CHALLENS:	Show her in, show her in. (*Mme Claire leaves and shows in Mme Le Goff. She is an elderly lady, very distinguished.*) Good day, Madame. How are you keeping? Very well, I can see.
MME LE GOFF:	Thank you, thank you. A little tired and weary. It's just my age.
MME DE CHALLENS:	Oh, you're still as strong as ever.
MME LE GOFF:	Well, I've nothing to complain about.
MME DE CHALLENS:	Please, have a seat, Madame. (*She points to the armchair.*)
MME LE GOFF:	Thank you. And you, Madame, are you not rather exhausted at the end of the school year with all the things you have to do?
MME DE CHALLENS:	Not at all. At least, not exhausted!
MME LE GOFF:	It must be a tricky thing steering this little ship through stormy seas.
MME DE CHALLENS:	Yes, of course, but our little ship is a thousand times better than the big one out there!
MME LE GOFF:	I admire you, Madame.
MME DE CHALLENS:	Goodness me! Whatever for?
MME LE GOFF:	Because in spite of being young, beautiful and rich, you have chosen this austere and scholarly existence over an elegant life in high society which is so full of temptations for an attractive woman.
MME DE CHALLENS:	I have no regrets. When Monsieur de Challens died, I bid farewell to such conceits. In my grief I found, if not consolation, then some comfort in the task to which I'd dedicated myself: the education of the young daughters of our aristocracy, threatened as they are by the moral standards of today, this dreadful modern spirit. My first pupils were the children of my friends. I'd known them all since they were born. I was godmother to the eldest one.
MME LE GOFF:	All the same, it was an act of self-denial.
MME DE CHALLENS:	A very easy one, I can assure you. (*Pause.*) Would you like to see your granddaughter?
MME LE GOFF:	Yes. You see, yesterday I received a letter from her. A very sad letter.
MME DE CHALLENS:	Sad?
MME LE GOFF:	Yes, she tells me that she is unhappy, that she wants to return home. She's frightened.
MME DE CHALLENS:	Frightened?

MME LE GOFF:	Yes. Well, I was concerned, so I came to check. Lucienne isn't poorly is she?
MME DE CHALLENS:	Not at all. I don't understand the reason for this letter. I'm not aware there's anything wrong with Lucienne. It doesn't make sense, not at all, except perhaps it's impatience for the coming holidays.
MME LE GOFF:	Yes, that's exactly what I thought. I know that since her poor mother has been ill, Lucienne has not been at her most cheerful. The little one takes it all to heart . . .
MME DE CHALLENS:	And how is Mme Le Goff?
MME LE GOFF:	Alas!
MME DE CHALLENS:	Still in the asylum?
MME LE GOFF:	Still there.
MME DE CHALLENS:	What do the doctors say?
MME LE GOFF:	They say they'll have their work cut out to detoxify her, given the state she's in. The poor thing is a slave to morphine. It's a terrible thing, isn't it?
MME DE CHALLENS:	Yes, yes, quite awful. (*Long pause.*) Would you like to see Lucienne now or wait until four o'clock when classes finish?
MME LE GOFF:	I'd prefer not to wait. I have to be in Paris before five and I don't like the chauffeur to drive too fast. I'm old-fashioned like that.
MME DE CHALLENS:	I'll send for Lucienne. (*She telephones.*) Hello? Could you bring Mademoiselle Le Goff across from Mademoiselle Louise's class?
MME LE GOFF:	I hope I'm not disturbing you?
MME DE CHALLENS:	Not at all. Not at all. On the contrary, I'm delighted that you've brought your child's inexplicable depression to my attention. We shall try to get to the bottom of it. Indeed we *must*.
MME LE GOFF:	Are you happy with her?
MME DE CHALLENS:	Yes. Her work is as good as anyone's. Oh, it's not fabulous, but her marks are above average. The only thing worth mentioning is that her character is . . . strong-willed, tenacious. But between you and me, I don't dislike that. I like to see energy and a strong will, even in a child.
MME LE GOFF:	Even so, one must be obedient.
MME DE CHALLENS:	Will you be coming to Prize Day, Madame?
MME LE GOFF:	But of course. Has the date been set?
MME DE CHALLENS:	The 28th. I'm sorry it's taken so long to confirm it and I know it's a nuisance for a lot of families who are going on holiday. It's most regrettable, but I had no option. I do want to put on a magnificent party. So I do hope I'll be forgiven.
MME LE GOFF:	You are already forgiven.
MME DE CHALLENS:	Thank you. Here's Lucienne.
	Mlle Claire ushers in Lucienne.
LUCIENNE	(*crying out*): Grandma!

She is about to rush forward, but Mme de Challens makes an imperceptible gesture which prevents her.

MME LE GOFF: Darling!

MME DE CHALLENS: Well! Give your grandmother a hug, Lucienne!

LUCIENNE: Grandma! Grandma!
She throws herself, almost convulsively, into her grandmother's arms.

MME LE GOFF: My dear, how pale you are! You're not ill, are you?
Long pause.

MME DE CHALLENS: Come now, Lucienne, your grandmother is asking if you're unwell. Answer her.

LUCIENNE (*with great effort*): No, Grandma. I'm well.

MME LE GOFF: You see, I came to make sure. Are you happy?

LUCIENNE: Yes, yes, I'm happy.

MME LE GOFF: Only a few more days and it'll be the holidays. That's good, isn't it?

LUCIENNE: Oh, yes, yes, Grandma!

MME DE CHALLENS: Lucienne, listen to me. Why did you write to your grandmother and tell her you were afraid? Who are you afraid of here? Tell me. Who are you afraid of?

LUCIENNE (*murmuring*): Nobody. (*She hides in her grandmother's arms.*) Grandma, Grandma, take me away . . . take me away!

MME LE GOFF: But why?

LUCIENNE: I beg you, Grandma, take me away.

MME LE GOFF: But whatever is the matter? What a carry-on!

MME DE CHALLENS: What's the matter, Lucienne? Why do you want to leave? Are you not well? Are you unhappy? You must tell me. Are you unhappy?

MME LE GOFF: Lucienne, my darling . . .

MME DE CHALLENS: Don't you like it here any more, Lucienne?

LUCIENNE (*without expression*): Of course I do, Madame.

MME LE GOFF: It's just a phase she's going through.

MME DE CHALLENS: Childishness. (*Enthusiastically.*) Will you be spending the holidays at Mantes?

MME LE GOFF: Goodness me, yes. Why go anywhere else? I know that Lucienne likes to travel, go to the seaside . . . but I'm too old for that kind of thing. I have my little ways, my ways of doing things. Besides, she has nothing to complain about. The estate is immense. The grounds are at least twice the size as here, with beautiful lawns and hundreds of trees. Lucienne can have a whale of a time there.

LUCIENNE: Will Jean-Jean be there?

MME LE GOFF: Of course.

MME DE CHALLENS: Who is . . . Jean-Jean?

MME LE GOFF: He's my gardener's young boy. He's younger than Lucienne and she winds him around her little finger.

LUCIENNE: I like Jean-Jean. He's kind.

MME LE GOFF:	You're not going to make me cross this year, are you? You're not going to get out of your depth in the pond or play going up and down the well shaft in the buckets?
MME DE CHALLENS	(*shocked*): Oh, no, not that! Not that! (*Suddenly much calmer.*) You mustn't go near the well, Lucienne . . . never . . . never. (*Long pause. She looks into the distance.*) This heat is unbearable, don't you find?
MME LE GOFF:	Yes. No doubt we'll have a storm this evening.
MME DE CHALLENS:	Let's hope so. This weather puts everyone on edge.
MME LE GOFF:	As far as I'm concerned, I never go out when there's lightning. And thunder frightens me, so it makes perfect sense. So I'm going to make sure I don't get caught in it! That's all there is to it!
LUCIENNE	(*sobbing*): Oh, no, Grandma. Don't leave me!
MME LE GOFF:	Now look here, my dear. You're not being reasonable. I shan't come back to see you if you're going to martyr yourself. Come on now, calm down. Give me a kiss. Just think that in five days' time, you'll be free. Five days. Less than a week! Quickly now, dry your eyes for me and come and see me off.
MME DE CHALLENS:	That's against the rules, but this once . . . *She rings the bell.*
MME LE GOFF:	Ah, well then, I don't want there to be exceptions to the rules. It has to be the same for everyone. Discipline is discipline. Say goodbye to me here, my dear. You promise me that you're going to be good? You're not going to worry your grandmother?
LUCIENNE:	No . . .
MME LE GOFF:	Until Friday . . .
LUCIENNE:	Yes.
MME LE GOFF:	And don't cry . . . or you'll make me cross.
LUCIENNE:	I'm not crying.
MME LE GOFF:	Goodbye, my darling.
LUCIENNE:	Goodbye, Grandma. *Enter Mlle Claire.*
MME DE CHALLENS:	Would you show Madame out? (*Accompanying Mme Le Goff.*) Children today also have their fits of depression— my best wishes, Madame, and a safe journey home.
MME LE GOFF:	Thank you. Goodbye. Goodbye. *Mme Le Goff and Mlle Claire exit. Mme de Challens watches them leave and then turns to Lucienne who gradually lifts her head.*
MME DE CHALLENS	(*going to the sofa*): Lucienne, come here. (*She sits down.*) Closer. Why did you write to your grandmother? Why did you tell her that you wanted to leave? Why did you cry in front of her?
LUCIENNE:	I . . . I don't know.

MME DE CHALLENS   (*taking hold of Lucienne by the hands*): Listen. I forbid you in the future to imply that you might be unhappy here. I want you to simply obey me at all times. Anything I ask for . . . whenever I ask for it . . . whenever I want it. I command you to do it. I order you to do it. Do you understand?

LUCIENNE   (*with a gasp*): Yes.

MME DE CHALLENS: You'll obey me at all times?

LUCIENNE: Yes, at all times.

MME DE CHALLENS: Give me a kiss. (*She pulls the child to her, then suddenly pushes her away again.*) Go back to your class. Wait. (*She wipes the child's lips with her handkerchief.*) There's some lipstick. Go into the bathroom on your way and bathe your eyes. There's no need to show your friends that you've been crying like a baby. Come this way.
She leaves with Lucienne. A woman appears, young, thin with brown hair, dressed in black. She carries a small suitcase. She stares into space. She puts down her luggage and stands motionless. Enter Mme de Challens.

MME DE CHALLENS   (*in a trembling voice*): Solange!

SOLANGE: Martha!
(*Very slowly, Solange opens her arms. Long embrace.*)

MME DE CHALLENS: Solange, Solange . . . it's you . . .

SOLANGE: Of course . . .

MME DE CHALLENS: How's your health?

SOLANGE: Not too bad. And yours?

MME DE CHALLENS: I'm well, thank you. (*Pause.*) I'm so happy to have you here with me.

SOLANGE: Really?

MME DE CHALLENS: I've missed you so much.

SOLANGE: Me too. I'm so happy to be back here with you.

MME DE CHALLENS: Sit down. It's very muggy, isn't it?

SOLANGE: Yes, I suppose so.

MME DE CHALLENS: Are you tired?

SOLANGE: Yes. The train was slow. I'm so on edge.

MME DE CHALLENS: It's the coming storm.

SOLANGE: Yes, no doubt.

MME DE CHALLENS: If I'd thought about it, I could have sent the car to pick you up from Paris.

SOLANGE: But why?

MME DE CHALLENS: Did you find my servant waiting at the station?

SOLANGE: Yes.

MME DE CHALLENS: Did he take care of your luggage?

SOLANGE: Yes.

MME DE CHALLENS: Did he show you to your room?

SOLANGE: I think so.

MME DE CHALLENS: Then come here. Look, you're a bundle of nerves.

SOLANGE: I'm such a nervous wreck.

MME DE CHALLENS:	Would you like to have a little rest?
SOLANGE:	No, it's no use. I just wouldn't be able to sit still.
MME DE CHALLENS:	Would you like a little green tea?
SOLANGE:	With a little orange blossom, perhaps? What do you take me for? A baby?
	(*Pause.*)
MME DE CHALLENS:	What have you been up to since I last saw you a year ago?
SOLANGE:	I've been giving lessons, here and there.
MME DE CHALLENS:	Why didn't you reply to my letters?
SOLANGE:	Your letters?
MME DE CHALLENS:	Yes.
SOLANGE:	You wrote to me?
MME DE CHALLENS:	Yes, of course.
SOLANGE:	I didn't receive them.
MME DE CHALLENS:	That's impossible.
SOLANGE:	No, Martha, I never had any letters from you.
MME DE CHALLENS:	That's strange.
SOLANGE:	Why?
MME DE CHALLENS:	Letters don't get lost themselves.
SOLANGE:	This proves that they do.
MME DE CHALLENS:	I was hoping you'd come and see me. I've been so unhappy without you.
SOLANGE:	I've been travelling a lot. I had a little free time. I needed to get my life back!
MME DE CHALLENS:	Ah!
SOLANGE:	Does that surprise you? It's quite normal.
MME DE CHALLENS:	Yes.
SOLANGE:	What?
MME DE CHALLENS:	It's odd. I don't know why exactly I've got this idea in my head.
SOLANGE:	What idea?
MME DE CHALLENS:	The idea that you're hiding something from me.
SOLANGE:	Come on, now . . .
MME DE CHALLENS:	Solange, please, come here. (*Solange goes to sit down.*) Listen, you don't have to tell me anything you don't want to, but sometimes when I think of you, I surprise myself.
SOLANGE:	Surprise?
MME DE CHALLENS:	Yes. You told me that you were a poor tutor, scarcely earning your keep, chasing after any kind of work.
SOLANGE:	So?
MME DE CHALLENS:	I don't believe it.
SOLANGE:	However . . .
MME DE CHALLENS:	No, Solange. It seems to me that the way you dress, so simply, so modestly, does a poor job of hiding who you really are. You are not who you say. You're a woman of the same social standing as me. We are of the same world. There are signs that don't lie. You're a fine lady, for sure.
SOLANGE:	Pure fantasy.

MME DE CHALLENS:	Not a bit of it.
SOLANGE:	But it is. Think about it. Look, don't you remember when I came here, how it was we got to know each other.
MME DE CHALLENS:	Yes. Last year I needed a dance teacher. I placed an advert in the newspapers.
SOLANGE:	And the advert caught my eye. So I came here, presented myself and was taken on.
MME DE CHALLENS	(*tenderly*): Solange . . . *She kisses her.*
SOLANGE:	And that's the whole story.
MME DE CHALLENS:	Our whole story. *Awkward pause.*
SOLANGE:	Well then! So where did you get the idea that I'm not who I say I am? What was it that is supposed to have given me away?
MME DE CHALLENS:	I don't know.
SOLANGE:	Let's leave it then. It's stupid. Tell me your news. What have you been up to this winter?
MME DE CHALLENS:	Nothing much. I had some time off. During the Easter holidays I spent a week at Sainte-Maxime. I saw some beautiful places. Including a magnificent opium den. A real nirvana . . .
SOLANGE:	Where was that?
MME DE CHALLENS:	In the house of a Russian exile, a lovely woman, a great artist and poet!
SOLANGE:	Good God, Martha, such enthusiasm!
MME DE CHALLENS:	You would understand if you had seen this magical thing she created. Just imagine that she knew how to renovate this old opium den.
SOLANGE:	Who taught you about the little pill of liberation?
MME DE CHALLENS:	My husband. He spent a long time in China.
SOLANGE:	Did he smoke much?
MME DE CHALLENS:	Enough to die of it at a young age.
SOLANGE:	Do you miss him?
MME DE CHALLENS:	For a long time I've missed his companionship. But as a husband? Never!
SOLANGE:	You can't smoke here.
MME DE CHALLENS:	No, certainly not. Versailles, perhaps? No, I go to Passy, to a friend's house, the Baroness of Bergue.
SOLANGE:	Madeleine!
MME DE CHALLENS:	You know her?
SOLANGE:	Yes, yes. I taught her how to dance the Cotillon.
MME DE CHALLENS:	And you call her Madeleine?
SOLANGE:	Why not? *She paces in agitation.*
MME DE CHALLENS:	Solange . . . what's the matter with you?
SOLANGE:	Oh! I'm so ill! *She opens her bag and produces a small morphine kit.* *She prepares her injection.*

MME DE CHALLENS:	You haven't given up then?
SOLANGE:	It's the only thing that works.
MME DE CHALLENS:	Morphine. I was never really one for that.
SOLANGE:	Why not? Because it's no longer fashionable? Does cocaine seem more modern to you?
MME DE CHALLENS:	No, I'm not a snob like that. It's a question of preference, that's all. (*Solange pierces her skin with the needle.*) Oh, that's enough now! Look . . .
SOLANGE:	I need this much. Otherwise I don't feel a thing. (*She tidies up the kit and sits down.*) Now, let's talk about why I'm here. You're throwing a party?
MME DE CHALLENS:	Yes, like the one that I wanted to give last year when all the trouble happened. *Long pause.*
SOLANGE:	That little one, all the same . . . to go and throw herself down the well.
MME DE CHALLENS:	And why?
SOLANGE:	Yes, why?
MME DE CHALLENS:	I think about it all the time.
SOLANGE	(*staring into space*): I remember . . . she was a pretty brunette. Her eyes shone like they were on fire. That soft voice, so musical, so tender. It was the evening I arrived. We were here, the two of us, like now. She came in. From over there. From over there.
MME DE CHALLENS:	I remember as well.
SOLANGE:	And the next day, she was simply adorable, so full of life. So wonderful. She was no longer the helpless little thing. Why? Why?
MME DE CHALLENS:	It's beyond comprehension. *The two women remain with fixed pained expressions. Very long pause. Solange stands up.*
SOLANGE:	Are there any interesting ones amongst the girls this year?
MME DE CHALLENS:	One in particular. I've never known one with a nature that is so passive, so malleable. She will do whatever I want. I only have to think of something and she'll obey.
SOLANGE:	Really?
MME DE CHALLENS:	The other day I was over there, writing at my desk. As it happened I was writing up some notes that concerned her. I thought of her and in she came!
SOLANGE:	That's not possible.
MME DE CHALLENS:	It is!
SOLANGE:	Just a coincidence, surely.
MME DE CHALLENS:	No doubt. All the same, it's bizarre. I looked at her, stared into her eyes . . . and she fell asleep!
SOLANGE	(*to herself*): What unfathomable mysteries haunt these little souls, these beings, so often carrying such terrible hereditary defects! Amongst this shop of little angels, how many of them are future monsters in waiting!

MME DE CHALLENS: That's right!

SOLANGE: In the meantime, how sweet they are. Such a deep pleasure to feel them near you, to caress them when they are obedient. It's good, isn't it?

MME DE CHALLENS: Yes.

The two women are holding each other's hands.

SOLANGE: And also . . . a young head, delicately balanced on the neck. Martha . . . Martha . . . you're so lucky to have all of that every day!

MME DE CHALLENS (*standing up suddenly with a hint of wickedness*): Perhaps. But sometimes it's a cruel thing too. The happiness of children is bad for those with a troubled heart. I hate them when they are happy. They make me sick. I like it when they cry, because I can console them. I love to see them suffer so that I can make them better with my love and attention. In the old days, there were good fairies who would come to their cradles. Golden-haired good fairies with golden wands and glimmering dresses. I would have liked to have been one of those!

Four o'clock strikes. A bell rings.

SOLANGE (*as if suddenly woken from a dream*): What? What's that bell?

MME DE CHALLENS (*in the same tone*): It's four o'clock—playtime.

Enter Mlle Claire.

MLLE CLAIRE: I've brought the bottle back.

MME DE CHALLENS: Thank you . . . well?

MLLE CLAIRE: The nose bleed has stopped, but the child is still complaining of a headache.

MME DE CHALLENS: Ah! I'll contact the doctor. You can supervise playtime. (*Mlle Claire exits. Mme de Challens replaces the bottle in the cupboard and telephones.*) Hello? Versailles one-nine, please, Mademoiselle.

A noise erupts outdoors.

SOLANGE: What's that noise?

MME DE CHALLENS: Playtime. Hello? Doctor Bernier? This is Madame de Challens. Is the doctor there? Ah, not yet? Could you please ask him to call by the school as soon as possible? Good. Thank you, Mademoiselle. (*Solange is looking outside. Suddenly she lets out a raucous cry.*)

SOLANGE: Martha, Martha! Look! Over there, amongst the trees! The big girl is hitting the little blonde one! (*Angrily.*) Go on, go on, hit her, hit her! You'll see, the little one will start crying. She's struggling. (*Crying out.*) Harder! Harder! Ah! What's that woman doing coming to separate them. (*They are huddled together, one against the other, trembling. A ball lands in the room.*)

CHILDREN'S VOICES: Oh! My ball! . . . It's Lucienne's turn . . . Go and get it . . . I daren't . . . Go on!

MME DE CHALLENS:	She will have to come and get it.
SOLANGE:	She won't come.
MME DE CHALLENS:	She will. If I want her to.

Turning towards the playground, she stares through the window, then slowly steps back. Lucienne appears, walking almost like a robot. Mme de Challens opens her arms towards her. The child continues to walk forwards, whilst the curtain slowly falls.

ACT TWO

The stage is as before. Storm. Lightning. Eleven o'clock strikes. The caretaker enters, wearing a cape that is dripping with rainwater. He puts his lantern on the desk and sits down. Enter Mlle Claire.

MLLE CLAIRE:	Who's there?
CARETAKER:	It's only me, Mademoiselle. Don't be frightened.
MLLE CLAIRE:	What are you doing?
CARETAKER:	I'm waiting for Madame. Where is she?
MLLE CLAIRE:	Madame? I don't know. I'm also looking for her. Well, have you found anything?
CARETAKER:	No.
MLLE CLAIRE:	This is insane. Don't sit there in the darkness. Put the light on.

She exits. The caretaker tries to find the light switch, but gives up. Mme de Challens enters, followed by the Police Superintendent, and switches on the light.

MME DE CHALLENS:	This way, Superintendent, please.
SUPERINTENDENT:	What room is this?
MME DE CHALLENS:	My office.
SUPERINTENDENT:	What does this bay window look out on to?
MME DE CHALLENS:	The playing field, look.
SUPERINTENDENT:	Where do the children play during break time?
MME DE CHALLENS:	Well, right here, in front of us.
SUPERINTENDENT:	So you can see them from here.
MME DE CHALLENS:	Of course. It's the main reason that I have the office here. I like to keep an eye on their antics.
SUPERINTENDENT:	Is there always someone in here?
MME DE CHALLENS:	Not always, no. But more often than not.
SUPERINTENDENT:	Apart from yourself, who also comes in here?
MME DE CHALLENS:	Mlle Claire, the school nurse.
SUPERINTENDENT:	And where is she now?
MME DE CHALLENS:	With the children, I expect.
CARETAKER:	Excuse me . . .
MME DE CHALLENS:	What? Speak up?

CARETAKER:	Mlle Claire has just left. Just a second ago. She was looking for you Madame.
MME DE CHALLENS:	Ah! Which way did she go?
CARETAKER:	That way.
SUPERINTENDENT:	What is this door?
MME DE CHALLENS:	It leads to inside the school. That one goes outside.
SUPERINTENDENT:	So, to go from inside the building to the outside, you always have to go through here?
MME DE CHALLENS:	Not necessarily. There's a corridor along the length of the building with an exit out into the garden.
SUPERINTENDENT:	Would you please show me the way, Madame. I can then speak to the school nurse at the same time.
MME DE CHALLENS:	Very good. If you would care to follow me . . . Jean, stay here. If anyone comes, deal with them. This way, Superintendent.
SUPERINTENDENT:	I'll follow you, Madame.
	They exit stage right. Alone, the caretaker goes to the desk for his lantern, rests a hand on the table and cries out.
CARETAKER:	Ah! I've stabbed myself! (*He looks at his hand and extracts something.*) What is that? A sharp pen nib . . . (*He throws it away and sucks his hand.*)
VOICE:	Is there anybody there?
CARETAKER:	Yes. Who is it?
	He goes to the door. The doctor enters.
DOCTOR:	Doctor Bernier.
CARETAKER:	Ah, excuse me, doctor. Good evening, doctor.
DOCTOR:	Good evening, Jean. Somebody called me this afternoon. I was away and have only just got back. Who is ill?
CARETAKER:	But . . . I don't know. I mean . . . I'll go and find Madame.
DOCTOR:	There's no point in waking up Mme de Challens.
CARETAKER:	Oh, but Madame isn't asleep. She's over there with Monsieur Levron.
DOCTOR:	Monsieur Levron?
CARETAKER:	Yes.
DOCTOR:	Not the police superintendent?
CARETAKER:	The very same.
DOCTOR:	Levron is here? But why?
CARETAKER:	Because of the disappearance.
DOCTOR:	What disappearance?
CARETAKER:	The disappearance of a pupil. The whole place is turned upside down.
DOCTOR:	Tell me all about it. Quickly.
CARETAKER:	Yes, Doctor, of course. Well, this afternoon during playtime at four o'clock, the girl was playing there in the playground with her friends. It seems that she went off for a moment to look for the ball that she had lost. And that was the last anyone saw of her.
DOCTOR:	No . . .

CARETAKER: Yes . . . nobody knows what has become of her.

DOCTOR: Now, look here—you say that at four o'clock she was playing with her friends?

CARETAKER: Yes.

DOCTOR: And at what point did anyone notice that she had disappeared?

CARETAKER: About five o'clock or thereabouts. That was the time when they came to ask me whether I'd seen her go out.

DOCTOR: And you didn't see anything?

CARETAKER: No and I didn't leave my post. And I'm certain that nobody walked by the door. It's possible that she could have escaped whilst I was paying the milkman, but it would have to be timed just right and it would need a stroke of luck.

DOCTOR: Yes, obviously. And they've searched around here?

CARETAKER: I think so. They've scoured the whole place. I went to the playground, the vegetable garden, the outbuildings, while Madame and the teachers searched the house. Ah, it's most bizarre.

DOCTOR: Yes, indeed.

CARETAKER: If you want my opinion, then the child has escaped. It's just that . . . how was she able to get away?

DOCTOR: What makes you think she's run away?

CARETAKER: Sir, it's just an idea that I have . . . because this very afternoon, the girl's grandmother came to see her and Lucienne wanted to go home with her. She told her so. She didn't want to stay here any longer. That's all. There's nothing odd about that.

DOCTOR: No . . . except that this is the second time such a thing has happened . . . and at the same time of year!

CARETAKER: Yes. Except last year it was suicide.

DOCTOR: Of course, of course. (*He walks around pensively.*) Strange . . . very strange. (*To the caretaker.*) Tell me, your mistress must be very worried?

CARETAKER: You would think so, Monsieur . . . and Mademoiselle Solange as well!

DOCTOR   (*with surprise*): What? That Solange woman is here?!

CARETAKER: Yes, Monsieur. Since this afternoon.

DOCTOR: Ah! Oh! Well . . . well . . . (*He appears anxious and upset.*) Look . . . go and tell Monsieur Levron that I'm here and that I want to speak to him straightaway.

CARETAKER: Very good, Monsieur.

DOCTOR: But listen. Be discreet about it. I mean without Mme de Challens knowing anything about it. Do you understand?

CARETAKER: Perfectly, Monsieur.

DOCTOR: Off you go, quickly, my friend. (*The caretaker exits. The doctor paces up and down, murmuring, 'Strange . . . a strange coincidence'. Arriving at the desk, he puts his hands down and pulls them away, crying out.*) Oh, Ouch!

(He looks at the palm of his hands and removes something which he examines anxiously.) Ah! I see! *(He looks at the desk.)* Oh! Oh! *(He takes his handkerchief, rubs a spot on the desk, looks at his handkerchief and exclaims.)* Oh! . . .
The voice of a woman singing in a strange melancholic tune can be heard. She stops as she arrives behind the door. The doctor turns out the light and hides. Solange appears. She moves like a robot, her eyes staring into the distance. She holds her arms out in front of her and crosses the stage.

DOCTOR:	No, no. It's not possible. Ah, the poor thing!
SUPERINTENDENT	*(outside)*: Is the doctor in here?
DOCTOR:	Yes, I'm waiting for you.
SUPERINTENDENT:	Ah, good evening, my dear chap, what fair wind brings you here to us?
DOCTOR:	It's more of an ill wind, I think. Good evening, Levron. *(They shake hands.)*
SUPERINTENDENT:	Have you come to see a patient?
DOCTOR:	Yes, and then I found out that you were here . . .
SUPERINTENDENT:	Well, a good job too. We might have need of you yet . . .
DOCTOR:	If only you knew how right you are. And yet I was the one who sent for you.
SUPERINTENDENT:	Quickly then. I must tell you first that I haven't a moment to waste.
DOCTOR:	Me neither. I haven't eaten yet and I've been out and about since eight o'clock this morning. If I remain here, it's for your sake. Sit down and listen very carefully.
SUPERINTENDENT:	That's a line straight out of a tragedy.
DOCTOR:	That's what we have here.
SUPERINTENDENT:	What?
DOCTOR:	I'll sum up the situation. A child has disappeared, pandemonium in the house, various theories, a runaway, an accident, a kidnapping, suicide, a crime. What do you think?
SUPERINTENDENT:	Good God, Doctor, you must be joking! A five-minute search, a glance here, a glance there and you think that I can solve it just like that? My dear chap, if only I'd had you here . . .
DOCTOR:	But that's it . . . I was here!
SUPERINTENDENT:	What are you trying to say?
DOCTOR:	I mean that I arrived well after you and I certainly know more about it.
SUPERINTENDENT:	About what?
DOCTOR:	About what has been going on here!
SUPERINTENDENT:	Bravo! Go to the top of the class!
DOCTOR:	Not at all. Tell me now, Superintendent, you know this place well? The children, the staff, the headmistress?
SUPERINTENDENT:	Well, yes, that's true.
DOCTOR:	Do you know Mademoiselle Solange as well?

SUPERINTENDENT:	The young woman who gives the dancing lessons?
DOCTOR:	That's the one, yes.
SUPERINTENDENT:	Well then! You want a description or what? That's easy: plain, distinguished, supple, big dark eyes, naturally curved eyebrows, hair worn up.
DOCTOR:	The *femme fatale*, in other words . . .
SUPERINTENDENT:	You must be joking! Surely you don't believe in *femmes fatales*? You know, in my book, outside the movies . . .
DOCTOR:	So, you don't believe in them?
SUPERINTENDENT:	Not at all, Doctor!
DOCTOR:	Then you're wrong, Superintendent!
SUPERINTENDENT:	Why?
DOCTOR:	Because . . . because you approach things in the exact opposite way, for the most part, to your police colleagues.
SUPERINTENDENT:	Well, what are all my police colleagues doing then?
DOCTOR:	Well! When there is a very trivial and insignificant matter, they always dream up the most tragic scenarios. Yourself, on the other hand, faced with a situation that I consider to be particularly serious, I see you perfectly relaxed and at ease.
SUPERINTENDENT:	So, what's the matter with my being relaxed then?
DOCTOR:	In my opinion, it's not appropriate to the situation.
SUPERINTENDENT	(*he smiles*): Excuse me, old boy, but you are funny!
DOCTOR:	Do you think I'm joking?
SUPERINTENDENT:	Of course!
DOCTOR:	It doesn't matter, then!
SUPERINTENDENT:	Perhaps you don't realize, but the way you exaggerate is rather amusing! Honestly, it is! I can assure you that it's fortunate that, contrary to your professional instincts which you have made all too clear to me, I won't follow you into this dark place you'd like to take me, because if I let you do that then we'd inevitably end up coming to this terrible conclusion that the missing child had not left the house.
DOCTOR:	Then you wouldn't be very far from the truth!
SUPERINTENDENT:	My dear friend, be careful. You may be able to say that to me here without any witnesses present. That's one thing. But you should realize that repeating it could have serious consequences, old boy.
DOCTOR:	Of course, of course.
SUPERINTENDENT:	Just think about it, for goodness sake. If you spread it around that Madame de Challens and Mlle Solange . . . have murdered their pupil . . .
DOCTOR:	Exactly.
SUPERINTENDENT:	My dear chap!
DOCTOR:	My dear friend, doesn't this make you think of the child who was found dead at the bottom of the well last year? Doesn't it strike you that this strange disappearance of another child has happened today, on the same date, in

	the same circumstances, added to which there's the most troubling thing—the presence of this Solange woman? What is she doing here? Eh?
SUPERINTENDENT:	Well . . . she's here for the fête . . . the prize-giving . . . the ball . . . it's well-known.
DOCTOR:	That's just a façade . . . a pretext . . .
SUPERINTENDENT:	What?
DOCTOR:	Listen. When I was at the asylum for the mentally deranged . . .
SUPERINTENDENT:	As an inmate?
DOCTOR:	I knew an inmate who was strangely similar to this Solange woman. Well, I thought I saw this patient again here just now, in the features of this Solange woman. OK, so let's assume that it's her. Shall I go on?
SUPERINTENDENT:	Don't put yourself out!
DOCTOR:	This woman is an unhinged, erotically obsessive morphine addict with a predisposition for sexual perversion.
SUPERINTENDENT:	Well that's a very fancy label! And how do you work that one out?
DOCTOR:	It's a little too difficult to explain. You should read the work of Dumas, who's a psychologist. He would explain it much better than I could.
SUPERINTENDENT:	Is there anything else?
DOCTOR:	Well, heredity, syphilis, ether, opium, eau de cologne, cocaine and so on. Everyone has their own favourite poison, don't they? Cigarette?
SUPERINTENDENT:	Thank you.
DOCTOR:	According to the theory, anything can excite the nervous system. Gradually the senses are dulled and softened and greater stimulation is needed. In the end things start to break up and become unhinged. Love, even acute stimulation, isn't enough. You see these women leaving their husbands and their children to go with another woman, and in their madness animals are introduced into the bedroom, but most commonly it's children.
SUPERINTENDENT:	Ah, the professional's ability to distort things! So, it's not only at the police station where such things are rampant, eh? That's specialists for you. Everywhere they look they see degenerates, lunatics, sexual inverts . . .
DOCTOR:	No, no . . . perverts . . .
SUPERINTENDENT:	Perverts, inverts, it's all the same.
DOCTOR:	Not at all. There's no similarity.
SUPERINTENDENT:	Really?
DOCTOR:	Absolutely: As degrading as it may be, sexual inversion is still a form of love, since it's limited to a psychological act between two subjects of the same sex. Whereas sexual perversion demands the most terrible acts: flagellation, bloodletting and even murder as a way of achieving the

ultimate pleasure. Children, old people . . . anything is legitimate to satisfy the desire.

SUPERINTENDENT: And Mademoiselle Solange is one of these?

DOCTOR: Yes. And that's before we even get started on our headmistress.

SUPERINTENDENT: Her too?

DOCTOR: The same diagnosis.

SUPERINTENDENT: No, no. On that point we can't agree. According to you these two women are supposed to come together every year to commit a crime.

DOCTOR: Come now! You can see it. You might not want to see it, but you can see it! Yes, my dear chap, what we have here is a cyclical and periodic case of madness. It's a rare thing, but it exists. The proof . . .

SUPERINTENDENT: The proof . . . The proof . . . We have to find the proof.

DOCTOR: That, old boy, is your job. I've done mine. Now it's over to you.

SUPERINTENDENT: You're playing a dangerous game. Accusing people of murder . . .

DOCTOR: Let me summarize. Mademoiselle Solange, former inmate of a mental asylum . . . I treated her previously . . .

SUPERINTENDENT: Don't boast about it . . .

DOCTOR: I wasn't the one who discharged her . . . who let her re-enter the world under the name Elsa de Rienza. That's not an assumed name. It's her real one!

SUPERINTENDENT: We're amongst aristocracy then!

DOCTOR: That may be a mitigating factor.

SUPERINTENDENT: So, in your opinion, Mademoiselle de Rienza and Madame de Challens are insane.

DOCTOR: Yes. This criminal insanity is fuelled by the grooming of certain favoured boarders, the worthy offspring of a rotten generation. Who knows the secrets of the dormitory, the passions of our young ones, the shared smiles, the wandering hands . . .

SUPERINTENDENT: Ah yes, the life of the convent!

DOCTOR: The promiscuous life! The communal life, the life of the dormitory and of confinement. Everything that will contaminate our children, bleed them dry, just as they are flourishing. It's the way of foreign drug-pushers who deal in certain establishments that you ought to be keeping a closer eye on, the way of the young parasites who hang around the street selling drugs, the way of the sex maniacs of all ages and backgrounds, who, from the bottom of the pile to the top of the social ladder, spread their pathological vices . . .

SUPERINTENDENT: Ah! So that's it . . .

DOCTOR: . . . and infect all those around them. It's the way of our own sexual fantasies when we were young. That can suddenly erupt later on due to a blow from an officer's baton or an expert mistress or the submission of a superior will.

SUPERINTENDENT: Nice speech!

DOCTOR: And given all this and knowing what I know, I tell you, do you hear, that I would stand up in court and swear that this is what has happened in this house. A wretched woman, a dangerous lunatic, because no one suspected her, slipped in, drawn by the love of young flesh. She has given in to her desperate tendencies and become unbalanced and it's the coming together of these two nightmarish things that holds the mystery of the double disappearance of these girls. There you have it!

SUPERINTENDENT (*ironically*): And when will the trial be, your honour?

DOCTOR (*seriously*): No, my dear sir, when will the padded cell be ready?

Pause.

SUPERINTENDENT: It worries me terribly, old boy, your story and your theories . . . as if things weren't troubling enough.

DOCTOR: I don't deny it.

SUPERINTENDENT: But all the same, it's a theory that I could find believable, except there are certain facts that just don't add up.

DOCTOR: Such as?

SUPERINTENDENT: Well, for example . . . look, let's accept that there has been a crime. This crime could only have been committed after four o'clock this afternoon. Those are the facts.

DOCTOR: Agreed.

SUPERINTENDENT: It's now half past eleven. Less than eight hours have elapsed. How do you explain Madame de Challens' calmness, her clear-headedness, the lack of emotion when she showed me in? She has been organizing the search party herself and hasn't left a stone unturned, I can assure you. This woman is not the born criminal that you say she is. And if she is mad, then nothing in her appearance or her behaviour would confirm it. There's not even a suspicion that she is suffering some mental disorder.

DOCTOR: Of course . . . the crisis has passed.

SUPERINTENDENT: What?

DOCTOR: At this moment, Madame de Challens remembers nothing . . . and to all appearances, at least to the lay person, she is as sane and well behaved as you or me . . .

SUPERINTENDENT: But even so . . .

DOCTOR: Now, listen . . . if you want to have a scientific discussion about madness, its many forms and manifestations, we'll be here all week. But we both have other things to do. For the time being I think I've explained things enough to you. It's now for you to use it as you see fit.

SUPERINTENDENT: Thank you. I shall continue with my enquiries. Will you come with me?

DOCTOR: If you like.

Mlle Claire enters.

MLLE CLAIRE:	Ah, gentlemen. The headmistress would like to speak to you.
SUPERINTENDENT:	Whenever she likes. This is her house. (*Mlle Claire is about to leave.*) Mademoiselle? (*Mlle Claire comes back.*) One moment, please. Do you know the exact time when Mademoiselle Solange arrived this afternoon?
MLLE CLAIRE:	The exact time? No, sir. I couldn't tell you. But if I were to say between half past three and quarter to four, I wouldn't be far off.
SUPERINTENDENT:	Did you see her at that time?
MLLE CLAIRE:	No, sir.
SUPERINTENDENT:	When did you see her first of all?
MLLE CLAIRE:	It was five o'clock. I'm absolutely certain of that. The clock struck and it was shortly afterwards that the alarm was raised concerning Lucienne Le Goff's absence, when she didn't return to class.
SUPERINTENDENT:	Where was Mademoiselle Solange whey you saw her?
MLLE CLAIRE:	Over there, in the corridor. She was going back to her room on the first floor.
SUPERINTENDENT:	Did you speak to her?
MLLE CLAIRE:	I said hello to her, but she didn't reply.
SUPERINTENDENT:	That's not very polite.
MLLE CLAIRE:	That's exactly what I thought.
SUPERINTENDENT:	Did anything strike you about her manner, her behaviour, the way she looked?
MLLE CLAIRE:	It certainly did!
SUPERINTENDENT:	What?
MLLE CLAIRE:	I thought she was . . . drunk! (*Enter Mme de Challens.*)
MME DE CHALLENS:	Ah, Mademoiselle Claire! Ah, good evening, doctor.
DOCTOR:	Good evening, Madame.
MME DE CHALLENS:	Well can you believe it, what a terrible thing! I don't know what to think!
SUPERINTENDENT:	Well, Madame . . . we need to try and see things clearly.
MME DE CHALLENS:	Oh yes. And I'm counting on you, believe me, Monsieur Levron. This is a terrible thing that's happened.
SUPERINTENDENT:	Assuming that the child has run away . . . In your opinion, is this a possibility?
MME DE CHALLENS:	No, Superintendent, not at all. I've told you already and I stand by that. It is actually impossible for a child of that age to escape. Our grounds are enclosed by a three-metre-high wall. Moreover, we are surrounded by other occupied properties that are also fenced off. The only way out onto Queen Street is by a gate. What's more, to pass through the gate, which is always locked anyway and only the caretaker can open it, you have to pass by his lodge.
SUPERINTENDENT:	So?
MME DE CHALLENS:	So . . . it's almost certain that the child can't have left the house.

DOCTOR:	I'm persuaded by that.
MME DE CHALLENS:	Unless there's something else that we haven't thought of.
SUPERINTENDENT:	Such as?
MME DE CHALLENS:	A ladder, a rope, maybe, that could be used to get into a neighbouring property. It's an absurd idea.
DOCTOR:	Ridiculous
SUPERINTENDENT:	Good God! Excuse me, Madame. At the end of the day, we must consider the evidence. Since six o'clock this evening we've gone through this place from top to bottom. We've been everywhere! The apartments, the classrooms, the dormitories, the cellars, the attics . . .
DOCTOR:	The well?
SUPERINTENDENT:	That too. I tell you, the child is either at home or she's on the way there. One way or another I'm going to find out. Paris has been informed and all the places in between. (*The telephone rings.*) Ah, there we are! That will be for me. If you'll allow me, Madame.
MME DE CHALLENS:	By my guest.
SUPERINTENDENT	(*on the phone*): Hello? Yes, it's me. Ah, it's you, Morin? Well?
MME DE CHALLENS:	(*anxiously*): Have they found her?
SUPERINTENDENT:	No sign? And the railway stations? And the bus from Versailles to the Louvre? Not there either? Her family? Nothing. I see. Carry on, Morin. Keep in touch with your colleagues in Paris and the suburbs. No, no. Telephone me as soon as you know anything. I'm not shifting from here. (*He hangs up.*) This is very worrying. (*Solange enters.*)
SOLANGE:	So . . . this child . . . is there any news?
MME DE CHALLENS:	I'm afraid not. It's all too much!
SOLANGE:	We have to keep on looking. She can't have disappeared just like that. *The doorbell rings.*
MME DE CHALLENS:	A visitor. Mademoiselle Claire, go and see. *Mme Clare exits.*
SOLANGE:	Perhaps there's some news . . .
MME DE CHALLENS:	I do hope so. I can't bear this agony. *They wait, in the grip of intense anxiety. Mlle Claire enters, running, out of breath.*
MLLE CLAIRE:	Madame, Madame . . . it's the young girl's grandmother . . . she's been taken ill in the lodge . . .
SUPERINTENDENT:	Doctor . . .
DOCTOR:	I'll go. Have you any ether or smelling salts?
MME DE CHALLENS:	Yes, in here. *She goes to the cupboard and opens it. A body falls out onto the floor. It is Lucienne. General horror. Mme de Challens screams and faints. Solange, gripped by a sudden attack of madness, rushes towards the corpse, which the Superintendent has carried over to the sofa.*

SUPERINTENDENT	(*calling out*): Bouvard, Garin, take this woman away and keep a close eye on her. Leave us alone. *The policemen, helped by Mlle Claire, lead away Solange and Mme de Challens.*
DOCTOR:	Well, my friend?
SUPERINTENDENT:	You were right. How did she die?
DOCTOR:	Strangled . . . in a frenzy of sadistic passion.
SUPERINTENDENT:	But she's covered in blood.
DOCTOR:	Fetishism. These women weren't doing things by halves. I understand it all. The table is covered in broken pen-nibs. You see, I was right. It's not prison that these wretched women need. It's a padded cell.
SUPERINTENDENT	(*as he is leaving with a bottle of ether that he has taken from the cupboard*): So, what's the difference?

THE END

The Eyes of the Phantom

(*Les Yeux du Spectre*, 1924)

by

JEAN ARAGNY

Drama in Two Acts

Preface

Jean Aragny was the pseudonym of the Budapest-born Eugène Aranyi, and between 1926 and 1936 he was a regular, rather than prolific contributor to the repertoire of the rue Chaptal. Over that time he produced on average a new play every two years, both single and co-authored, the most successful of which was *Le Baiser de Sang* (*The Kiss of Blood*) in 1929 with Francis Neilson (reprised in 1937) and the last of which, *La Machine à tuer la vie* (*The Machine that Kills Life*), premiered in the same month of his death.

Les Yeux du Spectre, however, predates his writings for the rue Chaptal and was first staged at one of the Théâtre du Grand-Guignol's rivals, the Théâtre des Deux Masques in the neighbouring St Georges area of the city on 3 November 1924 (ironically, the theatre closed down the following month). Nevertheless, it is a Grand-Guignol play to its very core and is an excellent example of the genre. In fact, one might suspect, given the number of Grand-Guignol signature tropes that Aragny fits into this short play, that it almost served as his calling card, demonstrating to the management at rue Chaptal his abilities as a playwright of the short horror drama. The play was also dedicated to Tristran (Pierre) Bernard, a lawyer and writer predominantly of comedies and vaudevilles, but most importantly a senior key member of the cultural establishment and acquaintance of Toulouse-Lautrec. Significantly, Bernard contributed two plays to the Théâtre du Grand-Guignol, *Octave, ou les Projets d'un Mari* (*Octave, or the Plans of a Husband*), a comedy from 1899, and *Les Amours d'un fauteuil roulant* (*The Love Affairs of a Wheelchair*), a melodrama from the following year. Aragny was possibly using the dedication to signal his own importance by association. It certainly paid off, as in little over a year later he was writing his first play for the rue Chaptal, *Le Spectre sanglant* (*The Bloody Phantom*), which premiered in 1926.

The action of *Eyes of the Phantom* takes place in an asylum, a hierarchical (and therefore disruptable) society, where the rational and irrational meet in their most extreme forms, and, understandably, a common setting for Grand-Guignol horror plays. In this, Aragny seems to be referencing at least one of André de Lorde's successful Grand-Guignol classics, *Le système du docteur Goudron et du professeur Plume*, where the (in)sanity of the medical staff and the patients is called into question. There are also striking similarities with *Un crime dans un maison de fous* (*A Crime in the Madhouse*) with its group of female inmates and an obsession with eyes. However, it is uncertain whether this is simple coincidence, as although de Lorde's play had premiered in London under the title *The Old Women* in 1921, as part of the London's Grand Guignol's fourth series of plays, it did not premiere in Paris at the rue Chaptal until June 1925. Nevertheless, Aragny seems to be flattering de Lorde with his imitation and use of tropes, from the sadistic nurse to the outwardly kindly senior doctor, as well as adopting the Gothic tropes (as Grand-Guignol often did) of the stormy weather and chiming night-time clock.

The character of the journalist, Jean Bardot, is also interesting in this respect. He is another stock character, that of the curious, but objective cynic, the inquisitive amateur with limited knowledge, to whom everything needs to be explained by the man of science. This allows Aragny to adopt another technique popular with de Lorde and other Grand-Guignol writers, namely that of incorporating contemporary science, especially understandings of psychology and psychiatry into their plays to give them authority and authenticity. Aragny uses the dialogue between Bardot and Tardier as a way of explaining a range of different manifestations of delusional mental illness.

One interesting aspect of Aragny's work, which is unusual in the Grand-Guignol, but clearly manifested here in *Eyes of the Phantom* and also in his later collaboration, *The Kiss of Blood*, is the relationship with the supernatural. As we have argued elsewhere, the Grand-Guignol rarely dealt with the supernatural, but preferred to root its horror much more in the everyday here and now. In tbis way the genre owes more to its roots in Zola-esque naturalism than it does to the Gothic tradition. Aragny, arguably, also does not pander to the supernatural, but he does make use of people's belief in, or fear of, the supernatural. There are supposed phantoms in both of these plays, whereas the solution to the mystery is finally exposed to be more mundane.

Whether or not Aragny's intention was to flatter through imitation and thereby tout for further commissions as a writer of Grand-Guignol (a strategy that seemed to work), he has composed here an almost perfectly constructed Grand-Guignol horror, resplendent with recognizable tropes, its growing tension as it journeys from naturalism to melodrama and its inevitable clash between the rational and irrational, the wild and the controlled, and order and chaos. It is perhaps surprising that it was never adopted and revived by the rue Chaptal itself.

THE EYES OF THE PHANTOM

(*Les Yeux du Spectre*, 1924)

by

JEAN ARAGNY

DRAMA IN TWO ACTS

First performed at the Théâtre des Deux Masques, Paris,
November 1924
This text follows that published as *Les Yeux du Spectre*
by Librarie Théâtrale, Paris, in 1926.
Translated by Richard J. Hand and Michael Wilson

'To my dear and good friend Tristran Bernard, whom I admire and love.'
Jean Aragny

Cast
Professor Tardier
Dr Codier
Jean Bardot, journalist
Beaujard, nurse
Denise, patient
Henriette, patient
Odette, patient
Louise, patient
Madame Marthe, nurse

ACT ONE

A ward in a lunatic asylum. Ward No. 8, Women's Section. Four beds are in a row. From Stage Right, the beds are arranged thus: Louise's bed; Henriette's bed, Odette's bed; Denise's bed. The windows have white curtains. There is a clock on the wall and there is a small table and two chairs.

As the curtain rises Dr Codier is skimming through the newspapers. At one point, as he is reading, he shakes his head with annoyance. A few seconds later Beaujard enters, dressed in his nurse's uniform. He carries some cards on a tray.

CODIER: Ah! Beaujard! Are the patients from this ward still out in the garden?

BEAUJARD: Yes, Doctor.

CODIER: Don't forget that the rounds have been organized for six o' clock. You know how Professor Tardier likes punctuality.

BEAUJARD: (*looking at his watch*): It's only half past five. The professor is doing his rounds at the moment—in Ward No. 7 with the new doctor, Doctor Rollin.

CODIER: Is Doctor Rollin now in charge of the second women's section?

BEAUJARD: Yes, Doctor. He's responsible for Wards 5, 6 and 7.

CODIER: It's about time that I was given an assistant. I can't cope any more . . . I'm overworked. (*Pause.*) I understand that Doctor Rollin comes from the asylum at Pau?

BEAUJARD: Yes, Doctor . . . but I heard a rumour that he was only there a few weeks. (*Confidentially*) It seems that something happened down there. He had no choice but to leave.

CODIER: Really? I didn't know anything about that!

BEAUJARD: Although the young doctor hasn't been here very long . . . the patients don't like him at all. He can barely tolerate the sick, you see. Sometimes he's even quite curt with the patients. Professor Tardier, who takes such matters very seriously, has already had words with him about it on more than one occasion.

CODIER: Patience is the most important quality in a psychiatrist. Unfortunately, complete patience with lunatics is only acquired over time. (*Pointing to the tray that Beaujard is holding*) What is that?

BEAUJARD (*handing over the business cards*): These gentlemen have come to see the professor . . . journalists.

CODIER: Again!

BEAUJARD: I told them that Professor Tardier was not available and they went away far from happy.
(*Codier makes a dismissive gesture.*)

CODIER: Well, Beaujard, these journalists have been turning up for the past two days . . .

BEAUJARD: Some of them will go to any lengths to try and get me to talk.

CODIER (*anxiously*): What have you said?

BEAUJARD: Nothing, rest assured, Doctor . . . not a word.

CODIER: You did well, Beaujard. Professor Tardier insists on absolute discretion in this business . . . not that we know anything about it . . . Just think, Beaujard, *The French Echo* this morning published a piece entitled 'Ghosts in the Asylum'. *The Morning Star* wrote, 'We find ourselves in the middle of a serious situation that requires thorough investigation and heads must roll. Undisciplined staff are terrorizing patients at night by dressing in white sheets.'

BEAUJARD: That's untrue. I know my colleagues.

CODIER: Even so, Professor Tardier is worried . . .

BEAUJARD: Well, he doesn't like publicity, does he? But they do say there's no such thing as bad publicity.

CODIER: I'm not so sure . . . his reputation as a psychiatrist, as an expert, is global. His dedication and professional sense of duty is beyond all doubt.

BEAUJARD: For sure there's no one who is kinder and gentler to the patients, or indeed anybody else, than he is. I beg your pardon, Doctor, but bearing in mind the situation, I would like to know if Dr Rollin is equally kind to the patients?

CODIER: I . . .

BEAUJARD: You will not be unaware that for the past few days, around midnight, a phantom has roamed through the wards.

CORDIER: What? A ghost!

BEAUJARD: I've seen it with my own eyes, Doctor! As soon as I started to approach it, it disappeared, silently . . . mysteriously.

CODIER: Or with great agility . . . Truth be told, Beaujard, I don't know any more about it than you do yourself. Up until this morning, I didn't believe in it . . . I suppose I just thought it was a conspiracy by the patients. Don't forget just how cunning they can be or the susceptibility of their imaginations. But since you swear that you've seen it yourself, I'm beginning to take it more seriously.

BEAUJARD: Nobody hears the sound of footsteps. They say that his feet don't touch the floor.

CODIER: Or perhaps he goes barefoot.

BEAUJARD: He walks through several wards that are all double-locked.

CODIER: He may have got hold of the keys.

BEAUJARD: At least he doesn't pass through the windows.

CODIER: They have bars on them, you see, Beaujard! (*Voices are heard off-stage.*) Go and see what that is. (*Beaujard exits and returns immediately.*)

BEAUJARD (*entering with a business card*): This gentleman insists on seeing Professor Tardier.

CODIER (*reading the card*): 'Jean Bardot, editor of *Today*'. (*To Beaujard*) You know our orders . . .

BEAUJARD: He's not interested in them and he won't leave. He said that *Today* is the most important newspaper of all.

CODIER: It's intolerable! I can't drop everything just like that. Professor Tardier will be along to do his rounds any minute now. (*Pause.*) Very well! Ask the gentleman to come in. (*Beaujard exits. Bardot enters.*)

BARDOT: Sir . . . I would like to see Professor Tardier.

CODIER: The professor is very busy, Monsieur, he's doing his rounds. I am the senior doctor in this establishment and if I can . . .

BARDOT (*dry*): Thank you, but I have come from Paris expressly to see Professor Tardier and I refuse to leave until I have done so.

CODIER: I am sorry. Orders are orders.

BARDOT (*as before*): Would you be so kind, Doctor, to pass on my card to Professor Tardier and ask him to give me five minutes of his time? If he does not grant my request to speak with him, you may tell him that tomorrow, on the front page of my newspaper, the following headlines will appear: 'Culpable Negligence of the Medical Profession', 'Professor Tardier Hides Away', 'An Enquiry is Needed'.

CODIER: I shall pass on your exact words to the professor myself.

BARDOT (*to Codier who is about to leave*): Thank you, Doctor.
(*Codier leaves. Bardot paces up and down. Professor Tardier enters, followed by Codier. He is a man in his fifties, distinguished, a little pale.*)

TARDIER: What's all this about, Monsieur?

BARDOT: It seems to me, Professor, that it would be advantageous and useful to you, for the good reputation of your establishment, to respond yourself to the unpleasant rumours that have become widespread.

TARDIER: I'm not worried about the reputation of my establishment.

BARDOT: Nevertheless, night after night a ghostly white apparition has come to disturb the peace of your patients.

TARDIER: You know as well as I do that there are no such things as ghosts.

BARDOT: Of course . . . but a practical joker could . . .

TARDIER: Nobody except the doctors and the nurses go near the patients and they are recruited to the highest standards.

BARDOT: Nevertheless, not long ago, a patient, an elderly woman, was found dead in her bed. She'd been strangled.

TARDIER: Indeed, a patient died here in mysterious circumstances that I was unable to explain, despite a thorough investigation, despite following extensive lines of enquiry, despite several hypotheses that I constructed.

BARDOT: And this ghost?

TARDIER: Absolutely no connection between this imaginary phantom and the unfortunate woman who died, alas! That's all there is to it.

BARDOT: But what about this white apparition?

TARDIER: Perhaps it only exists in the imagination.

BARDOT: However, Professor, many inmates have seen . . .

TARDIER: It may be that they experienced the same hallucination. We call this psychological phenomenon 'Collective Conviction'.

BARDOT: But a nurse saw it as well.

TARDIER: Perfectly sane people can also be victims. Even more so with those who are unwell with an over-excited imagination that processes information with an incredible facility and power. There are numerous examples. And legends can be created in this way. In pathological matters, just as in legal matters, nothing is impossible, all hypotheses are acceptable and it is necessary to consider them all . . .

BARDOT: And you really believe that . . .

TARDIER: Sometimes one sees anomalies, monstrosities of the imagination or ambiguities that challenge our preconceptions . . . and completely amaze us. Besides I'm going to question, in your presence, the nurse who saw this mysterious nocturnal visitor . . . and then you'll know as much about as I do. (*He rings the bell.*)

BARDOT: Thank you, Professor.

TARDIER: Here he is! (*Beaujard enters.*)

BEAUJARD: Professor . . .

TARDIER: Beaujard, this morning you told me that last night you believed you saw . . . Well, why don't you repeat your story for this gentleman? Don't leave a single detail out.

BEAUJARD   (*quietly*): Well . . . I was making my second tour of the women's section, as usual, as midnight was chiming. I got here and I saw in the moonlight shining next to Madame Denise's bed—she's already a very anxious patient—a white shape. I stood rooted to the spot, as it seemed so strange and mysterious. A minute later it vanished . . . not the slightest sound . . . nothing. I ran to the door at the back, the only possible way out . . . absolutely nothing . . . just silence and darkness. (*Pause.*) Professor . . . the patients don't scare me . . . for ten years I've regularly done my rounds through the wards, all alone. Death doesn't frighten me any more. I've risked my neck on more than one occasion . . . but last night my legs were trembling, my throat was dry. That white apparition was such a mysterious thing, almost transparent . . . in the moonlight . . . like a phantom . . . I don't know any more . . . I was frightened . . . an irrational and senseless fear, and I was shaking like a child who has been told a ghost story.

TARDIER: You have a vivid imagination, Beaujard.

BEAUJARD: It all happened so quickly that I believed that I must have been the victim of . . . an . . .

CODIER: Of an hallucination.

BEAUJARD: Yes, Doctor . . . but the cries and fear of Madame Denise convinced me of what I had seen.

TARDIER: Thank you, Beaujard.

BEAUJARD   (*taking his leave*): Monsieur, Professor . . . (*He goes to leave.*)

TARDIER   (*seemingly deep in thought for a few seconds*): One second. Beaujard. (*Pause.*) You said . . . you saw this white shape . . . in the moonlight.

BEAUJARD: Yes, Professor.

TARDIER   (*slowly*): And you're absolutely sure about that?

BEAUJARD: Absolutely sure, Professor.

(*A long pause. Tardier massages his forehead.*)

TARDIER: That's strange . . . (*Another pause. Dismissing Beaujard with a wave of the hand.*) Thank you, Beaujard. (*Pause. Tardier appears to be deep in thought.*) I hadn't thought of that. (*Slowly, as if to himself.*) I hadn't thought of that . . . It was only when he talked about the moonlight that the idea suddenly came to me.

CODIER: What idea, Professor?

TARDIER: The nocturnal visitor might be a somnambulist.

CODIER: Well, yes.

TARDIER: That which we found puzzling has become very simple . . .

BARDOT: Like someone caught in a dream, devoid of free will and reason . . .

TARDIER   (*interrupting*): But the somnambulist has free will, mental activity of great power, an extremely vivid imagination.

BARDOT: At the same time he risks his life running along the rooftops, whilst fast asleep, and along routes even more dangerous.

CODIER: His movements are, in fact, steadier, more confident, more precise.

TARDIER: Some may read, study, or even write. It is said that La Fontaine created one of his most beautiful, most moving, most touching fables, 'The Two Pigeons' whilst he was asleep.

BARDOT: And when he woke up, he had no memory of it.

TARDIER: Most times, there's nothing. Once the somnambulist is awake he remembers nothing, apart from having woken from a deep sleep.

BARDOT: Nevertheless, he has a conscience?

TARDIER: Yes . . . but a fleeting conscience.

BARDOT: So it's possible to be a somnambulist without knowing that you are one?

TARDIER: Perfectly . . . it is frequently the case.

BARDOT: Are there any somnambulists amongst your patients?

TARDIER: Not that I know of. I would have been informed . . .

MME MARTHE   (*entering*): It is six o' clock, Doctor, the patients are ready . . .

CODIER: If the professor would like to continue with his rounds . . .

TARDIER   (*to Bardot*): Would you like to come along?

BARDOT: Certainly, Professor, thank you.

TARDIER   (*to Mme Marthe*): We shall start with Odette and Louise. (*Mme Marthe exits. To Bardot.*) If you're interested in somnambulism, you'll come across some curious things in Nysten, Robin and even in Maine de Biran and Lelut.

MME MARTHE   (*to Louise*): Come, on Louise, just get a move on . . .

LOUISE   (*to Mme Marthe*): You're in quite a state today . . . have you taken your sedative?

MME MARTHE: Come on now, Louise.

LOUISE: You don't look well . . . stick out your tongue.

ODETTE   (*smiling at Bardot, singing*): Kiss me, Ninette, kiss me . . . I . . .

LOUISE   (*pointing to Bardot*): Another lunatic . . .

ODETTE: You're a pretty boy.

LOUISE: No doubt you've come for some information on the patients.

TARDIER: The gentleman is actually a journalist.

LOUISE: Well then . . . tell your readers that there are plenty of lunatics here who are cared for by dedicated staff. (*Pointing at Mme Marthe.*) Here is a patient who's a little overwrought. (*Pointing at Codier.*) Here's another serious case . . . a mad scientist . . . but we hope to save each and every one through kindness . . . and hypnotism . . . There's only one incurable patient here. (*Quietly.*) Alas, he's a lost soul. (*Pointing at Tardier.*) That's him. He thinks he's a great expert . . . a great psychiatrist. (*With compassion.*) The poor deluded soul . . . poor deluded soul.

ODETTE: Kiss me, Ninette, kiss me, etc . . .

TARDIER   (*to Louise who continues to play with the red shawl around her shoulders*): Well, Louise, what have you got for us tonight then?

ODETTE: My lover.

LOUISE: A silent white shape that crossed the ward and stops for a second by Denise's bed.

BARDOT (*quietly to Codier*): Why is she constantly playing with that red shawl around her shoulders?

CODIER: Why don't you ask her . . . but don't get too close. (*He makes a sign to Mme Marthe who goes and stands right next to Louise.*)

BARDOT (*to Louise*): Miss . . . I really like your red shawl . . . Would you like to give it to me for a minute? (*Louise lunges at him with piercing shrieks whilst trying to scratch him with her fingernails. Mme Marthe restrains her.*)

LOUISE (*crying out*): My shawl . . . your eyes, your eyes . . . I'll scratch out your eyes . . . thieves . . . cowards . . .

CODIER: You see?

BARDOT: But why?

CODIER: She's jealously guarding her secret.

BARDOT: She frightened me.

TARDIER (*to Mme Marthe who is leading Louise away*): Take her away.

ODETTE (*leaving, to Bardot*): Kiss me, Ninette, kiss me . . .

LOUISE (*crying out, as she is led away*): Let me go! I'll give you a shower and then put you into the straitjacket . . . the straitjacket!

BARDOT: These obsessions are a terrible thing.

TARDIER (*to Mme Marthe who has returned*): Bring in Henriette.

HENRIETTE (*lighting up suddenly with joy*): Ah, Doctor . . . have you any news of him? I've been so eager to see you . . .

TARDIER: Not yet, Henriette, but soon. I have written. You'll see him soon.

HENRIETTE (*ecstatic*): I will see him . . . I will see him . . .

TARDIER: Did you see anything last night?

HENRIETTE: My Pierre is the only thing that matters to me . . . my little Pierre. (*To Bardot.*) It's a nice name, isn't it, Monsieur? He loved me, you know. (*Smiling.*) He told me I was pretty . . . and when I went away with him . . . Mother wept . . . wept . . . and we were very happy. He kissed me . . . he made a fuss of me . . . he cuddled me. (*Sadly, her face suddenly becomes tragic.*) Then he hit me . . . here . . . (*pointing to her head*) it hurt . . . it hurt . . . Pierre . . . Pierre . . . I cried . . . cried . . . then he kissed me . . . I was happy . . . I loved him . . . I loved him . . . then he hit me again and again . . . I said nothing . . . nothing, because I loved him. One day . . . he left . . . for good . . . it was over . . . Mother had died . . . I was all alone . . . all alone . . . it's been a long time . . . Is he ever coming back? (*To Bardot.*) But I'm not mad, you know . . . it's only my body that is here . . . my soul . . . he took it away with him out there . . . out there to the stars. (*She raises an arm to the sky. She exits, repeating:*) Out there . . . out there . . .

BARDOT: The poor girl.

TARDIER (*to Mme Marthe*): Who else is there?

MME MARTHE: There is only Madame Denise.

TARDIER: Bring her in. (*Mme Marthe exits. To Bardot.*) A very seriously affected patient. Five years ago, her husband, an alcoholic, half strangled her, before dying himself in the midst of an attack of delirium tremens. Since then she believes that anyone who approaches her wants to strangle her.

BARDOT: It's by her bed that the white shape has stopped on multiple occasions?

TARDIER: Yes, exactly. Don't be alarmed by the severe way that I speak to her. I use kindness and gentleness with my patients in all circumstances, but she is the only one where most of the time I have to raise my voice and even use intimidation. It's the only way to calm her down. When I try to be kind . . . well, you'll see . . . here she is now. (*Denise stops in the doorway, fearful, and when Tardier gets up to approach her, she cries out in fear.*)

DENISE: Don't touch me, you're going to strangle me, you're going to strangle me. (*She protects her neck with her hands.*)

TARDIER (*gently*): Not at all, my dear Denise, nobody wants to hurt you.

DENISE (*crying out even more loudly*): Yes, you do, you're going to strangle me . . . Help! . . . Help!

TARDIER (*severely, raising his voice*): Silence! Be quiet! Nobody wants to hurt you.

DENISE (*crying out*): Help! Help!

TARDIER (*approaching her, he grabs her forcefully by the wrists*): I forbid you to cry out! Or else! (*She stops suddenly.*)

BARDOT: Oh!

TARDIER (*very gently again*): You see, Denise, when you're good, I don't want to hurt you.

DENISE (*trembling, her eyes full of fear*): But yes, yes! I'm going to be strangled, just like Berthe was strangled last month.

TARDIER (*severely*): I forbid you to say that . . .

DENISE (*immediately, quietly*): Oh . . . no . . . no . . . no . . .

BARDOT: Ah!

TARDIER: So, be sensible. (*Changing his tone.*) What did you see last night?

DENISE (*tragically*): The phantom came, he came . . . he was there . . . he came up to me to strangle me. (*She protects her neck from imaginary hands.*) I'm frightened . . . I'm frightened . . .

TARDIER: He won't come again . . .

DENISE (*her teeth chattering*): He will . . . he will kill me . . .

TARDIER (*raising his voice with authority*): He will not come back. (*Looking into her eyes.*) I forbid you to think about it or to believe it. I forbid you. I want you to stop thinking that someone is going to strangle you.
He looks into her eyes for a long time. A long pause whilst Tardier subdues her with his eyes. She is nothing but a poor, terrified wreck.

TARDIER (*to Mme Marthe in a loud voice so that he can be heard by Denise*): Very well. Take her away and if she says one more time that she's going to be strangled, you'll let me know.

DENISE (*looking at Tardier fearfully, like a captured animal, quietly, pleading to Mme Marthe who is approaching her*): Oh, don't tell him anything . . . I beg you . . . I beg you . . .

MME MARTHE: Of course not . . . of course not . . .

DENISE (*pleading in a low voice whilst the nurse tries to lead her away*): Oh, no, no, don't strangle me . . .

MME MARTHE: Come on, Denise! Let's go!

DENISE (*resisting*): Leave me alone! Leave me alone! You're going to strangle me. I'm frightened . . . you're going to strangle me! (*Mme Marthe leads her away.*)

BARDOT: The poor thing! It's terrible . . . I can see you're using fear to keep her safe, but has she really calmed down?

CODIER: At least she's exerting herself less.

TARDIER: She'll never be cured . . .

BARDOT (*getting up*): Professor, it only remains for me to thank you and then to write about all you have confided in me in my newspaper.

TARDIER: Thank you. I'll come down and get some fresh air. If you like, we can walk a little way together.

BARDOT: Of course.

TARDIER (*to Codier*): Don't forget my instructions for this evening, Doctor. You will sit up and keep watch with Beaujard. I'll come by myself before I go to bed. I want Doctor Rollin to keep watch too.

CODIER: Very good, Professor.

TARDIER: At the first sign of anything suspicious, you and the men will grab hold of this white apparition, if indeed there is such a thing at all. Do you believe in ghosts yourself, Codier?

CODIER: Well, you see, Professor . . .

TARDIER: If it is a somnambulist, of course you mustn't wake them . . .

BARDOT: Is it dangerous to wake them?

CODIER: Of course it is! They always fall unconscious. Sometimes they can even die from the shock.

BARDOT (*to Codier*) Goodbye, Doctor. (*Codier waves goodbye.*)

CODIER: Monsieur.

TARDIER (*drawing back the curtains at the window*): Oh, look at those clouds. Come here quickly, Codier. (*He goes towards the window, followed by Bardot.*) When the weather is overcast, the patients get very worked up . . . there's going to be a storm tonight.

CURTAIN

ACT TWO

The same scene. Night-time.

The ticking of the clock is the only thing that disturbs the silence of the ward when the storm abates from time to time.

Darkness, apart from the bluish glimmer of a nightlights that gives a little illumination. The patients are in bed. Mme Marthe is patrolling the ward. The rain is lashing against the windows, the wind can be heard blowing somewhat at the start of the act. The patients are on edge.

DENISE   (*in a hushed voice*): The storm . . .

LOUISE: My shawl would get soaked outside in this. (*She strokes her shawl which is stretched out on her bed.*)

HENRIETTE: You see, Odette . . . if Pierre comes this evening . . . despite the rain and the thunder . . . I'll leave with him . . .

MME MARTHE: A bit of hush, please . . . it's eleven o' clock and you should be asleep . . .

LOUISE: We don't want to sleep . . . in case the phantom comes . . .

MME MARTHE: Enough of that, there is no phantom.

DENISE: It was during a night just like this when . . . (*She says the rest in a low voice.*)

LOUISE   (*suddenly sitting up when Mme Marthe passes close by. With violence.*) Don't touch my shawl. (*She strokes her shawl.*)

MME MARTHE: Come on now, Louise.

LOUISE: I know you want to steal it from me, but you won't have it. (*Violently.*) You won't have it, you won't have it. (*Pause. To Henriette.*) The poor lunatics are going to be all worked up tonight. (*Pointing at Mme Marthe.*) Look how nervous she is.

MME MARTHE: How long is this chattering going to go on? I'd like to go to bed!

ODETTE: Who with?

LOUISE: I'll scratch out the eyes of the first person to try and take my shawl.

ODETTE: Even me?

LOUISE: Even you.

MME MARTHE: Louise, for the last time . . .

DENISE: It was a night just like this that he wanted to strangle me . . . he held my neck so tight . . . so tight . . . (*She continues very quietly. Mme Marthe goes to sit down at the back.*)

ODETTE: Kiss me, Ninette, kiss me . . .

MME MARTHE: Enough, Odette!

ODETTE: I feel like love tonight . . .

HENRIETTE: No change there then.

ODETTE: Oh, love! (*With passion.*) Oh, love!

HENRIETTE   (*very gently, very sadly*): Love, you see, it's not that . . .
it's something else . . . it's sad . . . oh, so sad. (*Propping
herself up on her elbow.*)

ODETTE   (*also propping herself up on her elbow*): Sad? I don't think
that's true at all.

HENRIETTE: Only if you believe what you read in novels. Then you
can imagine that it's all rosy . . . happiness . . . tenderness,
kindness . . . and then, it's the exact opposite.

ODETTE: Love is all about kisses and caresses.

HENRIETTE: Love is all about suffering.

ODETTE: Sensuality.

HENRIETTE: Tears.

ODETTE: Sometimes!

HENRIETTE   (*suddenly bursting into sobs*): Pierre . . . my dear Pierre.

ODETTE   (*moved*): My dear . . . don't cry . . . don't cry like that . . .
what do you expect . . . that's life . . . you have to accept it.

HENRIETTE   (*drying her tears*): Yes . . . yes . . . all the same, you never
think it will come to this, ending up here.
Pause.

ODETTE: Don't cry any more, my dear, don't cry any more.

HENRIETTE: Life? . . . Ah! . . . Life!

ODETTE   (*moved*): You lost sight of life a long time ago.

HENRIETTE: If only I could get it back.

ODETTE: You remember when we were little?

HENRIETTE: Yes.

ODETTE   (*very sadly*): They said that we were mad.

HENRIETTE   (*also sadly*): But we saw things clearly.

ODETTE: It didn't last.

HENRIETTE: Alas!
They both weep silently. The wind gets stronger.

DENISE: The storm . . .

LOUISE: The phantom will be here soon . . . I'm worried . . .
(*Suddenly.*) . . . in case anyone tries to steal my shawl.

DENISE: He's going to strangle me tonight . . . he's going to kill me.

MME MARTHE   (*energetically sitting up in her chair*): I forbid you to speak.

LOUISE: It's the mad woman . . . it's best to ignore her . . .

MME MARTHE   (*shouting furiously*): Louise!

LOUISE: Calm down, calm down! (*The patients laugh.*)

MME MARTHE: Ah! You're starting to get on my nerves.

LOUISE: The poor mad woman . . . the poor mad woman . . .
(*Laughter.*)

MME MARTHE   (*furiously*): Enough!

LOUISE: They should lock you up.

MME MARTHE   (*on her feet and approaching her*): If you don't shut up
right this minute, I shall take you to the showers.

THE OTHERS   (*fearfully*): Oh! Oh! The showers! They're cold!

LOUISE   (*boldly*): You're more in need of a cold shower than I am.
(*Laughter.*)

MME MARTHE	(*raising her arm in order to hit her*): If you don't shut up . . . you're such a nuisance . . .
	This time Louise curls up in her sheets whilst the others protest loudly.
ALL:	You don't have the right to do that . . . Coward . . . You wouldn't dare do it in front of the doctors.
	Enter Tardier.
TARDIER:	What's going on? What's all this noise at this hour?
MME MARTHE:	They won't . . .
	They all interrupt her, pointing their fingers at her.
ALL:	She was going to hit Louise.
LOUISE:	Yes, yes, she was going to hit me . . . that's right.
TARDIER:	A bit of hush, please!
MME MARTHE:	That's not true . . . the doctor knows full well . . .
ALL:	She's lying . . . she's lying . . . she was going to hit her . . .
DENISE:	It wouldn't be the first time.
TARDIER:	Calm down, everyone. (*To Mme Marthe severely.*) You've been warned about this. If it happens again then I shall have no choice but to dispense with your services.
ALL:	That's good . . . he's gentle, he's kind.
LOUISE:	It's all just for show . . . you don't show your true colours in front of the lunatics.
TARDIER	(*to Mme Marthe*): Do you understand?
MME MARTHE:	But, Doctor . . .
TARDIER	(*quietly to Mme Marthe*): You have to be patient, gentle with these poor souls . . . don't forget that.
MME MARTHE:	But . . .
TARDIER	(*as before*): Don't keep on about it . . . I want the patients to be treated with kindness . . . you must never lose your temper . . . (*Gently.*) Just make sure it doesn't happen again.
	Enter Codier and Beaujard.
TARDIER	(*to Codier*): Ah, there you are, Codier. Anything to report?
CODIER:	Nothing at the moment, Professor.
TARDIER:	The doors are all locked?
CODIER:	Double locked. All of them.
TARDIER:	The patients in the other wards are calm?
CODIER:	Not particularly . . . because of the storm, you see, nothing unusual there.
TARDIER:	They must be calmed down, reassured . . . This weather is hardly good for the patients . . . Look at the state Denise gets herself into. (*Gently.*) Denise . . .
CODIER:	It's best to leave her be.
TARDIER:	Yes, that would be best.
DENISE:	If the phantom comes tonight . . .
	A gust of wind blows open the window and blows out the night-light. A panic ensues with the patients shouting out phrases over each other. These words can be heard.

VOICE OF DENISE: He's going to strangle me, he's going to strangle me!

VOICE OF TARDIER: It's the storm!

VOICE OF DENISE: The ghost of my husband . . . he's coming for me. Help! Help!
Piercing cries.

VOICE OF TARDIER: Get some light, we can't see a thing.
Codier switches on the electricity and calm is restored. Mme Marthe closes the window that has been blown open by the wind.

TARDIER: Now then, everyone . . . don't be frightened . . . it was just the wind that blew open the window . . .

DENISE: It's the phantom . . .

TARDIER: There is no phantom . . . look . . . and now we're here . . .

LOUISE: Fat lot of good that will be!

TARDIER: Doctor Codier and Doctor Rollin will keep watch with Beaujard until the morning. They won't be far away. Madame Marthe will sleep in the next room. She'll be able to hear everything.

LOUISE: (*quietly*): She doesn't give a damn about any of that.

TARDIER: Now then, can I tell her to go to bed? That you'll be good? And reasonable?

ALL (*except Louise*): Yes, Doctor . . . Yes, Monsieur.

TARDIER: Go to bed now, Madame Marthe. (*To Codier*) Let them sleep . . . I'm going to bed too . . . Good night, everyone, be good.

ALL: Yes, Doctor. Yes, Monsieur. Good night, Doctor. We'll be good . . .
Tardier, Codier and Beaujard exit.

MME MARTHE (*quietly to Louise, once the doctors have left*): Sooner or later you'll pay dearly for that. (*She exits.*)

LOUISE: They're in a bad way, these lunatics.

HENRIETTE: Monsieur Tardier and Monsieur Codier are nice—I like them.

LOUISE: I don't trust them, myself. You can never be sure with these lunatics, that's for certain.

ODETTE: Codier is kind, Tardier is too old.

HENRIETTE: Well, I like him. He's very nice.

DENISE: (*very slowly*): He frightens me.

HENRIETTE: Rollin is evil.

ALL THE PATIENTS: Ah, yes, Rollin is evil, he is evil, he is evil.

DENISE: I wonder if the phantom will come tonight.

ODETTE: It will be right on midnight—the hour of the dead and tormented souls. (*She bursts out laughing.*)

DENISE: I'm frightened.

ALL: Enough! That's enough! (*Silence. A clap of thunder.*)

LOUISE (*suddenly crying out*): I saw him! I saw him!

ALL (*terrified*): What? Who?

LOUISE (*with dread*): The storm . . . he wanted to steal my shawl . . . but I was stronger than him.

ALL: Enough! That's enough!

DENISE   (*gently*): Perhaps it's the phantom that wants to take your shawl . . .

LOUISE   (*with dread*): I'll scratch his eyes out. Ah! I can't sleep.

ODETTE: Me neither. (*The wind blows strongly.*)

HENRIETTE: But if . . . I can't get him out of my mind . . .

ODETTE: Listen to Henriette!

HENRIETTE: Leave me alone! (*She puts her hands together.*) Dear Lord, let me see him once more, just once more. Forgive him for the hurt he has done me, just as I forgive him myself. Let him be happy, even without me. And Sweet Jesus, every now again, let him remember the one who loves him—and will always love him to the grave—even if he . . . (*Closing her eyes, she falls asleep, whilst gently stroking her pillow.*) My dear boy . . . my . . . (*The wind blows very strongly. Thunder.*)

DENISE: Will he come?

LOUISE: Perhaps.

DENISE: When?

LOUISE: Just like on previous days, when the clock strikes twelve.

DENISE: The hour when the dead come to strangle the living.

LOUISE: Do you remember the old woman who used to have your bed, Denise? It was one month ago today that she died right on midnight, on a stormy night . . . just like this.

DENISE: Oh!

LOUISE: Yes, at midnight. She let out a terrible cry—and that was all! A spirit, perhaps. They say that this place is haunted.

ODETTE: The souls of lunatics roam the corridors at night.

LOUISE: look, I've seen this curtain move more than once tonight.

ODETTE   (*looking at the clock*): It's nearly midnight . . . I can't see it very well . . .

LOUISE: Well . . . it doesn't matter anyway. I'm going to try and sleep. Denise is the only one in danger.

DENISE: Oh, don't leave me!

LOUISE: If he comes, it will be at midnight.

DENISE: Ah! . . . the hour of the dead . . .

Louise falls asleep, putting her hand on her shawl, which she holds in a clenched fist. A long pause. Lightning. The wind blows.

DENISE   (*the only one awake*): The hour of the dead . . . I'm the one who is in danger . . . (*She weeps.*) The phantom is coming to strangle me . . . tonight . . . yes, tonight . . . my husband's spirit will rise from his grave. (*A flash of lightning illuminates the ward, followed by a loud clap of thunder.*) I can feel him . . . I know . . . he will put his claw-like fingers around my throat . . . (*The wind blows violently.*) My God . . . have pity. (*Sitting up.*) What's that noise? Who's there? . . . It's him . . . it's him . . . no, it's the

storm . . . it's midnight . . . he's coming . . . I'm scared . . .
(*She wraps herself in the sheets, facing the audience.*)
Oh, my God, have mercy on a poor, unfortunate soul . . .
I don't want to die . . . Ah! I'm thirsty . . . it's so dismal
in here . . . the ghosts of the lunatics are roaming the
corridors . . . (*Terrified.*) It's midnight . . . (*Slowly and
dismally the clock strikes twelve.*) The hour of the dead . . .
(*On the twelfth stroke the curtain moves several times.*)
He's coming . . . he's coming . . . I daren't look . . . I'm afraid
to turn around . . . I want to look . . . but I daren't . . .
I want to look . . . I want to look . . . I want to . . .
*She turns around very slowly, trembling. A white shape
suddenly appears behind the bed . . . the fingers held out
like claws, menacingly, behind her. Then they grab her
round the throat . . . She lets out a heartrending cry, at
which all the patients wake up. She cries out in desperation
whilst the white shape continues to grip her throat. Odette
and Henriette run screaming through the door at the
back. Mme Marthe rushes in, then Codier and Beaujard,
immediately followed by Odette and Henriette. The
Phantom continues to strangle Denise. She has torn away
the sheet that has been covering his face. Throughout this
scene Louise continues to scream.*

LOUISE: Oh! Oh! Help!

CODIER: The lights! The lights! Quickly!

Mme Marthe switches on the lights.

CODIER (*quietly, terrified*): It's Tardier.

BEAUJARD: The Professor . . . Ah!

THE PATIENTS: Ah!

CODIER: Him! (*Seeing Denise strangled, with her head lying over the
edge of the bed.*) Dead . . .

LOUISE: He's strangled her.

THE PATIENTS: Oh! Oh!

Robot-like, Tardier moves towards the exit.

CODIER (*to Beaujard who is about to grab hold of Tardier*):
No, stop . . . you mustn't . . .

LOUISE (*crying out*): It's Tardier!

*Hearing his name, Tardier stops suddenly as he is about to
leave. With a start he then falls into the arms of Codier and
Beaujard. Mme Marthe brings over a chair into which the
unconscious Tardier is placed. Codier listens to his chest.*

CODIER (*to Mme Marthe*): Ether!

*Mme Marthe passes him the ether with which he brings
Tardier round.*

TARDIER (*gently coming round*): What? What's going on?

CODIER: Nothing, nothing, Professor.

TARDIER: Why are you looking at me like that?

CODIER (*trying to lead him away*): This way, Professor, this way.

TARDIER: Hold on a minute . . . What am I doing here?
            (*Turning round, he sees Denise, strangled.*) Ah! . . .
            Denise . . . Is she dead? Who did this? Answer me . . .
            Answer me, I say . . .
CODIER: The somnambulist.
TARDIER: Who is it? A patient? Which one? Which one?
            I want to know now!
CODIER   (*gently*): It's not a patient.
TARDIER: What? Who then? A nurse? A doctor? (*Codier lowers his
            head.*) You're not answering me. Why are you looking at
            me? (*He suddenly stops and looks at his own appearance.
            The colour drains from him and his eyes glaze over . . .
            He staggers backwards, shaking convulsively, staring
            wide-eyed at Denise.*) Shut up . . . shut up . . . shut up!
            *He steps back and collapses onto Louise's bed, right onto
            the red shawl. Louise, shrieking, digs her fingers into his
            eyes and scratches his face.*
LOUISE: The eyes! The eyes! (*She laughs. The patients cry out
            deafeningly.*)
            *Henriette repeats, 'She is dead, she is dead.' Louise shakes
            the red shawl between her teeth. Odette sings furiously,
            'Kiss me, Ninette, etc.' In the meantime Codier, Beaujard,
            and Mme Marthe go to help Tardier. They pull him away,
            his face is covered in blood, his eyes torn out, crying out
            in agony.*
LOUISE   (*standing on her bed, whilst Beaujard tries to bring her
            under control*): I always said that he was mad . . .
            The patients continue to cry out whilst the curtain falls.

CURTAIN

The Lover of Death

(*L'Amant de Mort*, 1925)

by

Maurice Renard

Preface

Over the years, the Grand-Guignol succeeded in recruiting celebrated authors to join the ranks of its regular playwrights (above all, the prolific André de Lorde) in the creation of original works for the repertoire. Hence, following the contribution made to the repertoire by authors such as Gaston Leroux and Octave Mirbeau, in 1925, another notable writer, Maurice Renard, wrote a stage play for the legendary horror theatre: *L'Amant de Mort*. Renard was a popular novelist and remains an important figure in the rich tradition of French science fiction and fantasy. Arthur B. Evans (1994) signals that although Renard was a giant of French science fiction between 1900 and 1930, his literary achievement has been unduly overlooked, especially in Anglophone cultures. For Evans, Renard's remarkable work represents the transition between the nineteenth and twentieth centuries, realism and surrealism, spanning Gothic, realism and popular genres of crime and science fiction, and, most profoundly, as a bridge between the 'two fundamental sides of the human psyche—the rational and the irrational' (392).

In 1920, Renard published what remains his most famous novel: *Les Mains d'Orlac* (*The Hands of Orlac*), a paradigmatic example of twentieth-century Gothic horror in which a concert pianist is seriously injured and receives the transplanted hands of an executed murderer and becomes a killer himself. The novel has been directly adapted into the films *Orlacs Hände* (1924), *Mad Love* (1935) and *The Hands of Orlac* (1960). The fact that the lead actors were Conrad Veidt, Peter Lorre and Christopher Lee respectively bears testament to the rich and heightened nature of this classic horror role. Moreover, the central theme of the *Orlac* tale—advanced surgery leading to possession—recurs as a horror subgenre on screen from *Hands of a Stranger* (1962)—effectively another adaptation of Renard in all but name—the optical-themed *The Eye* (2002) and its various sequels/remakes through to British comic parodies such as the penis transplant-themed *Percy* (1971) and in 'Voodoo Feet of Death' a television episode in Steve Coogan's affectionate parody of the portmanteau horror form, *Dr Terrible's House of Horrible* (BBC, 2001). As much as Maurice

Renard was bringing arcane folklore and traditional tales of curses and possession into the sterilized surgeries of the twentieth century, he was also acutely aware of genuine scientific developments. Although *Les Mains d'Orlac* is a tale of a 'mad scientist', a trope as old as the modern Gothic itself, it was partly based on reality: Renard's insane, surgical genius—Dr Cerral—is a very thinly veiled allusion to the real surgeon Alexis Carrel who won the 1912 Nobel prize for his pioneering work in surgery, including laying the foundations for transplant surgery. Hence, Renard is animating a very primal fable of possession, but he is also producing a work that is satirical, perhaps reflecting contemporary anxieties and controversies about the ethics of medical progress.

The achievement of *Les Mains d'Orlac*—a brilliant melding of current (or certainly conceivable) science and Gothic tropes of possession, revenge and murder—is an impetus that can be detected in his one play for the Grand-Guignol, *L'Amant de Mort*, a play about lust, death—and hypnotism. Just as he researched medicine and surgery in *Orlac*, in his treatment of hypnotism, Renard was exploring a well-established practice but one that had recently gained some notoriety. This was owing to the psychologist Pierre Janet who had discredited the practice of hypnotism in his works *Les Médications Psychologiques* (1919) and *La Médecine Psychologique* (1923). Janet is cited by Christine Guilloux as leading a backlash in the medical community that began to accuse those who used 'the practice of suggestion through hypnosis of being immoral' (Guillox 2008: 58) with the consequence that hypnosis became out of vogue in France (albeit not elsewhere) for many decades. In the light of this, Renard's Grand-Guignol play would have been seen as a topical presentation of a controversial practice by its original audience. This is evident in Robert's line in the play 'This authority of one will over another seems to me to be . . . to be a crime.'

Renard's play, however, is not a diatribe in dramatic form. The play reveals him to be a master of atmosphere and the modern Gothic stage. There is an eerie quality to the play that takes on a grotesque and surrealistic quality in scenes such as the arrival of the two revellers, dressed as clowns, and William dressed as a devil. In addition, the well-developed characters and their motivations—especially the unscrupulous Robert—lend the play an inexorable intensity.

The finale of Renard's play has the potential to be a *coup de théâtre*: having heard the voice of the deceased Simone, '*Suddenly in the darkness, the audience can see what Robert has seen*' and the mangled body of Simone lurches towards him. This is literally the last seconds of the play, but it presents a shocking climax. It might be a populist thrill tactic, like the final jump scare in a horror movie, but it also ramifies in a highly regarded modern Irish play: Conor McPherson's *Shining City* (2004). In this contemporary classic, John visits a therapist Ian and recounts how he keeps hearing and seeing his late wife (killed in a car crash) in their home. In the final sequence, the audience briefly beholds this spectacle:

> *In the darkening gloom of the afternoon, we see that* Mari's *ghost has appeared behind the door. She is looking at* Ian, *just as* John *described her; she wears her red coat, which is filthy, her hair is wet. She looks beaten up. She looks terrifying.* (McPherson 2013: 56)

The impact on audiences was evident, with the *New York Times* describing it as 'the most shocking ending on Broadway' through which 'McPherson has found an inspired alternative to those inadequate tools of communication called words' (*New York Times* 10 May 2006).

For Benedict Nightingale, reviewing the premiere at London's Royal Court Theatre in *The Times* (11 June 2004), *Shining City* demonstrated 'acting and writing at its most riveting', but he had reservations about the finale, which he discussed without any 'spoilers':

> At this point I'd better reveal that there is Grand-Guignol ending that is either cheap or deep but, either way, doesn't make clear what we are finally meant to think of Ian or John. Let's just say that it's a powerful if confusing image of suffering womanhood. But before this there is genuine excellence.

We could argue that decades before this undoubtedly shocking (and, for some, troubling) denouement, the Grand-Guignol pioneered the power of such strategies, taking the audience through carefully poised dialogue and atmospheric set-up into a moment of sudden, absolute terror.

THE LOVER OF DEATH

(*L'Amant de Mort*, 1925)

by

MAURICE RENARD

First performed at the Théâtre du Grand-Guignol on 11 February 1925
Translated by Richard J. Hand and Michael Wilson
This translation was commissioned by the Molotov Theatre Group

---

Cast
Robert Samoy
William Darvières
Masked Figure 1
Masked Figure 2
Louis
Simone Darvières
Ginette Barjot
Maud Risner

ACT ONE

The boudoir of Simone Darvières. The lamps have been lit. Simone serves tea to her visitors, Ginette and Maud.

GINETTE: Tell me, Simone, are you free at eight o' clock on Saturday?
SIMONE: Saturday at eight?
GINETTE: Yes. That's the day I'll have my Spanish model with me.
MAUD: Oh?
GINETTE: You can't imagine just how gorgeous he is! I met him in Cadiz when we were there last year. He was selling watermelons in a doorway. He's come to Paris to seek his fortune. I asked him round to my place to pose for me. I started by studying his profile, and then . . .
MAUD: And then . . .?
GINETTE: And then he wanted to do a full *life study*! Ah, what a marvel, my darlings! You should see him! An Adonis! A bronze Adonis! And a natural instinct when it comes to posing!
MAUD: You're making my mouth water!
GINETTE: He's a force of nature! As natural being naked as a beautiful fruit, or a pebble on the beach.
SIMONE: My dear Ginette, please don't get yourself worked up!

GINETTE: Oh, you're just incapable of appreciating the wonders of modern art. You're still under the influence of your husband who has never been able to *unlearn* the lessons of the Academy! William Darvières will never be more than an artist of the establishment!

MAUD: Why don't you just come out with it and say it's kitsch!

GINETTE: What I mean is that his technical ability . . .

SIMONE: Of course, neither of you follow the same artistic movements . . .

GINETTE: Anyway, I'm counting on you . . . on both of you, if the master will allow you to come along.

SIMONE: Alas, my dear Ginette, I'm truly sorry but I won't be in Paris on Saturday.

MAUD: Are you leaving?

SIMONE: Yes. On doctor's orders! I've never fully recovered from the bout of flu I went down with at New Year. I still wake up coughing in the morning and by the evening I sometimes run a bit of a temperature. So William has insisted that I spend a few weeks recuperating on the Riviera.

GINETTE: Is he going down there with you?

SIMONE: No, quite impossible. He has started on a portrait of Lady Hamilton. He can't possibly be disturbed.

GINETTE: Well then, that's headline news! The perfect couple is splitting up! The 'model lovers', as everyone calls you, are going their separate ways!

SIMONE   (*seriously*): It will be the first time that we'll have been apart since we got married. And the doctor really had to bully me into agreeing to leave Paris without William.

MAUD: Will you be staying at the coast for long?

SIMONE: Oh no, just a few weeks. Just long enough for me to rest up.

GINETTE: Rest up? No one goes to the South of France to *rest*! I know you—you'll be in the casino every day!

SIMONE: Bah! You know they drink tea there as much as anywhere.

MAUD: So, you're going to leave your husband here alone, just like that? Beware!

SIMONE   (*simply*): I trust him.

GINETTE: The fact is, he loves you so much!

MAUD: Exactly! It's terrible when a man loves his wife so passionately. He gets used to being loved and it becomes a habit, just like any other. I wouldn't be so relaxed about it if I were Simone.

SIMONE   (*with irony*): You're very kind, my dear. Thank you.
No doubt I'm a very proud woman, but I'll leave William in Paris without the slightest apprehension.

GINETTE: After all, he's so busy . . .

SIMONE   (*ringing the bell*): Yes, exactly. There are his lectures, his classes, the portrait of Lady Hamilton . . .
Enter Louis.

LOUIS: You rang, Madame?

SIMONE: Take away the tray . . . have you put out the dustsheets in the dining room?

LOUIS: Yes, Madame. We're protecting all the polished surfaces.
SIMONE: Very good. Thank you.
             Louis exits.
GINETTE: Are you closing up the house? But surely . . .
SIMONE: William will be taking his meals at the club whilst I'm away.
             It will be more pleasant for him over at Volney rather than alone
             here in our dining room. Besides, I'm leaving him the smoking
             room . . .
GINETTE   (*with a hint of a smile*): Perhaps his good friend, Robert Samoy,
             will come and keep him company . . .
SIMONE: I don't know. Robert doesn't get out much anymore. It's ages
             since we saw him.
GINETTE   (*mischievously*): Perhaps that's all for the better!
SIMONE: Why do you say that?
GINETTE: Oh, I'm just saying . . .
SIMONE: You are a funny one! What do you mean by that?
GINETTE: Me? Nothing . . . After all, you know that I'm a terrible gossip.
SIMONE: Have you seen Robert recently?
GINETTE: Oh, well, I suppose so, yes.
SIMONE: Where did you see him?
GINETTE: At the Georgian Night Club.
SIMONE: Did you speak to him?
GINETTE: No chance.
SIMONE: Why?
GINETTE: He had his elbows on the table and he was slumped against some
             awful redhead with dark eyes and a vacant stare. I tell you, it was
             a sorry spectacle.
SIMONE: Robert? Him?
GINETTE: He had one of those faces. You know, women, alcohol, drugs. It
             seems that he will lose himself in anything.
MAUD: What do you mean, 'lose himself'?
SIMONE: What you're saying isn't possible!
GINETTE: I've seen him!
SIMONE: Oh, but he's such a kind man, so considerate, so affectionate . . .
             to have sunk so low! Why, oh why, has such a change come over
             him now?
GINETTE   (*as an afterthought*); Problems. No doubt. The drugs numb the
             pain . . .
MAUD   (*continuing*): Even the pains of love!
SIMONE: Oh! Do you think that Robert . . .?
GINETTE: Maud is right. It only takes one disappointment in love to explain
             such a transformation.
SIMONE: That's terrible. William will be upset to hear that his friend . . .
             Enter Louis.
LOUIS   (*discreetly*): Madame . . .
SIMONE: What?
LOUIS   (*still discreetly*): Monsieur Robert Samoy asks if Madame will
             receive him.

SIMONE   (*shrill*): He's here! He's here! (*To the two young women.*)
           It's him! (*Ginette and Maud exchange a smile.*)
           Robert enters.
ROBERT   (*kissing Simone's hand*): My dear Simone. I've just seen William
           and he told me of your imminent departure. I didn't want you to
           leave Paris without my saying goodbyes . . .
SIMONE: You're too kind . . . you know these ladies, I believe?
           Madame Ginette Barjot. Mademoiselle Maud Risner.
ROBERT   (*bowing*): I've already had the honour of being introduced to
           Mademoiselle Risner at the latest private view of the Humourists.
           As for Madame Barjot, we are old acquaintances from our youth!
SIMONE: Well, that is excellent!
MAUD   (*getting up*): My dear Simone, it just remains for us to wish you a
           pleasant journey . . .
GINETTE   (*doing likewise*): And a safe return home.
SIMONE: What? Are you leaving already?
ROBERT   (*to the young woman*): I do hope that it's not my arrival that is
           causing you to leave?
GINETTE: Not at all, my dear friend. I have a meeting with a model at
           six o' clock.
ROBERT: A model of virtue!?
GINETTE: You are so impertinent, Monsieur Samoy! (*To Simone.*) Well,
           then, goodbye, my dear. Don't forget about us now! Send us all
           your news!
SIMONE: I shall. Goodbye, my dear . . . Goodbye, dear Maud.
MAUD: Goodbye.
           *Ginette and Maud exit. Simone sees them out and then returns
           almost immediately.*
SIMONE   (*returning*): Excuse me. I had to see my friends out.
ROBERT   (*ironically*): Those are your friends?
SIMONE   (*ringing the bell*): Of course! Why shouldn't they be!?
ROBERT: You're not too picky then!
SIMONE: That's the secret of happiness.
ROBERT: And are you happy?
SIMONE: Completely.
           Enter Louis.
SIMONE   (*to Louis*): Could you bring in the port, please? And could you
           tell Justine that Monsieur Samoy will be joining us for dinner?
LOUIS: Very good, Madame.
ROBERT: But no . . . I can't possibly—
SIMONE: Nobody asked for your opinion. William would be furious not to see
           you again. Besides, I hope you're not going to abandon him whilst
           I'm away? I'm absolutely depending on you to keep him company.
           *Louis places the tray, laden with glasses and a carafe, on the
           coffee table and leaves during the following exchange.*
ROBERT: You can rest assured. I'll keep an eye on the poor lonesome soul.
           Is it tomorrow that you're leaving?
SIMONE: That's right.

ROBERT: And when are you planning to return?

SIMONE: In five weeks exactly. On Shrove Monday.

ROBERT: Perfect, perfect! Such an eye for detail—I'd forgotten just how it was in your nature to be precise, punctual and . . . thoughtful!

SIMONE: A glass of port?

ROBERT: No, thank you.

SIMONE   (*about to ring*): A cup of tea, then?

ROBERT   (*stopping her*): No, no, nothing. Thank you. (*Nervously lighting a cigarette.*) May I?

SIMONE   (*watching him*): But whatever is the matter, my friend?

ROBERT: It's just . . . that you're leaving. That's what's the matter.

SIMONE   (*smiling*): It's not such a terrible thing . . . We did decide on it at short notice. . . .

ROBERT: The suddenness of the trip doesn't make it any the less disagreeable.

SIMONE: For you, perhaps. For me, as you know, I'm rather pleased to be leaving Paris with its constant drizzle and the fog that clings to you, for the beautiful countryside that awaits me down south. If it weren't for the fact that I'm leaving William behind in this miserable place, I would be leaving with a joyous heart.

ROBERT: You're such an egotist, like all happy people.

SIMONE: My God! It's so irritating to hear you endlessly moaning on. You have every reason to be happy as well!

ROBERT   (*with bitterness*): Yes! (*Seriously.*) Do you think I have everything, Simone?

SIMONE: I would think so! How miserable you are today! (*Changing her tone.*) Well, to cheer you up I'm going to give you a present.

ROBERT: A present?

SIMONE   (*taking a photograph out of the sideboard drawer*): Yes, here you are. Look what I just found as I was going through the drawers.

ROBERT: A school photograph!

SIMONE: I'm giving it to you.

ROBERT: Thank you. What a memento!

SIMONE: I knew you'd like it. What date is it?

ROBERT: 1910. We were having a party at the Lalou Studio, your husband and I. It's all rather ridiculous! Each of us is wearing something to symbolize our own particular talent, or striking a pose that illustrates our temperament.

SIMONE: Why is William wearing a crown of turnips?

ROBERT: Because a turnip is synonymous with a watercolour in artist's slang. Your husband's family was insistent that he became an architect and he was immediately sent away to the Lalou Studio. But William only ever dreamed of painting. Hence the crown of turnips.

SIMONE: And why are you holding out your hands towards that pale young man sitting in front of you with his eyes closed?

ROBERT   (*bristling, after a pause*): At that time I was just starting to get interested in hypnotism.

SIMONE   (*surprised*): But you didn't carry on with it?

ROBERT   (*as before*): Yes. I did.

SIMONE: You never told me that. Neither did William. Does he know?

ROBERT: No.

SIMONE   (*shocked, but mockingly*): Does hypnotism work then? Are these moving tables, mediums, apparitions for real? Come off it, Robert, do you really believe in all that? (*She laughs.*)

ROBERT: Don't laugh. Don't laugh. I'm talking here about hypnotism, not spiritualism. A mesmeric trance, produced through the will of the hypnotist. An extraordinary state of being, during which commands are spoken to the subject that will determine their future behaviour . . .

SIMONE: But is that really possible?

ROBERT: You see how right I was to keep quiet about it. I give you my word of honour that hypnotism is not a case of smoke and mirrors. It should be considered as a science, albeit an emerging one, but nonetheless authentic, the unknown depths of which frighten us, a science of unimaginable possibilities . . . I have seen its power with my own eyes . . .

SIMONE   (*very interested*): Really?

ROBERT: Let's talk about something else.

SIMONE: Oh, Robert, tell me, please! Tell me, so that I can believe in hypnotism. I want to believe in it. It must be so exciting!

ROBERT: It is more than exciting. It's agonizing. Those that fall into a trance, their eyes become blank and their faces lose all expression—totally—it always makes me shudder. This authority of one will over another seems to me to be . . . to be a crime.

SIMONE: But a kind of crime that you have sometimes carried out!

ROBERT: I admit it. I have often used hypnotism for experimental purposes, because if we knew more about it, hypnotism could do so much good . . . And besides, you see, it's not just about the pursuit of truth, but so that we know as much about it as we do about magnetism . . . what is the nature of the force . . .? Is it conducted through fluids or vibrations? . . . And what might be the consequences? . . . For example, imagine, one evening . . .

SIMONE: One evening? Go on, tell me . . .

ROBERT: What are we afraid of? I only mean that hypnotism is a strange and terrifying discipline.

SIMONE: But can it be used for medical purposes?

ROBERT: In the same way that certain poisons or electric shocks can be. But these poisons must be administered in microscopic doses. Or the voltage of the current must be carefully monitored . . .

SIMONE: Oh, you're so infuriating! I can see that you know so much more than you're willing to tell me!

ROBERT   (*warming to his theme*): Yes, electricity is very similar to hypnotism. It has its uses, but we don't really know what it is. But gradually, through hard work and observation—sometimes down to luck as well—we find out about sparks, currents, its astounding energy and . . . immeasurable possibilities . . .

SIMONE: Oh, I would love to witness these experiments in hypnotism. What happens?

ROBERT   (*quite cheerfully*): So you want me to give you a scare for fun? Well, no, such mysteries are no laughing matter. We'll have a serious discussion about it when you return. Today, I respectfully request that we talk about something else.

SIMONE   (*disappointed*): So be it! As you wish, let's talk about something else. In the meantime, though, I shall hang on to the photograph!

ROBERT: Simone!

SIMONE: Don't you 'Simone' me! I shall put it back in the drawer. You shall still have it. You just have to be more open with me.

ROBERT: I see! Can a man really be open with a woman?

SIMONE: Why ever not?

ROBERT: Isn't lying a necessity of everyday life? Do you think that there would be harmony between men and women if lying did not underpin our gestures, our words, our thoughts?

SIMONE: Not at all. I can very well imagine a world without lies.

ROBERT: You're joking! Without a little necessary social dishonesty, where would you and I be right now?

SIMONE: What do you mean?

ROBERT   (*upset*): Nothing . . . Goodbye, Simone.

SIMONE: What? Are you leaving?

ROBERT: Yes . . . Goodbye, my dear Simone . . . I hope you'll be happy down south.

SIMONE: Your voice is trembling . . .

ROBERT: Be happy, you lucky thing! Have fun and spare an occasional thought for those of us left behind, those of us who . . .

SIMONE: Robert, you look troubled. What on earth is the matter?

ROBERT: Nothing!

SIMONE   (*emotional and confused*): I'll see you soon, Robert. When I get back!

ROBERT: No!

SIMONE: What?

ROBERT: No! I shan't be coming back. I don't want to see you again.

SIMONE: But why ever not, Robert? Why ever not?

ROBERT   (*seriously*): Because I love you.

SIMONE   (*as if insulted*): Robert!

ROBERT: No, no, don't tell me to be quiet! I can't do it anymore! It's suffocating me! I can no longer keep this secret quiet . . . it's killing me! I love you, Simone! I have loved you since the first day I saw you!

SIMONE   (*confused*): Be quiet!

ROBERT: Ah, that first day! That first day! William and I had been invited to spend the evening at the Morels' place.

SIMONE: The Morels' place?

ROBERT: Yes, a musical soirée. An evening in your honour. I can remember it. I can remember everything about it. William went to order us a taxi. On the Quai des Grands-Augustins a bus nearly hit us. Our taxi had to swerve. William said to me, 'That was a lucky escape!' Since that evening I have often regretted that the bus didn't crush us!

SIMONE: Don't say things like that! How dare you talk like this, Robert!

ROBERT: And then there was the emptiness of the days that followed.
I was completely paralysed. I could no longer work. I could only
think of one thing: seeing you again! Then one morning William
knocked on the door and told me, 'You remember that beautiful
blonde woman from the other evening, the one who played the
piano at the Morels? Yes? Well, I'm going to marry her, old boy!'
And that was that. The misery of my life was complete!

SIMONE   (*pityingly*): My poor friend!

ROBERT: Don't pity me! Your marriage with William was a perfectly
natural thing . . . William is rich after all, isn't he?

SIMONE: Oh, surely you don't think that . . .

ROBERT: A Darvières! What am I next to my friend? A miserable little
fourpenny architect, a sort of glorified bricklayer, a complete
loser, eh? Well what more was there to say? And I said nothing.

SIMONE   (*deeply moved*): Robert!

ROBERT: I said nothing. And I was even a witness at your wedding.
Yes, Fate delivers such ironies. I put on my white gloves and
I signed the register at the town hall and then at the church.
'With all my good wishes! Congratulations!' Oh, those
declarations were sincere enough in the moment.

SIMONE: Robert, be quiet! You're frightening me!

ROBERT: Frightening you? Well now! It was at that moment that you
should have been frightened, sensing my despair and panic.
But you hardly paid me any attention. You were too wrapped up
in your happiness! Your own happiness! What did it matter to
you that a miserable soul was left with his heart bleeding on the
platform whilst the train took you away on your honeymoon?
Ah, if only I had been able at that moment to tear you away from
William and take off with you! What joy! What joy!

SIMONE: Shut up! Shut up!

ROBERT: Oh, those terrible weeks! Those weeks when you were with your
husband in Algeria. I tried everything during those weeks to make
myself forget. Women, gambling . . . I passed the nights in the
gambling dens. I went to some dive or other and I won. Won!
That was another of life's little ironies—this winning streak, this
luck that attached itself to me and overwhelmed me. 'The Happy
Gambler!' Ah! It meant nothing! And when gambling wasn't
enough, when I was sick of drinking, then I fell in with the drug
addicts . . .

SIMONE: Oh!

ROBERT: Does that appal you? Well, just forget it!

SIMONE: Robert, I beg you . . .

ROBERT: Nothing could be done. Nothing could cure me of you.
I ended up with my nerves frayed and just as unhappy as before.
Everything! I tried everything, even damned science . . .
Alas! There is no possible remedy for my kind of pain.
I love you so much, Simone. I love you too much!
He collapses into an armchair, sobbing convulsively.

SIMONE: Shut up! Or somebody will hear you!

ROBERT   (*getting up suddenly and taking her by the hands*):
And then what? I don't care if anyone hears me.
He looks at her with intense pain.

ROBERT: I won't come back here! Never! Never! (*She tries unsuccessfully to break free of him. There is some pity in her weakness. And then, despite herself, she returns Robert's gaze, looking deeply into his eyes.*) Ah! Your eyes! Your eyes! Look away! Look away, I tell you! You're hurting me! You enjoy hurting me, don't you?! You're hurting me terribly! Turn your head away! Go on, turn your head away! Oh, my God, what's the matter with you? (*He lets his hands fall by his side and takes a step backwards. Simone is silent and motionless, her eyes staring ahead. She seems to be rooted to the spot.*) What's the matter? Simone? (*To himself.*) No! No! That's not possible! Just like that? Without her consent? Without fixing her gaze? She's pretending, surely? (*Calling out.*) Simone! (*Expertly he places his hand on her forehead.*) It's true! She's asleep! (*An evil thought causes his features to tense. An internal struggle is playing out.*) No! I can't! That would be unspeakable! But yet . . . but yet . . . (*Impulsively, rejecting with a gesture all moral objections, he goes up to Simone and speaks in an authoritative voice, whilst looking deeply into her eyes.*) Simone! You will obey me! It is my desire. In five weeks' time you will return. In five weeks, at this time exactly, you will come to my house. And you will be mine! All mine! (*Momentarily taking hold of her hands again.*) Awake! Simone, who shivered slightly as Robert spoke, slowly comes out of hypnosis. She places a hand on her forehead. Her posture relaxes. She starts to smile, unaware of what has just happened. Robert, hiding his anxiety, plays along with the situation.*

ROBERT   (*in a forced tone of indifference*): Ah, well, you're quite right, Simone. It's true, I don't know what came over me!

SIMONE: At last! You're back to your old self again! You had me quite frightened there with your glaring eyes and erratic gestures . . .

ROBERT: I beg your forgiveness.

SIMONE: I shall happily forgive you. But on one condition! That is that never again—you hear me, Robert—never again are you to speak of such madness!

ROBERT: I promise.

SIMONE   (*holding out her hand to him, which he takes*): That's perfect. (*A door is heard closing.*) Here's William. (*Simone goes to the door to meet her husband. William enters.*)

WILLIAM   (*embracing his wife*): Good evening, darling!

SIMONE: Darling!

WILLIAM   (*seeing Robert, with delight*): Well, well, look who's here!

ROBERT: Yes, indeed, old boy. Simone has insisted that I stay for dinner . . .

WILLIAM: Quite right too! So then, what's new?

ROBERT: Nothing much. I arrived here right in the middle of the preparations for leaving and I've been playing my usual role of being an old bore!

WILLIAM: What on earth do you mean? You know full well that you're always welcome here. Isn't that right, Simone?

SIMONE   (*pouring William a glass of port*): Of course!

WILLIAM   (*to Simone*): I've booked your seat for tomorrow.

SIMONE: You didn't have too much trouble, did you?

WILLIAM: Yes. Everything was fully booked until twelve. But if you grease the right palm then anything can be sorted out! At the moment it's as if there's an exodus to the Côte d'Azur.

ROBERT   (*to Simone*): Your return journey will be more relaxed.

WILLIAM: Certainly. People stay on the Riviera until the carnival is over, so I think it's an excellent idea to return to Paris the day before Shrove Tuesday.

ROBERT   (*to Simone, with meaning*): Are you not tempted to stay for the festival?

SIMONE   (*wiping her forehead with her hand, distractedly*): Oh, no. I can't abide masquerades. All that noise and hustle and bustle. Nothing could be less pleasurable!

ROBERT: Pleasure is like happiness: it varies according to one's mood.

SIMONE   (*who only has eyes for her husband*): You're right. As far as I'm concerned, I can only imagine one thing—at home, in my house, with William.

WILLIAM   (*embracing her with a look of adoration*): Simone!

SIMONE: There's no other pleasure, there could not possibly be another . . . (*Wiping her hand across her forehead.*) For me . . . (*She clutches her forehead with a painful look on her face.*)

WILLIAM   (*alarmed*): What's the matter? You've gone all pale . . .

SIMONE   (*collapsing onto the sofa with a distraught look and holding her head*): It's nothing. Just a slight migraine. It's extraordinary. It suddenly came upon me.

WILLIAM   (*to Robert, whilst leaning over her*): Robert, would you ring the bell?

ROBERT   (*furrowing his eyebrows*): Certainly.

WILLIAM   (*to Simone*): You've exhausted yourself with all this sorting out of the house.

SIMONE   (*increasingly distraught, anxious and wailing*): Yes, yes, that's it, for sure. That'll be it.

Enter Louis.

WILLIAM   (*to Louis*): Quickly, an aspirin and a glass of water!

Louis exits. Simone struggles in pain against the mysterious affliction that overwhelms her.

WILLIAM   (*anxiously*): My darling! What's wrong? Simone! What's the matter with you?

SIMONE   (*pummelling the cushions, sobbing and wringing her hands, overcome with nerves, she desperately cries out*): I don't know! I don't know! I don't know!

CURTAIN

ACT TWO

A ground-floor architect's studio in Montmartre. On the right, a window onto the boulevard and a door. On the left, a bookshelf and a divan. Next to the divan, a small table with a drawer in it. On top of the table is an illuminated lamp. It is twilight and the room is dimly lit by the lamp and the flickering flames in the fireplace. By the end of the act, night has fallen.

As the curtain rises, Robert is anxious, sitting on a chair next to the fireplace.

ROBERT   [*murmuring*]: It's impossible . . . Impossible . . .! It's just a nightmare . . . [*He stands and walks slowly and aimlessly around the room. Suddenly*] I'm suffocating! I can't breathe in here . . .! [*He opens the window and the curtains float in the breeze. Singing and laughter can be heard from the street, filling the room*] Singing! Masks! All the tacky pleasures of the carnival . . .! How tawdry . . .! [*The noise grows more distant. Robert, leaving the window open, picks up a poetry book from the small table, flicks through the poems then reads.*]
The secrets of Death are terrible and dark
And before Her even Jesus turns pale
Sepulchre! Who can say, in your abyss of shadows,
What may happen?
Death . . .! [*He stops reading, with terror*] Death . . .!
Suddenly, two revellers, dressed as masked clowns—one black and one red—climb over the windowsill into the room, laughing and cavorting wildly. Robert leaps to his feet

MASKED FIGURE 1:   Good evening!

MASKED FIGURE 2:   Do you want to play with us?

ROBERT   [*his voice is dry and curt*]: Who are you? What is this?

MASKED FIGURE 1   [*very merrily*]: But it's us . . .! Come on! You're not being very nice to your friends now are you? Am I right, Master Bob!?

MASKED FIGURE 2   [*in hilarity*]: Yes, Master!

ROBERT   [*brutal*]: What do you want? Is this some sort of joke?

MASKED FIGURE 1   [*realizing their error*]: Oh, I'm so sorry, sir . . . Does that mean that Pradel, the sculptor, doesn't live here?

ROBERT: No, he doesn't! Off you go.

MASKED FIGURE 2   [*taken aback*]: He invited us to his costume party . . .

ROBERT: Well, it's not in here. It's in that pavilion . . . over there . . .

MASKED FIGURE 2   [*to Masked Figure 1*]: We got this so wrong . . .

MASKED FIGURE 1   [*making excuses to Robert*]: We saw the open window . . .

ROBERT: Yes . . . yes . . . [*Pointing at the door*] Pradel's studio is at the bottom of the garden. You can cut through there. It'll save you from going all the way around.

MASKED FIGURE 1:   Thank you, sir. I can't tell you how sorry we are . . .

MASKED FIGURE 2:   Yes . . . please forgive us . . .

ROBERT   [smiling very sadly]: It's carnival; everything is forgiven . . .
The masked figures leave. Distantly, music and joyous celebrations can be heard. Robert goes to the window.

ROBERT: The carnival . . .! Dancing . . .! Singing . . .!
He slams the window shut. It is [peaceful. Then, in the silence a knock on the door is heard. Robert is startled. Another knock. After a hesitation in which the terrified state of Robert is evident, he goes to the door anxiously and opens it, slightly at first and then he swings it wide open when he sees who's there.

ROBERT   [relieved]: William!
William is dressed as a devil. He comes in slowly, walking across the room and sitting on the divan.

ROBERT: Poor William!

WILLIAM: Yes. Poor William. I have come from the cemetery. I was praying there.

ROBERT: My poor friend!

WILLIAM: I have come to say farewell.

ROBERT: Farewell? What . . .?

WILLIAM: Yes. I cannot live like this any more. I have tried . . . But, no . . . It is impossible!

ROBERT: What are you going to do? Travel?

WILLIAM: Yes, that's right. I'm going to travel—far, very far.

ROBERT   (after a heavy silence): For five weeks . . . I've waited desperately to see you . . . but you would see no-one . . .

WILLIAM   [wildly]: No-one!

ROBERT: Not even me . . .

WILLIAM   (still wildly): Not even you! [Pulling himself together] Please forgive me . . . I couldn't help it. It's driven me to despair. I've been completely distracted . . . and also in torment! The weight of the world is on my shoulders . . .! I know it's crazy but I can't help it. I feel it's all my fault; I feel that I could've prevented the accident from happening; that I should've stopped her from going, that woman I loved so much, she meant the world to me . . . and I found her body, burnt and mutilated . . .

ROBERT: Come on—stop.

WILLIAM: A nightmare! A nightmare that will follow me to the grave! Oh, it's torture!

ROBERT: Stop! Enough . . . [Pause] When I read what had happened in the newspaper, I realized she must've been on that train and I ran over to your house . . . You had already heard what had happened . . . And you weren't there . . .

WILLIAM: Yes. I heard the news on the street. I stopped a car and said to the driver 'Laroche!' He didn't understand but I begged and pleaded so much he drove me there . . . When we got there . . . Oh, my friend, the horror . . . The horror! Hour after hour I dug my way through wreckage and corpses, searching for her body . . . My clothes and hands were red with blood and gore . . . Oh, the faces, crushed and pounded! The eyes gouged out, hanging down over the torn and shredded cheeks! The jaws smashed open with broken teeth, looking like they were still screaming for help . . .! Then suddenly . . . in the rubble I saw a hand outstretched towards me . . . a woman's hand . . . I grabbed it . . . I pulled . . . And the hand and arm came out of the wreckage . . . Torn off at the shoulder . . . And I never knew which poor soul it belonged to . . .

ROBERT: How terrible!

WILLIAM: How did I have the strength to carry on searching through this carnage? I don't know! The power of nervous despair is unstoppable . . . Finally, I saw her . . . Amongst the dead. They had taken her mangled body to a railway station where they turned one of the halls into a mortuary. They had covered her body with a sheet . . . All my joy, my life, lay crushed beneath that shroud . . .!

ROBERT: Are you sure . . .? Are you sure it was her . . .? Did you recognise her . . .?

WILLIAM: Yes.

ROBERT: Her face?

WILLIAM: Yes, I was sure. She was horribly mutilated, but I could still make out the features of her face . . . Not her body—it was too badly disfigured . . . She had been trapped and crushed between two rows of seats . . .

ROBERT: Oh!

WILLIAM: It was horrific . . . But I couldn't be mistaken—it was her . . . I also found some things on her body . . .

ROBERT: What?

WILLIAM [pulling some objects out of his pockets]: Here.

ROBERT: A gold cigarette case? But that could belong to another woman. If this is all you found . . .

WILLIAM: And this?

ROBERT: Her handbag!

WILLIAM: You see! There can be no doubt. You recognize this bag . . . Simone's bag. Her hands were clenched around it, her fingers tight with rigor mortis . . . I had to break the bones to release it . . .!

ROBERT: Ah . . .!

WILLIAM: The next day, I returned to Paris with the body of my poor darling . . . I had her buried in my family tomb next to my mother. I didn't let anyone know . . .

ROBERT: Then what did you do?

WILLIAM [exalted]: I locked myself away at home. I spent hours in despair and madness . . . I took her clothes, her jewellery, everything she wore. I breathed in their scent. And I stayed there hour after hour, like a lunatic, like a maniac, relishing in the spirit of her soul, her perfect soul . . .

ROBERT: Yes, yes, she was adorable!

WILLIAM: How could you know?

ROBERT: Yes . . .! It's a terrible loss . . .

WILLIAM: An irredeemable loss . . .! [*Pause*] Look at her little mirror . . . You know, she was terrified of breaking this mirror. It was in the bag, intact and undamaged, right next to this revolver . . . This revolver I gave her for protection if she was ever alone in the villa . . .

ROBERT   [*a little nervous*]: Is it loaded?

WILLIAM   [*gravely*]: Yes, it is. It is there, a solution to life, to memory, to sorrow . . .

ROBERT: William!

WILLIAM: And when the day comes when I can't take it any more, when I can't bear this misery . . . On that day . . .
[*He puts the revolver to his chest*]

ROBERT   [*leaping up and struggling to take the revolver off him*]: William!

WILLIAM   [*fighting back*]: No, I can't live any more! Let go of me!

ROBERT: You're losing your mind! I won't let you do it . . .

WILLIAM: You can't stop me! You have no right to stop me!

ROBERT: Stop!

WILLIAM   [*letting go of the revolver*]: But I tell you, I can't go on!

ROBERT   [*putting the revolver in his jacket pocket*]: It will take time, your sorrow will abate, you'll come to terms with it. I beg you, it will abate, you'll come to terms with it. I beg you, William, calm yourself!

WILLIAM: Give it back! Give me the gun!

ROBERT: No!

WILLIAM: If you have any pity, give it back!

ROBERT: Too late. You'll get it back when you have calmed down. William, you must stay alive! You just try to carry on!

WILLIAM: Ah, it's over. My life is destroyed . . . I loved her so much . . .! Goodbye!
They shake hands with great emotion. William exits. Night has fallen. The lamp and the fireplace casts only a feeble, reddish light. Lots of shadows in the corners and behind the furniture.

ROBERT   [*after a time of sombre reflection*]: I feel your agony . . .! But I don't have the right to cry out! What an abomination! To love someone more than anything in the world, to see her disappear and yet not be able to scream out in despair! *Silence. Seized in paroxysms of despair, Robert seems to be fighting against an idea. He hesitates several times and then makes up his mind. He sits on the divan and searches through the drawer in the little table. He finds a syringe and*

prepares it. He injects himself in the left forearm. He lolls
back onto the cushions and soon starts speaking as if in
a dream.

ROBERT: They found her . . . crushed between two rows of seats . . .
And . . . to take her handbag, her . . . bones . . . had to be
broken . . . the little bones . . . in her fingers . . .! Ah! I can
hear them cracking . . .! I don't want to . . . I don't want to
hear them breaking! [*He thrusts his head into the cushions.*
Then he gradually begins to seize on a desperate idea] Tell
me you aren't dead . . . I'm waiting for you . . .! Today is
the day, now is the hour that I told you to come to me . . .
Suddenly a gust of wind makes the window smash open;
breaking the glass. Robert is horrified and leaps up wildly
as if someone entered with the gust of wind. He stares in
horror as if he can see someone in the void, someone he can
hear in the silence.

VOICE OF SIMONE: Robert . . .! Robert . . .!! Robert . . .!!!

ROBERT   [*trembling*]: Who's there?

VOICE OF SIMONE: It's me. Voice of Simone.

ROBERT   [*scared*]: Voice of Simone . . .? It cannot be!

VOICE OF SIMONE: Yes. It's me. Don't you recognize my voice?

ROBERT   [*staring at a vision*]: But it's impossible!

VOICE OF SIMONE: I'm doing what you told me to do.

ROBERT: Go! Go away!

VOICE OF SIMONE: But you told me to come to you . . . I was scared I'd be late.
It was very difficult to come to you from *down there*!

ROBERT   [*terrified*]: From *down there* . . .!? [*Reasoning with himself*]
Oh, it's just a nightmare! As if hypnotism could work
beyond the grave!

VOICE OF SIMONE   [*laughing hideously*]: Ha! Ha! Ha . . .! Beyond the grave!

ROBERT   [*tripping over*]: Go away!

VOICE OF SIMONE: You want to force me away from you . . .?

ROBERT   [*recoiling*]: Don't come any nearer!

VOICE OF SIMONE: I obey. You're my master, my only master.

ROBERT   [*to himself*]: Yes, it's just a nightmare—a terrible nightmare.
[*He recoils again*] Please! I beg you! Please!

VOICE OF SIMONE: Do you feel guilty?

ROBERT: Yes . . .! Please, leave me alone . . . I beg you . . .!

VOICE OF SIMONE: But I have come to you—as you commanded me to.

ROBERT: Keep back!

VOICE OF SIMONE: Love is stronger than anything—even *death*!

ROBERT   [*forcing himself to take control*]: I command you to return
from whence you came . . .

VOICE OF SIMONE: You cannot command the dead. The dead command you.

ROBERT: Oh, make this nightmare end! For that's all it is, a
nightmare, a delusion in my mind . . .!

VOICE OF SIMONE: There's nothing you can do to stop me: I am dead.

ROBERT   [*sinking into his hallucination*]: I can escape you! I am alive!

VOICE OF SIMONE: Escape me? No, you cannot. I am coming to you . . .
I am coming to you . . .
*Robert is mad with fear, recoils again in the face of this
unreal visitor. He stumbles into the table and falls to the
floor in front of the divan. The lamp has fallen to the floor
and gone out. In the shadows, the flickering reddish light of
the fireplace is the only source of light.*

ROBERT: Ah! No! Not that!

VOICE OF SIMONE: I am coming to you!
*Suddenly in the darkness, the audience can see what Robert
has seen: the hideously mutilated corpse of a woman that
lurches towards Robert, touching him with hands stripped
of flesh.*

ROBERT: No! Don't touch me! Don't touch me! Let go of me! Aaaah!
No! NO!
*He shoots himself in the heart with the revolver. As he dies,
the vision begins to fade away, disappearing with the mind
that invented it. Through the window we hear the laughter
and singing of the carnival.*

CURTAIN

Orgy in the Lighthouse

(*L'Orgie dans le phare*, 1956)

A Grand Guignol Drama in One Act

Adapted by Eddie Muller from Alfred Machard's
L'Orgie dans le phare (**1956**)

First performed at the Hypnodrome, San Francisco, 2000

Preface

Orgy in the Lighthouse was translated and adapted by Eddie Muller for per-
formance by Thrillpeddlers as part of the Shocktoberfest of 2000. It was
revived in 2015, shortly before the closure of the Hypnodrome in early 2017.
The original play, *L'Orgie dans le phare*, premiered at the rue Chaptal in
July 1956 in a programme that otherwise consisted of well-established, early
Grand-Guignol favourites: *La Fiole*, a 1900 comedy by Max Maurey, which
appeared in eight seasons in total between 1900 and 1958; *La Dernière
Torture*, André de Lorde and Eugène Morel's 1904 drama set during the
Boxer Rebellion; and *Isolons-nous, Gustave!*, a comedy from 1917 by André
Mouëzy-Éon, who wrote over a dozen plays for the Grand-Guignol between
1908 and 1955. Its author, Alfred Machard, was the husband of Raymonde
Machard, the writer, essayist and feminist, who was in charge at the rue
Chaptal from 1954 to 1960.

Although Machard was 66 years old at the time, *L'Orgie dans le phare*
was his first play for the Théâtre du Grand-Guignol. His only other contribution was a comedy, *La Noce à papa*, which played in November of
the following year. Principally Machard was a writer of popular fiction, as
well as a screenwriter, director and occasional actor and his early novels
concerned themselves largely with the escapades of the Parisian criminal
underclass, the very same subject matter that had been the raw material
for Méténier and the other naturalist and early Grand-Guignol writers of
the *comedies rosses*. Novels such as *La Marmaille* (*The Gang*, 1935) and
Bout-de-Bibi, Enfant terrible (1917), as well as the romantic modern fairy
tale *La Femme d'une nuit* (1929), which was made into a film in 1931,
featuring Antonin Artaud, were all published by the respectable publishing house Flammarion, which had published Zola and Maupassant. Other
novels, published with the major publisher of pulp fiction J. Férenczi, such
as *Printemps sexuels* (*Sexual Spring*, 1926) and *Le Syndicat des fessés* (*The
Spankers' Union*, 1928), suggest an overtly erotic side to his writing that is

also evident in *L'Orgie dans le phare*. Raymonde Machard also published essays with Flammarion in the 1920s and 1930s, and a novel, *L'Œuvre de chair* (*Act of Flesh*, 1924) with Férenczi.

L'Orgie dans le phare was not the first occasion that the Grand-Guignol had employed the services of a pulp fiction writer. Between 1953 and 1955 Frédéric Dard, the writer of more than 300 novels, plays and screenplays, 175 of them concerning the adventures of his fictional detective Antoine San-Antonio, effectively operated as a writer-in-residence at the rue Chaptal, working alongside his friend and collaborator, the director Robert Hossein. During his eighteen-month tenure Dard wrote six plays for the Grand-Guignol, including *Les Salauds vont en enfer* (*The Wicked Go To Hell*, 1954), which was subsequently adapted into both a novel and a film (directed by Hossein) within two years, *La Chair de l'orchidée* (*The Flesh of the Orchid*, 1955), adapted with Marcel Duhamel from the novel by James Hadley Chase,[19] and *Les Assassins de Montchat* (1955), an adaptation from a novel by Paul Gordeaux.[20]

Nevertheless, the positioning of *L'Orgie dans le phare* within a programme made up of Grand-Guignol classics, serves as a reminder that it sits at a very important juncture in the later development of the Grand-Guignol. While Raymonde Machard was trying to arrest the decline of the Grand-Guignol by bringing in new writers with a background in popular fiction, she was still relying to some extent on the traditional repertoire to draw in the audiences. The shift towards the more sensational was completed the following year with the arrival of Eddy Ghilain at the rue Chaptal; he dominated the final years of the Grand-Guignol, as writer, actor and director, with his more overtly sexual displays of horror.

Although culturally the lighthouse is used as a symbol of hope and refuge, in the Grand-Guignol it evokes a more sinister atmosphere. Here the reference is to the lighthouses that adorn the rugged and storm-battered Atlantic coastline of Brittany, which stand out in the mind not only as places of resistance against the untamed and sublime forces of nature, but are also linked with ideas of remoteness, isolation and vulnerability. In the Grand-Guignol the lighthouse is a prison more than a sanctuary, a place that is outside normal society.

In the first instance, *L'Orgie dans le phare* refers back to the classic Grand-Guignol lighthouse play *Gardiens de phare* (*The Lighthouse Keepers*) by Paul Autier and Paul Cloquemin, which had become a much-revived

---

[19] Marcel Duhamel was an actor and writer who also founded the *série noire*, a series of hard-boiled detective novels focusing on American writers such as Raymond Chandler, Dashiell Hammett, Ed McBain, Chester Himes, Jim Thompson and the English thriller writer James Hadley Chase. One legacy of the series is the widespread use of the 'noir' to describe novels and films of the genre.
[20] Paul Gordeaux was a writer, journalist and humourist who was also the first editor-in-chief of *Paris Match*.

favourite of the Grand-Guignol repertoire since its premiere in 1905 and memorable for its innovative use of sound effects to evoke fear among the audience (see Hand and Wilson 2002: 109–20). In some ways *L'Orgie dans le phare* is an updated version of the earlier play, introducing a more overtly erotic storyline that would have been more acceptable to a 1950s audience than to one of the *belle époque*. Whereas it is an invasion of rabies that ultimately does for the unfortunate father and son team, Bréhan and Yvon, in *Gardiens de phare*, it is an invasion of sexual promiscuity and drunkenness that seals the fate of Legonadee, Yann and Yves.

Both plays also document the decline into madness, provoked by the isolation and prison-like circumstances that the characters find themselves in. Their mental fragility is tested and ultimately broken by the circumstances of being outside the safety of normal society, and the storms that batter the lighthouses in both plays are assaults on their states of mind, as much as on the lighthouse itself. It is not the lighthouse that represents sanctuary, but the community back on land that they have left. In this sense, *L'Orgie dans le phare*, in particular, is a play about being 'on the edge' in all senses of the phrase—geographically, mentally and morally.

In addition, of course, the lighthouse stands as a potent phallic symbol, and in both these plays the lighthouse is an undeniably male space. In fact, in *L'Orgie dans le phare* it is the breaching of the male space with the arrival of Rosa and Nini that initiates the descent of Yann and Yves into sexual depravity and of Legonadee into an alcoholic stupor. In spite of the lighthouse symbolically standing resolute and erect as it weathers the storm, inside the men show themselves to be weaker and more vulnerable. Interestingly, these themes of isolation, mental breakdown and boastful, yet fragile masculinity are also the core themes of Robert Eggers's evocative black and white film *The Lighthouse* (2019).

On another level *L'Orgie dans le phare* can be read as a 'siege' play. The three lighthouse keepers themselves are under siege from their own psychological and moral demons in the form of sexual depravity and alcoholism, while at the same time the lighthouse itself is under siege from Mother Nature in the form of the tempest that has been unleashed, so preventing their escape. It is interesting to note that *L'Orgie dans le phare* was programmed alongside *La Dernière Torture*, another classic siege play from the Grand-Guignol repertoire. The plays are, of course, very different in terms of scale and scope, but they are both siege plays nonetheless. In *La Dernière Torture* the relief, in the form of the Allied Forces, arrives to lift the siege, but ironically a moment too late to avoid tragedy, whereas in *L'Orgie dans le phare* the one hope of rescue, in the sense of the one hope of restoring the lighthouse keepers' moral integrity (as well as saving the lives of Rosa and Nini), by preventing Guermane's boat from sinking, is literally dashed on the rocks below. In both cases the conclusion is played out in terms of complete mental and moral collapse.

ORGY IN THE LIGHTHOUSE

A Grand Guignol Drama in One Act

Adapted by Eddie Muller from Alfred Machard's
L'Orgie dans le phare (1956)

First performed at the Hypnodrome, San Francisco, 2000

Cast
Legonadee
Yann
Yves
Rosa
Nini

Lights up on the control room of a lighthouse, which also serves as home to the light's operators. The room has three entrances: a trapdoor in the floor, which leads to the long spiraling stairway down; a door at the rear which opens onto an exterior catwalk, and a staircase to the turret above, which houses the massive lamp—at the top of these stairs is a trapdoor that opens into the ceiling. The only widows are small portholes on either side of the rear door, and in the side walls.

The room is monastically spare: a pair of cots, two stools, a single small table. The cupboard contains only enough plates and cups for two men. A phonograph is the sole source of entertainment. Against the wall stand a row of kerosene cans, used to fuel the lamp. The walls are hung with nautical gear, a barometer, buoys, life jackets, foul-weather attire. There is also, conspicuously adorned and lighted, a shrine—with burning candles—to the Virgin Mary.

Legonadee, the wizened veteran lighthouse operator, peers through a hand-held telescope toward the shore. Yann, his young assistant, kneels praying before the Virgin.

LEGONADEE: What a mob! The streets are packed from the wharf all the way up the hill.

YANN: As it should be for the holiest feast of the season.

LEGONADEE: Quite the festival. Indeed.

YANN: Too bad we can't be ashore this evening when the bonfires are lit. And the girls come out to dance.

LEGONADEE: So, Yann—are you devout, or just horny?

YANN   (*embarrassed*): I just like to dance.

LEGONADEE: No need to play dumb with me, kid. I was young once too, you know. Trust me, I know what it's like to be here weeks on end without a woman. But after a while . . . well, let's just say that it if I was ashore tonight . . . I might seek out a drop or two of Calvados.

YANN: Ah, that's your vice, Legonadee.

LEGONADEE: Vice? Since when is it a sin to enjoy something good?

YANN   (*rising, going to window*): Hey, take it easy. Give me the telescope.

Legonadee hands it over. Yann peers through it.

LEGONADEE: What's going on now?

YANN: They've reached the pier. The priest is leading the farmers.

LEGONADEE: He'll bless the boats.

YANN: Yeah. Everybody is kneeling now.

LEGONADEE: The benediction!

In the distance, the faint sound of bells. Legonadee whips off his cap and kneels. Yann quickly drops to his knees before the Virgin Mary. Both men cross themselves, and begin murmuring a prayer:

LEGONADEE AND YANN: Hail Mary, full of grace, the Lord is with thee, blessed art thou among woman and blessed is the fruit—

A head pops through the trapdoor in the floor, blowing a loud blast from a toy trumpet, startling the praying pair. The man (Yves) clambers into the room through the trapdoor. He's wearing a sailor's suit festooned with decorations from the festival. He's a little tipsy.

LEGONADEE: Jesus, Mary and Joseph!

YVES: Did I scare the hell out of you?

LEGONADEE: Yes!

YVES: Good! Saved you all that time praying!

Yann strides forward and wraps the man in a warm embrace.

YANN: Yves! It's so good to see you!

YVES: Thought I'd drop up for a visit. Not everybody's kid brother lives in a lighthouse.

LEGONADEE: Next time, forget the horn.

YANN: Are you on leave?

YVES: Forty-eight hours of liberty.

YANN: But how'd you get out here?

YVES: Sailed, of course. Straight through the reef.

YANN: Are you crazy? The current is murder this time of year!

YVES: It's shorter . . . for a good sailor.

Legonadee slaps Yves' shoulder proudly.

LEGONADEE:	And you made sure to tie the boat up good and tight?
YVES:	I know what I'm doing. I know the tides are bad. That's why they need you out here.
YANN:	Where'd you get the boat?
YVES:	Rented it. At Guivic.
YANN:	You sailed out from Guivic?
YVES:	After I took the train from Brest.
YANN:	You saw Mama.
YVES:	She wasn't home.
	Yann looks dejected.
YVES:	She'd already left for the Isles this morning.
YANN:	I can't believe she'd miss the festival.
YVES:	Are you kidding? There are bigger festivals over there. She went over on Guerman's boat. The steamer.
YANN:	That piece of junk?
YVES:	What's wrong with it? I've been on it.
LEGONADEE:	It's ancient, that's what wrong with it. I saw the damn thing just this morning, not more than a stone's throw away, this side of the black rocks. Wheezing against the current like it was on its last legs!
YANN	*(forlorn)*: If I'd known Mama was aboard I'd have gone out on the catwalk and waved. If they were that close she'd have seen me for sure. She probably looked up here as they passed.
LEGONADEE:	I'm sure she waved, Yann.
YVES:	The apple of his mama's eye . . .
YANN:	I wish I'd known . . .
YVES:	Well, I was told they're not coming back till tonight, so I didn't want to stay in Guivic.
YANN	*(smiling again)*: So you came out to see me.
YVES:	Here I am.
YANN	*(seriously)*: But you did go to church first, right? It is a feast day, after all . . .
YVES:	Sure, sure. I know.
YANN:	Why didn't you join the procession?
YVES:	I don't know . . . I felt like coming out here instead.
YANN:	It's bad luck not to join the procession. And then sailing out here alone. My God, you took a chance.
YVES	*(slow smile)*: Who said I came alone?
	Yann and Legonadee stare at each other. Yves lifts the trap in the floor. He blows his trumpet into the void. Far below, a toy trumpet replies.
YANN:	Who came with you?
LEGONADEE:	Guys from your ship?
YVES:	Now what would I bring them for?
YANN:	Yves, who is it?
YVES:	Well . . . it's some . . . girls.
LEGONADEE:	Girls! You know better than that! You know the rules! No visitors! And certainly no female visitors!

YVES:	Take it easy! Are they up here? I made them promise to stay below.
YANN:	You missed the procession to come out here with girls?
YVES:	Well, I wanted to catch the tide . . .
YANN:	. . . On a festival day . . .
YVES:	You used to do OK with the girls on festival days. At the bonfire.
YANN:	Yves—that was after the procession. How many are there?
YVES:	Two.
LEGONADEE:	You know the rules! A lighthouse is government property!
YANN:	And they're just waiting down there, huh?
YVES:	Both of them. Two.
YANN:	Still in the boat? I'd see them if I looked over the catwalk?
YVES:	They're inside. At the bottom of the steps. *A louder trumpet blast comes from below, followed by the sound of female laughter.*
LEGONADEE:	Oh my God, they're coming up!
YVES:	If I tell them not to, they won't.
YANN:	Two of them, huh?
YVES:	A pair. Two.
YANN:	Young?
YVES:	No—I dragged a couple of old broads out here.
YANN:	Pretty?
YVES:	And that's not all. (*He indicates large breasts.*) These girls are the real stuff. And what's even better . . .
LEGONADEE:	If you think that (*he mimics the breast gesture*) is a reason to break regulations— *Legonadee moves to slam shut the trapdoor.* *Yves stops him with a hand on his shoulder.* *Legonadee stares at him angrily.*
YVES:	How about. . . . (*Yves pantomimes drinking.*) *Legonadee's face softens.*
YVES:	They've got a few bottles with them.
LEGONADESE:	Bottles of what?
YVES	(*winking at Yann*): Calvados. Four bottles, to be exact.
LEGONADEE	(*incredulous*): Really?
YVES:	Would I tease about such a thing, Pop?
LEGONADEE	I suppose not . . . but still . . . it's against the rules.
YVES:	But, Pop—I brought them all this way for you. I paid good money in town.
LEGONADEE:	That was a lovely, generous thought.
YVES:	And besides, who will know if they do come up here? There's just the three of us, and we're not going to say anything.
LEGONADEE:	Ah, it'd just . . . the regulations . . .
YANN:	They're not exactly enemy spies, you know.

LEGONADEE: So you know these girls well?

YVES: Ah, yes. I'd say I know them intimately.

YANN: It's not like we'll be getting a surprise inspection today.

LEGONADEE: OK . . . let them come up.

YVES: (*calling down*): Come aboard, maties! (*to Legonadee*) You won't regret it, Pop.
The girls' horns sound—very close—and suddenly they burst through the space in the trap.

LEGONADEE (*aware he was being played*): Well that was a quick trip!
First in is Rosa—earthy, dark and sluttishly dressed. Trailing is Nini, a pale, ethereal blonde with a lovely face and figure. Each woman is toting two bottles.

ROSA: Jesus Christ! Any longer and my ass would be branded by those steps! (*she rubs her lush derriere as she surveys the scene*) Which one's your brother?
Yves points to Yann.

ROSA (*a long look at Legonadee*): Thanks heaven for small favors. (*She eyeballs Yann up and down.*) OK, you did all right, Nini. He's cute. (*to Yann*) Hi, Yann. This is Nini . . . my cousin. She may not look it, but she's smart . . . About everything.

NINI: (*shyly*): How do you do?

YANN: (*shaking hands*): How are you?

YVES: And this would be Legonadee. I told you about him.

ROSA: Papa. Hello, Papa.

NINI: Pleased to meet you.

YVES: I promised them they'd see a real working lighthouse.

LEGONADEE (*proudly*): This one is mine, ladies. The most beautiful lighthouse on the entire coast. It stands forty meters tall—

ROSA: Save it. I climbed every goddamn step on my hands and knees. What shall we do with these? (*She waves the bottles.*)

LEGONADEE (*gathering the bottles from both eagerly*): Allow me, allow me.
Legonadee sets the bottles on the table and avidly pulls the cork from one, sniffing the contents ecstatically. Meanwhile, Yann steps toward Rosa, noticing something on her cheek.

YANN: What happened here?

ROSA (*evading him*): Nothing—it's just a scratch.

YANN: The blood's still fresh. Did you cut yourself coming up?

ROSA: Ask your brother.

NINI: Actually, it was pretty funny. This morning as we were watching the procession go by, Rosa looked right at the priest and said—

YVES: SHUT UP!

ROSA (*gesturing to Nini*): Yeah. It wasn't as funny as all that.

NINI: Is it me, or is it really hot in here?

ROSA   (*examining the place*): Hot as the hinges of Hell.
             Doesn't it make you crazy. Being cooped up inside a
             lighthouse?

NINI: I didn't imagine it like this at all.

ROSA: What the hell'd you imagine?

NINI: I thought there'd be a big light, you know?

LEGONADEE: Oh, of course—the big lamp. Yes, it's most interesting!
             Nini looks around, perplexed.

ROSA: I don't see any big lamp.

YANN: (*pointing*): Above us.

YVES: Pop, why don't you show the girls your big lamp. Explain
             how it works. Then when you come down, they'll be so
             grateful you'll get a little snort of their Calvados.

LEGONADEE: Yes! Yes, certainly. I'd like that. This way, ladies.
             *He leads them up the stairs and through the ceiling trap.
             Yves and Yann admire their backsides as they ascend the
             steps and disappear.*

YVES: Well? What do you think?

YANN: They seem all right.

YVES: Which one do you want?

YANN: I don't know . . . they're both fine, I guess.

YVES: Rosa, the dark one, she's my girl.

YANN: Oh, you should have said. Well, the blonde is nice.
             Different.

YVES: She goes for you. I can tell.

YANN: No. She's just . . .

YVES: Trust me. She's got it for you.

YANN: You think? Do you think she might . . .

YVES: I know it.

YANN: She's not married or anything?

YVES: Married? These girls?

YANN: Well, it's a holy day, and I don't want to commit a sin.

YVES: Yann! What do you think these split-tails are?
             They work the Pompadour in Brest.

YANN: What's that?

YVES: Oh, c'mon. It's a whorehouse.

YANN: Oh, the Pompadour.

YVES: Yeah, right.

YANN: Uh, huh.

YVES: Look, Yann—I made a bet with a couple of my mates:
             Jacques and Le Ruedee, the helmsman on my boat.

YANN: What kind of bet?

YVES: That I'd bring a couple of these snatches from the
             Pompadour home with me. That was the bet.
             What was I supposed to do? They said 'You'd never
             dare take girls like that home for the feast,' and I said
             'Like hell I wouldn't.'

YANN: What was the bet?

YVES: A round of drinks. But that's not the point.
I couldn't back down. It was a matter of honor!

YANN: Whose honor?

YVES: Mine! And theirs, of course! Theirs!

YANN: You brought them to Mama's house?

YVES: What do you think I am? An idiot? I left them at a bar
near the station when I went home. I told the guys in
the bar they were waiting for their husbands. Since
Mama wasn't home, we decided to come out here.
Hell, I thought I was doing you a favor!

YANN: Then I guess maybe Nini . . .

YVES: Listen, brother—don't tie yourself in knots trying to figure
how to . . . you know. That's what she was made for.
*Legonadee and the women descend from the floor
above.*

ROSA: OK, knock off the low mass down here. (*she blows her
toy trumpet*)

LEGONADEE   (*proudly*): She thinks my lamp is spectacular.

ROSA: Biggest I've ever seen.

NINI: And I'm gonna get to see it lit.

LEGONADEE: This evening, my dear. This evening.

NINI   (*to Yann*): He said that lots of birds kill themselves
up there.

YANN: The light blinds them. It happens a lot.

NINI: I think it's cruel, that light.

YANN: What would be better? To let the sailors pile into the
rocks down there?

YVES: The coast is very dangerous here, especially at night.

LEGONADEE: From up here the rocks look like pebbles . . .
but they'll split a ship wide open.

YVES   (*pulling Nini over to him*): Why are we talking about
rocks? (*He pushes Nini over to Yann.*) How do you like
my kid brother?

NINI   (*studying him*): He's a good-looking boy.

ROSA: You want to kiss him?

NINI: If he wants to.

ROSA: Kid? You want to kiss her?

YANN   (*acting macho*): You kidding? Sure.

ROSA: Well, get to it.
Nina goes to Yann. He kisses her lightly.

ROSA: That's a kiss? Show him, Nini.
*Nini takes Yann's face between her hands and kisses him
passionately, pressing her body into his. Yann laughs
nervously.*

ROSA: Wow, you sure don't take after your brother.

NINI   (*made uneasy by Yann's embarrassment*): It's awful
stuffy in here—can't you open a door or something?

YANN   (*bolting to the door*): No problem! How's that for a
            view! (*He scans the horizon.*) Uh, oh . . . looks like a
            storm brewing. (*Checking the barometer.*) Falling.

YANN   (*moving next to Yves*): A seven-point drop since
            morning. Could be a big blow.

NINI: What are you talking about? What's going to happen?

ROSA: You heard—a storm. (*She walks to the doorway, looks
            out.*) Yves, come look at the sea.

NINI: We have to go. I'm scared to be in boats when the
            sea is bad.

YANN: There's lots of time. Anyway, it might pass right by here.

NINI: No. No. I want to go. Rosa!
            *She heads toward the door, following Yves and Rosa
            onto the catwalk.*

LEGONADEE   (*to Yann*): You better make your move, kid.
            She's scared. Reassure her.

YANN: But she wants to go . . .
            *Nini comes wobbling back into the room from the
            catwalk.*

NINI: I can't . . . Oh my God . . .

YANN: What's the matter? Are you all right?

NINI   (*swaying*): We're so high up! It's such a long way down!
            I . . . I'm dizzy.

YANN: You're just not used to it.

NINI: My God, if you fell off . . .

YANN: You'd make a lot of fish happy.

NINI: How can you joke about it!
            *During this whole exchange, Legonadee has surreptitiously
            uncorked the bottles and lovingly inhaled their bouquet.
            He then opens the sparse cupboard.*

LEGONADEE: We're not used to company. We only have two glasses.
            So sorry.

ROSA   (*re-entering arm-in-arm with Yves*): I think we can work
            it out, Pop.

LEGONADEE: I'd be happy to just drink from one of the bottles and
            leave you the glasses. I don't need to be fancy for just
            one little mouthful.

YANN: Pop . . . just a short one, all right? No more.

LEGONADEE: It's feast day, kid. Celebrating is encouraged.

YANN: I'm not going to stand your watch! (*to Yves*) When he's
            lit you can't do a thing with him. He goes out cold.
            Might as well be dead.

LEGONADEE   (*filling the glasses*): A drink for our guests!

ROSA   (*taking hers*): About time. Maybe this'll liven things up.
            You said we'd have some laughs up here.

YVES: Okay, let's laugh! (*He blows his trumpet.*)

ROSA: Have a drink, lover. (*To Nini.*) What's up with you, kid?
            Can't get him in the mood? You must be slipping.

NINI   (*affronted*): He likes me fine. He's just not ready yet.

ROSA: How can you not be ready living out here all alone?

NINI   (*offering Yann her glass*): Here, have a drink. Put your lips right where mine were.
Yann does as she says.

ROSA: Oh, Christ. Hey kid, why don't you ask her what's on her mind?

NINI   (*pressing against Yann, touching him*): He knows just what I'm thinking . . . You're thinking it too, aren't you, honey?
Yann's resistance fades; he starts caressing Nini.
This excites Rosa, who takes up with Yves.

ROSA: That's more like it. How 'bout some for me, tiger? C'mon . . .
While the amorous pairs entangle, Legonadee takes to his beloved Calvados, savoring several long swigs.

ROSA   (*suddenly breaking away from Yves*): Whew! Suddenly I'm feeling a little faint.
She falls onto the bunk and stretches luxuriously.

NINI   (*coming out of a heated kiss with Yann*): See? Nothing to be afraid of.
Yann pulls her back to him, and kisses her harder. Clearly aroused.

ROSA   (*beckoning Yves*): C'mere . . . bite my neck. The way I like it.
Yves descends on Rosa, but she teasingly pushes away.

ROSA   (*laughing*): Savage pig!

NINI   (*to Yann*): You're a good kisser. And a nice guy. I think I could really like you.

YANN   (*impatient*) Yeah, I like you too.

LEGONADEE   Care for another?

YVES   (*face in Rosa's bosom*): Maybe later.

ROSA   (*pushing Yves off her*): Let's have it, old man! I never turn down a drink.
Rosa fills a glass and holds it out to Yves.

ROSA: Down the hatch!
Yves leers at her, sloshes down half the drink, hands it back. She teases him with her looks and body language all through the following. Silently, he stalks her around the cramped space as she feigns disinterest in him.
They're gearing up for something nasty.
Across the room, Nini lifts her blouse.

NINI: I've got nice skin. It's soft. Go on, touch it.

YANN: It's so smooth . . .

NINI: Do you like me?

ROSA   (*looking at the cans against the wall*): What's all this stuff?

YVES: Kerosene for the lamp.

ROSA: That's a lotta fuel.

LEGONADEE   (*pointing upstairs proudly*): That's a lotta lamp.
Rosa notices the phonograph.

ROSA: Hey, how about some music. I could dance for you . . .
you'd like it.
*Hearing that, Yann, excited, moves for the small stash
of records.*

LEGONADEE   (*stopping Yann with a glare*): No music. Only
instructional records. Government issue.

ROSA: Jesus Christ! I sure wouldn't want to live here all the
time!

LEGONADEE: You'll want to especially avoid it in the winter.

ROSA: Bored to death . . . what a life! Huh, Nini?
Nini is engrossed with Yann.

NINI: I could get used to it.
*Legonadee slips something from the cupboard while all
eyes are on Nini and Yann. He plunks it on the table
loudly, regaining Rosa's attention. It's a woman's shoe.*

ROSA: What's with the shoe?

LEGONADEE: A souvenir. Of our last visitor.

ROSA: Ah! So you get women up here? (*She inspects the shoe.*)
Where's the other one? Maybe they'll fit me. (*to Yves*)
You'd like me in these.

LEGONADEE: She only had one.

ROSA   (*noticing something wrong*): Why's it all stained?

LEGONADEE: Sea water.

ROSA: Sea water?

LEGONADEE: The tide brought her to us. On the rocks.

ROSA: She was drowned? Dead?

YANN   (*suddenly out of his amorous spell*): She was young.
Blonde, with a lovely figure.

NINI: Prettier than me?

LEGONADEE: Hard to tell. The crabs had gotten most of her face.

ROSA AND NINI   (*in unison*): Oh my God! Stop!

YANN: That's right, a nest of them. In her head.
*Nini looks like she's going to be sick. She turns away
from Yann.*

LEGONADEE: Yann, take it easy. It'll be OK, little lady.

YVES: Guess she's not used to that kind of thing.

ROSA   (*she consoles Nini*): Who is?

YANN: I'm sorry.

YVES   (*pulling Yann aside*): Idiot! You wanna ruin everything?

LEGONADEE   (*pouring another drink and taking it to Nini*): I'm sorry,
too. It's just that out here we're more familiar with
funerals than celebrations. That's how it is with the sea
and the tides and the currents. (*He gives her the brandy,
but she turns back to Rosa, rejecting it.*) It'll improve your
outlook.

ROSA: I think it's the heat making her sick. Here,
c'mon—let's get some air.
Rosa nudges Nini to do as she does: slip off her dress.
Beneath they wear camisoles.

YVES   *(to Yann)*: Don't say I never brought you anything.
She's yours. Get to it.

YANN: Do you think she'll tell?

YVES: Tell who? What are you talking about?

YANN   *(puffing up)*: Yeah. You're right.
Legonadee brings each woman a Calvados. Surveying
them, he can't help a smile and a sigh.

ROSA: You getting ideas, old man? At your age?

LEGONADEE: I'm not as old as you might think. There's still some
ammo in the gun.

ROSA   *(she throws an arm around him)*: Ha! You married,
Pop?

LEGONADEE: With eleven children.

ROSA: Christ! You're not a man—you're a plague!
The women laugh.

LEGONADEE: I've had it all. This is all I need now. *(He cradles his
Calvados.)* I'll just slip upstairs and prime the wick, as it
were. *(Laughs.)* Get to it, boys. All this is yours!
Legonadee climbs the stairs.
Yves pulls Rosa into his lap, shoves Nini toward Yann.
He and Rosa clutch and kiss.

NINI   *(to Yann)*: I can't believe I'm so shy with you. That
means I really like you. I'd even let you give me a
ventilator.

YANN: A what?

NINI: Don't you know what a ventilator is?

YANN: No idea.

NINI: Jeez, he really doesn't know . . .

ROSA: Shut up and show him already.

NINI: Open your mouth.
She gives him a sensual, open-mouthed, tongue kiss.
While all this is happening, Legonadee has silently
descended the staircase and lifted another bottle of
Calvados. He admires it the way Yves has admired
Rosa's body. He kisses the bottle as he climbs through
the trap and closes it behind him.

ROSA   *(breaking from Yves' embrace)*: I still feel like dancing.
(She leafs through the records.) Hey! There is music!
This is a tango!

YVES: Like at the Pompadour!
Rosa puts the record on and starts dancing a sexy
come-on.

NINI   *(to Yann)*: You wanna dance?

YANN: I like to dance.

NINA: Really? You know how?

ROSA *(dancing over to Yann)*: Who taught you—the old man?
*The women laugh, then Rosa scoops Nini into her
arms and they tango together across the room, stopping
dramatically (in time to the music) before the shrine to
the Virgin.*

NINI: Look . . . *(pointing to the statue)* Who's that remind
you of?

ROSA *(quietly, just between girls)*: Oh shit—she looks just like
Madam Gitaud!

NINI: Don't she, though? We oughta take it back as a gift!
They both howl with laughter.

YANN *(protecting the shrine)*: Why are you laughing?
You mustn't laugh at her!

YVES *(taking Rosa in hand)*: Yeah, let's not have a repeat of
this morning!

YANN *(angrily)*: What were you saying about her?

ROSA *(tauntingly)*: Want to know what she said? Really?

YANN: Tell me what you said!

ROSA: Nini said: 'Gee, she looks just like the virgin at home
we say our prayers to every day.' You got a problem
with that?

YANN *(to Nini)*: Is that true? Is that all you said?

NINI: Well . . . yeah. Honest.

ROSA: You got a Bible around here? She'll swear on it.
So will I!
*Shrugging off Yann's anger, she turns to Yves and
gives him a shove. Drunk, he stumbles backwards
and collapses on the bed.*

NINI *(to Yann)*: Hey, c'mon-I thought we were gonna dance.

ROSA *(as she approaches Yves)*: Go on you two-get to it.
(sotto voce) The Virgin Mary wants to see you going at
it. *(louder, to Yves)* C'mon, tiger. Show me some moves.

YVES: No. You come down here.

ROSA *(pulling Yves to his feet)*: Get up here! You know how
I like it.
*She takes charge, putting one of Yves' hands on her ass,
encouraging his lust. Outside, the sound of the storm
rises, competing with the music. Across the room,
Nini has been dancing with Yann, and she uses Rosa's
aggressiveness as her cue.*

NINI: You can hold me tighter, too. Don't worry . . .
I don't bite.
*Yves starts manhandling Rosa: pulling on her hair,
squeezing her waist, grinding his hips against her . . .*

ROSA: Oh, yeah. That's it. Hurt me, baby.

NINI *(quietly to Yann)*: You will write to me, won't you?
Promise?

YVES: Uhhh . . . the room is spinning.

ROSA: I love that feeling. The world goes upside-down.
         *Outside, the distant sound of screeching cries within the
         storm. Nini stops dancing.*

NINI: What was that?

YANN: What? Why'd you stop?

NINI: It sounded like screaming.

YANN: That's just the seagulls. They always come back to shore
         just before a storm.
         The storm grows louder.

NINI: I'm scared.

YANN   (*tenderly*): Trust me, there's nothing to be afraid of.
         I promise.

ROSA   (*genuinely concerned for Nini*): Hey, kid . . . it'll be
         OK. Quit worrying. (*She turns off the phonograph.*)
         Remember the song the madam used to sing?
         (*She sings.*)
         There was a little hunchback
         Who had a twisted spout
         He was so all screwed up
         The Madam said 'Get out.'
         She wouldn't let him in
         In spite of all his gold
         She left him standing on the stoop
         With his spout out in the cold.
         *Yves guffaws. Nini manages a wistful laugh, despite her
         fear. Yann joins in, a little embarrassed.*
         A crash of thunder startles everyone.

NINI: Oh my God!

ROSA: I knew it was coming. Felt it in my bones. We're safe up
         here, right?

YVES   (*very drunk*): It's a lighthoush! Safest place in a shtorm.

NINI: Is that true, what the old man said? That the drowned
         people wash up here?

YANN: I've found five since I've been here.
         *Nina sits on the bed beside Yann and buries her head
         in his chest. She whimpers like a child. Yann strokes her
         hair tenderly, then lowers his hand to her breasts. As
         she's helpless, he takes full advantage. She responds.
         Rosa, the fire out of her, looks away from them. She
         tries to reignite herself to ward off the storm's threat:*

ROSA: C'mon, you bastard. They're not gonna have all the
         fun! (*She flops down on the other bed—and cries out in
         pain.*) Ow! What the hell!
         *She lifts herself up and pulls from beneath her the
         drowned girl's shoe. She rubs her bottom while
         observing the shoe—then hurls it across the room.*

ROSA: Goddamn dead girl's shoe!

Yves looms over her and Rosa lies back, beckoning.
Yves turns down the gas lamp on the table and the
room darkens. The four fold into each other as the
storm RAGES—
Howling winds. Booming thunder. Screeching gulls.
Waves pounding the rocks. Gradually, the silhouetted
sex subsides, and the figures lie still. Yves slides off the
bunk onto the floor. Rosa is passed out. Yann and Nina
are blissfully entwined, like true lovers, sleeping.
After a long pause, Yves stirs.

YVES   (*dreaming drunk*): Hey you guys, pay up! I did it! I took
          them home with me. Right through the streets. You got
          the next round. And the next! (*A clap of thunder.*) Hey!
          The guns! (*He staggers up.*) Hit the deck! They're firing
          the four-oh-sixes! (*Lightning flashes.*) How'd I end up
          down in the hold? Where are you guys?
          Yves staggers to a porthole and peers out.

YVES: This weather! Mother Nature-you bitch. (*He opens the*
          porthole and feels the wind on his face.) Ah, you feel good!

ROSA   (*singing*): There was a little hunchback who had a
          twisted spout . . .
          Yves turns into the darkness, seeking the voice.

ROSA: He was so all screwed up. The madam said 'Get out.'

YVES: The lighthouse! We're in the lighthouse.
          A siren blares out, audible over the raging storm.

YVES: Legonadee! Where are you? Old man!

ROSA: Forget that old fart. C'mere and kiss me—the way I like it.
          The siren grows louder.

YVES: Can't you hear that?

ROSA: It's seagulls, baby. C'mon back to bed. Love me.

YVES: Shut up! (he slaps her face) Listen!
          The siren—even more insistent.

YVES: It's a siren!

ROSA: So, it's a siren. Jesus.

YVES: That means a boat is in trouble! Out there somewhere!
          (*He runs to the porthole.*) It's so damn dark! Where's
          the hell's the light? (*Stunned realization.*) The light is
          out! The light is out!

ROSA: What are you talking about?

YVES   (*charging up the stairs*): Legonadee! (*Banging on the*
          trap.) Legonadee! Turn on the light! (*Bangs until he*
          gives up, starts down.) Yann! Yann! Where the hell
          are you!
          The siren grows louder.

ROSA: Jesus! It's close!

YVES   (*looking through the porthole*): They'll hit the rocks!
          (*A flash of lightning.*) It's Guerman's boat! Oh my
          God, Yann! It's Guerman's boat! Headed straight for

the rocks! They'll all be killed! Legonadee!!! (*He bolts up the stairs again.*) Legonadee! (*He beats on the trap door.*) Wake up, Legonadee!!!

NINI (*waking*): What's happening? Rosa?

ROSA: I'm here.

YVES: LEGONADEE!!!

NINI: What's going on?

ROSA: A ship's in trouble.
Yann is slow to awaken, grunting.

YVES (*down the stairs, to Yann*): Yann! Wake up! Wake up!

YANN (*still drowsy*): Mmmmm . . . take it easy.
The siren is very close. The siren continues throughout the following. Nini screams and buries her head in Yann's chest. Yves rushes to his brother and shoves Nini away. Yann looks at Yves, bewildered.

YVES: Yann! The siren! Listen! It's Guermane's boat, calling for help! Guermane's boat! (*A beat.*) Mama is on that boat!

YANN: Mama?

YVES: And the lamp is out!

YANN: What?

YVES: Legonadee is drunk! He must have passed out!

YANN: It's Guermane's boat?

YVES: He can't find the passage in the dark! He'll hit the rocks! (*Rising.*) Mama!

NINI (*clutching Yann*): I'm so scared!

YANN (*barely noticing her*): Let go of me.

NINI: I'm so afraid. What can we do?

YANN: Get away! (*He slaps her.*)

YVES: Screw that bitch! We have to have light! We have to get Legonadee! (*Yann staggers up the stairs.*) He must have locked it! It won't budge!

YANN (*pounding on the trap*): Legonadee! LEGONADEE!

NINI (*running to Rosa*): I'm scared, Rosa. I'm so scared.

ROSA: Shut up, Nini. So am I.

YANN: The bastard! He must be out cold! (*The siren wails.*) Oh dear God—spare them!

NINI: I wanna get out of here. Please, get me out of here . . .

ROSA: Take it easy, kid.

YANN (*striding to Nini—he hits her again*): Bitch! Shut up! Shut up! (*Moving to Yves.*) Can't we get out of here? Please?

YVES (*shoving her*): Get away! This is all your fault!

ROSA: My fault? What did I do?

YANN: The two of you! Coming here with your filthy mouths! A couple of dirty whores! On a holy day! With your dirty talk and your dirty songs!

ROSA: Screw you, choir boy! You didn't mind us till this minute!

NINI: You said you liked me.

YANN: Didn't I tell you to shut up? You're worse that she is—
        laughing at the Virgin! Blasphemer! That's why all this
        is happening now!

YVES   (*pointing at Rosa*): No! It was her! She's the one!
        At the procession today, she insulted the sacrament!

YANN: What!

YVES: Father Andre heard it, clearly. He looked right at me
        and said: 'Get away from here with that woman—she's
        doing the devil's work.' And he pointed right at Rosa!

YANN: Father Andre? Called her the devil?

ROSA: You're both crazy.

YVES: Yann! The Virgin! Your statue of the Virgin is gone!
        They stole it! (*To Rosa.*) Give it back or I'll kill you.

ROSA: What is the matter with you? The both of you.
        Those people need help!

YVES: You're gonna die.
        The brothers close in on Rosa.

ROSA: Wait, wait . . . Listen to me! I'll tell you the truth!
        (*A beat.*) She did it! She's the one!

NINI: Rosa?

ROSA: She thought your statue looked like the madam at
        the Pompadour . . . (*Lightning flashes.*) And at the
        procession? She was the one . . . she told me to laugh
        when the procession went by.

NINI: Rosa . . . I didn't. Oh my God, I did not do that.

YVES   (*turning on Nini*): Maybe it was you all along.

ROSA: That's what I'm saying.

YANN: Wait, wait! (*Pointing to Rosa.*) She's lying.
        Father Andre said it was her, right? Right?

YVES: Yeah, yeah.

YANN: And we know that the Devil always lies.

YVES: Of course! Liar! (*He grabs Rosa.*)

NINI   (*screams and shrivels into the corner, terrified.*):
        Let me go, Yves! Please, dear God . . . I haven't done
        anything to you.
        *From a scabbard in his boot, Yves extracts a six-inch
        utility knife. Without hesitation he slices Rosa's throat.
        Blood cascades down her chest. Yves and Yann drag the
        thrashing Rosa to the door.*

YANN: We'll throw her off. Into the sea.

ROSA   (*gurgling*): I have done nothing to you!

YVES: Open the door!
        *Yves clutches Rosa to him, an ugly reflection of their
        earlier embrace. Yann yanks the door open. The sound
        of the waves and the wind are deafening.
        The brothers hurl Rosa over the railing.*

NINI   (*whimpering*): Oh, Rosa . . . Rosa . . . Rosa . . .

Yves and Yann slam the door shut and stagger to their knees in the center of the room.

YVES   (*praying:*) Lord God, we have killed the devil for you.

YANN: We pray that you calm the storm and spare our beloved mother!

YVES & YANN: Hail Mary, full of grace, the Lord is with thee. Blessed art thou amongst women and blessed is the fruit of thy womb—

The siren suddenly stops. The brothers stop praying and listen.

YANN: It's stopped.

YVES: The boat must have missed the rocks. They're safe! Thanks be to God!

A horrifying crash is heard—followed by the screams of several people, whipped upwards by the savage winds.

YVES: Get the buoys! C'mon!

As they start to gather gear, Yann stops when he sees Nini cowering in the corner. Yves opens the door to peer down from the catwalk.

YANN: So it was you all along.

YVES: It's too dark! I can't see!

NINI: Yann, you're talking crazy . . . please . . .

YANN: You're the devil. You mocked the Virgin.

Nini crawls on her hands and knees across the floor, to the bed where Rosa slept.

NINI: Look . . . look here . . . under her pillow. See? See? It was Rosa. (*She pulls out the statue of the Virgin.*)

YANN: Don't you touch her, you filthy whore!

NINI   (*sick of it all*): Here's your goddamn Virgin! (*She throws the statue across the room.*)

YVES: I can't even see where to throw the buoys! We need light!

YANN   (*seizing Nini*): We'll have plenty of light!

NINI: What are you doing! Let me go!

YANN: Yves! Gimme your rope!

YVES: What are you going to do?

YANN: Here, grab her.

YVES: What are we doing?

YANN: Tie her to the hooks on the catwalk.

NINI   (*screaming*): No! No! No!

YANN: We're going to purify this devil.

Yann and Yves quickly lash Nini's wrists to the catwalk.

YANN: Get the kerosene.

NINI: Oh God, No! Don't let me die like this! I have done nothing wrong! God help me!

Yves brings a tank of kerosene and douses Nini with it.

NINI: I'm not the devil! I don't deserve this! Have pity!
For God's sake, have pity!
*Yann strikes a match from a big box in the cupboard
and moves toward the door.*

YANN: Close it.
*As the door closes, Yann tosses the match at Nini.
A huge ball of flame brightens the night outside the
portholes.*

NINI   (*screaming in agony*): Oh Jesus, I'm burning!
Murderers! Murderers!
*Yann and Yves gather up their gear and head for the
trapdoor. At the last moment, Yann yanks open the door
to the catwalk. Nini is dangling from the hooks, still
writhing in flames, screaming insanely.*

YANN: To hell with you, Devil!
*He slams the door. Yves and Yann clamber through the
trapdoor leading down.*

YVES AND YANN: Holy Mary mother of God, pray for our sinners now
and at the hour of our death, Amen!
*The STORM grows louder as Nini's screams begin to
ebb. The light outside the portholes dims, then fades to
black.*

LIGHTS OUT

The Sticking Place (2008)

CONCEPT BY ALEX ZAVISTOVICH

Script by Lucas Maloney and Michael McMahon, with Alex Zavistovich

Preface

The Sticking Place was Molotov's second major production and won the prize for Best Play at the 2008 Capital Fringe in Washington DC. Molotov's original press release described the play as a cross between *Macbeth* and *American Psycho* (https://www.prweb.com/releases/2008/06/prweb1040174.htm). It is an extremely dark comedy that explores contemporary media and sadomasochism and features some explicitly violent sequences within its witty and satirical script. In terms of an audacious Grand-Guignolesque set-piece, *The Sticking Place* features an onstage disembowelling which Alex Zavistovich explains:

> The disembowelling was actually quite an easy effect. We have always found that the easiest effects are the ones that are self-working. And in this case, the actor wore a plastic bag around his waist that had been cut and then resealed and filled with stage blood, and chitterlings from the butcher. The chitterlings were labelled 'very clean', but I think the meat industry has a lot to learn about cleanliness because these chitterlings were horrible. As the show proceeded, we threw other things in there, such as corn, because there's always corn isn't there? Even if you haven't eaten it for a month, there's corn, isn't there? At the allotted time, we thrust a stage knife into his belly, his pants were already down because he had been caught in a lewd act, his shirt was open and someone thrust the knife in and then pulled on a tab and the whole thing poured out. It was great! It was meant for laughs, so it wasn't completely horrifying. (Interview, 24 April 2015)

Even if this gutting is the major effect demanded by the play, Zavistovich reflects on the audience reaction to a far subtler moment of violence:

> In *The Sticking Place*, we see a couple with little razor blades on the palms of their hands as a prelude to pain-filled sex. And the audience all palpably reacted, I mean you could feel a sugar rush run through the audience, at the palm cutting scene. Not at the disembowelling, that was 'too big' for them to process, but everyone knows what a

paper cut feels like or has had a small cut, but seeing it enacted in that way, close-up, there was a sort of swooning in the audience. Oh, not all out fainting, but definitely a *queasiness*. (Interview, 24 April 2015)

This phenomenon of 'less being more' in horror theatre, especially when the visceral dimension is relatable, has been exploited elsewhere in Molotov's inventive repertoire of horror. One of the subtlest, but most impactful, effects featured nothing more than lipstick:

> We did a play called *Fat Men in Skirts* in which a character has to eat a lipstick. So, we took a regular lipstick and replaced it with some almond paste painted with red food colour. And people were *repulsed* by it. All they could imagine what that disgusting, waxy taste would be like in their mouths. But the larger effects just pass them by inasmuch as they were taken out of the moment in trying to work out how the effects were achieved. But they just assumed that the actor was literally willing to eat sixteen lipsticks for a role. (Interview, 24 April 2015)

Molotov has developed a panoply of effects, from elaborate mechanical devices to the concoction of liquids, as Zavistovich reveals: 'we have a recipe for anything you secrete or excrete or ejaculate, at different viscosities depending on what we need to do'.

Molotov places its effects within a core 'triumvirate' of acting, effects and violence. Regarding violence, Molotov uses stage fighting but emphatically titles it *brawling* to capture the fact that it needs to look 'sloppy and dangerous'. The ugliness of the encounter should not detract from the discipline and training that underpins it:

> We often include acrobatic moves and physicality. Our fights often include people flipping. I've found that including one aerial move—a flip, a toss or something—the audience think it's the most remarkable fight they have ever seen. Because they are so used to people on the ground trading punches one for one, throw in one flip and they're yours! They would not believe the amount of time that goes into just one fight. (Interview, 24 April 2015)

To return to the Molotov triumvirate, it is the integration of the three elements: 'the *acting*, the *effect or gimmick* and *brawling* are all part of what give us our style. Within this there is definitely a through line of magic and a very specific physicality.'

The Sticking Place captures the essence of Molotov. It is a play that is, by turns, horrific and humorous. It searches for laughs as much as shudders, thriving on the intimacy of the theatrical experience. With its various showcases of traditional Grand-Guignol—usually titled *Blood, Sweat and Fears*—Molotov has created a time tunnel to the *belle époque*. With *The Sticking Place* the audience is immersed into a very familiar world and a very modern story.

Figure 5. Molotov Theatre Group, poster for *Blood, Sweat and Fears*, 2016 (copyright Alex Zavistovich)

THE STICKING PLACE (2008)

CONCEPT BY ALEX ZAVISTOVICH

Script by Lucas Maloney and Michael McMahon, with Alex Zavistovich

First performed in Washington DC, 10 July 2008

The Place
Washington DC

The Time
Now-ish

The Cast
Darren—A sleazy Channel 4 news anchor.
Richard—A soft-spoken underling
    at Channel 4.
Debbie—Aspiring yuppie type. A real
    "girly" girl. Richard's girlfriend.
    Also low on the Channel 4
    totem pole.
Jane—Debbie's friend, roommate, and
    Richard's ex. A tough, cynical
    "goth" type.

SCENE 1 (THE NEWSROOM)

DARREN: This is Darren Davidson with a Channel 4 special news report, giving you a glimpse into the seedy underbelly of the District of Columbia. It's called bloodletting, or bloodplay, and it's the hot new trend of the underground social scene. But this startling new fad isn't restricted to teenagers wearing too much eye makeup and black clothing. No, bloodplay has attracted a following of young, hip urban professionals leading normal lives by day but meeting in sinister clubs and online chat groups by night to indulge in the darker side of their sick fantasies.

    It's considered a fringe activity even among the burgeoning bondage and sadomasochist clubs so popular among today's youth. Leather whips, cat-o-nine tails, strapado, rubber ball gags, dog muzzles, assless chaps, elaborate swings and ceiling restraints, thumb cuffs, foot screws, candle wax, edible underwear, pheasant under glass, sister on sister scat play, snake in the grass, Viking Dungeon, the rusty trombone, the 4 Point Sling Stand, the Crimper, Japanese Clover Nipple Clamps—NONE OF THIS IS NECESSARY to carry out an evening of debauchery, ending in the ultimate act of self-mutilation: bloodplay.

It's frighteningly simple. Walk to the kitchen, select your favorite paring knife, and the night has begun. Bloodletters often call the moment of realization of one's need to self-mutilate as their own personal "awakening," when they finally embrace and revel in previously forbidden desires. Participants will often agree on a "safe-word" beforehand, in an attempt to regulate the act of bloodplay. A commonly used system is based on traffic lights. Green means "Go ahead and keep cutting me." Yellow means "Hey, slow down there." And red, ironically, means, "Stop what you're doing and put down that knife, because you've gone too far." But really, any agreed-upon word or phrase that would not normally be used in the course of erotic events fulfills this purpose

Aside from the more obvious risk of blood-borne disease and infection, there is always the danger of taking things too far and causing serious injury or even death. Channel 4 Investigative News has discovered a staggering increase in hospitalizations due to recreational stabbings in the DC area over the last six months, including a 14 percent surge in the month of December alone. These figures indicate that merely crying "red light" does little to make such a risky and violent activity, by any reasonable social standard, acceptable or . . . safe.

For Channel 4 news, this is Darren Davidson wishing you a pleasant tomorrow. Goodnight.

VOICE   (*from off-stage*): And, cut!

DARREN   (*throws script up in the air and exclaims disgust*): Christ! (*to off-stage*) THIS is what I get to report on? Spoiled college grads all grown up and playing with knives in the city? Really? When am I gonna get to cover some real news, huh? When that next hurricane hits the Gulf, are you going to see me strapped to some telephone pole as the wind and rain soaks me to the bone? No. I'm gonna be sitting here reporting on teenagers huffing paint fumes and old ladies who leave millions of dollars to their favorite Chihuahua. This is pathetic. And Richard, you degenerate fuck, is it too damn much to ask to have some fucking Skittles on set? Once you get that right, maybe you can graduate to coffee . . . OR EVEN BAGELS! Stupid chicken shit.

Darren rises from his chair and stalks out of the studio, shaking his head and mumbling to himself.

SCENE 2 (RICHARD'S PAD)

Debbie and Richard enter the apartment. They are laughing after an exhilarating night of fun. Their clothes are spattered with blood, Richard has a rolled-up coat tucked under one arm. He throws the rolled-up coat on the couch and they stand facing each other.

DEBBIE: Oh my God that was intense . . .

RICHARD: I don't even have the words. (*They begin to kiss and grope each other. Debbie breaks away.*)

DEBBIE: We need music! (*She bolts offstage and starts flipping through record albums, looking almost frantically. She runs back out with an armful of records.*)

RICHARD: Just put something on!

DEBBIE: OK, OK! (*Bolts back offstage and we hear a record scratch and needle drops. Debbie runs back to the couch and pushes Richard down.*)

RICHARD: Wait, wait!

DEBBIE: What, what is it?

RICHARD: We need wine! (*Gets halfway across the room and stops in his tracks, wheels around.*) All I have is whiskey and absinthe.

DEBBIE AND RICHARD (*in unison*): ABSINTHE!

RICHARD: Right! (*Bolts off stage. We hear the sound of glasses clinking together and ice dropping into them. He strolls back casually with two glasses filled and hands one to Debbie. They drink and place glasses on the table. They resume their frantic kissing and thrashing about.*)

DEBBIE (*gasping for air*): And to think I almost didn't come out tonight. This has been so . . . so . . . oh my God, I'm so hot right now.

RICHARD: I know.
They resume.

DEBBIE: Wait . . . do you think anyone saw us leave?

RICHARD: How could they? No one was paying attention to us. Everyone was drunk. Babe, don't worry about it.

DEBBIE: I'm sorry, my mind's going a thousand miles an hour right now, it's all so exciting and new.

RICHARD (*buried in her neck and muffled*): Mmmhmm.
They resume.

DEBBIE: Wait, wait . . . hold everything . . .(*Teasingly and seductively.*) . . . what are we going to do about my shoes? (*Dangles them out in front of Richard.*)

RICHARD (*panting*): What do you mean?

DEBBIE: Well, look at them. (*Holds up blood-spattered shoes.*) Do you know how much I paid for these? Before we go any further, we have to clean my shoes.

RICHARD: Are you serious? It's 2:30 in the morning and you're on a shoe-shining mission? There's a time and a place, and this is neither.

DEBBIE: Come on, this won't take long.

RICHARD: How do you even CLEAN shoes like those?
What do you use, Windex?

DEBBIE: Are you retarded? I didn't buy these out of some back alley where they sell handbags and pleather knockoffs. These cost almost a week's salary.

RICHARD: Well, if you're the expert, tell me what to use and I'll give 'em a buff.

DEBBIE: Do you have any mink oil?

RICHARD: I'm not even going to answer that. Give them here, I'll take care of it.

DEBBIE   (holds shoes protectively against her chest and pushes Richard down onto the couch, straddling him suggestively): What are you gonna do?

RICHARD: Whatever I can. (Pulls Debbie close to him and they embrace, kissing long and hard and moaning with passion. Petting ensues.)

DEBBIE   (breaks away): All right, fuck the shoes (Tosses them off to the side and they resume their embrace. After a few moments, they finally separate.)

RICHARD: Damn, look at all this.

DEBBIE: I didn't think it was going to get all over us. It's everywhere.

RICHARD: Isn't that half the fun?

SCENE 3 (THE HEN HOUSE)

Lights up on Debbie and Jane's apartment. Debbie and Jane are sitting together, sipping glasses of red wine and talking casually. There is music playing gently in the background.

JANE: Is he really into that?

DEBBIE: Yeah, and if you think about it, it isn't all that surprising.

JANE: Compared to what?

DEBBIE: Never mind.

JANE: I had no idea. When I went out with Richard he was so . . . boring. In the end, that's what fucked everything up. I tried. But nothing he did ever excited me. Basically, I just got sick of him.

DEBBIE: So what pushed you over the edge?

JANE: Nothing in particular . . . with Richard, it was just everything in GENERAL. He didn't want to listen to me, he didn't want to talk to me, and he didn't even want to try. So I ended it. No regrets.

DEBBIE: Well, you did what you had to do.

JANE: Did he REALLY say that he wanted to try that kind
of stuff?

DEBBIE: He started dropping these weird hints and eventually
I just called him on it.

JANE: Mmm.

DEBBIE: Yeah.

JANE: Fucking right, yeah. More wine?

DEBBIE: Sure! (*Pause.*) Shit . . .

JANE (*pause*): Yeah.

DEBBIE: I mean, OK, it's weird coming from him. It's WEIRD.
But there's something about him when he talks like that . . .
it just . . . and I . . . ahhhh . . . God . . . you know what
I mean?

JANE: No, I wouldn't, remember?

DEBBIE: Right.

JANE: Bitch.

DEBBIE: Oh for Christ's sake, come on, what are you, like twelve?
I've seen some of the guys you've been out with after
Richard—or the ones BEFORE him. Remember Dirty
Steve? You two were like the Angelina and Billy Bob of
fucking H street.

JANE: Well, it is a very arts-friendly community . . . and Steve
was an animal in the sack.

DEBBIE: Well, whatever. I'm just saying.

JANE (*mulling it over*): Richard?

DEBBIE (*suddenly remembers something*): Oh! Like this one time,
I go over to Richard's just to pop in, and you know he
never locks the door—

JANE (*overlapping*): --never locks the fucking door . . .

DEBBIE: --locks the door. Right? And I yell for him, and I hear
this shuffling sound and he slams his bedroom door. He's
rustling around and banging into things, and after all that
he finally lets me in. All right, get this . . . He's sweaty, his
shirt's undone and . . . he's got this enormous hard-on.

JANE: Was he alone?

DEBBIE: Mm-hmm. He says hello, he's out of breath, and then
he darts off to the bathroom. But as he was leaving,
I noticed there was a little trail of blood coming from a
cut across his arm.

JANE: Hmm . . .

DEBBIE: So you don't have to be a genius to figure out what's been
going on.

JANE: I guess not. So what did you do?

DEBBIE: What could I do? I—. (*A knock at the door.*) Hold that
thought. (*She walks to the door.*) Who is it?

RICHARD: It's Richard.

JANE: Well, well . . .

Debbie opens door, Richard enters, dressed in a suit and overcoat.

RICHARD: Ladies.

JANE: *RICHARD* . . .We were just talking about you.

RICHARD: Good stuff, I hope.

JANE: Of course it was. What brings you here, all decked out?

RICHARD   (*ignores Jane, addresses Debbie*): I've been trying to call you since I left home but your cell phone's off.

JANE: Girls' night in.

RICHARD: Whatever. (*To Debbie.*) Look, are you going to the party? Everyone assumes that we're coming and we have to at least make an appearance.

DEBBIE: You know I hate those things. Everyone just gets drunk and tells the same stories over and over. Anyway, I already told you I wasn't going.

RICHARD   (*chuckles*): I know DARREN will be looking forward to seeing you there.

DEBBIE: Christ. Stalker. Why don't you ever say anything to him about that?

RICHARD: He has my career by the balls. It comes with the territory.

JANE   (*sarcastically to Debbie*): What do you expect him to do? Stab a local celebrity with a letter opener to defend your honor?

RICHARD: Jane, please remind me again why we broke up?

DEBBIE   (*hurriedly*): Look . . . maybe we can just stop in for a drink. Let me throw on something to wear.

JANE: No, don't change. I thought Juicy sweats were all the rage at Georgetown cocktail parties.

DEBBIE: I'll be right back. (*Runs out of the room, exposing "Juicy" brand on her sweatpants.*)
Richard sits down casually on the couch next to Jane. They regard each other for a few beats.

JANE: So. Richard.

RICHARD: So. Jane.

JANE: It's been a while since we had a chance to talk.

RICHARD: Has it? I didn't know we had anything to talk about.

JANE: Things change. So, what's NEW with you?

RICHARD: They moved me to copy editor at Channel 4. You know all those sleazy stories about things in food that can kill you, and Chinese baby formula laced with arsenic? I get to "fact check" those. It pays well, but it isn't very satisfying work.

JANE: So, did you sell out for the money or the fame?

RICHARD: Hey, I get to work my way up. Maybe one of these days I can be one of those blow-dried, talking heads you see on the news, instead of just plunking away on a keyboard in a cubicle.

JANE: Well, at least it seems like things are going well with Debbie.

RICHARD: Debbie's good. Things are good with Debbie.
Why . . . has she said anything about us?

JANE: Oh, you know Debbie . . . she never says anything really interesting like that. Not a big talker.
Debbie enters, looking flustered, shoes in hand and frantically putting earrings in her ears. She pauses, hopping on one foot and then the other to pull on one shoe, and then the other. She looks back and forth at Richard and Jane who gaze back at her.

DEBBIE: Ready?

JANE   (*looks at her watch*): Wow, that was record time.

RICHARD: Look, you don't have to rush, we can be a little late to this thing . . .

DEBBIE: No, no . . . we can go. (*Fixes her hair with her hands and breathes out deeply.*)

JANE: So can I expect you later?

DEBBIE   (*hurriedly*): Maybe. We're not going to be out all night, are we?

RICHARD: Probably not . . . Let's just see how it goes.

JANE: Well . . . I'll be here, I guess. All alone.

DEBBIE: OK, bye! (*Pulls Richard out by the arm.*)

RICHARD   (*over his shoulder*): Night, Jane!
Jane is left sitting in silence and looking angrily cheated.

SCENE 4 (PARTY IN GEORGETOWN)

Lights up on Channel 4 office party. Music plays in the background as Debbie and Richard enter. They face the audience as they stand awkwardly, having entered a rather drunken scene they were unprepared for. Richard halts Debbie as they walk and they gaze into the audience.

DEBBIE   (*tentatively*): Do you think we got here too late?

RICHARD: I think this is about as interesting as it's gonna get.
Why, what's the problem?

DEBBIE: Let's see: It's a bunch of sweaty old drunk men hitting on young, impressionable interns. The secretaries are dressed like sluts. All the other women look like Margaret Thatcher. And I'm none of the above.

RICHARD: Oh great, here comes Darren.
Enter Darren, jigging to the music and balancing a martini glass awkwardly in one hand.

DARREN: HEYYYY. Look who just dropped by . . . looking good, Debbie. Looking DELICIOUS. (*Gestures with his hand and slops most of his martini over the glass.*)

DEBBIE: Thanks.

RICHARD: Hi, Darren, what's the good word?

DARREN: Richie, what's up guy? Can you do me a favor and get me a refill? I'm about to give my big toast. Gonna give it up for the man in charge . . . Darren-style. Know what I'm sayin', bro? (*Pushes glass into Richard's hand.*) All riiiight. Dirty vodka martini, Ketel One.
Richard looks at the glass in his hand and walks away towards the bar.

DARREN   (*moves close to Debbie*): Hey, Debs. I like your threads.

DEBBIE: It's just a black dress.

DARREN: Yeah, but you're all up in it. Brings out the beast in me. (*Moves a hand down to her hips and she grabs it slowly and pushes it away.*)

DEBBIE: You really know how to charm a girl, Darren.

DARREN: Call it one of my many gifts. I got bigger gifts to show you later on, if you want. They're MAMMOTH.

DEBBIE: I thought mammoths were extinct.

DARREN: They are, but I'm bringin' 'em back. Bones intact.

RICHARD   (*balancing three drinks*): Here we go . . . (*Hands a martini to Darren who grabs it impatiently. Hands a drink to Debbie and keeps one for himself.*) What did I miss?

DARREN: Everything. Just kiddin', chief. All right, guys. I gotta go do this thing here. CLEAR A PATH, people, CLEAR A PATH.
Darren swaggers to the opposite side of the stage. Debbie and Richard watch him go.

RICHARD: So what did he have to say?

DEBBIE: The usual. At least he didn't put his hands all over me this time. Just my hips.

RICHARD: Wait, this ought to be good. Let's see if he can get through this without cursing.

DARREN: OK, people we all know why we're here. We're HERE to CELEBRATE the . . . (*Pauses, turns angrily.*) Hey, can you guys turn that shit OFF? I'm tryin' to make a toast here. (*Music cuts off abruptly.*)

RICHARD   (*to Debbie*): Guess not.

DARREN   (*swaying slightly*): Like I was saying, we're here to celebrate the passing of the torch. As we all know, Jimmy Burns, Channel 4's star personality, the King of DC morning news, just announced that he's retiring at the end of the month after twenty-five solid years as the face of Channel Four. Taking his place as the star of Channel 4 news is, of course, me. But tonight isn't about me and my carrying on of the great tradition set in stone by big Jim. This isn't about maintaining solid principles of bedrock journalism and unbiased objectivity.

No, this is about Jimmy Burns, and if you'll just indulge me for a few minutes, I'd like to say a few brief words about his noble service to this station. (*Takes a swig of his martini absentmindedly.*)
Now, even though I have a father, he's still alive and everything, Jim has been like another father to me. Someone I can confide in, bring my problems to, share my achievements with, and there's been a lot of great things to share. I've gotta say, Dad, if I can call you that, in this . . . context, uh, you did a lotta things right. Does everyone remember when the news division got caught fucking with the brake lines on that fleet of mid-size sedans to show negligence in Ford manufacturing? We all thought that Corporate was gonna string us up by the balls for that one, right Jimmy? But guess who didn't panic? Guess who kept steering the ship? Guess who was at the helm, holding strong against the wind and riding those waves? Battling through tides and foam like a damn Viking? That's right . . . Jimmy Burns, a man of mettle, with eyes of steel, balls of brass, and let's not forget that big old heart of gold. Heart of frigging gold, ladies and gentlemen.

DEBBIE: Where's he going with this?

DARREN: You're probably all wondering where I'm going with this. You know, as that guy in Hamlet says, man is a piece of work. And if there's one thing that Jim Burns knows all about, it's work. And principle. This man lives for Channel 4, for all of us, all the way from me at the top to the grunts, like Ritchie . . . oh! And that hare-lipped guy working in the mail room, sorting through . . . mail. Ponder that. For twenty-five years, Jimmy's been in the trenches, diggin' deep. Which brings me to another story . . .
Darren's speech goes into pantomime as he continues to gesture with the glass. We now hear Debbie and Richard conversing.

RICHARD: Christ, last year at the Christmas party he went on for twenty minutes.

DEBBIE: Someone should really shut him up.

RICHARD: How about us?

DEBBIE: How are we going to do that?

RICHARD: All right, after he's done with this toast, I'll go off to the bar. You go over to Darren and tell him what a great job he did, or some bullshit. Really kiss his ass. Then, bring him out to the back alley. I'll be waiting.

DEBBIE: Yeah, right.

RICHARD: I'm serious about this. Get him outside, and I'll take it from there. This is the perfect opportunity, no more talking about it, let's just do it.

DEBBIE   (*beat*): OK.

DARREN   (pantomime ends): And then Jim goes, "Goddammit boy, that's the biggest turkey sandwich I've ever seen!"
And you guys know the rest of the story. Here's to ya, Jim . . . And the rest of you, drink up! Open bar closes in thirty minutes!
Debbie and Richard look at each other. They kiss. Blackout.

SCENE 5 (THE ALLEY)

Lights up on Darren and Debbie, alone in an alley.

DARREN: So what's out here for me to see, Debs?

DEBBIE: Mmm . . . use your imagination, Darren.

DARREN: Well, we are in an alley. Good a place as any for a fun-rub. (*Unbuckles his pants and drops trow. Leans back with his hands behind his head and closes his eyes and sighs.*) Do it.
Debbie starts to rub his leg tentatively, while Darren starts moaning increasingly louder. Debbie inches her hand up while looking disgusted. He continues to moan. Richard emerges and seizes Darren by the testicles. Darren screams in a high-pitched howl of anguished pain.

RICHARD: What's up, bro?

DARREN   (*looking panicked*): She brought me out here. Say goodbye to your future in television, Richard.

RICHARD: Sorry, Darren.
He spins Darren around and slashes open his stomach, causing his intestines and stomach gore to hit the floor. Darren gasps and drops to his knees, and then falls on his side. Richard props him up against a garbage can and passes the knife to Debbie. They kiss violently and she breaks away. Richard seizes Darren by the hair with one hand and with the other hand holds open Darren's eyes, forcing him to watch Debbie stab repeatedly at his torso. Each thrust causes Darren to emit a gurgling noise.

DARREN: Please stop! Call an ambulance!
Debbie pulls out the knife. She and Richard stare down at Darren's body. Debbie notices blood on her shoes and pulls away.

DEBBIE: Oh my God . . . you got blood all over my Jimmy Choos! (*She pulls off one of her shoes and throws it at Darren.*) Do you have any idea how much these cost? They're RUINED.

RICHARD: Take it easy. Go and see if there's a rag in the trunk. I'll be along in a minute.

DEBBIE: Fine. (*She stomps off, stopping to retrieve her shoe.*)
RICHARD   (*watches Debbie leave and then looks down at the body*):
You know Darren, I was thinking this has been the best
time I've ever had hanging out with you.
*Richard sits down cross legged next to the body and slaps
Darren playfully on the knee. Darren is momentarily
awakened by the slap and makes a pitiful attempt to paw
at Richard. Richard slaps away at his hand and shoves
him over onto his side.*
    That's enough of that. You probably think I'm one
sick fuck right now. What, you got nothing to say?
Fine, I'll take that as a yes. No hard feelings, Darren.
None at all. You know that was a great speech you gave
in there, I feel like I got to know you a lot better. So let
me tell you a little more about myself.
    When I was in eighth grade, my class went on a field
trip to this lake in Maryland. There was a dock you
could jump off, you could fish, horse around, play water
volleyball . . .whatever. It was good times. Me and a
bunch of kids took turns doing cannonballs. We had
this teacher, Miss Garwood, she must have been fresh
out of college. You know, twenty-one, twenty-two years
old. Redhead. Tender. So she was having as much fun
as the rest of us, laughing and swimmin' around in this
little two-piece bathing suit. I mean, for a teacher, she
was hot. The guys used to draw naked pictures of her
and pass them around at lunch. Anyway, Miss Garwood
was pulling herself up on the dock after doing this really
cool swan dive and, I don't know, she must have caught
herself on a nail or something because she gives this yell
and we all look over. She's got this really deep cut right
above her belly button. Blood spread out all over her
stomach, just this little crimson trail getting bigger and
bigger. It must have hurt like a bitch because she flinched
a little, and this big, fat drop of blood slides down her
stomach and stains the bottom of her two-piece.
I couldn't take my eyes off of it. None of us could.
Temporarily abandons his story.
    Hey, are you listening to me? Trying to tell a story
here. (*He props Darren back up against the trash can.*)
So where was I? Oh yeah. Fast forward about five years.
When I was in college, my girlfriend was into field hockey,
lacrosse, you know, she was a jock. She'd always come
back from games and practice all banged up and riding
high from this huge adrenaline rush. So after a really
hard game we'd have this crazy monkey sex and it was
just incredibly intense. And sometimes I'd duck into the
bathroom after we were about halfway through, saying

I was going to powder my junk or whatever. Then I'd take a razor and make this little, tiny cut on my palm. I'd squeeze it just to get the blood flowing a little bit and then go back to the room. Then, when we were really getting into it, I could look back and forth between her, my arm, back to her, and—oh man, especially on days when her lacrosse team really got its ass kicked . . . you get the point. *Stops and gets to his feet, paces away like he's going to leave and then turns back as if to get one final thought off his chest.*

It's so hard to meet people, you know? Oh, that reminds me . . . SKITTLES! (*He produces a bag of Skittles, opens the bag and crams the whole bag into Darren's mouth.*) How are those working out for you, BRO? Good? (*Darren spits out Skittles and blood.*) Good!

I mean, take Debbie for instance. She was a find! (*Kicks at Darren.*) It's so difficult to find someone you have something in common with, someone who won't get up your ass about the things you like to do, let alone someone who actually shares the same interests. Hell, most women are so uptight, they won't even offer to pop a zit on your back. And believe me, you don't ever want to offer to pop one of theirs unless you've got time for a twenty-minute argument about how gross you are. (*Sighs wistfully.*) Relationships are complicated. *Richard slaps Darren one last time on the knee and walks offstage.*

SCENE 6 (THE HEN HOUSE)

Lights up on Jane and Debbie's apartment. Jane is alone and sitting on the couch. She is wearing an oversized T-shirt and swimsuit bottom. She has one foot propped up on a coffee table, and is painting her toenails black. Cotton swabs between her toes. Light gothesque music plays in the background.

JANE   (*humming along to the music*): Shit! I always fuck up on the little one! (*Stretches out her foot to get a better look.*) Ah, screw this. (*Stops painting.*) There's nothing more pathetic than drinking wine and painting your toenails by yourself on a Friday night.
She sits back and looks around bored. After a few beats, she resumes working on her nails. Mimicking Debbie.

"Oh, Jane, it'll be great, just the two of us. We'll sit around, order food, drink some wine and just have a girls' night in. Forget Richard, tonight it's just the two of us. Look, I'm even turning off my phone. I'm not even going to text him! You are me, Jane . . . you and me." (*Resumes normal voice.*) What happened to our night in, Debbie? Are you having fun with RICHARD? (*Takes a swig from the wine bottle.*) She's so dick-whipped. (*Takes a bigger swig.*) But it's OK. I'm not even going to call her. (*Grabs her cell phone and hits a button, then slams it back down.*) I'm not even going to TEXT her. (*Looks at her watch.*) Two in the morning, and not a word. The bars are closed, and they're probably back at Richard's place having drunk sex. Boring, pathetic, predictable drunk sex.

Jane grabs a TV remote and flips on the "TV". She leans back nonchalantly and after five or six seconds turns it off.

All right, this is driving me crazy. I need to eat something. (*Grabs her phone and starts looking through numbers.*) Henry's? Closed. Damn. Really wanted their sweet potato pie. Papa John's? Too many carbs. Three Brothers from Nepal? I don't even know what that is . . . Well, it's Yums be default. (*Presses "Send" and sits back impatiently.*) Wonder what the happy couple ate tonight? Some huge catered spread, I bet. Debbie probably wouldn't even bring me back some bread wrapped in a napkin.

Yes, can I get a delivery? Yeah, I'll hold . . . (*Sighs, swigs from the wine bottle.*) I can't believe I'm ordering from this place by myself, I could kill Richard and Debbie for this. Yeah, hi, can I get an order of hot and sour soup, and a dozen chicken wings. Loads of mumbo sauce. I mean, really pour it on. Wait, you're out of hot and sour soup? You're a Chinese restaurant, how can you be out of the most generic Asian soup? Yeah, I'll hold . . . AGAIN . . . yes, thank you, let me get . . . what do you mean, you're CLOSED? Since when does Yum's close at 2 am? You were just taking my order a second ago. No, don't hang up on me. I just want to . . . hello? HELLO? DAMMIT. (*Hangs up the phone and puts it down angrily.*) Great. My fucking night has officially hit rock bottom. I've been rejected by YUMS.

All right, enough of this . . . (*Pulls cotton swabs out from her toes and starts pulling on her clothes, zipping up her boots and primping her hair.*) There's only so much rejection a girl can take. Sorry, Richard, if you're going to ruin my night, consider yours ruined as well. You're not the only person who can drop in unannounced.

Finishes pulling her clothes on and checks herself out in the "mirror."

Fucking hot. Mmm. . . .

Claps hands over her head and the lights go out.

SCENE 7 (RICHARD'S PAD)

Lights up on Richard and Debbie embracing on the couch, picking up where they left off in Scene 1.

DEBBIE (*breaks away*): All right, fuck the shoes (*Tosses them off to the side and they resume their embrace. After a few moments, they finally separate.*) I didn't think it was going to get all over us.

RICHARD: Isn't that half the fun? (*He grabs Debbie.*) Hit me. (*She does.*) Harder! (*She does. They make out.*) *Richard takes Debbie by the hair at the back of her head, other hand around throat. He pulls her up to her toes. Sexual moment, tinged with hints of violence. He rips her blouse open. She pushes him back.*

DEBBIE: What happened to the knife?

RICHARD: It's in my coat. (*Kiss.*)

DEBBIE: Are you sure?

RICHARD: Go see for yourself.
Debbie grabs the coat. It is revealed to be riddled with slashes, drenched in gore. Debbie finds the knife.
The coat is thrown to floor. A violent kiss is shared. Debbie pushes Richard onto the couch.

DEBBIE: Trust me?

RICHARD: Yes.
Bloodplay. Debbie cuts Richard's palm deeply. Richard takes the knife from Debbie.

RICHARD: Trust me?

DEBBIE: Yes.
Her palm is cut. Same reaction. They join hands. Lick each other's palms. He stands her up, pulls her hair. She hits him hard. She pushes away. She tears at his shirt. Sucks at her cut palm and spits. She pushes her bloody hand down the front of his pants.

DEBBIE: Did you hear him scream?

RICHARD: Yes.

DEBBIE: Did you hear him beg us to stop?

RICHARD: Yep.

DEBBIE: How did you feel?

RICHARD: Like a million bucks. I want you. Now.
There is a knock on the door.

JANE (*from outside*): Hello! Are you guys there? I just happened to lock myself out of the apartment and decided to drop in to see you guys. (*She enters.*) What the hell is going on? (*Pointing at the coat.*) What's this?

DEBBIE: Nothing. (*She drops the knife. Beat.*) Sorry you got locked out. Do you want my key?

JANE: No, I don't want the key, I want a fucking explanation!

RICHARD: Let's just say that Darren Davidson probably won't be
           the new face of Chanel 4 Morning Edition.

JANE: No way, no fucking way! I can't believe you've done this.
           Are you messing with me, because this is NOT funny!
           (*To Debbie.*) I can't believe you went along with this!
           How could you?

DEBBIE: I'm sorry, no one was supposed to find out.

RICHARD: Jane, don't do anything stupid. Calm down.

JANE: How am I supposed to calm down. I come in here
           expecting, at WORST, to see you guys naked and asleep
           on the couch, and instead I walk into this.

DEBBIE: I think I'm going to be sick.

JANE   (*picks up the knife and jacket from off the floor*):
           Is this all from Darren?

RICHARD: Most of it.

JANE: So he's dead.

RICHARD: I'm about 99 percent sure.

JANE: Oh my God.

DEBBIE: I'm sorry.

JANE: You think saying you're sorry is going to fix this!
           You really fucked up this time. (*She goes to leave.*)

RICHARD: Where are you going?

JANE: I'm getting out of here!

RICHARD: Just stay here for a little till you calm down.
           (*He moves towards her.*)

DEBBIE: Please listen to him.

JANE: I don't even want to look at either one of you now.
           Stay away from me.

RICHARD: Easy. (*Approaching.*)

JANE: I mean it, stay away from me.

RICHARD: You're hysterical. This isn't all that bad.

JANE: I'm warning you, stay away.

RICHARD: Shhhhhhh. You know I would never hurt you.
           I still care about you, you know. God, you're hot
           when you're angry!
           Debbie is covering her eyes and making weird noises.

JANE: Shut up.

RICHARD   (*changing tactics*): Give me the knife. What do you thinks
           going to happen if you don't calm down? What do you
           think we just did . . . for fun. If we did it once, we can do
           it again. Stop this bullshit and think things through.

DEBBIE: Richard, don't talk like that.
           *Richard lunges towards Jane. There is a brief struggle,
           and Jane stabs Richard. Richard falls on the ground.
           Debbie screams.*

RICHARD   (*lets out a guttural cry. Beat*): God damn it, Jane! That was
           deep! (*He realizes the severity of the wound.*) Oh shit!

JANE: I warned you to keep away from me. (*Jane kicks him. Richard groans.*)

RICHARD   (*to Debbie*): Please, help me.

JANE: Shut up.

Jane kicks Richard, stomps his hand and tries to restrain him. He grabs her and they struggle. Debbie is petrified on the couch with fear and interested disbelief. Jane slowly pushes the knife into Richard and pulls it back out. She stands up, looking down at Richard's body. She pokes Richard's body. Debbie stands and approaches Jane. Jane slaps Debbie. Beat.

DEBBIE: Harder.

Jane slaps her harder. They kiss. Beat.

JANE: You hurt me.

DEBBIE: I know.

JANE: This will take some time.

DEBBIE: How do you feel?

JANE: Weird, but good. Like I don't know what's happened. (*Beat. Angrily.*) You promised that your first time was going to be with me!

DEBBIE: I'm sorry. I didn't plan on things going this way. One thing just led to another, and it happened. He was really the one who initiated things. Everything was moving so fast. There was no way to stop it.

JANE: That's no excuse. It was supposed to be something special for us. You didn't even join in this time!

DEBBIE: I'm so sorry.

Beat.

JANE: He screamed. (*Moving to the couch.*)

DEBBIE: Yes. (*Also moving to the couch.*)

JANE: Did you hear him beg us to stop?

DEBBIE: Yes. (*They kiss again.*) Where's the knife?

JANE: On the floor.

Debbie picks up the knife.

DEBBIE: Trust me?

JANE: Yes.

Debbie cuts Jane's arm and touches the blood. They take off each other's shirts.

JANE   (*to Richard's body*): No peeking, you.

She throws the coat over Richard's head. Jane turns to Debbie and examines the knife. They watch it together, look at each other seductively and turn out the lamp.

BLACKOUT

A Room With No View (2009)

by

JAMES COMTOIS

Preface

Based in New York City, Nosedive Productions was a theatre company
co-produced by Pete Boisvert, Patrick Shearer and James Comtois. Tagging
itself with the slogan 'theatre for sick little monkeys', James Comtois
was the company's lead writer, producing intense thrillers and works of
dark satire as well as adaptations of *A Christmas Carol* (2004). Comtois's first explicit attempt to write a horror show was *The Adventures of
Nervous-Boy (a penny dreadful)* (2006), and in his playwright's note he
explains:

> (This) is a play for anyone who has felt a constant and steady fear of
> dread, who's felt that the water is up to his or her eyeballs and rising.
> A play for anyone who's felt at times that they're always in the wrong
> place doing the wrong thing; who's felt alienated and isolated despite
> being surrounded by people all the time.
>
> A play for people who have had their heart broken and have never
> been able to mend it properly and move on; who have wanted to go
> on a rampage after a week from hell.
>
> This is a play for anyone who has wondered if we are indeed in hell.
> (Nosedive Productions Archive https://www.nosediveproductions.
> com/the-adventures-of-nervous-boy)

This play was a summer production. Nosedive's next show was in
October 2006 and continued the exploration of horror theatre. However,
in contrast to the journey into contemporary angst of *Nervous-Boy*, the
new production *The Blood Brothers present . . . An Evening of Grand
Guignol Horror* presented a package of short plays introduced by the
bald and red-eyed hosts of the title, mixing classic works such as Maurice
Level's *The Final Kiss* and Jean Aragny and Francis Neilson's *The Kiss
of Blood* along with all-new works. As Comtois explains, the company
enjoyed instant success with the show:

> We got a good response from the audience and it was fun to do,
> so we made it an annual tradition every October. But each year,

we'd add a new theme or angle to *The Blood Brothers present . . .*
anthology series. One year we adapted old EC Comics. Another we
adapted short stories by Stephen King. But through the series, we'd
create original horror plays every year, many of which would show
off new gore effects designed from scratch by our producer Stephanie
Cox-Williams.

(Interview, 13 May 2021)

Nosedive built an audience for itself in New York with its dynamic mixture of scripts, performance and special effects. It continued to be a prolific
company before winding down in 2013, suitably concluding its story with
a final October horror show: *The Blood Brothers present . . . Raw Feed*
(2012).

Although the *Blood Brothers* formula was inaugurated with a selection
of Grand-Guignol plays, the company would not return to staging classic
works but crafted its own horror repertoire with adaptations and numerous original works by Comtois. In this regard, Comtois explains that his
'primary horror influences are movies—particularly horror films from the
1970s and 1980s—and the work of Stephen King and Clive Barker', though
he recognises that as 'many of those influences were themselves influenced
by the original Grand Guignol, so I suppose you could argue it was an
indirect influence' (interview, 13 May 2021). Even if the Grand-Guignol
repertoire did not materialise on the Nosedive stage after the inaugural
Blood Brothers show, the Grand-Guignol formula of the *douche écossaise*;
the nuanced journey of horror and comedy; and the playful relationship
with the audience in creating an intense experience. On this latter point,
Comtois signals the necessarily 'visceral experience' of theatre as whole
and horror theatre in particular:

when done right, theatre can—and should—be a visceral experience.
So, horror is a genre that fits right at home on the stage. Having the
actors perform only a few feet away from the audience in a small
black box theatre can create a tense claustrophobic feeling that's ut-
terly unique to the medium. Watching staged violence, be it a big,
choreographed fight or someone slicing their finger, can be an intense
and engaging audience experience. And in my experience, audiences
love seeing blood and gore effects done live, and love when they're in
'the splatter zone'. It's an added layer of fun.

(Interview, 13 May 2021)

The play we are including in this collection was written for *The Blood
Brothers present . . . The New Guignol* (2009). It had a powerful contemporaneous resonance, being based on the true case of Josef Fritzl
that had come to light in 2008 and concluded with Fritzl receiving life

imprisonment in 2009. Fritzl had imprisoned his own daughter Elisabeth in a secret area within the cellar of the family home in Austria. He kept her imprisoned for twenty-four years during which time he assaulted and abused her and fathered seven children with her. It was a profoundly shocking case that had global notoriety: horror mixed with fascination was evident in the media and the popular imagination as details emerged about the decades of suffering of Elisabeth Fritzl; the psychological, physical and sexual sadism of her father; the apparent ignorance of the authorities and the neighbourhood (including the rest of the family living directly upstairs). Equally shocking was Fritzl's lack of remorse, apparently telling a journalist who interviewed him in prison that although he confessed to everything he feels that he is the victim of a miscarriage of justice, and if you 'look into the cellars of other people, you might find other families and other girls down there' (*Daily Mirror*, Matt Roper 'Josef Fritzl's daughter's secret new life revealed 10 years after he was jailed' 19 March 2019 https://www.mirror.co.uk/news/world-news/josef-fritzls-daughters-secret-new-14141500).

As well as media fascination, there was cultural response, most famously Emma Donoghue's novel *Room* (2010), which was adapted into a film directed by Lenny Abrahamson in 2015 with the screenplay written by Donoghue herself. The author subsequently adapted the screenplay into a stage play premiering at the Theatre Royal Stratford East in 2017. Other adaptations have included the film *Girl in the Basement* (2021). Of course, it is worth noting that the theme of incarceration is a horror and thriller trope, and there are countless examples from Stephen King's *Misery* (1987) to recent examples such as *Split* (2016) and *Run* (2020).

James Comtois's short play about the Fritzl case was produced just a few months after the trial and no one in the audience would have missed the reference. As Comtois explains, 'Like with many original Grand Guignol plays, this was a story that was "ripped from the headlines", so it was based on a real event that garnered a lot of media attention' (interview, 13 May 2021): the Grand-Guignol practice of using news stories and *faits divers* as source and inspiration continues to be a valid practice in producing the contemporary Grand-Guignolesque. The effect on an audience when they realise they are about to witness a dramatic interpretation of a true and recent event can be powerful. In the case of *A Room With No View*, Comtois recalls that 'audiences were sufficiently creeped out and upset by the play (which was, of course, the goal)' (interview, 13 May 2021). At the same time, Comtois pays homage to the creative team:

> Cast members Robert Leeds and Becky Byers totally committed to the roles and didn't shy away from its more disturbing elements. And even though it was based on a true story, director Abe Goldfarb did a fantastic job leaning into the fractured fairy tale aspect of the show.

Ultimately, because of the subject material, and the cast and director committing to the story's inherent horror, we didn't need to rely too much on gore effects.

(Interview, 13 May 2021)

The Grand-Guignol at its most successful should not hinge upon stage blood and its effects but is a theatre of committed acting and psychology. At the same time, even when dealing with the horrifying realism of true events, it is forum for stagecraft and fantasy (in this case the fairy tale metaphor).

A ROOM WITH NO VIEW (2009)

by

JAMES COMTOIS

First performed in New York City, October 2009

In a room that has a handful of amenities, including a table and chairs, ELISABETH, a young woman, cradles a crying baby. There are a couple of surveillance cameras throughout the corners of the room, watching her.

TITLE CARD:[21] *This is not a true story.*

ELISABETH: Come on, sweetie, come on, shhhh-sh-shhhh . . . don't cry, please don't cry. We'll make it all better, I promise. Just please, shhhhh . . . (*To the cameras, intense but not so loud to scare the baby.*) Hello? We need help down here. Hello! I think she's sick! Can you hear me? We need help! (*To the baby.*) Lemme tell you a story, you wanna hear a story? It's about a sweet and gentle princess who one day, came across an old man needing help carrying supplies into his house. The princess felt bad for him, and thought he seemed gentle enough, so she offered to help. (*To the cameras, a little more loud.*) Hey! Help! (*To the baby.*) He was grateful, and asked her if she could carry a large wooden door to his cellar. Since he seemed frail, she obliged. But it was a trick. He wasn't a gentle old man at all, but a shape-changing ogre. Once the princess was down the stairs in the cellar with the heavy door, the ogre revealed his true form, and locked the princess down in the cellar. The evil ogre vowed that he would keep the princess down in the cellar until the end of her days. Oh, oh, oh, don't be scared. It does have a happy ending, I promise. We'll get to the part where the handsome prince comes and rescues her, don't worry—
JOSEF, an older man, enters. Elisabeth stops telling the story and looks startled.
JOSEF: *Have you finished it?*
ELISABETH: *Oh. Oh! She's sick. I think she's sick!*
JOSEF: Have you finished it?
ELISABETH: *I think we need to take her to a hospital, she needs—*
JOSEF: Have you finished it?

---

[21] Playwright's note: When this was originally staged, we used an on-stage narrator instead of title cards. Both options (in my mind) work just fine.

ELISABETH: What?

JOSEF: Have you finished it?

ELISABETH   (*realizes what he means*): Almost.

JOSEF: Finish it. (*Exits.*)

ELISABETH: But wait wait wait what about—
It's too late: he's locked the door behind him.

ELISABETH   YOU SONOFABITCH! (*She bangs on the door, but it's no use.*)
Let me out of here! LET ME OUT OF HERE!
*The baby's cries are louder now. She stops banging on the door
and gets herself together. To the baby.*
Sorry, sorry, don't be upset. Shhhh-shhhhhh . . . mommy just got
a little . . . emotional. You know how mommy gets sometimes.
There, there. Don't' be sad. Please sweetie, don't be sad . . .
just . . . please, please . . . stop crying . . .
*She carries the baby over to the table, where a pen and pad of
paper await her. She sighs, and then writes.*
'Dear Mother and Father. I hope this letter finds you well, as
I want to assure you that I am healthy and alive. I am still with
friends in Braunau, and still don't wish to return home. Perhaps
that will change, but for now, I will ask that you continue to
respect my wishes of being away from the family. Although
I harbor no ill will . . .'
*She clenches up and needs half a moment after that,
then resumes writing.*
'. . . and don't blame you, the environment at home was
incredibly stifling and oppressive, and I would like to be free
from that for the time being. Please do not try to look for me, or
I shall leave the country. Fondly, Elisabeth.'
*She stops writing and resumes tending to the sick and crying
child. To the baby.*
The evil ogre kept her down in the cellar against her will for
years. Often, he would have his way with the princess, and they
would have children. But the ogre rarely let the princess keep
them. She bided her time, waiting, perhaps in vein, for her prince
to come and save her.
*The door opens. Elisabeth looks vaguely hopeful in spite of
herself. And . . . no. It's only Josef. It was silly of her to get caught
up in her own fairy tale.*

JOSEF   (*sees the letter*): Ah. Is that . . .?

ELISABETH: Yes.

JOSEF   (*takes it and reads*): Good girl. We wouldn't want your mother to
worry. Or at least, start looking.

ELISABETH: Yes. Yes. Now, I did what you asked, so please, she needs
medicine, she's sick!

JOSEF: Oh, now, Elisabeth. You're being emotional . . .

ELISABETH: I'm not! We need to get her to a doctor. We need to get out of
here. This is no place for—

JOSEF: Let me see . . .

Elisabeth is reluctant.

JOSEF: Elisabeth, please. If she's really sick I should see for myself.
After a pause, Elisabeth hands the baby over. Josef looks at the baby.

ELISABETH: She needs to see a doctor! Please . . . don't let her die.

JOSEF: You think I'd let my granddaughter die?

ELISABETH: Granddaughter?

JOSEF: Watch your tongue.

ELISABETH: I'm sorry, I'm sorry, I'm sorry, just . . .please. Help her. And . . .
don't . . . take her away from me. Just . . . please . . . give her
back. Give her back!
Josef exits with the baby.

ELISABETH: No! No! Please! Let me keep her! At least just let me hold her
one last time! NO! PLEASE!
She bangs on the door again, and again, it's no use.

ELISABETH: PLEASE! WHY ARE YOU DOING THIS? I'M YOUR OWN
DAUGHTER, FOR GOD'S SAKE! PLEASE!
*She falls to the floor and cries. After a moment, she finishes her fit.
What else can she do? She gets herself together and dries her eyes.*

ELISABETH: One day, after the ogre had taken yet another one of her children
away from her, a horrific realization dawned on the princess.
There would be no handsome prince to come to her rescue.
No Fairy Godmother. No genie granting her wishes of freedom.
There was no one to come to save the princess, because, thanks
to the letters the ogre forced her to write, there was no reason for
anyone to believe she was missing.
Josef is holding an evening gown.

JOSEF *(indicating the gown)*: I thought, since Rosemarie is heading out
for the night, that we could dine together. Please, don't be mad,
darling. Would you put this on? Please? I'll prepare a fine meal
for both of us. How does that sound?
*Elisabeth says nothing. Josef puts the dress over the chair.
He pulls Elisabeth close, who's reluctant, but decides not to fight.*

JOSEF: Please . . . don't be mad . . . we'll have a fine meal.
*He runs his fingers through her hair and breathes in her scent.
She looks disgusted but again, doesn't fight. He rubs his face up
against her cheek and massages her tummy.*

JOSEF: You'll forget all about that sick child.

ELISABETH: Just like I forget all of them.
Josef examines her face.

JOSEF: Was that sass?

ELISABETH: . . .

JOSEF *(snickers)*: What I always loved about you. Your ability to show
sass and spunk, even when you're being all grumpy. *(Pause.)*
You know I do love you, right, Elisabeth?
Josef resumes holding and pawing at Elisabeth. She doesn't resist.

JOSEF: You've always been . . . special to me. Really. Special. You
understand that, right, sweetie?

ELISABETH: Uh-huh . . .

JOSEF: That's why we have this special arrangement. Your mother would never understand. She'd be too . . . meddlesome. Too intrusive. It's better this way. This way, we have each other to ourselves. I don't have to share you with your mother.

ELISABETH: . . . Yes . . . daddy . . .

JOSEF   (*grabbing her jaw, threatening*): Watch yourself, love. You're still emotional.

ELISABETH: Sorry . . . my . . . darling.

JOSEF   (*loosens his grip on her jaw*): Not at all, my love. (*Caresses her face.*) Now. Please. Prepare yourself. I'll be back with our meal shortly. (*Exits.*)
Elisabeth looks at the dress with contempt.

ELISABETH: The walls to her prison were thick, and she realized she was too far under the ground for people in the house to hear her screams. She knew the ogre was in the mood to do unspeakable things to the princess that night, as he had done many times before.
She goes over to the dress. Cautiously and uncomfortably, she gets out of her clothes and changes into the dress, turning her back on the cameras, painfully aware of their relentless leering.
As she changes, we see scratch marks, welts and bruises all over her back. She changes into the dress, now as ready as she'll ever be for dinner.

ELISABETH: It dawned on the princess that it was going to be up to her to escape her prison. And the terrible fate that await her after the meal. (*She looks at the candles.*) Fortunately, she had an idea. It wasn't going to be pretty.
She sits and waits for Josef. Her eyes glance over at the pen that's still on the table. She snatches it and hides it. Josef enters with a tray of food and bottle of wine. The plates are paper and the cups and cutlery are plastic.

JOSEF: Ah, look at you, my love. You look radiant. I hope this is to your liking. I was originally hoping to prepare steak, since I know that's your favorite, but cutting it all to size just takes so much time. And we can't have you using the steak knives, since you tend to get . . . emotional . . . when the children have to be brought upstairs for safe keeping. You understand.

ELISABETH   (*pause*): Of course.

JOSEF: Lest we forget about that last time you deliberately ruined the evening.
They sit down to eat.

ELISABETH: Yes.

JOSEF: Those cameras aren't cheap, you know.

ELISABETH: No, I know. I'm sorry. (*Pause.*) How is she?

JOSEF: She'll be taken care of.

ELISABETH: How are they all doing?

JOSEF: I'm sorry?

ELISABETH   (*sighs*): Our . . . children. Are they healthy? Are they happy?

Josef looks enraged, but isn't going to let such sass ruin the mood. He forces a smile.

JOSEF: Rosemarie's spoiling them.

ELISABETH (*haughty*): How is my mother?

JOSEF: !!!

ELISABETH: We don't have to talk about this if you don't want. I just figured we should talk. If we're dining together.

JOSEF   (*a dig/warning*): She misses you, but respects your wishes to not be sought after.

ELISABETH (*fuck fuck fuck*): Okay. I was just curious. (*Pause.*) I'm glad to hear our children are doing well.

JOSEF: They are. Wine? (*She doesn't respond.*) It's not . . . spiked, my sweet. Here. I'll have some myself to show you. (*He pours himself a cup and drinks.*) See?

ELISABETH: Sure. (*He pours her a cup.*)

JOSEF: I must say, I'm beginning to regret that we're not able to spend as much quality time together like before.

ELISABETH: It's not like you don't know where I am.

JOSEF: Watch yourself.

ELISABETH: I didn't mean it like that, I'm sorry. (*Pause.*) Sorry if I've been hostile.

JOSEF: Think nothing of it.

ELISABETH: You know how I tend to get . . . emotional.

JOSEF: I do indeed, I do indeed.

ELISABETH: Could I have some more, please?

JOSEF: Why, certainly. (*Refills her cup.*)

ELISABETH (*downs the wine*): This is just lovely.

JOSEF: Is it?

ELISABETH: Yes.

JOSEF: I'm so glad you approve, my love. (*Pause.*) I know I do repeat myself, Elisabeth, but I must say, you are simply stunning in that dress.

ELISABETH: Well. You picked it out.

JOSEF   (*leering*): But I couldn't have imagined how . . . you'd fill it out.

ELISABETH: Really?

JOSEF: Yes. Oh, yes . . .
             Now's the time. She needs to get ready. This could be her one shot. She'd have to play along.

ELISABETH (*to herself*): The princess knew what to do. It's not like she hadn't had to do it before.

JOSEF: What was that, my darling?
             Throughout the following, she becomes coquettish and coy.

ELISABETH (*in a little kid's voice*): Nuffin', daddy.
             She moves her chair over towards Josef, hikes the dress up slightly and starts to spread her legs. Josef's breathing gets heavy and shallow. She continues using the little kid's voice until otherwise indicated.

ELISABETH: Is it okay for me to call you daddy again?

JOSEF: Oooh, you're all frisky . . .

ELISABETH: It's the wine, daddy. You shouldn't be letting little girls drink wine. They get all silly.

JOSEF: That's true, that's true . . .

ELISABETH: You like the way I look in this, daddy?

JOSEF: . . . Absolutely . . .

ELISABETH: You ready for dessert, daddy? Yeah? (*Josef nods eagerly.*) You like it when I talk like this, daddy? Is your baby girl being naughty?

JOSEF (*crawling over to her*): . . . Oh . . . yes . . . but don't worry . . . I won't punish you too hard.
Pulls him up by the chin to have him face her.

ELISABETH: I know, daddy. But . . .
She pulls him closer.

ELISABETH: I still need to be punished a little . . .

JOSEF (*stroking her hair*): Okay, my sweet . . .

ELISABETH: Please, daddy. You know what to call me. You like that. It gets you all excited . . .

JOSEF: Okay . . . okay . . . I'll punish you a little . . . my daughter.

ELISABETH: Okay, daddy . . .
She pulls him in for the kiss. As she does so, she jams the pen into his ear. Blood shoots out as Josef falls back and howls in agony.
She now drops the little kid's voice.

ELISABETH: You still mad, daddy? You going to punish me worse now?
Josef lunges at her, but he misses.

JOSEF: You . . . fucking . . . I'll fucking KILL YOU, YOU BITCH!
She takes the bottle of wine and turns over the table and uses it as a shield as he comes after her.

JOSEF: FUCKING . . . KILL YOU . . . BITCH!
He plows through the table to get to her.
She hits him with the bottle. Blood pours out of his head. He collapses to the ground.

JOSEF: . . . Fucking . . . Bitch!
She hits him with the bottle over and over again.

ELISABETH: FUCK YOU, YOU FUCKING OGRE! I'M YOUR FUCKING DAUGHTER! HOW DARE YOU! HOW FUCKING DARE YOU!
Elisabeth continues beating him until it's clear he isn't getting up.
TITLE CARD. This was not a true story.
She stops, looking down at the messy mutilated corpse of her father.
TITLE CARD. This was a fairy tale.
She drops the weapon and goes through his pockets. She finds the key.
TITLE CARD. The true story:
TITLE CARD. Josef Fritzl held his daughter Elisabeth captive in a concealed part of the basement of the family home for 24 years.
TITLE CARD. They had several children together.
She then slowly staggers toward the door, in a daze.
TITLE CARD. Three of their children had been imprisoned along with Elisabeth for the whole of their lives.

TITLE CARD. Josef and his wife raised three other children conceived by Elisabeth in the upstairs home. Josef engineered their appearance as foundlings discovered outside his house.
TITLE CARD. When Elisabeth's eldest daughter became seriously ill, Josef took her to a hospital, triggering a series of events that eventually led to the discovery of Elisabeth's imprisonment.

ELISABETH: At long last, the princess was free from the ogre's prison. After preparing to round up her children, she thought it'd be nice to see the sky again. It had been quite a long time, after all.
Elisabeth opens the door. The light pouring in is blinding. She shields her eyes and exits.
TITLE CARD. There was no dramatic escape.
TITLE CARD. Josef is still alive.
TITLE CARD. Sources: Wikinews, CNN.

BLACKOUT

The Ghost Hunter (2013)

by

STEWART PRINGLE

Preface

Stewart Pringle and Tom Richards, who had become interested in Grand-Guignol while still students at Oxford, established Theatre of the Damned in London in 2010 as a company dedicated to 'the neglected world of the Théâtre du Grand-Guignol'. Most of their productions played relatively short runs as part of the London Horror Festival, which they were instrumental in founding. In 2012 they performed *The Horror, The Horror*, a Lovecraft-inspired show in the (at that time) unrestored Wilton's Music Hall in London's East End.[22]

However, it was arguably *The Ghost Hunter*, a simply staged one-person tale of the supernatural, that was the company's greatest commercial success, premiering at The Old Red Lion Theatre on 30 April 2013, where it ran for four weeks, before a successful run at the Pleasance Courtyard at the Edinburgh Fringe in August and then an occasional national tour that visited towns and cities as diverse as Salford (The Lowry), Broadstairs, Worcester, Cambridge and York, among others, before finishing back in London in May 2014.

The hour-long production, directed by Jeffrey Mayhew and designed by Alice Saville, featured Richards in the role of Richard Barraclough, a failed actor and alcoholic, who plies his trade leading ghost tours through the medieval streets of York. Reviewer Graeme Strachan described it as 'a genuinely haunting experience' and 'a great old fashioned ghost tale' (www.britishtheatreguide.info/reviews/the-ghost-hunte-pleasance-court-9166).

The Ghost Hunter is interesting on a number of levels. It is, of course, a ghost story, and the Grand-Guignol has traditionally steered well clear of the supernatural, even though it has been a regular feature in wider horror culture from the early Gothic onwards. Where the Grand-Guignol did stray into the supernatural, it did so either with a degree of ambiguity (for example, in Gaston Leroux's *The Man Who Met the Devil*) or with

---

[22] Wilton's formed the inspiration for 'The Grand Guignol Theatre', a fictional blood and thunder melodrama house in John Logan's TV Series *Penny Dreadful* for Showtime/Sky (2014–16).

an exposition of any supposed revenant as a natural phenomenon, such as in Aragny and Neilson's *The Kiss of Blood*. This ambivalence towards the supernatural—the horrors of the Grand-Guignol were always very much set in the real world—emerges from its origins in late nineteenth-century naturalism and modern Grand-Guignol theatre companies seem less concerned with such limitations, being much more willing to use whatever might be available to the makers of horror theatre. And yet *The Ghost Hunter* is not a straightforward play about the supernatural, and some of that Grand-Guignol ambivalence is evident as the story unfolds: it is as much a story about fakery, the gullibility of the audience to believe and non-ghosts, as it is about real ghosts.

Pringle is very aware of the dangers of overreliance on the supernatural as a tool for creating atmosphere, yet in writing *The Ghost Hunter* was also aware of the role that it plays in the horror lexicon, especially among horror audiences. While television shows such as *Inside No. 9* (2014 onwards), embrace elements of the supernatural, in terms of theatre in particular, the most successful 'horror' shows in recent years have both been supernatural plays: *The Woman in Black*, which has been running at the Fortune Theatre since January 1989 and is now the second longest-running show in the West End after *The Mousetrap*, and Jeremy Dyson and Andy Nyman's *Ghost Stories*, which premiered at the Liverpool Playhouse in 2010 before successfully transferring to London. Furthermore, the production of horror theatre in recent years has, not surprisingly, focused around Halloween, and Theatre of the Damned found that their forays into the supernatural were the most popular with audiences and the best critically received plays in their repertoire:

> we actually found the most successful of the evening was the supernatural play. The others, most of the others, did fine but the reviews and the critical response was very much the supernatural play is the highlight [. . .] We kind of found that we got a stronger reaction from that and so we sort of started moving more into looking at, yeah, the supernatural and the cosmic horror and moving slightly further away from the murder and revenge, and violence aspect.
>
> (Interview, 31 August 2016)

One ambition of Theatre of the Damned was always to try and build a regular and sustainable audience for horror theatre and exploiting Halloween formed an important part of that strategy. *The Ghost Hunter* was their first real attempt to produce horror theatre all year round and Pringle admits that it was a challenge, explaining that

> when we did *Ghost Hunter* around Halloween in Wilton's and places we sold out, but when we did it in May we really struggled, because

nobody was looking for a ghost story because it was the middle of the summer.

(Interview, 31 August 2016)

It was, however, the very consideration of the economics of production and building a sustainable model of production that could support a professional company, working in the small, intimate venues that horror performance often demands, that in part led to *The Ghost Hunter* in the first place:

> *The Horror, The Horror*, at Wilton's, that was commissioned by Wilton's so was all covered by Wilton's financially as an in-house deal. The next year we looked at the financial implications of building a horror show and, basically, the one thing we could make money back on was doing sort of a one-man ghost story show. So I wrote a play called *The Ghost Hunter*, which we toured and commercially that worked, but only just and that was one man with a hat, not eight people and gallons of fake blood and laundry bills.
>
> (Interview, 31 August 2016)

In a sense, this consideration of the economics of theatre-making is similar to the way in which the Théâtre du Grand-Guignol in Paris also had to operate, with a careful control of the company size, a regular change in repertoire to ensure returning audiences and a watchful eye on the laundry bills.

The play is also Grand-Guignolesque in its economy of writing. *The Ghost Hunter* is a finely crafted monologue that is written to fit into the durational limitations of London pub theatre or the Edinburgh Fringe. As was the case at the rue Chaptal, it was the economics and context of the production that determines *what* is done and *how* it is done in a fusion of the realities and the mechanics of theatre-making.

As with the best examples of Grand-Guignol, *The Ghost Hunter* is also a playful script. It is itself a story of artifice, trickery, theatrical myth-making and the relationship between performer and audience—all very much part and parcel of the Grand-Guignol form. It is a piece of meta-theatre, referring to its own theatricality and artifice, a piece of storytelling that enters into a game with the audience. Even the description of the atmospheric walk through York's medieval old town is a kind of homage to the renowned walk through Pigalle from the metro to the rue Chaptal that was essential to building the necessary atmosphere and a critical part of the whole Grand-Guignol experience.

THE GHOST HUNTER (2013)

by

STEWART PRINGLE

First performed at the Old Red Lion Theatre, London, 30 April 2013

Cast
Richard

The back room of the Black Swan, a public house in York. Present day. A table and stool stand centre-stage.

Faint light up. Richard sits at the table, he wears a long black coat and top hat. There is a near-full pint of ale at his hand, and a black leather bag at the side of his stool.

RICHARD: They came just after midnight. There were no lights in the windows, there were no sounds. Even the coughing had pretty much stopped. And they gathered outside with pots of red paint and brushes, and with nails and long wooden boards. They came with a minister and he stood by the house and read a long prayer in Latin for the souls of those afflicted that dwelled inside. Or perhaps he prayed for himself, and the men from the city who had already begun branding the doors and windows of the little house on College Street with the red cross. X marks the spot. Plague. It must have woken them up when the first board was nailed into place, one of the poor souls must have heard it, but if they did they were too weak to move.

    Perhaps they did call out, perhaps they did cry for help or mercy, it's not recorded. Nobody wrote that bit down. Nobody would have written any of it down, I don't expect, except for what happened in the top room. This was 1551, and the plague had swept through York with dreadful ferocity. In the poorest districts of the city there were bodies mounting in the streets, and men, women and children would shuffle back and forth with rough bandages on their bitter, suppurating wounds. When the plague struck a house in the city centre, in an unaffected road like College Street that stood in the shadow of the Minster, this is what was done. Always in the dead of night, always with a prayer and a handful of long iron nails. It was a family in this one; two parents, one grandparent and three children, and they'd all got it.

They tried to keep it under wraps, they always did, but word got out, it always did.

It were a week later when someone spotted it. A tiny hand pressing against the glass in the top window, palm flat against it, banging again and again. Then a tiny face, wide eyed and weeping. The youngest girl, five or six years old, she'd recovered. It happened from time to time. Lucky her. Not so lucky. Children pointed as they walked past, but the grownups just turned their faces away and hurried on. Nothing to be done. And in that top room a little girl pushed her face to the glass and cried out until her throat stung. And she went to her father and her mother, slumped in their beds, and she tried to wake them, over and over again until the smell got too bad. And then she got hungry. And then she died.

Now the first recorded sighting wasn't until 1890, when a young man new to the city knocked on the door of the little house by the Minster and a servant answered him. 'Who's that little girl in the top window?' he asked, 'And why is she crying?' But there was no girl in the window, there was no girl in the house at all. After that she was seen quite regularly. Always in the top window, always at night, always crying with a hand against the glass. There's an elderly couple living there now, and a few times a year, without fail, a stranger knocks on the door and asks them the same questions. Who's the girl? Why's she crying? They've even heard her from time to time, a quiet sobbing from the top of the stairs. They'd rush upstairs, knocking teacups from laps and barging through the door of the little room. There's nothing. There's nothing there at all.

Lights rise.

Now, the thing with Abbot is, it makes you want to piss like a bloody racehorse. Excuse me.

Standing up.

Why is that? It's not like a pint of Hen makes you piss. Pint of Hen makes no difference at all. But Abbot's practically a diuretic. Like it does it on purpose. Excuse me.

Retires backstage. We hear the sound of him pissing into a toilet.

That's it. Just talk amongst yourselves. Not bad, that one. Bit of history, bit of tragedy, not much comedy but then it's a bloody Ghost Tour so it don't really matter, and a creepy child at the end. The old couple who own the house are actually personal friends of mine, and they leave a lamp on in the room so when I point to it everyone can have a good peer and spook themselves out a bit. I send them a bottle of wine every Christmas to say thanks or whatever.

Returns, wiping his hands on his coat.

Good people. And every year when I drop it round I ask how she's getting on, that little girl, and there's always another story. They've always had a knock at the door or heard little footsteps and sobs from the top room. Not bad at all.

But punters don't come for not bad. And they don't come for that bollocks Harry Martindale spins about the ghostly romans wandering about in a cellar, either. They come for him. They want to hear about George Pimm.

It could only work as a closer. You couldn't put it anywhere else. It's the big one, the big guns. You save those till last. I don't know anyone . . . I don't know anyone on the circuit who'd put it anywhere else. Some of them miss it out altogether. The softer lot. The 5.30's. Pre-dinner. Family crowd. You wouldn't want to face your Bella Italia for four after that, would you? It's the one they go home talking about. It's the headliner. It's not just the story, but it is a great story. It's the place. The name.

Bedern.

Bloody perfect.

Blackout. Atmospheric music. Lights rise. RICHARD is removing his coat and hat.

It all started in 1840 when George Pimm was appointed Parish Beadle and walked down Goodramgate with the keys to the Ragged School in his pocket. Pimm took the keys from his ragged old pocket and turned them in the front door of the school.

Or maybe it started back in 1805 when George Pimm was born with a crook in his back to a butcher who drank and who beat him with the end of a thick leather belt.

Or 1812, a Monday, George Pimm finds his neighbour's cat on the street and takes it home. Tuesday, morning, Pimm cuts one of the cat's ears off with one of his father's knives. Afternoon, 5pm, Pimm panics, tries to drown the cat in a barrel of rainwater in his father's yard. 5.05pm on a Tuesday afternoon in an unseasonably harsh October in the year of our Lord 1812 George Pimm is caught in the act of catricide by his father, the butcher, who beats him, savagely.

1840 and George Pimm has installed himself like a tick in the centre of a sprawling, stinking city. It's two streets over from where he grew up, but his father's shop isn't there any more, it's been taken over by a tanner. There are still plenty of butchers, of course. That's what the Shambles are. They're butchers streets. The pavements have a channel that runs right down the middle of them to catch the blood that floods out of the butchers' shops six days a week.

George Pimm has his little patch of land in the middle of a swamp of blood and offal. Pimm's got two whole rooms to himself, with a big open fire in one of them. Then there's two dormitories on the ground floor, and a long gallery that's used for lessons. Pimm watches a young lad up a stepladder painting the sign, forming the letters on the board as he wobbles back and forth, York—Industrial—Ragged—School.

It's the summer of 1840 and Pimm is moving in his furniture. A lectern. A few chairs and desks. Slates, assorted. A wardrobe.

It's more than one hundred and fifty years later. A man turns from Bedern, numb with fear and pale as death, and totters into the night.

York.

That's what it's built on. It used to be built on trains, then chocolate, now it's only the ghosts holding it together. 1978 and there were already a few of them. I remember the signs all cable-tied to lamp-posts with grainy pictures of Bela Lugosi or a face with the skin all hanging off and great boogly eyes. Names like 'Spoooooky Tours', spelled like that with four O's, and you'd see the crowds of punters led by men in black, awkwardly criss-crossing each other in the narrow streets. This is before the Dungeons opened up, there was just a House of Horrors in the waxworks down Friargate with Crippin and a lot of the London types. This was when it had just kicked off, really.

Produces a manila folder from his bag, opens it and removes a few thin tourist guides: 'Walking Haunted York', etc.

I saw these in some museum gift-shop. My father didn't want me to have them, just a load of gruesome tat, but I kept on at him and eventually he caved in. Some of these I've had since then, some of them are new. It's turned into a sort of collection, I suppose. Just cheap stuff. Just rubbish. 'The Bloody Jews of Clifford's Tower' . . . site of an anti-Semitic massacre in the 12th century—'visitors walking past the ruined tower in the dead of night have reported strange howling and wailings imanating', well they've spelled that wrong. That should be with an E that should. 'Emanating from the shadowy recesses of the tower.' Well there's not much strange about that because that's where we used to go to cop off, that is. That's where I copped off with Julie Featherstone, Bonfire Night 1985.

'The Tragedy of the Shambles Girl', spirit of a young girl who tumbled down stairs and broke her neck at some party, conveniently first manifested when the gift shop downstairs had had a particularly bad season and punters were a bit thin on the ground.

'The Body Shop Poltergeist' . . . I mean that one's actually branded; it's a branded ghost! (*reading.*) 'Visitors to the Body Shop have been known to see objects fly through the air, find objects in places they had not been before, and others in their possession to disappear entirely.' Which adds a much needed frisson of danger to a store that largely specializes in unwanted Christmas gifts and ecologically minded body butter.

'The Headless Woman' . . . well, speaks for itself, that one.

Puts the books aside.

Now, as you may have gathered from this publicity material I am in fact a Ghost Hunter. To be more precise I am and have for the last eighteen-odd years been a Ghost Tour Operator, or in layman's terms, a failed actor. I was born in Milton Keynes

in 1971, and moved age seven to York. I lived there until I was
eighteen when I spent two years of disillusionment and afternoon
drinking at a non-accredited London drama school operated by
a drug addict and a Baby Jane-esque harridan with an irritable
poodle named Christopher and an Evian bottle filled with neat
gin. I returned to York three stones heavier with my heart broken
and no money whatsoever. In the biography of my drinking
problem, this short break in the capital serves as the prologue,
and the rest of the chapters more or less wrote themselves.

I began as an occasional fill-in on The Haunted Tour of York,
which began at 8pm every evening except Mondays from just
outside the Minster. It was what you might call a mid-level ghost
walk, with relatively low footfall through the winter months and
a small uptick near Christmas. Bank holidays were packed and
we were busy through most of the summer. Started in the late
1970s by an ancient bastard called Ronald who used to work
in the education department of the Yorkshire Museum until he
was summarily fired for cutting pictures of Lord Fairfax out of
antique books, which he pasted into a scrapbook for no reason
I have ever managed to ascertain. Regardless, Ron possessed
an encyclopedic knowledge of York's criminal and paranormal
history, and all the stage presence of a stick insect. He was a dry
and desiccated sort of man with a reedy voice that was buffeted
about by the wind: he wore a coat three sizes too big for him
and carried a silver-topped walking stick which had become less
ornamental and more structural as the years rolled on and Ron's
arthritis began to bite.

Ron and I met in the bar of the Black Swan, a pub which
famously played host to a range of black magic rituals in the
18th century, and which runs regular lock-ins on Wednesday and
Thursday evenings. It was at just such a lock-in that I found Ron
lodged under a low table, which he'd ventured under in search
of a stray 20p coin only to find that his knees had locked. Falsely
regarding himself to be a man of some dignity, he had been
unable to bring himself to call out for assistance, and so when I
sat down at the table with Dave Henderson I accidentally hoofed
Ron in the gut. After helping him to his feet and treating him to
a half pint of mild we got talking about the job, and by the time
we staggered out into the birdsong of a chill April morning he'd
offered me a one-week trial subject to training, the majority of
which was delivered in a snug of the Black Swan, Ron holding a
confused sort of court and me scribbling down the ten or twelve
stories in his repertoire into my notepad.

That's how it started. And this is how it starts . . .
*Lights out. Sound. Then lights slowly rise. He steps forward from
the shadows upstage.*

Good evening, ladies and gentlemen. Step a little closer if
you please. That's it, huddle together, closer. Huddle together for

warmth—not that close madam, this is a public thoroughfare.
Now, welcome one and all to The Haunted Tour of York.
My name is Richard Barraclough and I am to be your guide this
evening. Now, before I begin I must assure you that though there
are rather a lot of you here this evening you will all be able to see
me and you will all be able to hear me. I must ask you to take
care when moving as we will be crossing several roads, I must
ask that you all stick together and do not go wandering off into
the ghoul-ridden night, and that you allow any children in the
audience to move down to the front where they can enjoy an
unrestricted view.

And we're off. Minster Yard to Denegate, Plague House,
Goodramgate and the lost and headless Earl. Colliergate,
Coppergate, Coney Street, Stonegate, Low Petergate, Aldwark,
Bedern. George Pimm and the Ragged School.
Takes a hefty gulp from his pint.

It was renovated in the 1970s, but whatever building the
school had been in was long gone by then. Now it's all a Barratt
Homes sort of thing. Red brick, new builds, everyone's got their
own parking space, you know. Mainly older folks. You come
straight from the cobbled shambles and through a low sort of
arch and suddenly you're not really in York any more, you're in
the outskirts of Doncaster. It's not what you'd call attractive, and
it's not what you'd call atmospheric either. You'd walk straight
past it and never give it a second glance. Boring, really. But it
doesn't matter what you build on somewhere like that. It don't
matter what you put over the top of it. You could build an out
of town shopping centre on somewhere like that and there'd be
women fainting in TK Maxx. You can't just scrub out something
like that, like Bedern. It's gone wrong for good.
Another gulp of ale.

They used to ask me, especially the Americans, used to ask
me 'What scares you? What's a Ghost Hunter scared of?' And
I used to look at them. Just stare at them for a second, and then
I'd reach out my hand and gesture like this.
Shows beckoning gesture.

And I'd wait for them to come to me. Bit closer.
Continues to gesture.

And I'd say: 'The thing that strikes cold terror into the heart of
every free working man of York.' And then I'd lean in to their ear
and whisper . . .

H . . . M . . . R . . . C.

I think most of the buggers thought it was a secret code.
Drinks.

By 1994 there were more than ten tours operating within
the city walls, and you had to do quite a bit to stand out. Most
of the guides would end up in the same handful of pubs of an
evening, and they made an odd crowd. Bunch of middle aged

men in top hats and cloaks swapping stories about dead kings
and complaining about the weather or the council. There were
some bloody good story-tellers and there were ones who just
paid a couple of students five quid to jump out of the shadows
in a Freddy Krueger mask. Ron never bothered with it, he was a
private sort of man when he wasn't performing, but I'd go along
for a chat. It's a lonely business, otherwise.

I was watching the football in the King's Arms with a mate
called Clive who works on a haunted riverboat. It's not actually
haunted, obviously, it's just been painted black on the inside. At
Christmas it's not haunted at all, it's a Christmas Cruiser and
they paint it red and green and string tinsel up. But this wasn't
Christmas so it was a haunted boat and Clive was working on it
most evenings. And it was a Sunday afternoon and I was standing
at the bar and enjoying my pint, and not enjoying watching
the football much because I support Brentford and people who
support Brentford rarely do, and I notice my hat is not where
I left it. And it's not just any old hat, it's this hat. It's a very
important hat. And I've got a tour in a couple of hours and I'm
buggered if I'm doing it without . . .
Indicates hat.

Then I spot it, just outside the window. It's on a woman's
head. She looks like she's had a few. And she's posing and there's
a bunch of lasses with her all in matching T-shirts. Bloody hen
parties. I go outside to talk to her, I'm a bit cross and I'm a bit
addled as well so I just snatch it off her head. 'Oh, is that yours?'
she asks. Well of course it's mine, it was standing right next to
my pint. And besides, how many other men are there watching
Brentford versus Carlisle wearing full Victorian formal dress?
She laughs. She's pretty.

And then she says, 'You do one of those Ghost Tours, then?'
I tell her I do, and I'm about to turn away when she says,
'Brilliant! Could I have a word with you about it?' and she sits
me down. She's a teacher at Fishergate Primary and she wants
me to do a tour for her class. End of term treat. I say we'll sort
something out.
Drinks.

Now, I have to confess, I am not a fan of school bookings.
They don't bloody listen and they walk too slowly. So that
night after my regular tour I ask Ron if he'd mind taking it for
me. I thought for a minute he was going to have a heart attack,
practically choked on his beer and it's not like him to waste good
beer. 'Not up my street,' he says, 'not up my street that one. And
I'd leave it well alone if I were you . . .' Well, I'd said we'd sort it
for her so that just left me.

Fix it for the next Thursday and it's a scorching hot day and
she's brought dozens of them. Must be two classes worth at least.
They're chattering and running ahead, they're not in the least bit

scared because it's the middle of the afternoon and they're too busy faffing about with their cartons of Ribena and Mini Milks to bother much with the stories. Until I got to the end. Until I got to Pimm. And they started to cry. I've had criers before, I think it's the walking that does it, mainly. But this wasn't one or two. It was all of them. Crying and balling and the pretty teacher's scolding them and trying to make a joke of it and explain, but it was no use. They were terrified. I had to cut it short, couldn't finish it. And I caught the teacher's eye as she was leading them out of the little courtyard. Angry, I think. Not apologetic, anyway. It was almost . . . Well, funny lot, teachers.

Now, as they say, for the science bit.

Reaches into his bag and retrieves a strange box that resembles a wireless with assorted wires and cables glued to it. A small black microphone is attached by a black cord.

Control yourselves. Now, I'm keenly aware that the Background Psytronic Galvometer is not in fact particularly convincing, so I'll ask you to bear in mind that it was constructed in 1992 when everyone was mad on *Ghostbusters* and that it was usually getting a bit dim by the time I wheeled it out. I'd hold this bit and I'd hand the receiver to a kid or a giggling lass and ask them to hold it while I waggled the aerial round. Just leave it on an empty station. It's just a wireless. It was just white noise but if you'd built it up right they loved it. They'd all listen to this fizzing sound and I'd tell them that if you listened just right you could pick up voices, spirits. Hang on.

Turns on the Galvometer. White noise.

I'd do it by that tower and tell them to listen for the sound of flames flickering in the distance, screaming. And I'd just wait. And they'd just listen. And there was nothing there, but the longer they listened, the more they concentrated. Willed it.

White noise increases. Pause. RICHARD suddenly clicks the device off.

Then one night I caught the dial with my sleeve and treated them to a burst of 97.2 Slade FM, and that was the end of that.

But I was serious about it, in a way. About things, bad things, being stored up somewhere. Something happens and it gets in the stones. In the ground. Or it just gets in the people and stays with them. Persists. I don't drink in the Kings Arms anymore, I don't even like going near it in case I bump into that teacher again. With that look. We've all got our private hauntings. And in a city, one like York that's just graveyard laid on graveyard, some of them are very public. Some of them are shared out, like a birthright. Viking invasions. Sloughs of skin nailed to church doors. Clifford's Tower. It's surprisingly contagious, mass murder. It's difficult to shake off.

The Catholics know what they're at. They know people need places to put things. Ways to sort of tell stories. Like with

Clitherow. Margaret Clitherow, saint and martyr. The pearl of
York. Patron saint of martyrs, converts, and for reasons which
are rather unclear, businesswomen. Caught harbouring Jesuit
priests and pressed under a door. There's a shrine to her down
the Shambles, and they've got it all written up on like a fake
parchment done with calligraphy and that and people come there
and they pray. Praying that it's haunted, or to make it haunted.
But what the sign doesn't tell is that she wasn't some hellfire
and brimstone mother superior neither, some old martyr with a
wimple—she was a thirty-year-old mother of two. She married
a well-to-do butcher, a Protestant, when she was sixteen year
old. And they took her, these men, these old lecherous bastards
and they stripped her naked and they covered her with a slab of
splintered oak and stamped it down and piled lumps of masonry
on it till her ribs broke one by one and she choked on her own
frothing blood.

What happens next? To that room where they did her in? How
do you live in that room? How do you smile in that room, ever?
People cross the little street to give it a wide berth. Nobody'll
have it. No new owners. No new tenants. Nobody wants to wash
it down or sweep it out. Put in a few shelves and turn it into a
chandlers or a butchers or . . . It's like a crossroads where they
used to burn witches, or an old tree with the rope marks still cut
into the bark. Cursed places. Shunned. Bad for business.

So you don't sweep it out. You don't try to gull some bloke
into taking it on. You say, 'this is the shrine of Saint Margaret
the blessed martyr. And here's a bit of her hair, here's the hand
they lopped off her, here's a bit of bone or a splash of blood.'
She haunts the place and we let her, we encourage her. Because
what else can we do? What choice do we have? Make it a story,
pass it on.

Or like with the Jews in that tower: 'What happened to the
Jews in that tower? What did you do to them? Why? Why did
you do it?' 'Well I'm not quite sure, to tell you the truth, but don't
worry, they're still here. Listen closely. Listen at night.'

They're like sticking plasters, like stitches when a town cuts
itself open. There's always a grain of truth in them. Usually a
great boulder. Do you know what they mean, ghost stories? Ron
asked me that the first time I met him. 'Do you know what they
mean? Do you know what they are? They're a place to put things
you're too scared to look at any more.'
Picks up one of the guidebooks. Finds a page.

1841. In York's litany of terrible things this one's about the worst.
Puts book down.

The Ragged School is full. It's more than full, it's over-full.
38 children, all aged between six and twelve. The two dormitories
are roughly covered with straw and tatters of sackcloth and the
straw and the cloth is soaked with filth and urine. The rooms

were intended to segregate the boys from the girls, but the state of hygiene and the proliferation of infectious diseases around the blood-stained Shambles and necrotic Ragged School has seen a large number of the thin and sallow-faced children fall ill. The second room has become a sort of neglected hospital, where the sick are carried by their classmates so that their coughing does not make sleep impossible. The summer is hot and thick, and the air is filled with the smell of decay and urine, together with the sickly smell of animal offal that drifts from the butchers' shops nearby.

George Pimm rests in his living quarters, plush with the money he earns from the children's care. The city awards Pimm one shilling per month for each of the children who attend his school, and allowing approximately one penny per head per week for the meagre gruel he serves each child, he makes a tidy profit on their keep. Lessons take place between 8am and 5pm each day, readings from the Bible about obedience, humility and self-sacrifice. Pimm is quick to anger, and the lessons are punctuated by savage beatings.

The first to die is a nine-year-old boy. He slices open his foot on a nail left poking through the floorboards, and it goes bad. He's suffering from malnutrition, but then they all are, but the lack of food combined with the unsanitary conditions in the school means that he rapidly develops what would now be termed gangrene. He calls out through the night, and his cries are loud enough to wake Pimm from his drunken slumber, and the beadle turned schoolmaster beats him with his thick cane until he faints dead away. The other children pretend they're asleep. Until he leaves and they crawl over the straw and try to wake him. He rouses once, just before dawn, and then expires. When Pimm pulls the shutters open in the morning and sticks his boot into the tiny crumpled body he finds it stiff as a board. Pimm panics, and in the bright sunshine of an August morning just before 7am Pimm takes the boy outside, wrapped in a scrap of sackcloth, and he buries him in the rough patch of land outside the school. *Light shifts.*

Now there are 37 children in the Ragged School at Bedern. But when Pimm goes to collect his shillings he takes 38, and the little boy is forgotten. More follow. The younger ones, the weak ones die first. Before long there's a little graveyard in the patch of earth outside the school. Shallow graves. Hardly graves at all. And still 38 shillings in Pimm's ragged pocket. Numbers getting thin, Pimm takes in more. 40 shillings, 45. And when he closes his eyes he can see them, and when he tries to sleep he can hear them. So he drinks, he drinks to forget and to silence the crying in his head. And he locks the door of the school and vanishes for days and nights at a time, drinking and whoring. Leaving his wards to pick amongst the scraps of bread and plates licked clean of gruel in those two bare rooms. And they continued to die.

The winter came, and it was a hard one. And they died faster. The rooms were filled with coughing and . . . crying. But now when one of the poor buggers popped their clogs, the ground was too hard to bury them. Pimm could hardly crack the surface however hard he tried. So he began to stick the little bodies in the big oak wardrobe that sat in the corner of his pantry. By Christmas-time there were four or five in there, and as the winter bit into March there were nearly a dozen. Still Pimm took in more children, and still Pimm took his pocket full of shillings.

One day a constable turns up in the yard and Pimm spots him from the window, spots him asking questions of one of the boys. He's out there in a shot, pushes the brat back indoors. 'What seems to be the matter, constable? Can I help you?' And the constable's not bothered, he's passing by, killing time, he'd best be off, and he never notices Pimm scuff nervously at the earth beneath him with the tip of his cane.

It was the 2nd of April, and still cold as ever when a small boy, new to the Ragged School, found himself so terribly hungry that when Pimm was out drinking and carousing, he snuck his way upstairs and into his master's chambers. He ignored the protests of his fellow captives, his stomach ached so terribly and his limbs were stiff with weakness and the cold. He made his way into the plush rooms, filled with empty bottles of wine and scraps of cheap periodicals and newspapers. He crept into the panty and shovelled a great hunk of bread into his mouth, when his eyes fell on a wardrobe in the corner, barely a shadow the gloom. He edged towards it, like he was drawn to it. Like a lost friend of his was calling out. His hand had reached the doorknob when the sound of someone crashing up the stairs made him jump backwards. Spitting oaths and drunkenly stumbling, Pimm made his way up to his rooms. And the little boy had nowhere to hide, nowhere except the wardrobe. And he flung himself inside it and the door swung closed and latched behind him. And the smell was unbearable . . .

Pimm kicked off his boots and flung himself into his bed. And that's when he hears the knocking. And the voice crying out from the pantry. His eyes snap open, and his hand reaches for the cane. And he creeps across his room and into the cold chamber next to it. Knock, knock, knock. From the wardrobe. From the wardrobe stacked to bursting with the bodies of his victims. The cane falls from his hands. And Pimm's mind collapses.

They found him in the morning. There'd been complaints, you see, from the houses around and about the Ragged School. Complaints of screams and howls, banging and shouting. 3rd of April the door was smashed down by two members of York's constabulary. They found Pimm standing in the middle of a pile of tiny bodies. Bloody cane in hand. Eyes bulging out of his head. He'd butchered them all. Pimm lived out the rest of his days in an asylum, and the Ragged School was flattened to dust.

Pause.

Except it wasn't. And Pimm never went to the wardrobe because the wardrobe was never there. And Bedern fields never filled up with little bodies because there never was a Ragged School.

Because it didn't start in 1840, or 1805 or a Monday in 1808. It started with me and Ron with a couple of pints of Abbot in the snug of the Black Swan on a rainy afternoon in 1995. I hadn't seen him since he left the tour to me about 18 months before. He'd had a bit to drink, well we both had, and he proposed a competition, to tell the spookiest story. It wasn't the first time. Ron had made up half a dozen of the best ones in his repertoire, said it was his favourite bit of the job. And he was always clever at it.

I got a round in and he started on his. At first I'm not really listening because I'm wracking my brain trying to think of my own, but I catch bits of it. Something about a craggy old beadle, a schoolmaster in old York. And a school that stood in a cold hard cemetery of its own making. And it's good. It's really bloody good. So I started jotting it down. I don't remember what mine was, it can't have been much cop. So Bedern started there. *Picks up a handful of the guidebooks.*

Or to be strictly accurate it started one night when it was pissing it down and I decided to take the tour back round to the Shambles to get out of it, and I dragged them into the archway by Bedern close to wait for the rain to ease off. When I opened my fat gob and before I knew it I was laying out that story from my notebook, and it flowed out so beautifully, full of tiny embellishments Ron hadn't even imagined. And they were enraptured. And they were afraid. And so I went back the next night, and the next. And the crowds got bigger, and I kept on telling it.

Or maybe it really started when Mad Alice, who was one of those strange backward women who carry a shopping bag full of other bags and cameras all wound on too far, maybe it started when she set up her own little tour and charged 75 pence, which is frankly just mental, and she tagged Ron's Bedern story, our Bedern story, on the end.

Or when it had gone round the block a few times and some chancer picked it up and put it in their little guide. Fiction pressed into fact when the rollers start rolling. *Opening a book.*

Page 43, George Pimm, the Butcher of York. *Another.*

Double page spread, with picture cribbed from the York Dungeon who used to have a full reconstruction of the event in fiberglass. Pimm staring out at the punters with wild cartoon eyes. Because you don't just tell a ghost story, not in York, you sell it on. Good business, ghosts. Intangible resource. You can build an

industry on them, you can build a city on them if you're careful, if
you don't ask too many questions.
Another.

Page 12 to 15, George Pimm and the Weeping Children of
Bedern.
Another.

And again. Pimm.
Another.

Pimm. Pimm. The children. There's even talk of putting up
a plaque. 'Dedicated to the Memory of the Children of Bedern
Industrial Ragged School.'
Laughs, not warmly.

The sightings started in about 1996, far as I can tell. Late at
night. Coming home from the pub, putting the bins out, putting
the cat out, taking the cat in. Whatever. It would be dark but
they've got lamps everywhere and if you so much as move three
security lights flick on like you're a prisoner of war making a
break for it. So it's never dark. And you've got some fellow taking
his dog for a walk and he hears this noise. Quiet. Just round the
corner. And it's some kid laughing.

Or maybe a couple of them, like they're playing a game or
singing a skipping song. And it echoes a bit because everything
echoes in Bedern, and it's a bit strange because it's far too late for
children to be playing on the streets. It's a quiet estate but it's not
as safe as it looks. So you go to check, tell them to get themselves
indoors. But there's no one there. They've vanished, like they were
never there at all.
Lighting shifts.

Now I've had people come up to me, after the walk, and tell
me that they've heard them. One woman, said she lived round
there, said she'd seen one of them. A little girl in a tattered dress
with filthy arms and legs just bawling to herself, like she was
lost. Said she'd seen her suddenly turn around as if she'd heard
something. That she'd called out to her but she was running in
the opposite direction. As if someone was chasing her.

You know, I almost felt guilty. The first time someone told me
that they'd seen something or . . . or heard something. I felt like
laughing in their faces.

Bloody fools.
Drains the last of his pint.

One last story. It's 2001 and a man walks alone through
what's left of Bedern. He's been here before. He's been here
hundreds of times and he's told the tale of the children to
thousands of people. He's not scared of ghosts. Ghosts are his
business. He's not scared of Pimm because Pimm didn't exist until
the name was scribbled on the top line of his jotter on a rainy
afternoon in '95. It's not raining now, it's a summer's evening
and he catches scent of something in the thick air. He thinks it's

a barbecue at first because it's strong and sweet, but then he gets another whiff and it stops him in his tracks. And it's cold, all of a sudden it's not a summer's evening, it's cold and the man's afraid. And he's sad, too. His eyes are burning. And there's nothing there, there's nothing to see. But he's afraid. And he stuffs his hands deep into his pockets to warm them.

And then he feels something tugging, ever so lightly, tugging on the end of his sleeve. He doesn't look down to his side. He can't. He keeps his hand clenched deep in his pocket. And it tugs harder. He closes his eyes and holds his breath tight. And then he feels an icy little grip, the size of a doll's, or a child's, close around his wrist. And he tries to pull his hand away but he can't. And he tries to move his feet but they're stuck fast. And the smell. Straw and piss, something gone bad.

Lights begin to dim.

And then I hear it. Like laughing. Skipping songs. Children playing. A dozen of them. Boys, girls, voices I can't make out.

It changes. The singing stops. The little hand starts tugging on mine. They're running away, running round the twisty cul-de-sacs and corners of Bedern. They're screaming and they're running, but not from me. They want to take me with them, and I want to follow because I'm afraid. I can feel him. I can feel him behind me, I can almost smell him, with his boozy breath. I can hear his cane clip against his boot. And the little hand tugs harder. Desperate. Squeezing.

Eyes snap open. White noise stops.

'Evening, Richard.'

'Evening, Ron.' He's got two Tesco bags in one hand and his stick in the other. It's been a few years since I've seen him and he looks so thin and wizened I barely recognize him.

'You coming in?'

The words don't register at first.

'You all right, Dick? How long's it been?'

Still nothing coming. His eyes narrow, frowns.

'Years.' I just about manage.

'Really? That long? Well . . .'

He's talking but I'm not listening. He's asking about the tour, about business. I don't really hear.

I'm thinking about the shrine of Margaret Clitherow, and the Jews in Clifford's Tower. He's put his hand out and the little hand's gone so I've taken it. He's hobbling away, his cane's clacking on the neat brick paving. I'm thinking about that story tumbling out, I'm thinking about ghosts.

Ron is crossing a patch of grass towards a squat little porch. I can't be sure but I feel like he stops, just for a moment scuffs at the turf with the tip of his walking stick.

I know he looks back over his shoulder and tips me a nod.
I know he takes his keys from his pocket, unlocks the door once,
twice, clambers clumsily inside and closes it behind him.
Bells in the distance. Richard *bows his head.*

SLOW FADE TO BLACKOUT

We'll Fix It! (2013)

By

LES WILLIAMS

First Performed as Part of License To Thrill Theatre Company's
FEAR (2013), 19 October 2013

Preface

License To Thrill Theatre Company (LTT) was established in Liverpool, UK, with its first public performance in 2013. The creative director and lead writer of LTT is Les Williams. LTT present Grand-Guignol theatre, usually new works in the genre occasionally interpolated with plays from the classic repertoire. Interestingly, after two years of shows coinciding with the Halloween season, LTT left the increasingly crowded 'horror events' calendar and placed its annual horror show towards Christmas. Packaged as 'Tis the Season', the LTT Grand-Guignol has developed a cult fanbase—as well as 'virgins'—relishing their horror stories for the season of goodwill. LTT has used effective venues in Liverpool: the no longer extant Actor's Studio in Seel Street for its premiere production, an evocative venue on an atmospheric street; a couple of seasons at the Lantern Theatre, an intimate venue with a well-stocked bar on a backstreet near the Wapping and Queen Docks; and—in a rare foray away from Liverpool in 2016—in the intimate Old Laundry Theatre in Bowness-on-Windermere. In 2017, LTT presented a horror show in the perhaps unlikely venue of the Royal Philharmonic Hall's Music Room (the first theatrical performance ever to take place in the space) which nonetheless proved to be a highly suitable small space within the grandiose venue, especially when prepared by the LTT team. According to Les Williams, the custodians of the Royal Philharmonic Hall became increasingly anxious about the notoriety of LTT and the content of their shows, and ultimately refused to associate their name with LTT and their publicity despite the venue having been booked. What seemed like a marketing disaster became something of a coup: the show was publicized through word of mouth and the run of the show enjoyed excellent attendance with a detectable frisson among the spectators who arrived discreetly, drawn by rumour and being among the lucky ones who were 'in the know'. It went to show that although fliers and posters may be the standard mode of publicity 'on the street', a lot can be achieved by using, effectively, oral storytelling: the ensemble and its associates spread

Figure 6. Licence to Thrill, poster for *'Tis the Season* 2016
(copyright Les Williams)

rumours and lured potential spectators with the whispered words 'Did you know there's a top secret horror show at the Royal Philharmonic this weekend . . .?'

LTT relishes the *douche écossaise* blend of humour and horror that the Grand-Guignol inaugurated. They frequently package their shows with playful preshow antics, building up an atmosphere of 'horrality'. Their premiere production was a Grand-Guignol show called *FEAR* and included aspects of framing narrative, such as openly discussing common fears with the spectators while a gigantic spider was slowly lowered towards the head of an unsuspecting member of the audience who wondered why the crowd seemed to be laughing and pointing at them. LTT's comedies are frequently 'gross out' with excesses of blood and other authentic-looking bodily emissions. Their horror plays can surprise the viewer with the intensity of their theme. A case in point is the play *We'll Fix It!* in the *FEAR* production. After the playful horror and humour of the showcase, the audience was startled into intense, shocked silence as they realized the theme of the next play.

Sir Jimmy Savile was an English 'national treasure', a hugely successful television and radio personality lauded for his services to entertainment and charity. After his death, hundreds of allegations of paedophile abuse perpetrated by Savile came to light and led to the commencement of 'Operation Yewtree' in 2012, a thorough investigation by British police into child abuse by Savile and others. It is worth remembering that despite Savile's status as an establishment figure, rumours had circulated about his paedophile activity during his lifetime. Figures such as the musician John Lydon made allegations in the 1970s and the comedian-magician Jerry Sadowitz did so in the 1980s, but found themselves censored or threatened with prosecution. Even Savile's autobiography—*Love is an Uphill Thing* (1976)—seems to confess to acts of misconduct. There were even various police investigations into Savile that were closed owing to lack of substantiation. The fact that Savile spent his life acting with impunity despite the allegations, rumours and quasi-confessions fuelled the fury that emerged when, soon after his death, his victims were finally given a platform and believed. There was public rage at what Savile did and deep regret that he died before justice could be served.

We'll Fix It! alludes to the title of Savile's television series *Jim'll Fix It* (1975–94) and is a drama of revenge. It is a bitter narrative of 'wish fulfilment' that imagines that Jimmy Savile has been kidnapped and is brutally punished for his misdemeanours. Savile's name is never mentioned in the play—he is simply the 'Victim' wearing a tracksuit (typical of Savile) and a hessian bag over his head throughout the play. The play opens with a song by Gary Glitter—another celebrity guilty of child abuse—which gives a clue as to the theme of the play. It was too much for some members of the audience—just a year after Operation Yewtree began—who left the auditorium. Quizzing those who left, Les Williams discovered that they were not angry with LTT or questioning the quality of the show, they had simply arrived at their personal limit: this was 'too much, too soon'. The original Grand-Guignol made the adaptation of recent news and social furores its stock-in-trade. It loved to shock—or satisfy the ghoulish fascination of—its audience while giving its actors great opportunities to demonstrate their skills. It would have been proud of LTT and its 'Jimmy Savile' play that placed a notorious and shameful scandal centre stage in an intensely performed and adroitly crafted script.

WE'LL FIX IT! (2013)

By

LES WILLIAMS

Characters
Stephen
Cathy
Victim

The location is an old warehouse, dirty, unused for many months (years). Old tea chests and wooden crates are scattered about. There is a fluorescent light that hangs and flickers randomly. A man (Victim) in a tracksuit is sat USC in an old, battered armchair. His wrists and ankles are tied to the arms and legs of the chair. He has a hessian bag over his head with a badly drawn face scrawled onto it (the face looks pathetic—the mask should resemble something from a bad nightmare). Another man (Stephen) is stood reading a newspaper SL next to a kettle, which is boiling on top of a couple of stacked crates. A radio, milk, tea bags, teaspoon and two mugs are next to the kettle. There is a pile of newspapers scattered around other boxes, crates positioned SR.

TRACK: 'I'm the leader of the Gang'
LIGHTS slow fade up
Radio plays 'I'm the leader of the Gang' by Gary Glitter. Stephen keeps reading—absorbed. The kettle finishes boiling, he makes the tea continuing to read. He stirs the tea, lifts up the newspaper and takes the hot spoon over to the Victim, looks down once to the Victim's left hand and presses down hard with the back of the spoon—the Victim screams—Stephen continues to press the spoon into the man's hand whilst reading his newspaper. Stephen removes the spoon from the Victim's hand and goes back to switch the spoon for his mug of tea. He moves SR, still reading, and sits down sipping his drink. A dishevelled looking woman enters holding a bag.

CATHY: Fucking hell, Stephen . . . (*She realises what is being played on radio and moves fast to switch it off.*)

STEPHEN: What?

CATHY: 'Do you wanna be in my gang?' (*Victim starts sobbing.*)

STEPHEN: Sorry, I was just . . . (*Cathy drops her handbag and moves fast to the man in the chair and grabs him by the throat.*)

CATHY: Stop whinging, you sick fuck! What I'm going to do to you . . .

STEPHEN: Cathy . . .

CATHY: . . .you're going to wish you were never born . . .

STEPHEN: Cathy leave it . . .

CATHY: . . . I bet we're not the only people whose lives you ruined, you evil bastard.

STEPHEN: Cathy stop will you. (*Get up and pulls her away. Victim starts sobbing uncontrollably.*)

CATHY: Get off, what are you doing protecting him? He deserves everything he gets.

STEPHEN: I know. He will. The law will see to that. But like we agreed, we both wanted to find out if there are anymore who went through what he did to us both. And then when we hand him over, they'll publicise why we did this and hopefully people will finally come forward. Not feeling afraid to tell their own story about what this monster did to them.

CATHY   (*pause*): Alright. (*Stephen moves SR. Cathy moves SL.*)
I can't believe he's here! We've got him. How long do you think we have before they'll come for us?

STEPHEN: Who?

CATHY: His millions of adoring fans. Who? The police Stephen, wake up.

STEPHEN: Three or four days max. Then we'll have to move on or hand him over. (*Short pause.*) I tried calling you earlier, have you got your mobile switched off?

CATHY: No, it's on silent. Strangely, Stephen, I'm not in the mood to talk or engage in polite conversation.

STEPHEN   (*pause*): Eh, it has its perks being a Property Letting Agent. This place has been on the market for months now and has no chance of being let any time soon. No one will ever suspect he's here.

CATHY: You hope.

STEPHEN   (*pause*): Well the media's having a field day. (*Holds up the newspapers and reads.*) 'National Treasure Missing', 'Icon Feared Dead', 'Kidnapper's might have known . . .' (*Cathy goes over and picks up 'Kidnapper' newspaper.*). I don't understand why the press are not telling the truth.

CATHY: Kidnappers? Kidnappers! So now we're the bad ones and this shit's the victim? Cheeky bastards! They haven't got a clue what he did to you and me when we were children . . . they haven't got a clue. (*She starts to cry. Stephen gets up and consoles her, sits her down.*) What if it was just you and me Stephen? And he really did do nothing to anyone else . . .? What if what he did was a one-off? . . . And he made a mistake.

STEPHEN   (*crouches down*): Don't believe it, Cathy. And don't make excuses for him . . .

CATHY: Well why haven't people come forward to report him . . . why?

STEPHEN: People did! They have! You've heard the rumours . . .

CATHY: Yes rumours . . . that's all they are.

STEPHEN   (*stands up and turns away*): No. It's real. He abused more children . . . I'm sure of it. Of course people knew. We've both heard jokes at work about him, people laughing. Not really understanding, not bothered, don't care. Whilst we smile through gritted teeth—hiding the truth, pain and anger what this . . . caused. Those pompous bigots from the big corporation chose to ignore the 'rumours'. Take them, discard and lock them up at the back of some . . . small murky, dark cupboard space, on an unused floor forever.

CATHY: 'Oh we wouldn't want to tarnish the brand's image now would we.' Pricks. I wish it was them he . . . instead of me. A little girl, that's all I was, ten years old. We both adored you. Watched you every Saturday night, millions of children did. You could do no wrong. The lucky few, whose dreams you made come true. It was a lottery, writing the letter and hoping . . . wishing more than anything else that yours would be chosen.

STEPHEN: I still remember the fancy envelope the reply came in. With the corporation's image neatly printed into the top left-hand corner— big bold letters. How beautiful they looked.

CATHY: The look of importance.

STEPHEN: The feeling I felt when mum gave the letter to us both after school was incredible . . . I've never felt so excited . . . so happy. And then opening the envelope . . . seeing the letterhead. That logo!

CATHY: The colours . . . bright red and gold.

STEPHEN: My god, what a feeling! We had both been chosen, out of millions of school children . . . us. Our dreams were about to come true . . .

CATHY: Nightmares! Our nightmares where about to come true. He was so nice. Can you still remember meeting him for the first time? (*Stephen acknowledges. She gets up and moves to sit next to Victim. He flinches.*) I was completely star struck . . .

STEPHEN: We all were . . .

CATHY: He was so nice . . . so nice. Such a gentleman. (*Starts slowly, caringly stroking his head. Victim starts to whimper.*) Your warmth . . . your kindness . . . your generosity . . . that friendly smile and famous charm . . . (*Stops caressing—pause.*) So come on! Tell us what you got out of it? Come on don't be shy . . . tell us what . . .

STEPHEN: Well it's bleedin' obvious. He got off on it! That's what people like him do. Prey on the vulnerable . . . the innocent. Gain their trust and make promises. Give them a sense of what we all desire—to feel safe, secure, wanted . . . loved!

CATHY: Loved? I'll give him 'loved', the sick bastard (*Cathy tries strangling Victim. Stephen grabs Cathy's arm and pulls her away—restraining her. The Victim is crying*). Let fucking go of me. Let go . . .

STEPHEN: Stop! What are you doing? Cathy calm down! We agreed we wouldn't do this? The truth will come out eventually.

CATHY: How? When?

STEPHEN: Soon. The phone call we made yesterday telling the police what he did, what he's like, why we kidnapped him? This will bring us justice. We're generating publicity. It's already headline news and he's only been missing three days.

CATHY: Yes, the wrong type of publicity . . . (*Holds up newspaper.*) The whole country thinks he's a national treasure! It's the wrong attention. We want the truth . . . justice.
          TRACK: Nokia rings.
          Burner phone. Both look at each other. Stephen picks up old Nokia phone next to the kettle.

CATHY: Who is it?

STEPHEN: Don't know the number's blocked!

CATHY: Well answer it. It might be the police (*Phone stops ringing.*)

STEPHEN   (*pause*): If it's important, they'll ring back. (*He places phone back down. Pause.*)

CATHY: We might have been just a one-off you know. Two unlucky children . . .

STEPHEN: Stop . . .

CATHY: In the wrong place . . .

STEPHEN: Stop it . . .

CATHY: At the wrong time . . .

STEPHEN: STOP IT!
          TRACK: iPhone rings.
          Stephen's personal mobile phone rings. Stephen takes phone out of pocket and looks at caller. Nods to Cathy to restrain Victim from shouting out when he takes the call—she does. Stephen briefly composes himself before answering.

STEPHEN: Alright Paul. What's up? (*Pause.*) Shit. (*Checks his watch.*) Sorry, totally forgot . . . I was busy looking after things . . . family problems. (*Looks at Cathy. Long pause.*) Yes I will. I'll be there in . . . (*Checks his watch.*) fifteen minutes. Sorry mate. Speak soon.
          Cathy lets go of Victim and sits down. Stephen types something into his phone, then puts it away in his jacket. He picks up Cathy's handbag and goes to her.

STEPHEN: Here's your bag, we're going.

CATHY: I'm not going.

STEPHEN: Come on we need to go.

CATHY: Why?

STEPHEN: Because I'm not leaving you alone with him . . . you tried to kill him two minutes ago.

CATHY: I wouldn't do anything when you're not here.

STEPHEN: How am I supposed to believe that? We need him alive, Cathy.

CATHY: I know, you're right. We do need him alive so people know what he did to us.
          Stephens mobile rings again. Gets mobile out and cancels call, puts phone away in his jacket.

STEPHEN: Listen I need to go now. I'm trusting you not to do anything stupid. (*Moves to door—exit SR.*) I'm late showing a client round. I'll be back later this afternoon. Don't answer the phone. Let me handle that. (*Short pause. Moves back to Cathy. Hand on her shoulder, crouches down.*) It'll be OK. We'll get through this. Don't worry Cathy. Things will work out for the best, you'll see. (*Gets up and kisses her on the top of her head. Exits to door and stops.*) I'll call you on your mobile if anything comes up. Eh, don't forget to take it off silent. (*He waits. She reluctantly takes out phone and turns off silent, places on side.*) Cathy . . . (*She looks round.*) you'll be OK won't you? (*She forces a smile at him, trying to be natural. He smiles back.*) Don't do anything stupid . . . *Stephen exits. Silence. Victim in chair sobs quietly—he is scared.*

CATHY   (*gently laughs*): Feels strange this. Weird even. Us both being alone together . . . again! Brings back all the memories when you invited me and Stephen back to your dressing room, straight after the show. You were so friendly, so charming! I was gobsmacked by your dressing room, the dressing table lights, the flowers . . . I even liked the smell of your cigarettes. You made me and Stephen feel so . . . special . . . providing us with sweets, cakes and drink. You sat there in this high-backed chair . . . observing, watching how we both were thrilled to grace your presence. It may sound strange, but it felt like you were smoking *slowly* . . . smiling . . . thinking. (*Pause.*) It was then you asked if I would like you to sign my autograph book. I was over the moon, my friends would be so jealous. You then told Stephen to leave and go to the canteen to get whatever he wanted and that I could go when he returns—so you and Stephen could be left alone. You gave him £10. We both looked at each other not believing how much you had given him. Stephen left the dressing room with the biggest smile I have ever seen on his face. You waited. Then quietly you got up and locked the door.

You sat back down, smiled and asked me to sit on your knee. Patting your left knee gently. You seemed so warm and safe. I sat on the edge of it. Then your left arm creeped around my waist and held me close, in a firm grip. Slowly, you slid me back against your body. (*Pause.*) I still remember how bony you felt and that your hair and clothes had a decaying stale smell of smoke. Your breath was repulsive, and your teeth were yellow. (*Pause.*) A living corpse. (*Pause.*) You then held me inside your arms, constricting, as you signed my book. It was then I felt your left hand tug at the back of my panties. I looked at you and froze . . . fearful and knowing it was wrong. I looked you in the eye. You knew it was also wrong, but you just smiled and carried on. Your left hand rubbing my lower back and then . . . then you slowly brought your right hand under my dress. (*Long pause.*) I think it didn't last long, but it felt like time had stopped, frozen . . . I remember just lying there . . . staring at a small spider's web under the dressing table, in the corner of the floor. (*Pause.*)

When you finished, you stood up and lit another cigarette. I sat there numb, with my head down, squeezing my autograph book . . . not sure if what had happened was *real*. Then someone tried to open the door. It was Stephen. You let him in. You acted like nothing had happened. (*Short pause.*) He was so happy . . . buzzing. And then you gave me £10 and quickly ushered me out to go to the canteen. I was silent, in shock walking along the corridor to the canteen—I didn't buy anything. I kept the £10. I did not warn Stephen, I did not warn him . . . and then it was his turn. Whatever it was you did to him. (*Short pause.*) He was never the same after that . . . we both weren't. A twelve-year-old boy who now suddenly started wetting the bed. I remember dad getting cross with him . . . but he never told mum and dad why it started. Mum and dad thought it was a bit strange how we never wanted to watch your show after being on it. They presumed the gloss had worn off and it wasn't such a big deal now that we had officially met you. But the pain still remained . . . (*Short pause.*)

You destroyed my life. It's only thanks to Stephen that I'm still here. He understands. He's my rock. If it wasn't for him I would not be here now. (*Pause.*) Already divorced—you screwed things up there, Cathy—I can't hold down a steady relationship . . . for fear of being hurt, betrayed, abused. My two children are in care, who I've not seen for four years now. I miss them, want them . . . my babies . . . I love them so much! (*She breaks down. Long pause.*) TRACK: *Cathy's mobile phone rings.*
She picks it up and stares but does not answer, the call stops. Cathy puts the mobile down next to her on a crate and stares straight ahead. Silence. She then calmly gets up, collects her handbag and moves to man in chair. Slowly moves round back and places hand on his shoulder. He whimpers.

Does this bring back any memories? The touch of a woman— or a little girl—who's no stranger to your touch! You know you like it. That soft touch . . . the foreplay.
She starts massaging his shoulders. He sobs. She moves round the left side and strokes his left hand. She holds it.

Do you remember that day holding my hand? Forcibly holding my hand down so you could do what you wanted to do. No . . .
She stands up and breaks his middle finger. The Victim screams and starts crying.

Oh dear . . . did that hurt. I'm not sorry. Let me give you something else to increase the pain . . .
She moves round the front and kneels down in front of Victim. She pulls down his trousers. Her back to the audience. She starts rubbing the top of his thighs. He sobs uncontrollably.

You told me this was your favourite position . . . you liked this the most. If you liked this the most, I wonder how many more innocent little girls you violated, you sick fuck!
She goes to handbag and takes out a large pairs of scissors with right hand. And places left hand in front so to hide from audience—this will look like left hand is touching groin.

Oh dear, what's happened here . . . you've gone all floppy!
That's not good.

She turns round and looks at the audience, smiling.

I think we'll have to fix that!

She raises the scissors and snips twice. Turns back to Victim and holds scissors aloft then brings them down slowly to cut. Victim hysterically screams as Cathy cuts off his penis—this takes longer than expected due to the Victim's struggle. Cathy then stands up and turns around and walks slowly towards the audience—trance like—holding the pair of scissors and the Victim's penis—she stares at it. She drops the penis and then looks straight into the audience—eyes glazed over. The Victim continues to scream and then appears to pass out with the pain—occasional groans.

TRACK: Phone beep voice message.

Cathy then 'wakes up' and moves to her phone, picks up and presses play.

TRACK: We then hear an automated voice message voice, followed by Stephen's message . . .

STEPHEN   (*laughing, happy*): Cathy . . . bloody answer your phone. Good news, it's started! He's done this before, I told you he had. It's just been on the radio two women have come forward after hearing about our news, saying he had also abused them—they reckon more might follow. This is it, Cathy. Everything's going to be OK. I told you we'd fix it. Now we'll finally see justice and that bastard will finally get what he deserves. (*Slight pause.*) Well done Cathy for staying strong . . . I knew you could. I won't be long. See you soon.

Lights start to fade to blackout midway through voice message.

THE END

Leviticus: Evil Resides Within (2014)

by

Antonio Rimola

Preface

Tin Shed Theatre Company was established in 2009 by three graduates of performing arts degrees at University of Wales (Newport): Justin Cliffe, Georgina Harris and Antonio Rimola. Continuing to work where they met in Newport, Tin Shed became a professional company and have produced a variety of educational and immersive theatre work. They always evince a passion for the theatre of the uncanny and the horrific, and signal that studying Grand-Guignol drama as part of their university syllabus is a key influence in this regard. Tin Shed's horror theatre has encompassed productions such as *Dr Frankenstein's Travelling Freakshow* (2012), a tremendously energetic physical theatre production encompassing arch-Gothic comic characters, puppetry and projected animation: a rich and eclectic performance, reminiscent of the pioneering multimedia theatre of Forkbeard Fantasy (1974 onwards) and the genre-redefining work of Circus of Horrors (1995 onwards). An inspired and imaginative retelling of Mary Shelley's *Frankenstein* (1818), its riotous comedy, atmospheric cabaret aesthetic and meta-theatricality made the production a perfect fringe show and it enjoyed success at the Edinburgh Fringe (performing, appropriately, in the unique Frankenstein pub), the London Horror Festival and elsewhere in the UK before touring to the USA in 2014 where it performed at the Thrillpeddler's horror theatre the Hypnodrome in San Francisco and won a prize at the 2014 San Diego Fringe Festival.

While *Dr Frankenstein's Travelling Freakshow* was a playful and audience-pleasing neo-Gothic spectacle with the frenetic theatricality and comic energy of commedia dell'arte, Tin Shed's immersive production work could not be more different in concept, tone and style. Core to the company's ethos has always been the theatrical exploration of 'empty buildings' and 'unusual spaces' (https://www.tinshedtheatrecompany.com/about), and frequently this has taken its spectators into very dark horror performance. *The Ritual* (2013) commenced as a production that seemed to 'go wrong': a power failure led to an offer of a refund, but a lift in a minibus turned awry with the driver taking the audience to a huge warehouse on an industrial estate. The audience had been 'abducted' and, treated like prisoners, discovered the horrors of the building through

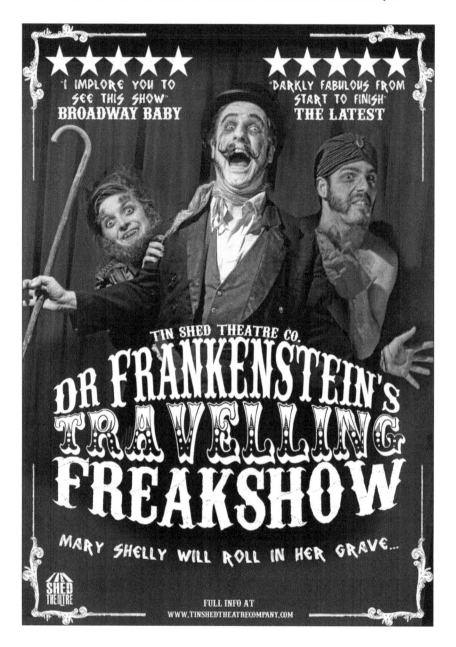

Figure 7. Tin Shed Theatre Company, poster for *Dr Frankenstein's Travelling Freakshow*, 2012 (copyright Tin Shed Theatre Company)

a variety of installations featuring chained victims as well as disturbing video and images of demonic craft. The cult who held the audience captive were evidently looking for a sacrificial victim. Ultimately selecting a (planted) member of the audience, the crowd observed a huge-scale ritual summoning an apocalyptic entity before running to freedom. Deliberately ambiguous—an overarching narrative and climactic ceremony that seemed part devil-worship and part Lovecraftian—*The Ritual* demonstrated an epic spectacle for a maximum audience number of fourteen with intense momentum, strong design, and moods that shifted from claustrophobia to agoraphobia and demonstrated a very impressive control of logistics.

Tin Shed's subsequent Halloween performance—the thirty-five-minute immersive performance *Leviticus: Evil Resides Within* (2014)—was as intimate as a full-evening experience of *The Ritual* was seemingly open and epic. Each performance of *The Ritual* relied on its locations/installations and sequences of script structured within realist improvisation. In contrast, *Leviticus* was carefully scripted for its four actors, placing the very small groups of spectators—only four per performance—into a horror experience as inexorably as a classic funfair ghost train or Dries Verhoeven's postmodern terror ride *Phobiarama* (2017). With minimal indication of the content of the show, the *Leviticus* audience were given a secret address in Newport—a small, Victorian terraced house—and a time slot. When the door opened, the audience was greeted by two priests, and the Biblical title to this Halloween-season production made it apparent that this would be a religious themed horror play.

The Book of Leviticus is in the Old Testament and features numerous rules appertaining to sacrificial offerings, food consumption and personal conduct. The Book spells out draconian punishments for transgressors. Of particular relevance, the Book warns against consulting with mediums and spiritualists, and the play will take us dangerously close to such dubious territory. As Tin Shed asserts, 'We wanted to explore modern themes and concepts that surround the phenomenon of practised exorcism in the western world' (www.tinshedtheatrecompany.com/theatre). Moreover, among citing numerous sexual transgressions, the Book warns against the grave sin of incest: a theme that ultimately becomes apparent in this horror play.

Leviticus is consciously allusive to William Peter Blatty's novel *The Exorcist* (1971) and William Friedkin's 1973 film adaptation. John Pielmeier's stage adaptation of *The Exorcist* premiered in Los Angeles in 2012 with continuing international productions. Although Pielmeier liaised closely with Blatty, the stage play is very much an experience that draws on the status and iconography of the 1973 film adaptation. It is inventively designed and playful, finding live stage effects equivalents to the famous set pieces in the film and, perhaps, succeeded in drawing an audience of horror fans more accustomed to cinema to the theatre. It is an example of the contemporary genre of commercial theatre that homages much-loved movies, proving that this phenomenon is not restricted to stage versions of Disney family favourites such as *The Lion King* (film 1994; stage adaptation 1997) or the innovative theatricality of Kneehigh's *Brief Encounter* (film 1945; stage adaptation 2007), but can produce an adults-only horror experience. Although *Leviticus* shares the same narrative theme as *The Exorcist*, its intimacy and immersivity demonstrated how live performance can make a familiar horror plot fresh, intense and terrifying.

Leviticus was, in Tin Shed's production, genuinely immersive. Eagerly welcomed into the humble and minimally furnished house, the quotidian normality of the environment gradually becomes transformed as the audience is drawn into the narrative of the possessed child upstairs. The audience's boundaries of spectatorship cross over into narrative participation. The use of sound was particularly well designed, with thumps and footsteps evolving into the use of a concealed audio system to augment and transform the up-close realism into the supernatural. The script we publish here reveals the creative dialogue between writer and production team: speculating on how the audience might react and what needs to happen for the successful exposition of the play.

Immersive theatre has now become an extremely popular concept—and possibly a (not always accurately used) cliché—in twenty-first-century performance. The theatre company Punchdrunk have been pioneers in this genre and companies such as The Guild of Misrule and DotDotDot have enjoyed great success with their immersive shows of, respectively, *The Great Gatsby* (2017 onwards) and *Jeff Wayne's The War of The Worlds: The Immersive Experience* (2019 onwards). While these shows, Tin Shed's *The Ritual* and landmark Punchdrunk productions such as *The Masque of the Red Death* (2007) and *The Drowned Man* (2013–14) worked on an epic scale, immersive theatre can be small-scale and intimate but no less spectacular. In this regard, Punchdrunk's *Clod and Pebble* (2008), a one-to-one performance in a furniture shop, Dread Falls Theatre's *Patient 4620* (2019), a performance in a small art gallery, and Tin Shed's *Leviticus*, in a terraced house in Newport, all take and implicate the spectator into the uncanny, transforming the ordinary into the supernatural.

LEVITICUS: EVIL RESIDES WITHIN (2014)

by

Antonio Rimola

First performed in Newport, Wales, 28 October 2014

Cast
Father Matthew
Father Simon
Phillip Jenkins (Father)
Sarah Jenkins (Daughter)

Audience knock on the door and Father Simon opens the door and greets them all.

FATHER SIMON: Good evening. I'm Father Simon. (*As he introduces himself, he shakes every one's hand and hopefully they will introduce themselves. He repeats their names back to them followed by . . .*) bless you. (*He allows for the audience to step in and makes sure he gets everyone's name.*) Please follow me into the lounge. (*He leads them to where Father Matthew is waiting to meet them all.*) This is Father Matthew.
Father Matthew steps forward and shakes each audience members hand and saying . . .

FATHER MATTHEW: Thank you all for coming. Peace be with you. It's good to finally meet you all in person. And this is Phillip, Sarah's father.
Phillip is sat down on the sofa looking exhausted and sad seeming almost like he is in mourning at a funeral wake. He stands up slowly and shakes the first audience member's hand.

PHILLIP: Hi, thanks for coming. (*He continues to shake the hands of the other three.*) Hi . . . cheers. Thanks . . . good to meet you, I'm Phil, thanks for coming, etc.

FATHER MATTHEW: Right, so, if everybody would like to just take a seat and make yourselves comfortable and at home we can begin with tonight's proceedings. Well firstly, welcome. Thank you for your response to my letter. I'm Father Matthew and I'll be leading tonight's proceedings. Father Simon is my curate and will be assisting me. I'd like to thank you all for giving up your time to be here tonight and I'm sure I speak for Sarah's father Phillip as well when I express my most sincere appreciation. What we're doing here certainly isn't easy and will be a true test of our faith. It's a very difficult thing for any human being to be faced with whether we are believers or nonbelievers, So, your bravery here tonight can only be commended and for that we thank you. And, of course, Phillip our thoughts are with you and with Sarah as well. We can only imagine what she must be going through.

PHILLIP: Thank you father. (*Breaking into tears.*)

FATHER MATTHEW: May God bless us all, and with the fruits of our Lord Saviour Jesus Christ, may he keep us safe and deliver us from evil. Amen.

FATHER SIMON: Amen.

PHILLIP: Amen. (*In tears.*)

FATHER MATTHEW: Now I need to remind you all that the things we discuss here tonight are completely confidential. Out of common courtesy, this is Phillip's personal life, and so we must respect that. So, with that confidentiality in mind can I make it clear to you all that nothing is to leave this house. Everything you may see and hear tonight is strictly kept within this congregation, am I understood? (*Audience may respond with 'yes'.*) Good. Phillip, is there anything you would like to add to that?

PHILLIP: Well I'd just like to thank you all again for being here really. It's been hard having to deal with this on my own. My wife, Melissa passed away only seven months ago, so . . . yeah, I've been struggling.

FATHER MATTHEW: With this being so difficult for Phillip he asked me earlier if I would speak for him this evening and explain to you all what has been happening over the past few weeks. So, Phillip, if you're still happy for me to do so, I will continue.

PHILLIP: Yes, go on.

FATHER MATTHEW: Right, so to start from the very beginning, or rather from what we believe to be the starting point of Sarah's condition . . . Sadly, as Phillip Just mentioned, seven months ago, Sarah lost her mother, to cancer. Sarah is only twelve years of age so as I'm sure you can imagine this has been a very traumatic time for her. She watched her mother deteriorate for months before eventually passing away, God rest her soul. A few days after her mother's funeral, Sarah woke up one morning and suddenly, without warning, refused to communicate with her father which made everyday life very difficult for Phillip.

PHILLIP: I couldn't even get her to go to school or leave the house for anything. When it first started I tried to get her outside by grabbing hold of her and she . . . she just screamed so loud and I couldn't stop her. She didn't stop screaming until I let go. And then it just got worse and worse and she started to . . . to (*Getting close to tears.*)

FATHER MATTHEW: Phillip, it's alright. You don't have to say anything.
I know this is difficult but Just try and relax. I don't mind
explaining. Sarah started becoming extremely aggressive
towards her father, punching, kicking, scratching and
biting and using lewd words that overall was very out of
character for Sarah. Despite these constant outbursts of
aggressive energy, Sarah is restless and never seems to get
tired. She stays up all through the night talking to herself
and laughing hysterically for hours and hours on end.
Phillip sought help from doctors who found no symptoms
of any medical condition. His next step of course was
to have Sarah see a psychiatrist, and not surprisingly
they put her behaviour down to grief and struggling to
come to terms with her mother's death. Phillip wasn't
convinced by this and Sarah's condition began to escalate
even more. Phillip contacted the church a month ago, He
explained everything that had been happening, and when
he described to us how things had escalated, we became
very convinced of Sarah's case. Phillip told us how Sarah
started walking into his room in the middle of the night
just shouting profanities at him and vomiting all over him.
Once he started locking his bedroom door at night this
aggravated the situation, and Sarah would stand outside
his door banging and trying to force the door open. She
has also been trying to harm herself and animals. So,
although we believe that the death of Sarah's mother has
been the trigger of all this, grief is certainly not the reason
for this sort of behaviour and it is not Sarah doing these
things. There are clear signs that a possession is taking
place inside Sarah's body.
*Suddenly a massive thump is heard from bedroom directly
above them. The heads of Phillip, Father Matthew and
Father Simon jolt upwards towards the ceiling and they
pause for a moment.*

PHILLIP: Shall I check on her?

FATHER MATTHEW: No. (*Still looking up at the ceiling and listening very
intently.*)
Slight sound of a young girl crying.

PHILLIP: But, Maybe she's hurt, fa . . .

FATHER MATTHEW: Shh shh (*Raises his hand to silence everybody. Another
pause and then above them again they hear hysterical
laughter.*) No, It's not safe. Not for you Phillip.
(*A young girl crying is heard again.*)

FATHER SIMON: Trust us, Mr Jenkins. Satan is a great master of deception.

PHILLIP: What are you saying?

FATHER MATTHEW: What he means, Phillip, is (*points his finger up to the
ceiling*) that is not your daughter you can hear crying up
there. But that's exactly what it wants you to think.

FATHER SIMON: It's playing tricks. It seems to want a reaction from you. Perhaps it's trying to get you to go upstairs, where it may possibly try and hurt you.

FATHER MATTHEW   (*quite annoyed by Simon*): Well actually that's not quite right, Simon. Apologies, Phillip, I think, what Simon is trying to say to you is that this demon that has taken your daughter . . . it seems to be directly meddling with you. At this moment in time we're not quite sure why that is, but for some reason it's very drawn towards you, like some strange attachment. Very unusual . . .

FATHER SIMON   (*interrupting*): Yes, and until we try and communicate with it, we won't know what it wants.

FATHER MATTHEW: So until then, Phillip, we must be careful and keep you safe.

FATHER SIMON: And remember that for as long as Satan has hold of Sarah's body it is he that speaks through her. Although it may sound like Sarah, your daughter is not there any more. (*Father Matthew gives Simon a look of disbelief and shakes his head sighing.*) Temporarily I mean. (*Awkward pause.*) You will have your daughter back by the end of the night.

FATHER MATTHEW: Phillip, I know you're scared, but I can promise you as a priest with the power invested in me by God that you will have Sarah back safe and unharmed. Sometimes to cast a demon out completely can take more than one attempt, but I can tell you I have performed numerous exorcisms and not once has God turned his back on those souls that the Devil has tried to take. I say to all of you now, that good will always overcome evil. The truth of the holy gospel and the holy light of God will overpower the Devil and free us from his evil wrath. We must all keep our faith. Remember that as long as God is present among us we cannot fail to cast the demon away. Father Simon, could you get everyone some tea?

FATHER SIMON: Yes, father.

PHILLIP: Oh, I'll have to take some more mugs out of the box.
Phillip gets up and leaves the room with Simon. Just Father Matthew and the audience left in the room together.
In this next section there are a number of different things we can do. We can either just have Father Matthew sit in silence with the audience for a while checking his watch, flicking through his Bible, walking over to the window and looking out, then coming back to the audience and saying in a hushed voice;

FATHER MATTHEW: Ladies and gentlemen, although you have very kindly responded to my letter and bravely brought your services here, to us this evening, I must remind you that we will be conducting an exorcism. You will see things tonight that, believe me, will be hard to forget. Although we are summoned here by God to do his work and absolve Sarah from this demon, there are certain things in this world that should, if we can avoid them, be left alone. We must keep our faith, but this is a difficult reality, and so if anyone here has changed their mind about being here tonight then I extend this as your final opportunity to leave this house before we take proceedings upstairs.

Before the audience can respond Father Simon and Phillip re-enter with the tea and break the moment.

So we can either play it like that or do the following of Father Matthew engaging in a bit of improvised conversation . . .

FATHER MATTHEW: So, how is everybody feeling?

This is a moment to completely improvise with the audience. If they respond saying they feel alright maybe respond with 'That's good. Just keep calm. We need to show this demon that we don't fear it.' If an audience responds with 'No, shitting myself a bit etc.' you may respond with 'Please let's all just relax. we are safe in the hands of God.' The house will be very cold and it's likely that someone will say 'It's a bit cold or I'm freezing' etc., so to that you can respond with 'Yes, the cold is one of the first signs of a paranormal presence. Please do try and keep warm. If you get too cold, Phillip may have something that you can throw on.'

Once a bit of conversation has taken place between you and the audience maybe we should make another sound from the bedroom above where Father Matthew can just look up again, but this time with a lot more fear and curiosity in his expression, like he is sensing something very unusual about this possession. Then after a decent pause look at each person in the audience still with fear in your eyes and either say nothing or say . . .

FATHER MATTHEW: We must keep our faith. Remember Satan is full of lies and deceit.

Father Simon and Phillip enter the room. Simon is carrying a tray with a teapot, sugar, milk and mugs. Phillip has two or three empty teacups in one hand and one more in his other hand which is his own and is already full of what the audience think is tea, but we are preparing to play a trick on the audience . . .

FATHER SIMON: Here you go, just help yourselves. Get nice and warmed up.

Allow for a short bit of time for people to pour themselves some tea but don't necessarily wait for everyone to have poured themselves one before continuing.

FATHER MATTHEW: So, Phillip, you need to know exactly what will be happening tonight because If at any point you change your mind and you no longer want us to go ahead with this then please do say. Legally under the authority of the church we cannot conduct this without your full consent.

FATHER SIMON: Yes, and we will also need you to sign this agreement form that we went through with you earlier. (*Pulls out a form and a pen and starts reading from it.*) So, Phillip, do you accept our final analysis following our investigations that your daughter's condition is not of any medical illness, physical or mental known to science but that it is a result of a spiritual intervention that can only be recognised and certified by the religious church of Roman Catholicism, as a demon possession?

PHILLIP: Yes.

FATHER SIMON: OK, so do you accept that the cure for your daughter cannot be given by a doctor who is qualified in the practice of medicine but rather in the form of an exorcism to be conducted by priests of the Roman Catholic Church who are given authorisation by order of the supreme pontiff Paul V and set forth in the order of *Rituale Romanum* of 1605? We explained that bit to you earlier, about the general procedure. Do you accept?

PHILLIP: Yes . . . thank you.

FATHER SIMON: OK, so then if you would like to sign here and h . . . (*Father Matthew interrupts.*)

FATHER MATTHEW: Phillip, you don't have to sign that now. By all means, you can choose to do it now or you can wait until I've explained a few more details. It's entirely up to you but I still have to make you aware that in some cases . . . (*Another noise from upstairs interrupts the conversation. Again they all look up. After a slight pause Phillip continues to talk but during which Father Matthew doesn't take his focus away from the ceiling.*)

PHILLIP: No, I'll sign it. I accept.

FATHER SIMON: OK, great. (*Handing over the form and pen.*) So just twice. By here and . . . here. (*Phillip signs the agreement, during which Father Matthew is still hooked to the sound upstairs.*)

FATHER SIMON: OK, Father Matthew, that's been done. Shall we continue then?
    No response. Father Matthew's gaze still fixed on the ceiling.

FATHER SIMON: Father. Father Matthew!
    Father Matthew turns sharply, a bit startled.

FATHER MATTHEW: Huh?

FATHER SIMON: Shall we continue?

FATHER MATTHEW: Oh . . . right, yes of course. (*Clears his throat and takes a nervous deep breath.*) Right, OK, so before we move on tonight I just wanted to check a few things. Is anyone here wearing any jewellery that may contain occultic or Christian symbols? If so then can you remove these and leave them downstairs. It's for your own protection.

FATHER MATTHEW: Also, I have to ask that if anyone has sinned in the past six months no matter how big or how small you must confess it now to God. We do not want Satan to sense any weakness in our group.

FATHER SIMON: There is no shame in this, as none of us are without sin. You don't need to share it with the group. Just close your eyes, repent your sins and pray for forgiveness. *Hopefully the audience will play along with this by at least closing their eyes, but it doesn't really matter if they don't. Both Father Matthew and Father Simon close their eyes and pray. Phillip, however, does not and Father Matthew notices.*

FATHER MATTHEW: Phillip . . . you haven't confessed.

PHILLIP: No . . . I just can't think of anything.

FATHER MATTHEW: No matter how small, Phillip . . . there must be something.

PHILLIP: Well, I actually don't think there is, father.

FATHER SIMON: Come on Phillip. We must confess to our Lord.

PHILLIP: Sorry, I really can't think of anything.

FATHER SIMON: Mr Jenkins, this is really important.

FATHER MATTHEW: Phillip, please.

PHILLIP: I . . . I just can't think.

FATHER MATTHEW: Are you sure?!

PHILLIP: Yes.

Phillip takes another sip of his tea whilst Father Matthew begins to speak . . .

FATHER MATTHEW: Right, well then you'll . . . (*suddenly interrupted by Phillip who begins choking violently and gagging. He chokes a load of blood all over the coffee table. Father Matthew turns to one of the audience members, picks up a box of tissues, hands it to them and says . . .*) Here, help him.

FATHER SIMON   (*to Father Matthew*): It doesn't make sense.

In that moment another sound is heard from upstairs. Father Matthew raises his hand to silence everyone. It's a really croaky cough that first sounds demonic and then starts sounding much more like an older woman rather than a young girl and it speaks. Upon hearing it, Phillip trembles with fear.

PHILLIP: Oh God . . .

Then the sound of tiny footsteps running really fast from one side of the room to the other.

FATHER MATTHEW   (*suspiciously*): Phillip what is it? Do you recognise that voice?

PHILLIP   (*with trembling fear in his expression and voice*): Yes, Sarah sometimes imitates her mother's voice.

FATHER SIMON   (*sparks up*): What did you say?!

PHILLIP: It sounds like her mother.

Both priests exchange really worried looks with one another.

FATHER MATTHEW: Phillip, let's talk about this outside. Sorry everyone, we won't be a moment. (*Phillip gets up and walks out of the room, both priests follow. They stand just outside the doorway so the audience can listen.*) Phillip, that voice that Sarah just used . . . is that Melissa's voice?

PHILLIP: Yes. It sounds just like her.

FATHER SIMON: Oh Jesus Christ! (*Immediately puts his hand over his mouth.*) Forgive me, father.

FATHER MATTHEW: Why haven't you mentioned this to us before?

PHILLIP: Sorry, father, I just didn't really think it was necessary.

FATHER SIMON: Well of course it . . .! (*Interrupted.*)

FATHER MATTHEW: Simon, please! Right, OK, Phillip, that's OK, you weren't to know. But tell me, how often does Sarah sound like your wife, Melissa?

PHILLIP: She, well, she does it every day, I guess.

FATHER SIMON: Ohh, Jesus no!

FATHER MATTHEW: Damn it Simon, Shut up! Right, OK, Phillip, so, every day . . . hmm, but how often?

PHILLIP: At least four, five times a day maybe. (*Pause.*) Does it really matter? I don't understand.

FATHER MATTHEW: Alright Phillip, alright. It's OK. Now, Phillip, you have to tell me the truth. Is there something we should know that you're not telling us?

PHILLIP: No, of course not, father.

FATHER MATTHEW: Swear it to me.

PHILLIP: I swear.

FATHER SIMON: Swear it by God.

PHILLIP: I swear I'm telling the truth.

FATHER MATTHEW: OK, Phillip, OK. Could you leave me and Simon to talk privately for a moment please?

PHILLIP: But what's wrong?

FATHER MATTHEW: Nothing's wrong, don't panic, we just need to . . . work something out.
Phillip re-enters the living room and slumps down on the sofa looking extremely nervous and upset. Father Matthew and Father Simon are still in the hallway having a private conversation, which this time the audience cannot hear except for little snippets.
Both priests re-enter and Father Matthew sits himself down right by Phillip.

FATHER MATTHEW: Phillip, Father Simon and I have decided that you should not be present for the exorcism of your daughter. It would not be safe.

PHILLIP (*weeping*): But she needs me.

FATHER MATTHEW: Please try and understand, that these things that keep happening to you are . . . very strange. Completely unexplainable! Even to me and Simon this is just so

unheard of. We have to be careful until we know why
this is happening to Sarah and what this thing wants
from your family.

FATHER SIMON: Or from you for that matter.

PHILLIP: What do you mean? What does he mean?

FATHER MATTHEW: Look, Phillip, it doesn't matter. Just trust us.
*A loud bang comes from another room and then lights
flicker and come back on. Extreme fear and terror in both
priests' eyes and then another sound is heard from upstairs.
This time it's really terrifying. It is a demonic voice almost
growling some words in a demonic tongue. Again the
priests look up with immense fear in their eyes.*

PHILLIP *(frightened and breaking down even further)*: Oh please . . .
please somebody tell me what's happening. Why me?
Why my Sarah?

FATHER MATTHEW: Phillip. (*Grabs him by the shoulders.*) Phillip! Listen to me!
You must stay strong and calm. This thing will thrive on
fear. (*Begins directing it towards audience.*) If it begins to
sense fear among our group the whole thing will fall apart
up there. Exorcisms achieve more success with a group of
people who have accepted the Holy Spirit into their hearts.
That is why you are all here! We must remain unified with
the power of the Holy Spirit, because you see then it will
fear us and we will succeed.

PHILLIP: But she needs me as well. I'm her father.
*Another sudden noise is heard, but not quite sure what.
Less of a reaction from Father Matthew who is trying to
keep his head. Father Simon, however, is extremely nervous.*

FATHER MATTHEW: Trust me, Phillip. We will protect her from harm.
Everything is going to be alright, but you must trust us and
stay downstairs.
*Phillip still trembling does not respond but nods his head in
approval.*

FATHER MATTHEW: OK, good. (*Pats him on the shoulder.*) faith Phillip. God is
with you. Right everybody, follow me. (*Father Matthew
leads the way and Father Simon waits for everyone to follow
and he tags along at the very back of the group. They begin
walking up the stairs. Father Matthew stops on the landing
and turns to everyone.*) OK, everyone, we're closer to its
presence, so you may start to get some strange sensations
around your body. Mostly rushes of heat down the back of
your neck and spine, a tightness around the throat, dizziness
and unpleasant odours, and of course you can expect these
sensations to get stronger once we're inside the room, but
don't worry these things cannot physically harm us. Right
now could everybody please link hands so we can pray
together. Father Simon, if you would like to lead the prayer.

FATHER SIMON: Father, do you really think we should go through with this after what Mr Jenkins just told us? If it's a Leviticus we cannot defeat it.

FATHER MATTHEW: I have never failed an exorcism, Simon. Lead the prayer.

FATHER SIMON: Yes, but this is different. There could be serious consequences.

FATHER MATTHEW: I have made a promise. Lead the prayer.

FATHER SIMON: But what if we're not quick enough?!

FATHER MATTHEW: Look, if it's a Leviticus then we need to act quickly! Lead the prayer!

FATHER SIMON: What if we're already too late?!

FATHER MATTHEW: She's just a child, Simon! We have to try! Look, we have everybody here, so we should stick to the plan. Lead the prayer!

FATHER SIMON: Sorry, father, I've just got a really bad feeling about this.

FATHER MATTHEW: Do not lose faith, Father Simon. Lead the prayer.

FATHER SIMON: Yes, father. OK, if everyone would like to just repeat after me. Lord have mercy.

ALL: Lord have mercy.

FATHER SIMON: Christ have mercy.

ALL: Christ have mercy.

FATHER SIMON: Christ graciously hear us.

ALL: Christ graciously hear us.

FATHER SIMON: Father in heaven, have mercy on us.

ALL: Father in heaven, have mercy on us.

FATHER SIMON: God the holy spirit, have mercy on us.

ALL: God the holy spirit, have mercy on us.

FATHER SIMON: Amen.

ALL: Amen

FATHER SIMON: Thank you. That's fine. Me and Father Mathew will continue the prayer. Holy Mother of God, pray for us. All holy saints, prophets and holy disciples of God pray for us.

FATHER MATTHEW: From all evil, deliver us, O Lord. From all sin,

BOTH PRIESTS: Deliver us, O Lord.

FATHER MATTHEW: From your wrath,

BOTH: Deliver us, O Lord (*This pattern repeats for the following invocations.*)

FATHER MATTHEW: From sudden and unprovided death . . . From the snares of the Devil . . . From lightning and tempest . . . From the scourge of earthquakes, plague, famine and war . . . From everlasting death . . .

BOTH: Deliver us, O Lord.

FATHER MATTHEW: O mighty God, we pray that you protect us now as we come face to face with our most dangerous enemy. God, by your might defend my cause. Hearken to the words of my mouth. Turn back the evil upon my foes and in your faithfulness destroy them. Give us the strength and may the power of the Holy Spirit work through us so that we may cast away the devil from the body of your servant. In the name of the Father, the Son and the Holy Spirit, Amen. (*Begins to sprinkle holy water on the audience.*) Once we're inside do not let go of one another's hands, don't touch anything, but most importantly whatever you do, do not look Sarah directly in the eyes. (*Father Matthew places his hand on the bedroom doorknob and pauses for a moment. Takes a deep breath and then opens it slowly. The bedroom is very dark with only two candles lit either side of the fireplace which is on the left-hand side of the room. The bed may be placed in the middle of the room. Not sure of its positioning yet. Hopefully we won't really be able to make out Sarah in the bed. Father Matthew leads the audience into the room. Father Simon closes the door behind them, leans against the door looking extremely nervous and does the sign of the cross. Father Matthew walks the audience over to the fireplace. He whispers . . .*) Everyone just stand here. Don't break hands. (*Father Matthew and Father Simon approach the bed together both doing the cross sign against their bodies as they approach. Sarah is lying on the bed or maybe not . . .*) Almighty God, Father of the Heavens, save this child who was created in your image. Let the enemy have no power over her. Lord send her aid from your holy place and watch over her from Sion. Lord heed my prayer and let my cry be heard by you.

FATHER SIMON: Lord, graciously hear us and have mercy on our souls. *For this final exorcism scene in the bedroom I know where I want to go with it, but I'm not entirely sure how we will get to that stage. We will probably have to devise this scene all together to see what will work, but here is some dialogue that I think should happen . . .*
The demon is pretending to be Sarah to fool the priests. Sarah has a few lines. Father Matthew tries to determine the name of the demon by asking it. He makes the sign of the cross over himself and then Sarah. He places the end of the stole on Sarah's neck, and putting his right hand on her head he says the following . . .

FATHER MATTHEW: Strike terror, Lord, into the beast now laying waste your vineyard. I command you, unclean spirit whoever you are now attacking this servant of God, by the passion and resurrection of our Lord Jesus Christ that you tell me by some sign your name, and the day and hour of your departure. (*The demon laughs. It's a terrifying sound.*) I command you to obey me, I who am a minister of God; I command you, reveal yourself to me!
The demon laughs again. Speaks in a demonic tongue unrecognisable to audience but the priests can understand. The sentence ends with the word 'Leviticus'. Upon hearing

it Father Simon steps back and grabs hold of the hand of the audience member stood at the end of the row and tells all the audience . . .

FATHER SIMON: Everyone come forward. We are servants of God the creator. Together we stand united in the power of our faith and protected by the Holy Spirit. Minion of the devil fear us! God Speaks through us, so fear his mighty sword upon our tongues.

As the audience approach Father Matthew at the foot of the bed he puts his hand out to the audience member on the opposite end of the row and says . . .

FATHER MATTHEW: Join me, Christian brothers and sisters, and let us call to our Heavenly Father, we who are servants of the truth. (*Everyone has linked hands, with Father Matthew and Father Simon stood on either end.*) Holy Lord, almighty father we humbly call on your holy name in fear, asking that you grant us steadfast faith and the power supported by your mighty arm, to confront this cruel demon with confidence and resolution. Amen. Father Simon, assist please. Everyone else stand firm and remember what I told you outside. (*Father Simon places one hand on Sarah's head and with the other he holds the stoop of holy water. Father Matthew places his one hand on Sarah's head and with his other he holds a crucifix.*) I cast you out, vile demon, in the name of our Lord Jesus Christ. Be gone and stay far from this creature of God. For it is he who commands you, He who flung you headlong from the heights of heaven into the depths of Hell. (*Father Simon sprinkles some holy water over the demon. Big reaction of pain from the demon.*) Hearken therefore and tremble in fear, you enemy of the faith, you foe of the human race, you corrupter of justice, you root of all evil and vice; seducer of men, betrayer of the nations, author of pain and sorrow. Why do you resist when you know Christ the Lord brings your plans to nothing? Be gone then, in the name of the Father, the Son and the Holy Spirit (*Father Matthew does the Cross sign on Sarah's head.*) Repel, oh Lord, the devil's power, put the unholy tempter to flight. By the sign of your name let your servant be protected in mind and body (*Father Matthew makes the cross three times on Sarah's breast.*) Lord, as we call on your holy name may the evil spirit retreat in terror and defeat. (*Father Simon sprinkles more holy water over the demon.*) I adjure you, ancient serpent, by the judge of the living and the dead, by your creator, by him who has the power to consign you to hell, to depart forthwith in fear from this child of God! . . . (*Failed attempt.*) I adjure you again by the might of the Holy Spirit to depart from this child of God. Yield therefore, yield to the minister of

Christ! It is the power of Christ that compels you. Tremble before that mighty arm that led souls forth to the light and depart from this child of God! (*Failed attempt.*) May the image of God descend on you. Make no resistance in departing from this child, do not think of despising my command. It is God himself who commands you. The majestic Christ who commands you. God the Father who commands you. Depart then transgressor! Leave this child now! (*Failed attempt, and demon keeps laughing and mocking the priests. Father Matthew becoming very nervous and impatient.*)

FATHER SIMON: Matthew . . . (*Very panicked.*)
They exchange looks. There is an understanding between them that things might worsen.

FATHER MATTHEW: Faith brother . . . faith. (*He attempts the exorcism again.*) Give place, creature, give way you monster, give way to Christ! For he has already stripped you of your powers and laid waste your kingdom. He has cast you forth into the outer darkness where everlasting ruin awaits you! To what purpose do you insolently resist?! To what purpose do you brazenly refuse?! For you are guilty before almighty God, whose laws you have transgressed. You Cannot take this child from her heavenly father therefore be gone! I am a minister of God! By my command depart then impious one, father of lechery, depart accursed one, model of vileness, depart with all your deceits for this is God's temple. Why do you still linger here? Give honour to God! It is he who casts you out, it is he who repels you. He who expels you. He who has prepared everlasting fire for you! Why?! Why do you linger here!? What do you want with this child?!
Demon laughs hysterically and very aggressively, even more frightening than before. It speaks.

DEMON: You fool. The child?! Not the child I want. (*Laughs.*)

FATHER MATTHEW: Everyone, get back! Keep away! Don't look it in the eyes. (*Father Simon pulls everyone back.*) What then? What is it that you want?

DEMON: You know what I want. (*The demon then starts to imitate Sarah's voice, crying and calling out . . .*) Dad! Dad, help! Please, dad, I'm scared! Help me, please, it's hurting me! *Father Matthew realises that Phillip has been the cause of everything, and suddenly Phillip bursts in the room.*

PHILLIP: Sarah! Has it worked?!
Phillip makes his way towards the foot of the bed. Father Matthew rushes over to Phillip and holds him back.

FATHER MATTHEW: Damn it, Phillip, get back! I told you to stay downstairs! *Suddenly the demon starts to imitate Melissa's voice.*

DEMON: Hi, hun. Do you miss me? Oh hun, do you still love me? Please hold me. You fucking sick bastard! Pervert! Screw

you! Screw you right in the mouth and in the fucking arse!!
Go on fuck her again! Fuck her again!
Father Matthew realises that Phillip must be hiding something.

FATHER MATTHEW: Phillip, what happened?! There's something you're not telling us!

PHILLIP: I told you everything.

FATHER MATTHEW: Don't lie to me, Phillip! Tell me! What happened to your wife whilst she was dying?!

PHILLIP: I . . .

FATHER MATTHEW: Tell me now, Phillip! You have to tell me! You must confess your sins now before it's too late! What did you do?!
(*Before Phillip can confess the demon starts freaking out, and then all of a sudden Sarah's body goes limp and she stops moving. The demon has left her body and taken Phillip's. We will have to choreograph something where Phillip flips out and Father Matthew tries to restrain him.*) Simon, get everyone out, quickly and lock the door behind you!

FATHER SIMON: What about you!? You can't cast it out! We have to leave!

FATHER MATTHEW: Go, Simon, just go!
Father Simon rushes the audience out of the bedroom and locks the door behind him. He makes the cross sign over his body.

FATHER SIMON: Quick everyone. (*He walks downstairs at a fast pace with audience following behind.*) Thank you for coming. Don't worry, Father Matthew and I will fix this. You must go now, it is no longer safe. (*Opens the front door.*) Speak of this to no one. May God go with you all, goodnight.
Rushes everyone out and slams the door shut.

THE END

Abel Hartmann's Grand-Guignol:
A History of Violence (2015)

by

DREAMCATCHER HORROR THEATRE

Preface

Dreamcatcher Horror Theatre was established in Devon, UK, in October 2005 with the expressed intention to develop horror theatre. The founders were Jon Lane and Carro Marren, both graduates of the Dartington College of Arts, a celebrated educational institution based at Dartington Hall near Totnes, south-west England, which specialized in offering education in the creative arts. Establishing itself as a small-scale horror group, Dreamcatcher has performed extensively in its local region but has also written plays for other theatre companies, including the horror play *Thank You* for the Molotov Theatre Group in Washington DC. Dreamcatcher has appeared at theatre festivals, notably the Edinburgh Fringe.

Abel Hartmann's Grand-Guignol: A History of Violence was first performed at the Edinburgh Free Fringe in August 2015. The Free Fringe operates at the same time as the more famous Edinburgh Fringe and was initiated by the comedian and producer Peter Buckley Hill (PBH) who was disheartened by the increasing cost of venue hire and ticket prices at the long-established Fringe. The principle of no hire charges and free admission (with post-show donations encouraged) proved a success, and the Free Fringe—also known as PBH's Free Fringe—has run with growing success since 1996. *Abel Hartmann's Grand-Guignol* was performed in a basement bar in Edinburgh and proved to be an effective example of Free Fringe horror theatre. The play is largely a monologue, as the audience listens to Abel Hartmann (played by Jon Lane in Edinburgh in 2015) telling the story of the original Grand-Guignol. The vivid details of the key figures, contexts and atmosphere of the Parisian theatre are complemented with occasional extracts from classic plays from the repertoire. Interestingly, this deployment of extracts within an overarching narrative is similar to Carl Grose's *Grand Guignol* (2009).

The Théâtre du Grand-Guignol was a remarkable theatre in terms of its venue, creative teams, genre and formula. It is a theatre that has a history—and a 'story'—that may be as compelling and as fascinating as any of its many plays and nights of *douche écossaise*. We have decided to conclude this volume with *Abel Hartmann's Grand-Guignol* as it represents an entertaining and gripping account of a long-gone theatre and, in so doing, presents a vivid example of the twenty-first-century *Grand-Guignolesque*.

ABEL HARTMANN'S GRAND-GUIGNOL: A HISTORY OF VIOLENCE (2015)

by

Dreamcatcher Horror Theatre

First performed at the Edinburgh Free Fringe in August 2015

Cast
Abel Hartmann (founding member of the
Dreamcatcher Horror Theatre Company,
and Grand Guignol aficionado)
Interns 1-4 (Four Interns/Volunteers/
Victims selected by Abel to aid him
demonstrate several examples of Grand
Guignol plays throughout its history)

The space is set up as follows: four chairs of the type used by the audience at the sides of the performance space—two on each side—and the director's chair, with leather straps at the wrist and ankle points, situated in the centre. Abel walks through the audience to the space, and begins.

ABEL: Ladies and gentlemen, decadents and deviants—I bid you welcome. To those of you who have not yet had the pleasure of my acquaintance, allow me to introduce myself. I am Abel Hartmann, founding member of Dreamcatcher Horror Theatre, and your guide for tonight's journey into the black heart of the human condition—a place I like to call 'home'.

Before we go any further, however, I need to call upon my assistants for tonight's performance. These enchanting, if somewhat naive, creatures will be instrumental in helping to illustrate several examples of what made the Grand Guignol, in its heyday, one of the top tourist attractions in Paris—and certainly the goriest. Ladies and gentlemen, I present to you—my harem. *Abel introduces each of his 'interns' in turn as they enter—four young women.*

Now, as lovely as these 'ladies' are, at present I have no need of their services, and so—(*snaps his fingers, and the girls all drop their heads into a hypnotic trance. Abel places each of them in one of the four side-seats*)—a little post-hypnotic suggestion

I planted with them before the show. I find it makes them so much more . . . biddable.

So, the stage is set, and we are ready to start. Oh—there is one final nicety we must observe. Our kind hosts have asked me to inform those of you in the (*pauses and mentally gauges distance*) front two rows that they are not responsible for any damage that might occur to your clothes, valuables, or other belongings due to arterial spray, vitreous humour, brain matter . . . or any other spilled bodily fluids. You have been warned.

To begin, then . . . Picture the following: in Paris, you get off the Métro at Pigalle, and walk south-west down the rue Pigalle, between the ranks of fishnet stockings and cigarette smoke, in the light of the neon signs and the sound of the music that emanates from the clubs lining both sides of the street. At the crossroads with the rue de Notre Dame de Lorette, the rue Chaptal and the rue Fontaine, you take a right down the rue Chaptal. The contrast is alarming; darkness and silence, a sad street, curiously barely-lit, without any shops, deserted. You can hear the sound of your footsteps on the pavement. Three hundred yards further along, invisibly, suddenly emerging on the right, is the cité Chaptal, a narrow dead-end alley, about a hundred yards long, culminating in the barely-lit façade of the Théâtre du Grand-Guignol.

Even before it became famous as the theatre of horror, the building had a dark and chequered history. It had originally been a convent chapel, before it was sacked and gutted during the Reign of Terror in 1791. When it was re-opened as a church, the Dominican priest who preached there was banned from sermonising by the church authorities, because of his unorthodox views. Thankfully, when it was converted into a theatre, much of the building's past was retained in the architecture and fittings: two giant angels gazed down on the audience from the rafters, as if in judgement on the proceedings below. The private boxes at ground level had grills on them, making them look and feel like confessionals. Audience members would swear they could still smell incense and wax in the air. This was not a purpose-built performance space: it was a place where God sat, weighing the souls of humanity, and found them lacking.

In other ways, the Grand-Guignol was not unlike this room here. The stage was a little larger than this, but the audience was very close to the action—as you are, now. It was said by one regular 'Guignoler' that the space was so confined, 'a front-row spectator could shake hands with the actors as he stretched his feet into the prompter's box'. (*Pause to shake the hand of a member of the audience.*) This led to a very focused and intense performance—and one where the inherent intimacy of the close space could become oppressively uncomfortable at the drop of a hat. For example . . .
During the next 'scene', Abel revives intern 1 and passes her a newspaper. As he describes the action, Intern 1 acts as though

she were in the scene; remaining in her seat, but letting her facial expressions and body language tell the story.

Let us imagine that sweet Viola here is a young prostitute, relaxing in her boudoir, waiting for her next client. She leafs through the city paper, filled with hair-raising stories of crimes and misdeeds. One in particular catches her eye—the lurid report of the latest murder and robbery, perpetrated by a scoundrel who has been terrorising the outlying districts of Paris. All the grisly details are given, along with a list of what was stolen from the victim. Also included is the news that the police have a suspect that they are searching for, and have called a city-wide manhunt.

Just then, there is a knock at the door. It is the brothel's madame, come to tell Viola that her next client has arrived. He comes in, full of nervous energy—so keen for privacy, that he insists that Viola lock the bedroom door. As part of the 'service' that she provides, Viola offers the man a glass of champagne; as the alcohol begins to take effect, the man starts to boast and show her pieces of expensive jewellery he has 'earned'—pieces that match items taken in the robbery-murder. Gradually, we and Viola both realise that she is locked in her bedroom with the killer—who has just casually revealed a revolver and a long butcher's knife. The intimate safety of her own boudoir has become, in minutes, a hellish place of extreme, life-threatening danger.

Abel returns Intern 1 to a sleep-induced hypnotic state.

This was the plot of one of the very first plays to be written and performed at the Grand-Guignol when it opened in 1897. Unlike the later plays for which the theatre became famous, however, this one did not end in bloody disaster for our beautiful young protagonist—the police come and the miscreant is captured in the nick of time, leaving her unscathed . . . physically, at least.

It would take a combination of the unique talents of three special people to unlock the potential of this theatre, and bring the public packing into its auditorium. The first critical ingredient was a new artistic director. The founder of the Grand-Guignol, Oscar Méténier, left after just a year, in 1898. His other jobs, as secretary to the police commissioner, and writer for the *fait divers* news journals—akin to the British 'Penny Dreadfuls'— informed his playwriting subjects of the criminal underclass, and themes that questioned the established bourgeoisie and theatrical moral conventions. But it was his successor, Max Maurey, who distilled this focus into a winning formula. Maurey heightened the levels of sex and violence within the plays, and established the tradition of 'la douche écossaise'—also known as the 'hot and cold shower', or more directly translated, ' the Scottish shower'— alternating short one-act horrors with bawdy farces. Many of the themes of the Grand-Guignol—sex, revenge, cuckoldry, hidden secrets—could be seen in both the comedies and the horrors: it was the approach and tone that changed.

The other area in which Maurey excelled was public relations. When it became apparent that several members of the audience had fainted during the more horrific moments of the evening's entertainment, Maurey's response was to hire a house-doctor onto the theatre's permanent staff, to be on-hand to administer first aid to those for whom the on-stage violence proved too much. This then led to the fateful occasion when, during one performance, the doctor was called for, to care for a woman who had collapsed—only for Maurey to call from the lobby, saying that no medical help was available, as the doctor himself had fainted from fright! Stories such as these enhanced the mythology of the theatre, as a place where audiences would flee from the stalls in terror, while blood flowed across the stage floor by the bucketful.

Of course, all of this publicity and attention would count for nothing if the plays didn't live up to the hype. Fortunately, when Maurey took over the reins of the theatre, he hired André de Lorde as resident playwright—a man who would become known throughout Paris as 'the Prince of Terror'. Most of the examples you will witness tonight flowed from the pen of de Lorde. In 25 years, he wrote over 100 plays for the Grand-Guignol, often in collaboration with medical professionals, to ensure the acts of physical violence were as realistic as possible. One of his frequent partners was his own therapist, Alfred Binet; and psychological horror was often a key ingredient of de Lorde's work. In 'The Last Torture', for example—set in China during the 1900 Boxer Rebellion—the French consul, fearing that the approaching clamour outside his embassy is the rioting Chinese, is forced to kill his own daughter rather than let her be captured and tortured by the rebels. Only then is it revealed that the approaching force is actually the Allied army, quashing the rebellion and saving the embassy. Realising what it is that he has done, the consul goes insane.

Many of de Lorde's other plays used psychology and its experts as the focus of the horror. As a new science, it was still largely unknown and mysterious to many, and a great source of inspiration for de Lorde—who was described by Binet as a terrible patient, always more interested in his latest play than in actually working on his ongoing treatment.

If Maurey created the atmosphere that got the heart pumping, and de Lorde delivered stories to chill the blood, then Paul Ratineau was responsible for making the blood flow. Although he was, first and foremost, an actor, and holds the distinction of the longest continuous career onstage at the Grand-Guignol; he also possessed an almost encyclopaedic knowledge of stagecraft and technical effects, especially those pertaining to horror. As such, he found himself in the role of stage manager for the theatre, and it was he who devised and created the myriad illusions and gadgets that allowed thousands of victims to be maimed, mutilated and murdered onstage throughout the Grand-Guignol's history. While the low lighting levels helped to obscure the devices from curious eyes, and the actors' performances onstage helped to 'sell' the illusion; the greatest tribute to Ratineau's work is that, even to this day, we have almost no idea how any of his effects were done.

I say almost . . . There is one effect which is documented, along with instructions on how it was performed. In the 1922 play, *The Torture Garden*—written by our beloved Prince of Terror, de Lorde himself—a young girl is punished for insulting a prestigious, and sadistic, customer of an opium den, by suffering the 'Torture of the Ribbon of the Flesh':

Abel wakes Intern 2 and Intern 3 to play the roles of 'Ti-Mao' (the torturer) and 'Ti-Bah' (the victim). The following text is taken from the play, and spoken by Abel.

'You see this knife, this little blade? A torturer like Ti-Mao does not need anything other than this to put her victims through the most atrocious suffering, and yet denying them the deliverance of death. She is going to make two long incisions down the length of Ti-Bah's back, and then, slowly, she is going to peel away a long strip of skin—just as you would peel a piece of fruit . . .'

Abel hands the knife to Ti-Mao, and takes hold of Ti-Bah's wrists, holding them high above her head as she kneels in front of the audience, facing them. Ti-Mao cuts up the back of Ti-Bah's blouse, and makes the two incisions down the length of her back, and then she and Abel turn Ti-Bah so that they can see the two cuts. Ti-Mao then takes the top end of the skin, and slowly begins to peel it away from Ti-Bah's flesh.

'Look . . . how she is suffering . . . listen to her crying . . . how she's suffering! And now, the blood is running . . . Ah, the blood . . . the blood . . . the blood . . .'

Abel returns both girls to their somnambulant 'trance' states, and uses the destroyed top to mop up any blood on the floor.

Ah, this brings back so many sweet memories . . . but this is no time for personal nostalgia.

Abel presses the bloodied, ruined top to the back of the mutilated girl, and covers her shoulders with a shawl.

When war broke out in Europe, in 1914, Maurey felt that the Grand-Guignol had had its day, and passed the baton to Camille Choisy and Charles Zibell. Zibell elected to be a silent partner, focusing on providing the financial capital for the venture, while Choisy became the new artistic director. Far from falling into decline, however, the Grand-Guignol entered what many called its 'golden years' in the post-war period. This is not so much down to what changes Choisy made to the format, but rather to what he did *not*. Camille recognised that Maurey's 'hot and cold showers', and the work of de Lorde and Ratineau, were all vital components for the continued success of the theatre, and he retained all three. What he *did* add to the mix were two names who would become superstars.

Georges Paulais was an extraordinary actor, who exemplified the style of Choisy's Grand-Guignol—a curious blend of naturalism, melodrama and Expressionism. Many of the great male roles of the 1920s were created by Paulais. But he was as nothing, compared to the woman who became known as 'the High Priestess of the Temple of Horror'—Paula Maxa. It is said that in the ten years or so that she appeared at the Grand-Guignol, she was killed over 10,000 times, in 60 different ways. Some of the more exotic methods of execution included: being cut into 93 pieces and stitched back together; crucified; burned alive; shot by firing squad; flattened by a steam-roller; and being devoured by a puma. Choisy's secretary, a meticulous archivist, recorded that Maxa cried 'Help!' 983 times, 'Murderer!' 1,263 times . . . and 'Rape!' 1,804½ times.

During its golden age, the Grand-Guignol became *the* place to be seen. Millionaires from every continent came to the theatre, as did many crowned heads: the King of Greece, Princess Wilhelmina of Holland, the Sultan of Morocco's sons and daughters, and several deposed and exiled rulers, could all be seen regularly within the Grand-Guignol. Another regular theatregoer, somewhat lower on the social ladder at the time, was a Vietnamese refugee, working as a pastry and noodle cook in a Chinese restaurant, by the name of Ho Chi Minh.

Let's take a look at another example of what made these great crowned heads return time and time again to the old chapel of Rue Chaptal. The following excerpt is from a 1912 play by Maurice Level, adapted from his own short story. It was so popular that it was revived several times during the Grand-Guignol's history, including at the height of Choisy's reign as director. It has gone under several different names through the decades, and been adapted many times. Even its original French title, 'La Baiser Dans la Nuit', has a delicious, sensual ambiguity to it, once one recognises that 'baiser' can mean either 'kiss' or 'fuck'. *Abel winds a bandage round his head and one side of his face, covering one eye.*

The story focuses on two ex-lovers, Henry and Jean. Some time before the play, Jean throws vitriol into Henry's face when he breaks off their relationship. Rather than press charges, however, Henry wishes to forgive her; and despite the unending agony she has caused him, he arranges for her to visit, for a reconciliation . . . or does he have something else in mind? *Abel performs the part of 'Henry', and wakes Intern 4 to play the part of 'Jean'*

HENRY: Jean—there's one last thing I wanted to ask you.

JEAN: What is it?

HENRY: It's . . . no, it doesn't matter. It wouldn't be fair on you.

JEAN: No, please, it's fine. After everything you've done for me . . . please, ask.

HENRY: I wanted . . . no, I can't.

JEAN: Please! Whatever it is . . . just ask. I will do anything.

HENRY: Anything?

JEAN: Yes . . . it's the least I can do.

HENRY: Then . . . before you go . . . could I have . . . one more kiss?
(*Jean starts back in shock.*)

HENRY: I'm sorry. Forget it—I was out of order.

JEAN: No! No, it's OK . . . I was just a little surprised, is all.
Yes, you can have a kiss before I go.

HENRY: Are you sure?

JEAN: Of course. (*Jean stands and faces Henry. Slowly, hesitantly, they move together and embrace. Henry bends his head to kiss Jean on the lips, but at the last minute, she turns her head away.*)
I'm sorry. I—
Henry gently puts his hand to Jean's cheek, and lifts it until they are looking into each other's eyes once more.

HENRY: It's OK, I understand. You don't have to do this.

JEAN: No, it's . . . you said it was what you wanted. (*Beat.*) OK, I'm fine.
They begin to move together once more, but Jean's head dips as before. This time, Henry's hand is quicker to move to her cheek, and slightly more forceful as he brings it back up again.)

HENRY: I thought you said you were fine?
Jean takes hold of Henry's hand and pulls it away from her cheek. Quickly, Henry shifts and takes hold of Jean's hair, pulling her head back and planting a kiss on her mouth. The two of them struggle for a moment, she trying to escape his grasp, he pulling her in closer. Jean finally knees Henry in the groin, and pushes him away as he sinks to the floor in agony.

JEAN (*furious*): What is wrong with you? Can't you take no for an answer? Couldn't you see I changed my mind? Or maybe you thought I didn't mean it—that I was just a little nervous, is that it? I don't care how long you've been on your own, but that was way out of line.
Henry remains kneeling on the floor, clutching at his groin.

JEAN: Oh, just get up, would you? This has always been your problem: you never had any backbone. Every time we got into a fight, you'd just back down and scuttle back into your hole. You never stood up to me. You were so meek, so polite—always happy to help others, even when it meant you'd come out worse off. You'd just shrug your shoulders and say, 'Well, that's life, I guess.' Well, I got news for you. Life is shit. And if you go around being nice all the time, sooner or later everyone else is going to drop all their shit on you.

Henry whimpers quietly, in pain.

JEAN: What did you expect from all this? That I'd fall into your arms
and we'd live happily ever after? This is the real world. And even
if I had come here with any ideas of getting back with you, the
whole desperate act got rid of them real quick. All this touching,
and stroking, and hugging, and dancing—it wasn't romantic, it
wasn't sweet—it was twisted! So that's what you've become—a
desperate, twisted, freak!
Henry still kneels motionless on the floor.

JEAN   (*realises what she has just said, the fight draining from her*):
Henry? I'm sorry, I didn't mean—Henry? Are you OK? Should
I get one of the wardens, or try and find some help, or something?
*Jean kneels down beside Henry, and places one hand on his
shoulder. Finally, he responds, turning slowly towards her and
taking her hand in both of his. After stroking it for a moment,
his hand moves to her wrist, where it tightens its grasp.*

HENRY: Got you.

JEAN: What -? Henry, let go. You're—it's too tight.

HENRY: Oh no, I'm never letting you go now. It's time for you to pay for
what you did to me.

JEAN: No! HELP! SOMEBODY HELP ME!

HENRY: SHUT UP! (*Jean does so.*) That's better. We wouldn't want
anyone to disturb us, after all. Not that it matters—the warden's
office is on the ground floor, and by the time they get up here to
find out what the noise was, it'll all be over. Now, you're going to
get what you deserve: but at my hands, not the decision of some
faceless jury! That's the real reason I dropped the charges—not
from any decency or sense of forgiveness, but because if you were
sent to prison, I would never see you again. And if that happened,
how would I be able to give you my parting gift? (*Jean struggles
to break free from the arm-locks, but Henry holds her tighter.*)
Stop struggling! It's pointless. (*Beat.*) Do you know, today was
the most nervous I've been since I first realised what to do. What
if you had decided not to come, to just put a line under our
chapter in the book and move on without a backwards glance?
I shouldn't have got so worked up about it, though: if there's one
thing I know about you, it's that you can't resist the nice guy,
right? And once you came through that door, I knew I had you
right where I wanted you. Even when you left—I knew you'd
come back. So now you've only got yourself to blame. (*Henry
takes both her wrists in one hand, and pulls out a small bottle
from a pocket.*) Do you see this? Do you recognise what it is?
You should—it's the same stuff you used on my face! Oh, don't
look so surprised—didn't I say the wardens here will get you
anything you need? So, now, we're going to let you see exactly
what I've been going through. I'm going to do to you what you
did to me.

Jean's struggling intensifies as she tries desperately to spit the gag out and break free, but Henry pushes her back into the central chair and holds her there.

HENRY: Now, let's have the face back towards me, there's a good girl. (*He pulls down on her arms, forcing her back to arch.*) That's better. And please, keep your mouth closed. I don't want any stray drops going down there and burning your throat away, do I? No, I want you to live through this. Are you ready? Here it comes! *Henry uncorks the little bottle with his teeth, and slowly pours it over Jean's face. Her screams suddenly take on a new pitch, of extreme agony. Henry releases her arms, and her hands fly to her face, as the skin begins to peel away from her cheeks. The screams get louder and higher as she buries her burning face in her hands.*

HENRY: Hurts, doesn't it? Well, get used to it: we're the same now, you and I. And the pain is going to last for a very long time indeed! *Abel returns the girl to her trance state, and unwinds the bandage from his face, putting it over her face and covering one eye.*

ABEL: In 1926, Charles Zibell's finances ran out, and he was forced to sell his share of the theatre on to a new director. His replacement, Jack Jouvin, would not be content to be merely a silent partner, however: he wanted complete creative control of this lucrative enterprise. For two years, he and Choisy argued and fought, until Choisy decided to start up his own theatre in competition, and Jouvin became the sole director. Nor was this the only change that occurred: Jouvin decided that 'la douche écossaise' was a tired old gimmick, and instead began to plan seasons based on particular themes. He also got rid of Paula Maxa, on the basis that she was 'too popular', and severely cut down on the number of plays written by de Lorde. Indeed, such was his determination to make the Grand-Guignol 'his' theatre, that he wrote and directed many of the plays himself. And the result? Audience numbers began to dwindle.

Now, not all the blame can be laid at Jouvin's door. Several other factors also played their part, two of which were especially significant. Firstly: three years after Jouvin took over, Universal Studios released *Dracula* and *Frankenstein*—the first horror films with sound. Suddenly audiences had a new form of entertainment to compete with the terrors of the Grand-Guignol; and the mesmerising glow of the magic lantern began to prove irresistible. As cinema audiences began to grow, the audiences for the spectacles of Montmartre began to decline.

The second element which cannot be ignored, is that the world was changing. The 1930s saw fascism rise, first in Mussolini's Italy, then Hitler's Germany, then Franco's Spain. The optimism of *la belle époque* and the Roaring '20s was gone, and a new mood of depression and uncertainty crept in. With the real-world fears that were everywhere around, the shocks and scares of the

Grand-Guignol began to pale in comparison. In July of 1938, Jouvin retired, spent and exhausted, beaten by a world that was heading inexorably towards war.

The Grand-Guignol never really found its feet again after that. Eva Berkson, an Englishwoman, took over the theatre from Jouvin, but during the Nazi occupation of France, she was forced to flee back to the United Kingdom, and it Camille Choisy returned to run it in her stead. The patronage of high-ranking Nazi officers, along with the horrors of war going on all around them, did little to entice theatregoers, however, and audience numbers began to fall alarmingly. After the war, wave after wave of owners tried unsuccessfully to revive the place: but as one of the later directors, Charles Nonon, lamented: 'We could never equal Buchenwald. Before the war, everyone felt that what was happening on-stage was impossible. Now we know that these things, and worse, are possible in reality.' Although it limped on for 17 years after the end of the war, in November 1962, the Grand-Guignol finally closed its doors for the last time.

Now, that seems a terribly dour and down-beat place to end our history lesson; so let's have one last slice of entertainment from the golden age of the Grand-Guignol. Perhaps one of the most famous plays written and performed at the theatre was 1925's *A Crime in a Madhouse*—and with good reason. It was written by none other than the Prince of Terror himself, Andre de Lorde; in collaboration with his stalwart therapist, Alfred Binet. As the title suggests, the play takes place in a madhouse, where—well, why describe it for you, when you can see for yourself?

Abel wakes up all four girls. Intern 1 takes the role of Louise; Intern 3 plays Hunchback, with the torn shirt on her back providing the necessary shape; and Intern 4 performs as one-eye; Intern 2 plays the part of La Normand.

ONE-EYE: Light!

HUNCHBACK: Here!

ONE-EYE: More light!

She puts a hand over Louise's mouth to silence her. Hunchback brings the bed lamp closer.

HUNCHBACK: *Voilà*!

Both Hunchback and La Normand lean over Louise.

LA NORMAND (*to Hunchback*): She holds her so firmly.

HUNCHBACK: She does!

LA NORMAND: What is she going to do?

HUNCHBACK: I don't know—but *she* knows!

ONE-EYE: Normand, do you have the cloth?

LA NORMAND: Here it is.

She hands her the torn-up piece of sheet.

ONE-EYE (*to La Normand*): Hold her hands! And give me a long needle!

HUNCHBACK (*searching the room*): A needle?

LA NORMAND:	The Sister's knitting needle! On the shelf!
HUNCHBACK	*(turning to the shelf)*: Ah, on the shelf.
LA NORMAND:	In front of the Blessed Virgin.
HUNCHBACK:	There it is!
	She gives the knitting needle to One-Eye.
ONE-EYE:	I can't see well enough to do my work!
	She jams the needle in the deep pocket of her asylum gown.
LA NORMAND:	I agree. It's too dark in here.
ONE-EYE:	Bring the bed light closer!
HUNCHBACK:	Here.
ONE-EYE:	Closer! *(Hunchback obeys.)*
LA NORMAND	*(staring at Louise)*: People say she's already dead. Yes, she is like a corpse.
ONE-EYE:	No. When I am finished, the cuckoo will return to us!
LOUISE	*(struggling against One-Eye's grip)*: Ah!
ONE-EYE	*(uncovering Louise's mouth)*: Do you know who I am, child?
LOUISE:	Where am I?
ONE-EYE:	Stop moving!
LOUISE	*(catching a glimpse of Hunchback and La Normand)*: What are you doing to me?
ONE-EYE:	Don't scream. We don't want to do anything to you . . . only to those two eyes.
LOUISE:	My eyes!
ONE-EYE:	Those are not your eyes!
LA NORMAND:	She thinks those are her eyes.
HUNCHBACK:	Ha! Ha!
LA NORMAND:	Ha! Ha!
ONE-EYE	*(with authority)*: Quiet, you two! Do you understand, my little one, it's a service I want to render you. You were crazy once, weren't you? Don't you remember?
LA NORMAND:	Of course she does!
HUNCHBACK:	She doesn't remember!
ONE-EYE:	While you were crazy, a bird got inside you, a cuckoo bird. She hid in your head. Behind your eyes!
LOUISE	*(struggling again)*: Ah!
ONE-EYE:	If you continue to scream, I am going to have to shut you up for good. So listen to me! I'm going to rid you of the bird. Do you understand? She has stolen your eyes. That bird has removed your eyeballs and put hers in your sockets! Do you understand now? *(Screaming.)* Those damned cuckoo's eyes are planning to rob me of my sight!
LOUISE	*(filled with terror)*: No, no! Have pity! Please!
ONE-EYE	*(calmly)*: Now you understand.
LOUISE:	I beg of you!
ONE-EYE:	It'll be good for you!
LOUISE:	Please! I don't want to die!
ONE-EYE:	You won't die!
LOUISE	*(struggling)*: Help! Help me!

ONE-EYE   (*her hand over Louise's mouth*): Shut up! (*To the women.*) Hurry, before the screams begin!
One-Eye gags her with the piece of cloth, which also covers her entire face.

LOUISE   (*resisting*): Ah!

ONE-EYE: Don't move, little one! It will be over soon. I only have to feel exactly . . . where your eyes are. (*Pause.*) But this cloth is too stiff! It's been starched!

LA NORMAND: What?

ONE-EYE: Too much starch in the cloth, idiot! Soak the damn thing in water and dry it on the stove! I must know precisely where her eyes are, Normand!
One-Eye grabs the cloth from Louise's face and flings it at La Normand. One-Eye again silences Louise with her hand. Now in a panic, La Normand repeatedly dips the cloth in a water basin and throws it on the stove, which sends up plumes of steam.

ONE-EYE: Why did you give me a starched cloth?

LA NORMAND: It's soft now! Look, it's completely soft!
La Normand spreads the steaming cloth over Louise's face.

LOUISE   (*screaming*): Ah!
One-Eye clinically touches Louise's covered face and smiles. With her other hand, she pulls the knitting needle from her pocket and quickly rams it through the cloth into Louise's eye-socket.

LOUISE   (*a new intense screaming*): NO!!!!

ONE-EYE: There! That's it! Blood is flowing on my hands. It's warm, it's good! It's just like the blood of an infant! A tiny, beautiful child! (*One-Eye stabs Louise's other eye.*)

LOUISE: Ah!

ONE-EYE: Like the old times!
One-Eye laughs hysterically and makes flapping gestures as she dances round Louise's tortured body.
In a reflexive motion the blinded Louise pulls the knitting needle from her second destroyed eye and leaps up from the bed, as the bloody cloth falls to the ground. Vitreous fluid flows down Louise's mutilated face, which is frozen in a silent scream.

LA NORMAND   (*confused as she runs towards Louise*): The bird? Where's the bird?

ONE-EYE: Ha! Ha! Ha! Ha!
Louise instinctively ignores La Normand, lunges toward the laughing One-Eye, and falls dead, holding the needle.

LA NORMAND   (*inspecting the corpse of Louise*): The cuckoo didn't fly out! Hunchback, did you see the bird?
The crones stare at each other in disbelief as One-Eye continues her demented dance. Realising that they had been tricked, Hunchback suddenly overpowers the ecstatic One-Eye and drags the uncomprehending ogress across the room to the stove. Hunchback forces the unseeing side of One-Eye's face down on the red-hot plate. The face sizzles away in a burst of bloody steam

as One-Eye screams wildly. Alarmed by the piercing shrieks,
Hunchback lifts up the ogress's oozing head by the hair and
smashes her one eye against the stove plate, killing her.
Long pause. Hunchback looks at La Normand.

LA NORMAND   (*coming out of her shock*): There never was a cuckoo!
(*Noise from the right is heard.*)

HUNCHBACK: Normand, listen! Footsteps!
Hunchback blows out the bed lamp and climbs into her bed.
The room is bathed in moonlight.

LA NORMAND   (*realising their predicament*): They're coming! They're coming!
She scrambles into bed and pulls a sheet over her head. A
moment's silence, as Abel returns to the space, and inspects the
dead bodies.

ABEL: Well, that certainly saved me some work. But we still have two
more to dispose of.
Abel steps over to each of the remaining girls, and calmly
breaks their necks, and then lifts the two dead bodies into their
respective chairs, covering them with sheets, as well.
You wouldn't believe how many of these 'interns' I get through
in a week. So, that just about wraps it up for today's show. I do
hope you've enjoyed our little jaunt through the dark streets and
back alleys of old Paris, and are not *too* unsettled by what you have
seen here tonight. Oh, who am I trying to fool? Of *course* I hope
you're unsettled. Horror is not meant to be cheerful, and come
with a happy ending. It's certainly not meant to be about so-called
'monsters' that sparkle in the sunlight and are just misunderstood,
waiting for the right woman to come along and tame them. Horror
is about twisting your guts into untold knots: it's about making you
realise that the world is a far less safe place than you walk around
pretending to yourself that it is; and waking you up to the fact
that one day, one night, on some dark street, or maybe even in the
comfort of your own home . . . *this could happen to you.*
Now, before you leave tonight, we must give our thanks to
everyone who has helped to make this show a possibility. We
are proud to be a part of the PBH Free Fringe, an organisation
which gives you, the audience, the chance to see some amazing
performances from some truly incredible people, for much less
than you would see them on the main Fringe. Most shows there
will cost you between ten and fifteen pounds for a seat: all we
have, is a bucket by the door on your way out. Please, think for
a moment about the star rating you would give this show, and
if you are able, please turn each of those stars into a pound. If
you're not able to do that, any donation will be most welcome:
and if you can't make any kind of donation, then please, just
come up and say thank you: we'll take your name and address,
and be round later.
A huge thank you must also be given to our hosts for this
show. Normally, I would also thank the other members of my

performance company, but since they are now all dead beneath their sheets, it seems a little pointless to do so.

During the final thanks, each of the girls rises from their seats, allowing the sheets to fall from them, revealing their mutilated and destroyed bodies as they begin to shamble forward towards Abel.

Finally, thank you to all of you, for coming to see this show. Do remember—if you are at all disturbed, sickened or morally outraged by what you've seen on our stage tonight . . . Please, do tell your friends, and write a review on the Fringe website. We're here all the way through to the end of August.

Abel realises he is not alone on the stage, and looks around him, seeing his victims poised to strike. Before he can escape, they grab him and pull him back forcefully into the chair, ripping his shirt open. One girl plunges her hand into his belly, ripping him open and spilling his guts across his lap. Two others bite into his chest and shoulder, tearing off huge chunks of flesh.

ABEL: Ladies and gentlemen; I have been Abel Hartmann—
GOOD NIGHT!

The last one takes hold of his head and, as his screams reach the peak of their intensity, she snaps his neck. With Abel now dead, the four reanimated corpses walk off-stage through the audience, ready to take people's money.

THE END

Bibliography

Christie, Agatha (1961) *The Rule of Three*, London: Samuel French.

Christie, Agatha (2013) *The Grand Tour: Letters and Photographs from the British Empire Expedition 1922*, London: HarperCollins.

Edwards, Martin (2016) *The Golden Age of Murder*, London: HarperCollins.

Ervine, St John (1933) *The Theatre in My Time*, London: Rich and Cowan.

Evans, Arthur B. (1994) 'The Fantastic Science Fiction of Maurice Renard', *Science Fiction Studies* 21.3: 380–96.

Galsworthy, John (1924) 'Introduction' *Laughing Anne and One Day More*, London: Castle.

Gordon, Mel (1997) *The Grand Guignol: Theatre of Fear and Terror*, New York: De Capo Press.

Green, Julius (2018) *Agatha Christie: A Life in Theatre* (rev. edn), London: HarperCollins.

Guilloux, Christine (2008) 'The Landscape of Hypnosis in France in the Twentieth Century', *Contemporary Hypnosis* 25.1: 57–64. https://doi.org/10.1002/ch.342

Hand, Richard J. and Wilson, Michael (2002) *Grand-Guignol: The French Theatre of Horror*, Exeter: University of Exeter Press.

Hand, Richard J. and Wilson, Michael (2007) *London's Grand Guignol*, Exeter: University of Exeter Press.

Hand, Richard J. and Wilson Michael (2016) *Performing Grand-Guignol*, Exeter: University of Exeter Press.

Harding, James (1989) *Gerald du Maurier: The Last Actor-Manager*, London: Hodder & Stoughton.

Holland, Samantha, et al. (ed.) (2019) *Gender and Contemporary Horror in Film*, London: Emerald Publishing Limited, 2019. https://doi.org/10.1108/9781787698970

Knowles, Owen and Moore, Gene M. (eds.) (2001) *Oxford Reader's Companion to Conrad*, Oxford: Oxford University Press. https://doi.org/10.1093/acref/9780198604211.001.0001

McPherson, Conor (2013) *Plays: Three*, London: Nick Hern Books.

Medawar, Tony (ed.) (2018) *Bodies from the Library: Lost Tales of Mystery and Suspense by Agatha Christie and Other Masters of the Golden Age*, London: Collins Crime Club.

Myers, Nicole (2007) 'The Lure of Montmartre, 1880–1900', in *Heilbrunn Timeline of Art History*, New York: The Metropolitan Museum of Art http://www.metmuseum.org/toah/hd/mont/hd_mont.htm (October 2007)

Partington, Wilfred (2000) 'Joseph Conrad Behind the Scenes', *The Conradian* 25.2: 177–84.

Phillippon, Jacques and Poirier, Jacques (2009) *Joseph Babinski: A Biography*, Oxford: Oxford University Press.

Pierron, Agnès (1995) *Le Grand Guignol: Le Théâtre des Peurs de la Belle Époque*, Paris: Robert Laffont.

Pierron, Agnès (2011) Maxa: la femme la plus assassinée du monde, Montpelier: L'Entretemps *éditions*.

Stokes, John (2000) 'Body Parts: The Success of the Thriller in the Inter-War Years', in C. Barker and M. Gale (eds.), *British Theatre Between the Wars, 1918–1939*, Cambridge: Cambridge University Press.

Witney, Frederick (1947) *Grand Guignol*, London: Constable.

Interviews

Blackwood, Russell, interview with Richard J. Hand and Michael Wilson, 31 August 2017.

Comtois, James, interview with Richard J. Hand, 13 May 2021.

Pringle, Stuart, interview with Michael Wilson, 31 August 2016.

Zavistovich, Alex, interview with Richard J. Hand, 24 April 2015.

Webography

All links checked on 31 May 2022

Resources and Theatre Company Websites

Vigor Mortis
https://www.vigormortis.com.br/sobre

Thrillpeddlers
http://thrillpeddlers.com/

http://www.grandguignol.com/

London Horror Festival
https://www.londonhorrorfestival.co.uk/

London Lovecraft Festival
http://londonlovecraft.com/

Molotov Theatre Group
http://molotovtheatre.org/

Carpet Theatre
http://www.carpettheatre.com/

Nosedive Productions
https://www.nosediveproductions.com/

Tin Shed Theatre Company
https://www.tinshedtheatrecompany.com/

National Edgar Allan Poe Theatre
https://www.poetheatre.org/

Center for Puppetry Arts
https://puppet.org/about/

Pandemic Collective
http://www.pandemiccollective.org/mission-statement.html

Web References

Great War Theatre
https://www.greatwartheatre.org.uk/db/script/606/

Brown Paper Tickets
https://www.brownpapertickets.com/event/445136

Extempore Theatre
http://www.extemporetheatre.com/past-productions/the-terror-seasons/
terror-2004/

BBC News
https://www.bbc.co.uk/news/entertainment-arts-20095581

British Theatre Guide
https://www.britishtheatreguide.info/reviews/grand-guignol-southwark-
playh-10851
https://www.britishtheatreguide.info/reviews/the-ghost-hunte-pleasance-
court-9166

World Radio History
https://worldradiohistory.com/hd2/IDX-Site-Early-Radio/Archive-World-Radio/
World-Radio-1935-04-19-S-OCR-OCR-Page-0028.pdf

Nosedive Productions
https://www.nosediveproductions.com/the-adventures-of-nervous-boy

Daily Mirror
https://www.mirror.co.uk/news/world-news/josef-fritzls-daughters-secret-
new-14141500

PR Web
https://www.prweb.com/releases/2008/06/prweb1040174.htm

National Edgar Allan Poe Theatre
https://www.poetheatre.org/our-shows

La Cinemathèque française
https://www.lemonde.fr/archives/article/1985/05/11/l-araignee-de-satin-filles-
fleurs-pour-baratier_3047470_1819218.html

Index

Printed in the USA
CPSIA information can be obtained
at www.ICGtesting.com
JSHW021531051123
51465JS00002B/76

9 781804 130803